The Intellectual Legacy of Michael Oakeshott

Edited by Corey Abel
and
Timothy Fuller

ia

IMPRINT ACADEMIC

Published in the UK by Imprint Academic
PO Box 200, Exeter EX5 5YX, UK

Published in the USA by Imprint Academic
Philosophy Documentation Center
PO Box 7147, Charlottesville, VA 22906-7147, USA

ISBN 1 84540 009 7

A CIP catalogue record for this book is available from the
British Library and US Library of Congress

Full details of additional titles in the Oakeshott Studies series:
www.imprint-academic.com/idealists

Contributors

Corey Abel, Adjunct Professor of Political Science, Metro State College of Denver

Josiah Lee Auspitz, Director, Philosophy of Institutions Project, Sabre Foundation, Cambridge, MA

Debra Candreva, Visiting Assistant Professor, Wellesley College

Wendell John Coats Jr., Professor of Government, Connecticut College

Douglas J. DenUyl, Vice President, Educational Programs, Liberty Fund

George Feaver, Emeritus Professor of Political Science, University of British Columbia

Paul Franco, Professor of Government, Bowdoin College

Richard Friedman, Associate Professor Emeritus of Political Science, University at Buffalo, State University of New York

Timothy Fuller, Lloyd E. Worner Distinguished Service Professor and Professor of Political Science, Colorado College

Robert A. D. Grant, Professor of Cultural and Political Thought, Department of English Literature, University of Glasgow

Eric S. Kos, Graduate Student in Political Science, University of Michigan and Visiting Assistant Professor, Alma College

Leslie Marsh, Centre for Research in Cognitive Science, University of Sussex

Kenneth Minogue, Emeritus Professor of Political Science, London School of Economics

Terry Nardin, UWM Distinguished Professor, University of Wisconsin-Milwaukee

Keith Sutherland, Editor, *Journal of Consciousness Studies*; Publisher, *History of Political Thought* and *Polis: The Journal of the Society for Greek Political Thought*

Martyn P. Thompson, Associate Professor of Political Science, Tulane University

Gerhard Wolmarans, Lecturer in Political Science, University of Pretoria, South Africa

Contents

Part III
Oakeshott Today

Timothy Fuller

Foreword

This volume presents essays on the work of Michael Oakeshott from the first two international conferences of the Michael Oakeshott Association, in London 2001 and in Colorado Springs 2003. The authors herein include both individuals who knew Oakeshott and younger scholars who did not have the chance to meet him but who have discovered his work. This is gratifying since this volume, in the company of a growing number of monographic studies of his work, anthologies of his unpublished writings, and doctoral dissertations, shows that international interest in Oakeshott's work is expanding significantly. Those of us involved in the Michael Oakeshott Association, and with long interest in his work, naturally see this as a major contribution to the field of political philosophy and to thinking carefully about politics, as well as a deserved tribute to the man.

These essays not only recognize Oakeshott's contributions to numerous fields of inquiry, but they also compare his work with other major thinkers. There was, in the past, a tendency for students of his work to consider Oakeshott in isolation, but no longer. As a result, not only do we now enjoy sympathetic and affectionate commentary, but also comparative and critical assessments and assertive questioning. This is all to the good. We remember that Oakeshott himself, while presenting his views directly and uncompromisingly, also was committed to conversation as an end in itself, as the most distinctive feature of being human. He was known to say that the philosopher may have a heavenly home but is in no hurry to get there. He did not expect closure on fundamental questions in the temporal sphere of human life even though he did think that, to be a good conversationalist, one needed to be clear on one's assumptions, taking care to know well what is likely to be said against them in dialogue. The idea that we could have a debate, and at the end of the day, discover a victor and a vanquished, was entirely foreign to him. Thus his self-characterization as a 'skeptic' and his philosophical approach to politics. He understood that in politics there are necessarily victors and vanquished, however fleeting and alterable these categories are. To study politics philosophically is thus to consider politics from a vantage point different from that of the politicians themselves, to focus on the ironies of the claims of politics in a way that would disable the politician.

In calling himself a 'skeptic,' Oakeshott meant, following St. Augustine, Montaigne, and Hume, skepticism about human pretensions to succeed in 'the pursuit of perfection as the crow flies,' to build towers into a putative heavenly kingdom, or to control and manage the contingencies of human existence. Such aspirations he admired in individuals seeking their fortunes as they defined them for themselves, but he deplored such aspirations in governments. He did so because he saw the state as a basically involuntary, but necessary, arrangement presiding over diverse peoples and interests. To invest in a single ideal in this involuntary circumstance imposes on some for the sake of others, suppressing the natural diversity that is the ground of human freedom. What is preferable, he thought, is a 'civil association' in which diverse people with diverse interests acknowledge and subscribe to a rule of law to insure the basic order they must have, with a view to affording the greatest freedom to live according to their own self-understandings. Oakeshott thought that this was the principal achievement of modern Europe, emergent in the fifteenth century, gaining grand theoretical expression in the seventeenth and eighteenth centuries, and persisting against fierce attacks in the nineteenth and twentieth centuries. One might describe this as the transformation of relations of command and obedience into relations of authority and acknowledgment, and it was possible because the ideal of the self-regulating individual, competent to pursue individual interests within mutually acknowledged procedural arrangements, not primarily dependent on coercive enforcement, was increasingly instantiated in practice in modern European history.

Nevertheless, as the technical and military power of modern governments began significantly to increase, they brought with them the temptation to invest modern governments with grand purposes for the redesign or reconstruction of social orders. This practical turn of events was encouraged theoretically by the influential growth of 'rationalism' in modern Europe under the influence of the thought of Francis Bacon, Descartes, Jeremy Bentham and the modern social sciences. Rationalism and its appearance in politics as ideology, as Oakeshott described it, advocates techniques or methods of reasoning, based on a mistaken conception of reason, by means of which we are to overcome the contingent character of historical existence. In extreme form, it holds that the hitherto endless activity of preserving and changing in politics can be brought to a satisfactory conclusion, and that this is to be done through a coalition of the intellectually enlightened with governments who are confident that they can use their power to steer people to the 'right' ends or end.

Thus modern politics is conducted in a charged field polarized between the skeptical attitude towards governmental power and the view that such power is the means to infinite improvement. The contest between the 'skeptic' and the 'rationalist' has so far proven historically interminable although Oakeshott thought that, in recent times, rationalism had clearly dominated. But because of the power in practice of the ideas of civil association, of rule of law, of authority grounded in acknowledgment, and because he thought these to be consistent with the human spirit, he believed that this remarkable modern achievement could persist. Modern politics is thus constituted in the tension between these competing understandings. They play off each other and the character of each is shaped by the presence of the other. Regardless of his personal preferences, Oakeshott thought that this is the reality of our situation.

For Oakeshott, the task of government is to keep the ship afloat, not to steer it to final port, so that individuals and voluntary associations could seek their fortunes, defining for themselves their personal destinies, constrained by a procedural structure of laws, and in a condition of dispersed power wherein the state, while not especially strong, and with few resources to distribute, would be strong enough to resist informal conglomerations of power that would turn civil association into a managerial enterprise, a modern Tower of Babel. In this one finds Oakeshott's 'conservative disposition.'

But a disposition is one thing, the vocation to philosophy another. The latter is higher than the former. Philosophy is the seeking, in detachment, to understand and to describe what is going on in the world. Conservatism is a particular practical response to the opportunities and perils of our modern life. Oakeshott thus provided a picture of the historical and philosophical context within which to identify more clearly what prompts the conservative disposition. He did not think philosophy could practically resolve the issues, but philosophy could clarify them in ways their advocates would likely not consider. In expressing a preference for one pole, however, he associated himself with an ancient tradition in the West, which denies to politics the highest honor. He called politics a 'necessary evil,' meaning thereby to say both that we cannot do without politics and that from its necessity does not follow its candidacy to be the source of all meaning.

In the essays that follow, these themes, and many others, are discussed intelligently and provocatively, bringing out both the subtleties and ambiguities that may be found in Oakeshott's thought. In addition, substantial effort is made to place Oakeshott in relation to Plato (Debra Candreva and Eric Kos), Aristotle (Corey Abel), Spinoza and Hobbes (Douglas Den Uyl), Hegel (Paul Franco), Spinoza and Hegel (Lee Auspitz), John Stuart Mill and representative democracy (George Feaver), all of whom were thinkers of great importance to him. His understanding of the rule of law (Richard Friedman) and of the prospects and limits of the social sciences (Terry Nardin) are discussed. Assessments of his arguments in terms of issues in contemporary philosophy are considered (Keith Sutherland, Leslie Marsh). Oakeshott's relevance to the modern African context is a remarkable addition to the discussion (Gerhard Wolmarans). Kenneth Minogue assesses current forms of rationalism. Martyn Thompson discusses the centrality of poetry in Oakeshott's thinking about modern civilization, while John Coats explores the poetic dimension of his philosophy of experience. Robert Grant critically assesses the coherence of Oakeshott's account of aesthetic experience. The widening intellectual landscape offered here gives promise to flourish even more in the future.

Special thanks must go to Corey Abel whose editorial assistance made the timely completion of this volume possible. We are also grateful for essential financial support from Colorado College, which helped to make both the 2003 conference and this volume possible. Finally, we want to express thanks to Leslie Marsh, whose indefatigable efforts to launch the MOA were indispensable to its existing at all.

Timothy Fuller
President of the Michael Oakeshott Association
Colorado Springs, November 2004

Abbreviations

C.Lec	'A Philosophical Approach to Politics: My First Course of Lectures,' LSE File 1/1/7
DSM	'A Discussion of Some Matters Preliminary to A Study of Political Thought', LSE File 1/1/2
EGP	Notebook titled 'Early Greek Philosophy,' LSE File 2/4/1
EM	*Experience and its Modes* (Cambridge UP, 1933)
FS	*The Politics of Faith and the Politics of Scepticism* (Yale UP, 1996)
HCA	*Hobbes on Civil Association* (Liberty Fund, 2000)
HCiv	*Hobbes on Civil Association* (Berkeley, 1975)
LSE	*A Study of Political Thought: A Series of Lectures by Michael Oakeshott,* LSE File 1/1/21
MPME	*Morality and Politics in Modern Europe* (Yale UP, 1993)
Nic I, II, III	Notebooks on the *Nichomachean Ethics,* LSE Files 2/3/1-3
OH	*On History and Other Essays* (Basil Blackwell, 1983)
OHC	*On Human Conduct* (Clarendon Press, 1975)
Rep I, II	Notebooks on the *Republic,* LSE Files, 2/2/1-2
RIP	*Rationalism in Politics* (Liberty Press, 1991)
RP	*Rationalism in Politics* (Methuen, 1962)
RPML	*Religion, Politics and the Moral Life* (Yale UP, 1993)
SPD	*The Social and Political Doctrines of Contemporary Europe* (Cambridge UP, 1939)
Spinoza I	Notebook titled 'Spinoza I,' LSE File 2/4/2
VL	*The Voice of Liberal Learning* (Liberty Fund, 2001)
VLL	*The Voice of Liberal Learning* (Yale UP, 1989)
WH	*What is History? and other essays* (Imprint Academic, 2004)

I

Oakeshott and the
Ancients

Debra Candreva

Oakeshott and Plato: A Philosophical Conversation

I

There is something about the activity of philosophy — and more, the attempt to describe that activity — that lends itself exceptionally well to the use of imagery. From the Platonic cave, to the Hegelian owl of Minerva and beyond, reflection has provided a seemingly endless assortment of poetic metaphors for the philosophic endeavor. Reading Oakeshott's work might suggest yet another image for the same pursuit, not because he explicitly mentions it, but rather because he seems to fulfill it. The image I have in mind is that of a palimpsest: that is, a tablet or paper whose surface has been written upon, erased, and re-inscribed again and again.

Admittedly, Oakeshott would probably object to the use of this image to describe either his own philosophy or the activity of thinking more generally. For one thing, it is a little too close to the image of the *tabula rasa*. He explicitly rejects this image, along with other similar ones such that of a painter working with colors, or a bricklayer laying bricks, for the same reasons: each ultimately suggests some material independent of or prior to the activity of working with it.[1]

The image, however, need not be taken to its logical conclusion in order to be illuminating; and in fact, it may reveal more if understood a little more poetically and a little less literally. This means that

---

[1]   'In thought,' he writes, 'there is nothing analogous to the painter's colours or the builder's bricks — raw material existing apart from the use made of it.' Oakeshott, *Experience and Its Modes* (Cambridge: Cambridge Univ. Press, 1933), 19. Hereafter: *EM*.

the image of the palimpsest may not accurately represent the process of Oakeshott's thinking, but it can say something about the end result of his writing. In this sense, Oakeshott's writings are like a palimpsest insofar as they seem to contain multiple layers in which many intriguing things are visible in fleeting and tantalizing glimpses, just beneath the surface, changing according to the 'light' in which they are viewed.

This quality to some extent explains the pronounced tendency of Oakeshott's commentators to interpret his thought in relation to a remarkable variety of thinkers. Some of the comparisons — for example, those between Oakeshott on the one hand, and Hobbes or Hegel on the other — are almost mandatory for understanding Oakeshott at any level. Beyond this, however, there is a rapidly growing list of thinkers with whom Oakeshott is compared, a list that currently includes (but is not limited to) Aristotle, Augustine, and Spinoza, as well as Bradley, Burke, Constant, Montaigne, Cervantes, Pascal, Nietzsche and Sartre.[2] Whatever the strengths and weaknesses of each individual project, this comparative approach clearly holds a strong attraction for those most interested in studying Oakeshott's thought.

In a recent example of this kind of approach, W. John Coats examines Oakeshott's thought in relation to a variety of thinkers who, in ways both more and less explicit, may be identified with Oakeshott's thinking. Coats designates these thinkers — who include not only Hobbes and Hegel but also Montaigne, Augustine, Constant, Rousseau, and Hume — as Oakeshott's 'contemporaries.' In so doing, Coats calls attention to Oakeshott's particular stance of active, critical and engaged response to these central figures in the history of political thought. Significantly, he uses the language of 'illumination' rather than 'influence' to describe this relationship, because it highlights the fact that these connections, though important and instructive, are also in some sense inconclusive.

For this reason, it is easy to see why one of Oakeshott's own favorite images for describing philosophy was not that of a palimpsest, but that of a conversation. For him, philosophy at its best is an 'intel-

---

[2]   For example, see Noel O'Sullivan, 'In the Perspective of Western Thought,' in *The Achievement of Michael Oakeshott*, ed. A. J. Norman (London: Duckworth and Co., 1993); Anthony Farr, *Sartre's Radicalism and Oakeshott's Conservatism* (NY: St. Martin's Press, 1998); and Timothy Fuller, 'Preface' and 'Introduction' to *Religion, Politics and the Moral Life* (New Haven: Yale Univ. Press, 1991), vii-viii, 1-26. Hereafter: *RPML*.

lectual adventure' rather than an exegesis. While it is related to other
forms of activity, it cannot directly prescribe action or direct practice.
Its value is not directly contingent upon particular ends, and like a
conversation, it can be fruitful and worthwhile without necessarily
being conclusive.[3]

I will argue that this attitude toward philosophy is something
Oakeshott shares most notably with Plato, and that for this reason,
Plato holds a place of special importance among Oakeshott's philo-
sophical interlocutors. In arguing this, I do not mean to suggest that
Plato's significance for Oakeshott is exclusive, or that his signifi-
cance renders less important any of the more traditional figures
through which Oakeshott's thought is generally understood.
Instead, I use Plato to call attention to a particular aspect of
Oakeshott's thought that generally goes unexamined: the connection between the substance and the form of his writing.

One obstacle to this argument would seem to be the obvious differences between Oakeshott and Plato, especially concerning politics. At first glance, it might seem that one would be hard pressed to
find similarities between the ancient designer of the 'ideal' city in
speech, with its noble lies and its philosopher-kings, and that most
ardent critic of the phenomenon known as 'rationalism' in politics.

Where Oakeshott learns most from Plato, however, is in the area of
philosophy rather than politics.[4] While the connections between the
two thinkers have not gone unrecognized entirely, they nevertheless
have been left relatively unexplored. Many of those who do see hints
of Plato in Oakeshott's thinking rightly acknowledge that these hints
seem to be concentrated more heavily in his earlier works. From this,
one could conclude — as some in fact have — that Oakeshott confines his affinities with a kind of 'Platonism' to the early part of his
career, and rejects them later on in favor of other views that are characterized as either Hegelian, Hobbesian, or a little bit of each.

This position, however, seems to me only partially correct. While
it is accurate to notice a change of some sort between Oakeshott's
earlier and later writings, one must be cautious about the meaning
one ascribes to this change.

As readers of Plato know well, both Plato and his Socrates are each
somewhat Protean. Proteus, the 'old one of the sea,' is the servant of

---

[3]   Oakeshott, *Rationalism in Politics and other essays, new and expanded edition*,
      ed. Timothy Fuller (Indianapolis: Liberty Press, 1991), 490. Hereafter: *RIP*.
[4]   This is an argument I make more fully in *The Enemies of Perfection: Oakeshott,
      Plato and the Critique of Rationalism* (Lanham, MD: Lexington Books, 2005).

Poseidon described by Homer who is capable of transforming himself into a number of different shapes, which he does as a means of evading those who ask too many questions of him. In a characteristic moment of irony, Plato's Socrates accuses his interlocutor of displaying this very quality. 'Really,' he admonishes Ion, 'you're just like Proteus, you twist up and down and take many different shapes till finally you've escaped me altogether.'[5] In reality, of course, it is Socrates and through him Plato who twist and turn, and elude us in significant ways, if not altogether.

This aspect of Plato could not have escaped, and did not escape, Oakeshott's notice. I contend that throughout his career, Oakeshott rightly recognizes the same thing that all careful readers of Plato recognize: that Plato's works contain a variety of competing, and often conflicting, viewpoints. To learn from Plato means accepting, not denying this characteristic, which in turn requires that one seek from Plato a manner of thinking rather than a particular thought.

Even in the earlier writings, where he refers to Plato most often, Oakeshott never attempts to smooth out the many variegated strands in Plato. Despite the number of isolated observations he makes about his philosophy, he never proposes an interpretation of Plato that would be less ambiguous than were Plato's own words. Thus, those who find Oakeshott 'rejecting' Plato after his earliest writings err in assuming that there is a singular Plato in his thought available for rejection.

Instead, any changes in Oakeshott's views should be understood in terms of emphasis rather than substance. The essays in which Oakeshott focuses on philosophical more than political concerns tend to contain references to the philosophical aspects of Plato — and hence, the connections appear as agreements. Other essays, in which Oakeshott addresses matters of a more directly political nature, contain references to the political aspects of Plato — and these, accurately enough, appear as disagreements.

If Oakeshott's references to Plato become increasingly critical in his later works, it is because his writing becomes increasingly political in its focus. However, this does not amount to a rejection of something he previously held to be true. To the contrary, the aspects of Plato that Oakeshott criticizes most strongly are aspects he would have criticized — and in many cases, did criticize — throughout his

---

[5] Plato, *Ion*, 541e, in *Complete Works*, ed. John M. Cooper (Indianapolis: Hackett Publishing Co., 1997). All subsequent references to Plato are taken from this edition.

career. The real difference, if any, is the frequency with which he does so.

None of Oakeshott's references to Plato are very complete or very systematic, and he very deliberately avoids taking a stance on the usual scholarly debates.[6] Nevertheless, I believe it still is possible to make some general observations about his stance toward Plato, and to draw a few conclusions from them. If I am correct about what I take to be his approach to Plato, it seems to me to be a very good one, which is very much in keeping with Plato's own spirit.

The same approach is also useful for understanding Oakeshott as well. It helps to highlight the 'Platonic' character of his philosophy as a conversation, which in turn can reveal something about the way Oakeshott matches his writing style to his philosophical content.[7] In the following section, I will lay the groundwork for this argument by outlining some of the most important ways in which Oakeshott's philosophy is, and is not, 'Platonic.'

II

Much has been said and written about Oakeshott's view of philosophy, and it is hardly necessary to point out that reactions to it, and interpretations of it, have varied dramatically. Most commentators would agree, however, that it is difficult to talk about Oakeshott's views on philosophy without addressing to some extent his understanding of Hegel. This theme has received a great deal of attention both recently and in the past, especially among those who have con-

---

[6] For example, he does not enter into debates about the so-called 'problem of Socrates,' which concerns questions about the accuracy or the historical validity of Plato's accounts. For an overview of some different approaches, see Mario Montouri, *The Socratic Problem: Its History – Its Solutions* (Amsterdam: J. C. Gieben Publishers, 1992). Further, though, Oakeshott does not draw a distinction between what is 'Platonic' and what is 'Socratic,' but instead treats them more or less interchangeably. For purposes of this essay, I will do the same.

[7] It also can help explain why there are so many conflicting interpretations of Oakeshott. Not only do his interpreters see a kaleidoscopic range of 'influences' on his thought; they disagree quite widely about the characterization of that thought. He has alternately been labeled a conservative, a liberal, and everything in between, and both neo-conservatives and postmodernists alike have appropriated his views for their own ends.

tributed to the long-standing controversy over the relative 'Hegelian' or 'Hobbesian' character of Oakeshott's thought.[8]

Important as this debate may be, however, it is not my intention here to contribute to it. There are several reasons for this, but I will limit myself to noting one in particular. Many of those who examine the Hobbesian and Hegelian currents in Oakeshott seem to assume that Oakeshott ultimately needs to choose between two competing traditions: that of the Will and Artifice, as represented by Hobbes; and that of the Rational Will, as represented by Hegel (*RIP*, 227-8).

To make this assumption, however, is also to assume that Oakeshott's philosophy is dialectic in the same way as that of Hegel. Specifically, it is to attribute to Oakeshott the Hegelian assumption that the different traditions that constitute the history of political thought progressively lead to, and will ultimately result in, synthesis. While it is true that Hegel believed his own philosophy could and ought to overcome the tensions in philosophies prior to his own, the same cannot be said of Oakeshott. For that matter, it is not clear that Oakeshott thought Hegel succeeded in this regard, either. Admirers of the Hegelian version of the tradition of the Rational Will, remarks Oakeshott, 'may be excused the belief that in it the truths of the first two traditions [Reason and Nature, and Will and Artifice] are fulfilled and their errors find a happy release' (*RIP*, 227).

It is true that some aspects of Oakeshott's view of philosophy make it easy to see the connections to Hegel, particularly as expressed in *Experience and Its Modes*. There, he describes philosophy as 'experience without presupposition, reservation, arrest or modification,' and an attempt to 'grasp firmly a single idea.' Above all, it is the attempt to assess the partiality of some 'modes of experience' in the attempt to achieve the coherence of the 'totality' (*EM*, 3).

Perhaps the simplest summary of Oakeshott's view of philosophy, however, is also the most direct: 'Philosophy is the elucidation of meaning.'[9] Viewed in this way, philosophy is an activity that emphasizes the process of articulation rather than that of discovery.

---

[8]   One well-known version is found in Paul Franco, *The Political Philosophy of Michael Oakeshott* (New Haven: Yale Univ. Press, 1990). Recent contributors include Steven Gerencser, *The Skeptic's Oakeshott* (NY: St. Martin's Press, 2000); W. John Coats, *Oakeshott and his Contemporaries* (Selinsgrove, PA: Susquehanna Univ. Press, 2000); and more recently still, Ian Tregenza, *Michael Oakeshott on Hobbes* (Exeter: Imprint Academic, 2004).

[9]   Oakeshott, 'The Cambridge School of Political Science,' in Luke O'Sullivan, ed., *What is History? and other essays* (Charlottesville, VA: Imprint Academic, 2004), 56. Hereafter: *WH*.

It is not the acquisition of completely new knowledge; rather, it is the clarification of something already known, if only partially so.

In other words, philosophy originates not on the imaginary blank slate of ignorance, but in the more realistic — and more compromised — world of half-truths and of opinions. 'Philosophy begins with the concepts of ordinary, everyday knowledge, and consists in an extended, detailed and complete exposition of those concepts, an exposition which is itself a definition'(*RPML*, 128).

Although one might attribute this view to a variety of sources — Hegel in the *Philosophy of Right*, or Aristotle in the *Nicomachean Ethics* — Oakeshott explicitly connects it with Socrates. 'A philosopher can establish his definition only by showing in detail the process of definition, and by showing his conclusion to be itself comprehensive,' he writes. 'This of course is the philosophical method and aim presented to us in the Socratic dialogues, and it is one with which I see no reason to quarrel' (*RPML*, 130).

This view remains consistent between his early and late writings. Most notably, in *On Human Conduct*, Oakeshott elaborates a view of 'understanding' with clear and powerful similarities to the views expressed by Plato in the *Republic*. Understanding, he writes, begins in a world of 'misty intimations of intelligibility when noticings become thoughts and when, in virtue of distinguishing and remembering likenesses and unlikenesses in what is going on, we come to inhabit a world of recognizables.'[10] These recognitions, he continues, are based in familiarity rather than in 'truth;' thus from a philosophical standpoint, they are often imprecise and unclear.

Gradually, however, these partially coherent understandings are 'gone over, rehearsed, revised, and refined' until, like the prisoners in the Platonic cave, we become able to recognize, identify and name the shadows of the various shapes passing before us. Indeed, the characteristics that Oakeshott says may be identified at this stage — 'shapes, sizes, colours, textures, movements, sounds, scents, tastes, etc.' — all are things the Platonic prisoners might be able to perceive (*OHC*, 3).

All of this is not meant to suggest that Oakeshott follows Plato precisely, without disagreement or reservation. In fact, the very Platonic set of passages in the opening pages of *On Human Conduct* are offset by several pages of fairly intense criticism of Plato (Cf. *OHC*,

---

[10] Oakeshott, *On Human Conduct* (Oxford: Clarendon Press, 1975), 3. Hereafter: *OHC*.

1-27, 27-31). The criticisms here may be summarized in two related points. First, Oakeshott objects to the radical division between philosophic knowledge and ordinary knowledge in Plato's image of the cave. According to Oakeshott, Plato rightly characterizes the movement of the philosopher away from opinion and towards something akin to truth, but he wrongly severs the 'ordinary' world of the cave from the 'philosophic' realm under the sun. The second critique, closely related to the first, concerns the relationship between theory and practice. While Oakeshott believes that philosophic knowledge does indeed transcend ordinary understandings, it is not superior to them in the sense that it ought to replace them, or that it ought to rule over them as suggested by the image of the philosopher king.

There is more to be said about these critiques, but for now the point may be made succinctly. Oakeshott is not one who is much given to the exegesis of the works of others; by his own standards, to devote five pages to a critique of Plato is a considerable thing. The fact that he does so, however, should not be mistaken for an unconditional rejection. Instead, the real point seems to be the opposite: such a deliberate explanation of the differences would not be necessary were there not so very many similarities in the first place. As Oakeshott puts it, his 'account of the engagement of understanding owes so much to the account in Plato (*Republic*, vi, *ad init.*, and elsewhere), that it may be instructive to notice its divergencies' (*OHC*, 27).

There are others among Plato's dialogues which are perhaps less conspicuously mentioned by Oakeshott but which nevertheless may prove illuminating. When Oakeshott rejects the *Republic's* division between the 'cave' and the 'sun' in *On Human Conduct*, he implicitly denies the view that anything other than philosophic knowledge may be dismissed as pure ignorance. 'In philosophy,' he writes, 'there is no such thing as a transition from mere ignorance to complete knowledge; the process is always one of coming to know more fully what is in some sense already known' (*RPML*, 128). At the same time, this generates a potential problem. 'The root from which all reflection springs is the paradox that we know and that at the same time we do not know' (*RPML*, 138). This view of knowledge, and of the difficulties that go with it, is reminiscent of the paradox of knowledge expressed in Plato's *Meno*. 'A man cannot search either for what he knows or for what he does not know. . . . He cannot search for what he knows — since he knows it, there is no need to search — nor for what he does not know, for he does not know what to look for.'[11]

In the context of the *Meno*, this problem is addressed through the myth of the immortal soul. The immortality of the soul, reasons Socrates, can easily resolve the incongruity. If the soul is immortal, then it can retain knowledge beyond death; in life, when we learn, what we are really doing is engaging in the process of recalling that knowledge. In this way, he suggests, we may be said to learn both what we do, and do not, know.

As is always the case when Plato's Socrates begins speaking about myths, it is difficult to tell whether he is more, or less, serious in this proposal. If nothing else, it certainly seems to beg the question of whether we are hearing a good argument or a bad one. As a solution to this particular philosophical problem, the myth of the immortal soul is particularly unsatisfying. Equally unsatisfying, however, is the difficulty for which the immortal soul is the purported solution.

Oakeshott explains very directly why the problem is not a genuine one. Citing this very same passage from the *Meno*, Oakeshott exposes the supposed paradox of knowledge as a simple trick of spurious logic. It is, he observes,

> equivalent to saying that 'in order to work iron a hammer is needed, and in order to have a hammer it must be made, for which another hammer and other instruments are needed, for the making of which other things are needed; and in this manner anyone might vainly endeavour to prove that men have no power of working iron.' The fact is a hammer has been made. We *can* come to know something of which we previously had no experience. (*WH*, 39)[12]

The problem we are left with is the same one that bedevils all readers of Plato. If we take seriously the unmistakably weak arguments, we are forced to accept as solutions those 'proofs' which are in fact simply assertions, and which thus actually do not prove anything at all. Yet if this is true, Plato and his Socrates appear as either philosophically clumsy or unforgivably dogmatic. On the other hand, if we do not accept at face value those arguments that seem especially weak or problematic, we still must find some way to make sense of them.

Oakeshott's more general observation that nothing may be dismissed as pure error in philosophy also may prove instructive here,

---

[11] Plato, *Meno*, 80e. Also see *Republic*, vii.
[12] Oakeshott attributes the paraphrase to Spinoza, *De Intellectus Emendatione*, §30.

even if we are taking it a little bit beyond its intended significance; and Plato's *Euthydemus* seems to be the perfect vehicle for doing so. This dialogue addresses many of the same themes as does the *Meno*, including both the paradox of knowledge and the idea of the immortal soul. Oakeshott was familiar with this dialogue, and with its connections to the *Meno* as well; he cites them together as sources for the logical 'trick' he exposes in the paragraph above.[13]

The *Euthydemus* is less well known than the *Meno*, but as is true of all of Plato's dialogues, its meaning is complex while its action is fairly simple. In it, Socrates reports to his friend Crito a conversation that had taken place the previous day. In that conversation Socrates and Clinias, the young cousin of Alcibiades, converse with the sophists Euthydemus and Dionysodorus, who are brothers. Ostensibly, the purpose of the conversation is for the two sophists to persuade Clinias to love and pursue wisdom and virtue, which they agree to do at Socrates' request.

What actually occurs, however, is something quite different. In the first conversation, Euthydemus asks Clinias what type of person is capable of learning: the wise, or the ignorant? As this question is posed, Dionysodorus leans over to Socrates and whispers, 'I may tell you beforehand, Socrates, that whichever way the boy answers he will be refuted.'[14]

To those already familiar with the writings of Plato, the warning is superfluous; but Clinias, to whom the warning might have been helpful, falls directly into the trap. The subsequent exchange is a tangle of refutations in which the only thing really made clear is the ability of the two sophists to overturn any argument they choose, including their own. Their methods are crude, but in their own way they are effective.

One of the striking things about this scene, and about this dialogue in general, is the remarkable similarity between the sophists' techniques here and Socrates' own techniques elsewhere. The sophists insist that Socrates only answer their questions, rather than asking questions of his own; and when Socrates objects it is difficult not to recall the objections of Thrasymachus to Socrates, who was doing precisely the same thing.[15] Even more striking, however, is the fact

[13] Plato, *Euthydemus*, 275d-276d, and 296d; the first of these is also cited by Oakeshott, *WH*, 39.

[14] *Euthydemus*, 275e.

[15] *Republic*, 336d. Also see *Clitophon*, 410c-d.

12 Debra Candreva

that Socrates in this dialogue fully explains the precise nature of the flaws in these arguments.

When Euthydemus sets his trap for Clinias, he does it by posing a question very similar to the one found in the *Meno*. 'Do those who learn learn the things they know or the things they do not know?' Euthydemus asks Clinias.[16] When Clinias chooses the latter for his response, Euthydemus quickly 'proves' him wrong. When someone dictates something to you, he says, he is dictating something you already know, because dictation consists in letters and you already know these. Dionysodorus then inverts the argument, by drawing a parallel between knowledge and acquisition. If a learner acquires knowledge, he claims, as he gleefully overturns the previous refutation, then he must lack it to begin with. All of this leaves Clinias understandably confused.

At this point, Socrates steps in. He first illustrates that the apparent success of the sophists' arguments comes from their manipulation of particular words. The sophists, he says, have used the word 'learn' to refer both to those who acquire knowledge, and to those who scrutinize an understanding they already possess.[17] Thus, by switching from one to the other, they can manipulate the argument as they wish.

Furthermore, Socrates makes a point not only of unmasking the faulty logic; he also dismisses this type of argumentation as pure 'frivolity.' Plato writes,

> Even if a man were to learn many or all such things [that is, such techniques of refutation], he would be none the wiser . . . but would only be able to make fun of people, tripping them up and overturning them by means of distinctions in words, just like the people who pull the chair out from under a man who is going to sit down and then laugh gleefully when they see him sprawling on his back.[18]

In raising this objection, though, Socrates seems to be revealing more than a flaw in Euthydemus' argument. Since he has used very similar arguments himself in other dialogues, and in fact does so quite often, it seems he is also revealing the secret behind some of his own rhetorical ruses.

The point gains even greater significance by the end of the dialogue. By the time the dialogue arrives at the concluding speech of the two sophists, it has degenerated into a monstrously ridiculous

[16] *Euthydemus*, 276e.
[17] *Euthydemus*, 278a.
[18] *Euthydemus*, 278b-c.

caricature of a typical Socratic conversation. Euthydemus reintroduces the same spurious argument about knowledge as before, though this time it is put in terms of whether one knows everything, or nothing, with no alternatives in between. This time, however, Socrates does not raise his previous objections, though he would be well justified in doing so. The result is that the discussion escalates into a claim by the two brothers to know all things, including shoemaking, leather stitching, and the number of teeth in each other's mouths. Finally, they arrive at the absurd conclusion of the sophists' absurd line of questioning. Interjecting suddenly, Socrates asks, 'And when you were children and had just been born, did you know everything? They both answered yes at the same moment.'[19]

This presentation of the issue contrasts sharply with the one in the *Meno*. In that dialogue, Socrates identifies Meno's question about the apparent impossibility of knowledge as a mere 'debater's argument.' However, rather than revealing the fallacy behind it, as he does in the *Euthydemus*, here he responds by immediately offering the argument — which is really an assertion — about the immortal soul.

It is hard to believe that Plato's Socrates takes seriously in one place an argument he justifiably discards in another. There is, however, one sense in which the myth of the immortal soul is a quite serious response indeed. We must not believe the debater's argument that knowledge is impossible, counsels Socrates, but not because it is wrong. Instead, we must disbelieve it because 'it would make us idle, and fainthearted men like to hear it, whereas my argument makes them energetic and keen on the search [for wisdom].'[20] In short, the truth of the claim may be less important for Socrates than its effect on those who hear it.

In the *Euthydemus*, the same argument is treated very differently, but in various ways the point both is, and is not, the same. One of the major differences is the element of parody so clearly evidenced in this dialogue, which is both well documented and well known.[21] The entire conversation is marked by moments of laughter, and Socrates

---

[19]   *Euthydemus*, 294e.
[20]   *Meno*, 81e.
[21]   See Ann Michelini, 'Socrates Plays the Buffoon: Cautionary Protreptic in *Euthydemus*,' *American Journal of Philology* 121 (2000): 517-20; and Robin Jackson, 'Socrates' Iolaos: Myth and Eristic in Plato's *Euthydemus*,' *Classical Quarterly*, n.s., 40, no. 2 (1990): 378.

repeatedly admonishes the two sophists to stop joking around.[22] Moreover, the arguments put forward by the sophists are vaguely recognizable as Socratic, yet are so outrageous that there could be no doubt of their fundamental absurdity; thus the brunt of the dialogue's mockery seems to be shared more or less equally by them and by Socrates. In other words, the effects of the dialogue's comedy are to clearly indicate the inadequacies of eristic argument, while failing to fully dissociate Socrates from it.

Despite its playfulness, the dialogue does seem to have at least one serious point, and it is the same as that cited in the *Meno*: the exhortation to wisdom. In some ways, the intended purpose of the conversation in the *Euthydemus* — to inspire Clinias to pursue wisdom — does not seem to be a success. In the end, it is unclear what if anything he has really learned. The arguments made by Socrates that are supposed to link happiness, knowledge and virtue either have failed explicitly, or have been accepted without being proven.[23]

The effects on Crito, to whom Socrates is giving an account of the prior day's conversation with Euthydemus and Dionysodorus, are somewhat different. When Socrates has concluded his story, and once again is speaking with Crito, Crito expresses some concern about the things that Socrates seems to take so lightly. He rightly is suspicious both of the methods of the sophists, and of Socrates' willingness to be associated with them. Primarily, he is concerned that these tactics will give philosophy — and anyone associated with it — a bad name; but he also seems to perceive something genuinely shameful in those tactics as well.[24]

Crito's more practical problem concerns his son's education. Given his misgivings about philosophy, he is confused about whether or not he should give his son a philosophic education. On the one hand, his friendship with Socrates suggests to him that philosophy is a noble thing; his observation of the antics of 'philosophers' like Euthydemus and Dionysodorus casts a good deal of doubt on that view.

[22]   *Euthydemus*, 278d; 283c; 288b-c.
[23]   *Euthydemus*, 290e. Rosamund Sprague argues that the dialogue shows the education of Clinias to be a success, and cites the argument at lines 288d-293a as proof of this. However, she does not address Crito's interjection at this point, or the following exchange in which he and Socrates suggest it was not Clinias who made these laudable arguments, but instead some 'divine being' who did so. See *Euthydemus*, 291a; and Sprague, *Plato's Use of Fallacy* (NY: Barnes and Noble, 1962), 20-2.
[24]   *Euthydemus*, 305a-b.

The advice Socrates gives him seems to contain an important message. 'Pay no attention to the practitioners of philosophy, whether good or bad,' Socrates tells Crito. 'Rather, give serious consideration to the thing itself: if it seems to you negligible, then turn everyone from it, not just your sons. But if it seems to you to be what I think it is, then take heart, pursue it, practice it, both you and yours.'[25] If the dialogue achieves its intended effects of urging either Clinias or Crito toward the pursuit of wisdom, it does so through means other than philosophic 'proof.'

This is precisely the critique of Plato made by Oakeshott in a number of places in his work. On one level, Oakeshott rejects the more dogmatic elements in Plato (such as the theory of Forms) for the same reasons he rejects rationalism. For Oakeshott, there can be no purely abstract principles to serve as guides for conduct. Thus, the claims found in Plato concerning the existence of abstract ideals such as 'justice' or 'the good' are for Oakeshott philosophically untenable.

On another level, though, Oakeshott discerns a second and less abstract difficulty with Plato's methods: namely, that his proofs obviously do not work. As Oakeshott points out, and as Plato's readers well know, the success of many of Socrates' arguments requires his interlocutors to accept outrageous assertions, of which the doctrine of recollection is only one among many examples.

Similarly, Oakeshott suggests that Plato's abstract principles about justice, the good, and the like are simply other versions of these same outrageous assertions, and which may in fact have precisely the same purpose. He makes the case for this using the *Republic* as an example:

> It is impossible to have the same sort of knowledge of a contingent situation as one may purport to have about *dikaiosune*. Indeed, Plato himself recognized this. He does not attempt to deduce the details of the life and education of the Guardians from the axiom of 'justice', because this would be impossible; he merely tried to persuade us that 'just' rule will be the probable consequence of rulers of this sort. Or again, he saw that in politics it would be necessary to win the compliance, by persuasion, of those incapable of appreciating proof, and he suggested that this could be done by telling them a convincing story. (*RIP*, 84)

The real critique in this seems to be less that Plato is inappropriately focused on ideals, and more that he resorts to myths to achieve certain results, when he knows full well that his philosophical proofs alone cannot do so.

---

[25] *Euthydemus*, 307c.

This is consistent with a point Oakeshott makes in *On Human Conduct*. Although he clearly accepts the Platonic view of philosophy as the unending interrogation of assumptions, he also reiterates the same critique: that Plato hints at the possibility of an achievement to which he is not fully committed. Again, he writes of the *Republic*:

> In stages, not all of which Plato divulges to us in detail, the theorist achieves, in the end, what Plato thinks of as a definitive understanding, in which the world acquires unconditional intelligibility in being understood in terms of the ultimate postulate, 'the Good.' I shall pass over the difficulties entailed in the notion of an unconditional understanding, which are, perhaps recognized in the visionary quality attributed to this final achievement; what is important is the critical inquiry into the conditions of conditions in which it is reached. (*OHC*, 29)

While he admires Plato's philosophy, Oakeshott dislikes what he views as his fanciful flights from it. The myths and visions to which Plato's Socrates frequently reverts are merely 'devices,' which Oakeshott says 'must be recognized, not as mere error, but as discourse appropriate to a certain sort of audience' (*RIP*, 94). Exactly what sort of audience might necessitate this form of discourse is not made clear; but it *is* made clear that this is *not* an audience engaged in the activity of philosophy.

III

Although Plato employs a form of demonstrative discourse in his writings, one cannot easily say that he is the proponent of any one particular philosophical doctrine. In part, this characteristic is the product of the particular manner — and form — in which Plato chooses to write. The Platonic dialogues are unique in a number of ways, including the fact that they allow their author to adopt different voices and different perspectives, many of which overtly conflict with one another. The benefit of this form is flexibility; the drawback, evidenced by the centuries of controversy about what Plato did or did not say, is some amount of confusion.

The connection between form and content in philosophy is not lost on Oakeshott. 'Not to detect a man's style is to have missed three-quarters of the meaning of his actions and utterances; and not to have acquired a style is to have shut oneself off from the ability to convey any but the crudest meanings,' he writes.[26] While he of course does not write dialogues, he does seem to learn a particular

---

[26] Oakeshott, *The Voice of Liberal Learning: Michael Oakeshott on Education*, ed. Timothy Fuller (New Haven: Yale Univ. Press, 1989), 56. Hereafter: *VLL*.

tactic from Plato, which allows him to capitalize on the benefits of the form while avoiding the worst of its drawbacks.

Oakeshott distinguishes between two general philosophical styles. The first is the didactic style, which he describes as the more expository of the two types. This form of philosophy, he writes, is 'already entirely freed from the doubts and hesitancies of the process of thought. It is only a residue, a distillate that is offered to the reader ... [and] if it inspires to fresh thought, it does so only by opposition' (*RIP*, 234).

Contemplative philosophy, on the other hand, is more dialectical than eristic. Authors using this style 'are less careful to send us away with a precisely formulated doctrine,' writes Oakeshott. 'Philosophy for them is a conversation, and, whether or not they write it as a dialogue, their style reflects their conception' (*RIP*, 234). Though he does not point to a specific example of this form of philosophy, he does not have to; there could hardly be a better exemplar for it than Plato.

Most superficially, of course, Plato's dialogues quite literally are — or rather, depict — conversations. Beyond this, though, they also function as conversations at another level. Because they contain a variety of viewpoints, as expressed through the words of the different characters, one cannot simply take in what is presented on the page. Instead, the dialogue requires that the reader actively participate in discerning which among those viewpoints is best, and which is most flawed. In this way, the dialogue becomes a conversation between the work itself, and the reader. As Jacob Klein puts it, 'a (Platonic) dialogue has not taken place if we, the listeners or readers, did not actively participate in it; lacking such participation, all that is before us is indeed nothing but a book.'[27]

The fluidity of some Platonic dialogues can sometimes give them an aura of spontaneity, but this appearance of artlessness of course is not entirely true. As Hegel observes, Plato's dialogues in fact are carefully constructed, much more so than actual conversations ever are, both in their questions and in their responses. Indeed, although Hegel believes the dialogues illustrate a 'beautifully consistent dialectical process,' he also finds this artistry unduly restrictive. 'Just as in the Catechism the answers are prescribed to the questions asked,

---

[27] Jacob Klein, *A Commentary on Plato's* Meno (Chicago: Univ. of Chicago Press, 1965), 6. See also the *Anonymous Prolegomena to Platonic Philosophy*, ed. L. G. Westerlink (Amsterdam: North Holland Publishing Co., 1962), 28.

so it is in these dialogues, for they who answer have to say what the author pleases.'[28]

Though Oakeshott observes in Plato the presence of the freer, more contemplative form of philosophy, I have shown in the previous section that he, like Hegel, also recognizes the periodic appearance of its opposite. This time quoting a selection from the *Phaedo*, Oakeshott writes as an example:

> 'I am confident that the dead have some kind of existence,' says Socrates with unwonted dogmatism; and Simmias, wishing to pass from authority which merely constrains opinion to reason which persuades and enlightens, asks, 'Do you mean to go away and keep this belief to yourself, or will you let us share it with you?' (*RPML*, 75)[29]

Once again, this shows Oakeshott's belief that Socrates' appeals to the immortal soul are both uncharacteristic and unfounded. When he makes these appeals, Plato's Socrates abandons the discourse of persuasive philosophical reason, and instead resorts to something less than philosophy. Surely, the immortality of the soul is one thing that can never be proved true; it can only be proved effective, and for this it requires acceptance rather than understanding.

Despite his dislike of these moments of 'unwonted dogmatism,' however, Oakeshott nevertheless admires the flexibility of Plato's dialogues, and incorporates some of this quality into his own writing. He does this not by mimicking the form exactly, but by choosing so frequently to write essays rather than treatises. The distinction between an essay and a treatise is suggested by Walter Pater, who writes that the effect of a treatise is to wither thought into a 'dogmatic system, the dry bones of which rattle in one's ears.'[30] The form most unlike the treatise, he continues, is the poem, which successfully captures the most intuitive and imaginative qualities of thought. The essay, however, occupies an intermediary position between the two; and this quality makes it most resemble the Platonic dialogue, which is dialectic throughout. 'The essence of that method,' he writes, 'is dialogue, the habit of seeking truth by means of question and answer, primarily with oneself.'[31]

---

[28] G. W. F. Hegel, *Lectures on the History of Philosophy*, trans. E. S. Haldane and F. Simson, vol. 2 (NY: Humanities Press, 1974), 14-17.

[29] Oakeshott here cites *Phaedo* 63c, *Republic* 345b, and Walter Pater, *Plato and Platonism* (NY: Macmillan and Co., 1895), chap. 7.

[30] Pater, *Plato and Platonism*, 156.

[31] Pater, *Plato and Platonism*, 158-9.

Other commentators have noticed the affinities between Plato's dialogues and Oakeshott's writings as well. W. H. Greenleaf explicitly highlights this connection, stating that 'Oakeshott's diverse writings may be seen as being rather like Plato's series of dialogues, the whole being united by a common manner of discussion rather than as parts of an architectonic system.'[32] This is a quality about his own work of which Oakeshott seems to be very much aware. In his preface to *On Human Conduct*, for example, he refers to that work as only a 'collection of essays,' a rambling path of 'footprints in the snow' (*OHC*, vii-viii). Similarly, in an earlier piece, he modestly compares his written thoughts to

> a choir of singers standing around the conductor, who do not always sing in time because their attention is diverted from him. But when they look at him, they sing well. So, these hints . . . partially express my meaning, but often I am conscious that they depart from that consistency and become isolated and feeble parts of a whole which does not exist. (*RPML*, 62)

One tangible effect of this style of writing is that it requires greater involvement from its readers. A treatise can be approached passively, and thus may allow us to 'to *forget to philosophize*, since we can all too easily devote our time to simply taking in the doctrine.'[33] In contrast, Oakeshott's writing seems to self-consciously oppose such a comfortable stance. As he puts it, 'a philosophical essay leaves much to the reader, often saying too little for fear of saying too much . . . it is personal but never merely "subjective" . . . and although it may enlighten it does not instruct' (*OHC*, vii).[34]

Without going too far, one nevertheless might venture to say that this is another respect in which Oakeshott is very much like Plato. It is true, of course, that Oakeshott does not explicitly adopt Plato's style; he does not speak through the voices of other characters; and he does not concoct conversations under the guise of recording them. While he does not furnish us with ready-made conversations, however, like Plato he offers texts that actively engage the reader in a form of 'discussion'.

In *On Human Conduct*, Oakeshott argues that all understandings are 'conditional platforms.' By this, he means that while many

---

[32] W. H. Greenleaf, *Oakeshott's Philosophical Politics*, (NY: Barnes and Noble, 1966), 15. Though he rightly makes this observation, he does not draw any further conclusions from it.

[33] Drew Hyland, 'Why Plato Wrote Dialogues,' *Philosophy and Rhetoric* 1, no. 1 (1968): 39.

[34] On the difference between information and instruction on the one hand, and judgment and 'imparting' on the other, see *VLL*, 51-62.

understandings can and should be treated as provisionally true, they are never absolutely so. Instead, all understandings may also be seen as invitations to further questioning rather than as 'truths' to be passively accepted. The understandings Oakeshott offers to us are no exception. If this standard is rigorously applied to his works, then they too become dialogues in so far as the reader accepts his invitations to inquiry and thus becomes an interlocutor of sorts.

This is why Oakeshott reminds us that his writings are more likely to 'enlighten' than they are to 'instruct.' For him, the task of philosophy is like that of education more generally: its success is not determined by the amount of concrete information it provides. Although its aim is to yield clarity, it is even more important that it help to cultivate an attitude and an aptitude for the pursuit of clarity in the future. If it encompasses a form of teaching, then it is one similar to that recommended by Plato in the *Phaedrus*. 'The dialectician chooses a proper soul and plants and sows within it discourse accompanied by knowledge… which is not barren but produces a seed from which more discourse grows in the character of others.'[35]

This is sure to disappoint those who seek something more substantial from philosophy, and it certainly accounts for some of the frustration felt by some readers of Plato, who may object to his Protean evasiveness. It should be recalled, however, that there is one way in which Plato is decidedly unlike Proteus. As Homer tells us, to one who can persevere through the terrible changes, twists and turns, Proteus will ultimately surrender, yielding his knowledge without any further challenge to the inquirer. With Plato, it is not clear that this moment of achievement will ever arrive; at no point can the reader ever really be satisfied that the effort of inquiry is over, and that wisdom has been acquired like a tame bird held in the hand. As the preceding pages have tried to show, this may be the central lesson Oakeshott learns from his encounters with Plato.

---

[35] *Phaedrus*, 276e-277a. In 'Teaching and Learning,' Oakeshott describes teaching as 'setting on foot the cultivation of the mind, so that what is planted may grow' (*VLL*, 47).

2

Eric S. Kos

Platonic Themes in Oakeshott's Modern European State

I

I am, no doubt, treading near a precipice; perhaps setting myself up to make 'a very great mistake' as Oakeshott himself put it in his first lecture at the London School of Economics and Political Science on the Modern European State, by lumping the modern European state together with the ancient Greek *polis*.[1] If, in fact, what I intended to do was to argue Plato's *polis* and Oakeshott's state are more or less analogous, a fatal step would be taken, though not without an insubstantial body of literature in this vein to cushion the fall. And it might even be an unforgivable mistake, for one of the central contributions Oakeshott makes to the history of political thought in the third essay of *On Human Conduct* is to argue that the 'pedigree of all modern European states is unquestionably medieval' (*LSE*, 387).[2] Fortunately, however, this is not at all what I propose to do.

---

[1]   Oakeshott, *A Study of Political Thought: A Series of Lectures by Michael Oakeshott*, 1950s-1960s, Oakeshott Archives in The British Library of Political and Economic Science, London School of Economics and Political Science (LSE), File 1/1/21, 387. This is a remarkable set of thirty-three lectures given at the London School of Economics and Political Science. They have recently been made available through the archives at London School of Economics. These lectures contain different iterations of many of the themes in Oakeshott's published writings. Citation of these lectures will be indicated by '*LSE*' followed by the page number. It is not clear the pagination was Oakeshott's. The pagination is continuous straight through the lectures, despite some pages clearly being out of order.

[2]   Cf. Oakeshott, *On Human Conduct* (Oxford: Clarendon Press, 1975), 198. Hereafter: *OHC*.

Rather, I hope to draw attention to the Platonic themes that per-
meate Oakeshott's third essay: themes that made an appearance in
the earliest expressions of his thought. This task has been made easier by the availability of Oakeshott's notebooks, which contain
rather extensive notes on early Greek political thought, Plato's
Republic, and Aristotle's *Politics* and *Ethics*, and by his lecture notes
both from his first course of lectures at Cambridge and from his lectures given at the London School of Economics and Political Science.[3]

Oakeshott shared with Plato the belief that the political regime is a
reflection of the moral character of the associates that make up the
regime. It is this belief and the idealism that it implies that underpin
both Platonic and Oakeshottian thinking.[4] Plato's idealism, however, mixes a disposition to be philosophical about the regime with a
disposition to reform the regime. It is Oakeshott's criticism of the latter that helps account for only a partial, but important, adoption of
Plato's theoretical treatment of the relationship of the individual to
the state. The disposition of Plato, to be both philosopher and
reformer, has an analogue in the way Oakeshott describes the dual
disposition of the associates in the modern European state.

II

As Oakeshott sees it, the office of government, in a modern European state, has a dual character objectified in the administrative history of the state. This dual character, in turn, is reflected in and is a
reflection of the dispositions of the associates that make up the state.
The state, Oakeshott says, is best viewed as 'an unresolved tension
between . . . two irreconcilable dispositions' (*OHC*, 201). One disposition makes plausible the analogy of the state as a *universitas*. Here

---

[3]   Oakeshott, Notebook titled *Early Greek Philosophy*, October [1923] 1925, LSE
       File 2/4/1 (*EGP*); Oakeshott, Notebooks titled *Republic I*, and *Republic II*,
       July 1923, LSE Files 2/2/1 (*Rep I*), and 2/2/2 (*Rep II*); Oakeshott, 'A
       Philosophical Approach to Politics: My First Course of Lectures,' 1931, LSE
       File 1/1/7 (*C.Lec*). I shall cite the notebooks using the abbreviations just
       given, followed by the page number and 'v' if the verso page. The lectures
       sub-titled 'My First Course of Lectures' as above followed by the lecture
       number and the page number.
[4]   This belief is not only important in understanding the state but powerfully
       contributes to the importance of education for Plato and Oakeshott. If the
       political regime is a reflection of the dispositions of the associates,
       meaningful changes in the regime come not from a rearrangement of
       institutions but from changes in the self-understanding of individuals.

the state is viewed as 'persons associated in respect of some identi-fied common purpose, in pursuit of some acknowledged substan-tive end, or in the promotion of some specified enduring interest' (*OHC*, 203). The other disposition makes the analogy of the state as a *societas* more appropriate. In this view, the relationship of associates in a state is understood 'not as an engagement in an enterprise to pursue a common substantive purpose or to promote a common interest' but that of 'loyalty to one another' denoted by the 'kindred word "legality."' The relationship is 'a formal relationship in terms of rules,' a 'pact or agreement . . . to acknowledge the authority of certain conditions of acting', but not determining the substantive choice of what actions to perform (*OHC*, 201). However, before exploring what Oakeshott could mean by the state as an unresolved tension between these two dispositions, there is an important con-gruence between Oakeshott and Plato in their presuppositions, or, more properly, a congruence between Oakeshott's assumptions and his understanding of Plato's assumptions.[5]

Though at times Oakeshott may seem to suggest it is the actual activities of governments and the great expansion of the power available to modern governments that are the significant factors in determining the character of the modern European state,[6] he is quite clear the primary source of the character of the state derives from the associates themselves. 'For, although the character of an association, that of the office of government (if any), and that of the associates are conditionally interrelated, each implying the others, it is the third which constitutes the *causa foederis*; and an associate is what he understands himself to be' (*OHC*, 234).

Oakeshott takes Plato to be coming from a similar position. In Oakeshott's notes on the *Republic* he records a passage from Nettleship's set of Plato lectures, a source Oakeshott relied on heavily.[7] Nettleship places great emphasis on the methodological path Socrates advances in the search for justice. Socrates suggests it

[5]   What should be clear is that the reading of Plato is the reading that emerges
       from Oakeshott's notebooks on Plato, which, like his interpretation of
       Hobbes, is not necessarily the familiar reading.
[6]   For example, he suggests that the number of individuals *manqués* is
       'proportionately greater than ever before, mainly because of the policies of
       governments' (*OHC*, 276).
[7]   Richard Lewis Nettleship (1846-92), was educated at Uppingham School
       and later Balliol where he became a student of T.H. Green (with Benjamin
       Jowett as tutor) and later a Fellow in 1869. He lectured mostly on Logic and
       Plato's *Republic*. He largely adopted the idealism of Green, but differed

might be better to look for justice in the city, which is larger, and once found it will more easily be detected in the soul, which is smaller. This is a critical turning point in the argument for Nettleship and for Oakeshott, for the latter records the following point from Nettleship's Plato lectures: 'To understand the import of this transition is to understand the principle of the whole argument of the *Republic*' (*Rep I*, 29).[8] That principle is not any of the usual suspects: that philosophers should rule, or that everyone has a distinguishable role to play in the natural, hierarchical organism that is society, or that democracy rules by opinion and not by wisdom or knowledge. Rather,

> The whole of the *Republic* is really an attempt to interpret human nature psychologically; the postulate upon which its method rests is that all the institutions of society, class organization, law, religion, art and so on, are ultimately products of the human soul, an inner principle of life which works itself out in these outward shapes. . . . Plato's position is that the life of the state is the life of the men composing it, as manifested in a way comparatively easy to observe. . . . The 'justice of the state,' then, is the justice of the individuals who compose it. . . . We must bear in mind throughout Plato's argument that there is no state apart from the individual men and women who compose it. (*Rep I*, 29)[9]

What is central to understand then, for Oakeshott (and Oakeshott sees this as the preeminent concern of Plato in the *Republic*), is the nature or the character of the individuals who compose the state. The two may diverge, as we shall see, on the character of these individuals, but what should be noticed here is the idealism that this view implies which drew Oakeshott and a host of other British Idealists to Plato.

Early British Idealists drew their inspiration from a rediscovery of Plato, from a reaction to what was perceived as the sensationalism and materialism of Hobbes, and from Berkeley, before Hegel made his way across the channel.[10] But, for later Idealists, like Bosanquet and Oakeshott, Hegel becomes a window through which Plato can

---

from Green in 'teaching philosophy more strictly from an educational point of view,' Richard Lewis Nettleship, *Philosophical Lectures and Remains*, in two volumes, A. C. Bradley and G. R. Benson, eds. (London: Macmillan and Co. 1987), xvii. Upon Green's death he wrote a memoir of Green and prepared his lectures for publication. A decade later he died in a snowstorm climbing Mont Blanc in Switzerland.

[8]   Nettleship, *Philosophical Remains*, 67.
[9]   Nettleship, *Philosophical Remains*, 68-9.
[10] See, John N. Murihead, *The Platonic Tradition in Anglo-Saxon Philosophy: Studies in the History of Idealism in England and America* (1931; reprinted, Bristol: Thoemmes Press, 1992), 14.

be understood. Oakeshott records in his notebook the following passage from Hegel's *History of Philosophy*:

> If we thus regard the content of the Platonic idea (i.e., looking below the surface of life to see whether its fundamental facts are grasped), we shall find that Plato did in fact represent the Greek moral system (*Sittlichkeit*) substantially as what it was; for Greek civil life is what forms the substantial basis of Plato's *Republic*. Plato is not the man to worry himself with abstract theories and principles; his true intelligence has grasped and represented real truth, and this could be nothing else than the truth in which he lived, of that one mind which came to life in him no less than in Greece. (*Rep I*, 3)[11]

What this passage and the earlier quotation from Nettleship capture is the notion that philosophy is the attempt to describe the whole of existence, experience, or reality by giving a reasoned account of the identity of, and relationship between, the particulars of that reality. The place to go for this reality is the thoughts and beliefs of individuals who lived at the time. It is not just the historical conditions but the meanings individuals placed on those goings-on that made up the historical conditions. As Oakeshott puts it in the first essay in *On Human Conduct*, an agent 'is what he understands [or misunderstands] himself to be, his contingent situations are what he understands [or misunderstands] them to be' (*OHC*, 41). One might recognize this as one of the fundamental postulates Oakeshott relies upon to theorize the state and human conduct, and he explicitly draws attention to this postulate again in the third essay (*OHC*, 235), but the immediate significance consists of two important points.

First, the locus of one's philosophical attention, in understanding the state or any other topic, should be squarely on the self-understanding of the individuals who compose the state, or on what we generally call today the political 'culture.'

Second, and closely related, this belief is a fundamental postulate of idealist thinking more generally. One's thoughts or ideas are the source of what gives a unity to reality. Thinking, in large measure, is an attempt to make more sense of one's reality. To follow the impulse of all thinking without reserve (i.e., philosophical thinking) is the attempt to capture the whole of existence, experience, or reality in thought. In short, philosophy is an attempt to achieve a concrete

---

[11] This passage is included in Bernard Bosanquet, *A Companion to Plato's Republic for English Readers Being a Commentary adapted to Davies and Vaughan's Translation*, 2d ed. (London: Rivington's, 1906), 16-17, as part of a series of passages students of Plato would do well to consider. Oakeshott relied heavily on Bosanquet's *Companion* in his notebook.

universal, a coherent map of the totality of experience that does not abstract from particulars but subsumes them in a monistic whole.

This understanding, the idealists hold, that reality is a complete and coherent whole (a unity in diversity, a many in one, or an absolute or concrete universal), may lead in two different directions, one more practical and the other more philosophical. That there is a relationship between the philosophical doctrine or explanation and the concrete particulars may suggest not just a philosophical approach, but a practical link from theory to practice. As David Boucher has pointed out, for the British Idealists, 'with a few exceptions, notably Bradley and McTaggart,[12] philosophy was integrally related to practical life and needed to be directed to improve the condition of society. They maintained that everything in experience was related to everything else. There could be no isolated individuals or facts.' As such, 'Idealism was able to provide a rational basis for belief which, together with its emphasis on the unity and development of human potential, provided a philosophical basis for social legislation.' So strong a basis in fact that 'British idealists were almost evangelical in their reforming zeal and saw their position as professional philosophers carried with it a social responsibility to identify and articulate the sources of injustice and depravity, and campaign for reform.'[13] Oakeshott did not follow the route of many of the other British Idealists, including Bosanquet whom he relied upon in his notebooks.

What is striking about Oakeshott's understanding of Plato's idealism is just how sensitive he was in his early thought to the varieties of idealism embodied in Plato's thinking. At a critical point in the discussion of the Good in the *Republic*, Oakeshott references McTaggart's essay on 'The Necessity of Dogma.' He is impressed with McTaggart's argument that 'Nothing is true merely because it is good. Nothing is good merely because it is true.'[14] Oakeshott understands Plato, however, to hold the 'idea of *knowledge* at the bot-

---

[12]   These two were a strong influence on Oakeshott. Oakeshott acknowledged a clear debt to Bradley in the introduction to his *Experience and Its Modes* (Cambridge: Cambridge University Press, 1933), 6. Hereafter: *EM*. McTaggart first introduced Oakeshott to philosophy as a student at Cambridge: See Robert Grant, *Thinkers of Our Time: Oakeshott*, Claridge Press, 1990), 13. One might include Oakeshott among these eccentric British Idealists.

[13]   David Boucher, ed., *The British Idealists* (Cambridge: Cambridge Univ. Press, 1997), ix-xi.

[14]   John Ellis McTaggart, 'The Necessity of Dogma' *International Journal of Ethics* 5, no. 2 (1895): 147-62, 150.

tom of all goodness. Truth at the bottom of the Good' (*Rep I*, 67v).
McTaggart makes a clear distinction between truth and goodness,
and argues that questions of truth and questions of goodness are 'independent and ultimate';[15] that the difficult duty of a thinker 'is to
avoid confusing the two great questions: Is this real? and Would this
be good?'[16]

This is not the only concern Oakeshott had about Plato's idealism.
He also worried about the mysticism implied in the monism of
Plato's idealism. In one of the rare moments in the notebooks on the
Greeks, Oakeshott poses a question. 'Is "justice" ever attained in
other than a mystic state?' referencing McTaggart's essays 'Mysticism' and 'The Necessity of Dogma' (*Rep I*, 56v). Mysticism,
McTaggart argues 'asserts a greater unity in the universe than that
which is recognized in ordinary experience, or in science'; he goes on
to note that there are two different kinds of unity that may be imagined.[17] 'The unity may be regarded as only one aspect of the universe, and as combined with diversity. Or it may be said that, in
reality, there is no diversity at all, but only unity.'[18]

There are then two separate questions about Plato's idealism that
Oakeshott is concerned with at the early stage in his thinking. The
one is that Plato collapses questions of goodness and questions of
truth into each other (a combination which is addressed more fully
below). The other is how to account for the unity (and thus the diversity) in experience. Oakeshott is keen, in addressing the latter question, to insulate Plato from the charge that he is an enthusiastic
mystic hoping for a release from every element of contingency. So,
Oakeshott is careful to follow Bosanquet's translation of the passage
where Socrates discusses the magnanimity of the philosopher. 'To
an understanding endowed with magnificence and the contemplation of all time and all being, do you think it possible,' Socrates asks,
'that human life seem anything great?'[19] Oakeshott remarks on this
passage that there is 'no thought here of "another" life or world' (*Rep
I*, 68). Bosanquet remarks that these passages should be handled

---

[15] McTaggart, 'Dogma,' 150.
[16] John Ellis McTaggart, 'Mysticism,' in *Philosophical Studies*, ed. S.V. Keeling
(London: Edward Arnold and Co. 1934), 64-5. Originally published in *The
New Quarterly* 2, no. 7 (1909): 315-39.
[17] McTaggart, 'Mysticism,' 47.
[18] McTaggart, 'Mysticism,' 50.
[19] *Republic*, 486a, quoted in Bosanquet, *Companion*.

carefully 'to avoid quietism.'[20] Oakeshott suggests one should not understand Plato to be arguing that there exists a mystical unity, the beholding of which annihilates the individual.

Or, consider Oakeshott's understanding of the Platonic Forms, which largely frees Plato from this mysticism and, interestingly, also from a correspondence theory of truth. The Platonic Forms are 'the elements of unity in the manifold objects or things which we apprehend by the senses' (*Rep I*, 66). This diverges from other readings of the Forms as 'things' separate from the actual objects of the senses; sense and thought cannot be separated. Bosanquet spends a good deal of time attempting to disabuse people of readings of Plato's Forms that come from sources other than the simple presentation of Plato himself: 'the conceptions which have been derived from Aristotle's account of the doctrine, from clearly mythical passages in Plato himself (as in the myth of the *Phaedrus*), and from vague echoes of Kantian "things-in-themselves."'[21]

At a minimum, Oakeshott's notes on these passages clearly show Oakeshott himself was aware of and sensitive to an idealism that is less absolute than some mystical, monistic absolutism. That there is a unity does not deny that the diversity is real. The earlier question of truth and goodness in Plato's idealism also is instructive, for Oakeshott is most critical of Plato for his practical bent that the mingling of the two implies.

III

Oakeshott's overall evaluation of Plato and his thinking can only be characterized as one of critical ambivalence. Oakeshott admired Plato's philosophical acumen and generally his understanding of the practice of philosophy and theorizing (*OHC*, 27). Oakeshott sees the *Republic* as a masterpiece of moral philosophy. However, and this aspect never ceases to provide occasions for comment by Oakeshott, the *Republic* is also 'a book of a <u>reformer</u>' (*Rep I*, 1). This evaluation of Plato as both philosopher *and* reformer was an enduring one for Oakeshott and he believed it was the zeal of the latter that compromised the former. This evaluation shows up in Oakeshott's first course of lectures at Cambridge in 1931. He praises Plato for his response to the Sophists and their abstract thinking, reading Plato to be urging the Sophists to 'think more concretely; have done with

---

[20] Bosanquet, *Companion*, 220.
[21] Bosanquet, *Companion*, 206.

abstract divisions like this of nature and convention. If you want to see the life of man truly you must see it as a single whole' (*C.Lec*, 8.3). Echoing Hegel's critique of Plato, which Oakeshott references later in his notebooks (*Rep I*, 49), Oakeshott criticizes Plato in the Cambridge lectures for not being idealist enough. Plato still 'speaks the language of morality — goodness, justice, what *ought* we to do?' (*C.Lec*, 8.3).

Oakeshott clearly sees the practical thrust of Plato's reflections on politics and the *polis*. Specifically Oakeshott identifies Plato with the political aim to 'awaken Athens to her desperate need of discipline.' 'Sparta he saw,' Oakeshott continues, 'took life seriously, was scientifically organized — for a purpose — war.... Athens must be disciplined, scientifically organized for the purpose of "the good life."' (*Rep I*, 3v). A primary event that animated Plato's philosophy, as many others have observed, was the death of Socrates and more particularly how the trial and death of Socrates underscores the 'errors of Athenian democracy.'[22] Oakeshott even places him within a political movement 'whose chief work was the criticism of the great 5th century and its statesmen.'[23] What is interesting though is the juxtaposition of this belief that Plato's philosophy is an attempt to correct Athenian democracy with Hegel's famous passage, to which Oakeshott immediately alludes in his notebook, from *The Philosophy of Right*:

> It is only when the actual world has reached its full fruition that the ideal rises to confront reality, and builds up, in the shape of an intellectual realm, that same world grasped in its substantial being. When philosophy paints its grey in grey, some one shape of life had meantime grown old: and grey in grey, though it brings it into knowledge, cannot make it young again. The owl of Minerva does not start upon its flight until the evening twilight begins to fall.

The force of Hegel's thought, of course, leans strongly against philosophy being prescriptive and rather toward philosophy's central activities being descriptive and explanatory, a belief Oakeshott never abandoned in his published or unpublished works.

Where Plato is being more philosophical (one might say Socratic) Oakeshott incorporates important insights about the state, and where Plato is wearing his hat as a reformer Oakeshott is critical. It is Plato's reforming zeal that Oakeshott believes distracts him from

[22] Oakeshott makes this point in his introduction to *Leviathan* (*RIP*, 226).
[23] He immediately references Pericles and his death in 429 B.C., the *Gorgias* 515e and 519a, and Hegel's evaluation that 'this marks the beginning of decadence (cf. Hegel, *Phil d. Rechts*. p. 20)' (*Rep I*, 2).

penetrating further than he does in philosophically working through the idea of the *polis*.

As indicated earlier, one of the criticisms Oakeshott had of Plato was that he didn't go far enough, and I want to pause a moment to notice what Oakeshott might mean by this. First, it should be noticed that Plato *did* go far to begin with, but far in what sense? Oakeshott's notes on Socrates help point the way. Oakeshott sees Socrates' response to the Sophists as significant in that it superseded the distinction between nature and convention. Socrates saw that what human beings *do* is a reflection of what they naturally *are*, so activities like living together and writing laws (conventions) is natural to human beings. Self-consciously making things, artifacts, whether a sculpture or a city with laws is natural to human beings, as Oakeshott puts it echoing Aristotle, 'Man's nature issues in all that he does' (*Rep I*, 24v). And, despite whether one believes there is a final cause or *telos* for human beings or the state, and regardless of the Greek understanding of fate, this belief is a central insight of Socrates that Oakeshott believed Plato largely internalized.

However, this Socratic insight is not taken to its logical conclusion, is not pressed far enough philosophically. Oakeshott records Hegel's criticism of Plato on this point from the *History of Philosophy*:

> People set it down as his defect that he was too ideal, but his defect lies much rather in this, that he was not ideal enough. For if reason is the universal power, and this is essentially intellectual; then as intellectual it involves subjective freedom, which had dawned on the world in Socrates as a new principle. Therefore, though rationality ought to be the basis of law, and is so on the whole, yet on the other side it essentially involves conscience, private conviction, in short, all forms of subjective freedom ... The element in general, this movement of the individual, this principle of subjective freedom, is in Plato in part disregarded, in part purposely violated, because it displayed itself as that which brought about ruin in Greece. (*Rep I*, 49)[24]

It is Plato's diagnosis and recommended treatment of Athens' ailment that leads his philosophical thinking in the wrong direction and toward advancing an ideal city that removes elements of diversity and to the purging of the city of all that distracts from its overall unity (what Oakeshott periodically refers to in his notebooks as Plato's monasticism). Interestingly, it is the Socratic side of Plato that gets pushed out. In Oakeshott's London School of Economics lectures on the Roman political experience he mentions that the Roman

---

[24] Here as elsewhere, Oakeshott drew the citation from Bosanquet's *Companion*.

notions of legality had very few counterparts in the Greek world, but in a handwritten bit of marginalia he references for comparison Plato's dialogue *Crito* (*LSE*, 244). Is Oakeshott suggesting that Socrates, despite the great barrier that the Greek moral view presented,[25] was able to grasp the outlines of law as having procedural authority? Perhaps, but what is clear is that Socrates is, for Oakeshott, the representative of the 'sceptical, enquiring, spirit' and the 'representative of the true philosophical spirit' (*Rep I*, 10). Plato, on the other hand, while reflecting this debt to Socrates especially in the early dialogues desired more of a system. Knowledge of the Good, for Plato, 'is a science, a system: it can be taught — true education. The raison d'être of the State,' Oakeshott notes (*Rep I*, 6).[26]

This invoking of Hegel's critique of Plato serves to draw attention to another Platonic theme in Oakeshott's thinking about the relationship of the individual to the state, and at the same time, the major difference between Plato's thinking about the *polis* and the modern understanding of the state. Oakeshott views Plato's reforming side as leading to his rationalistic insistence on system[27] and ignoring the interdependence of system and internal conviction: a rational objectivism that might deny subjective individualism. However, within Plato's argument insisting on the unity of the city, Oakeshott sees a truth many modern thinkers have ignored. Plato — and Aristotle — understand human beings to be the most they can be *within* a state. The *polis* exists, Aristotle says, not for living but for living well.[28] The thought here, as Oakeshott understands it, is that human beings are nothing without the state, that, quoting Nettleship, 'There is no such thing as an individual in the abstract, a human being liter-

---

[25] The Greek moral view was no doubt deeply impacted by its almost continual belligerence with its neighbors, a condition Oakeshott insists is alien to civil association and a powerful augmentation to the view of the state as an enterprise association (*OHC*, 273).

[26] This view is further reinforced, following Wincenty Lutoslawski, *The Origin and Growth of Plato's Logic, with an account of Plato's Style and of the Chronology of His Writings* (London, New York and Bombay: Longmans, Green, and Co., 1897), and J.A. Stewart, *Plato's Doctrine of Ideas* (Oxford: Clarendon Press, 1909). Stewart grouped the 'Socratic' dialogues as the earliest, followed by the later more 'Platonic' groupings as the systemization increases.

[27] In a later essay Oakeshott gives Plato the title of the 'father of demonstrative political discourse.' (See 'Political Discourse,' in Oakeshott, *Rationalism in Politics and other essays, new and expanded edition,* ed. Timothy Fuller (Indianapolis: Liberty Press, 1991), 82. Hereafter: *RIP*.

[28] *Politics*, 1252b29.

ally independent of all others' (*Rep I*, 63);[29] and quoting Bradley, 'The State without the individual is no more an abstraction than the individual without the State' (*Rep I*, 62v).

This view is reinforced in a number of places in Oakeshott's reading of the *Republic*. Thrasymachus' argument that 'Injustice, when it comes into being on a sufficient scale, is mightier, freer, and more masterful than justice'[30] is followed in Oakeshott's notebook with a reference to T. H. Green's lecture on political obligation. In this lecture Green is taking issue with the social contract theorists (Spinoza, Hobbes, Locke, and even Rousseau) in the separation they presume between individuals on the one hand and the state on the other.[31] Green's argument is that individuals (the rights they have and the freedoms they enjoy) are inseparable from the community they are in, that the community finds its unity in a shared understanding of what is good, and that the formal governing apparatus of the state is an attempt to give fuller reality to that conception of the good.[32] Or again, Oakeshott's critique of Glaucon's social contract is that, though it captures some truth about the community being a tacit contract and that 'society must have force to back it up,' nevertheless, referencing Green again, it is will — not force — that is the basis of the state (*Rep I*, 25v-26). Or, again in Adeimantus' objection that these people are hardly made happy and Socrates' reply that happiness is a harmony — like the beauty of a statue it is not an abstraction but a relation (*Rep I*, 50) — we see the embedded social nature of the individual.[33]

---

[29] Nettleship, *Philosophical Remains*, 177.

[30] *Republic*, 344c.

[31] It is not surprising that the line of argument is very closely followed by Bosanquet in his *Philosophical Theory of the State*, which Oakeshott references a number of times in the notebooks. Bosanquet singles out in addition to the usual social contract theorists, Mill, Spencer, and Kant as positing the atomistic individual *versus* the state.

[32] Thomas Hill Green, *Works of Thomas Hill Green*, vol. 2: 'Philosophical Works,' ed. R.L. Nettleship (London: Longmans, Green, and Co., 1886), 428, 430-1, 444.

[33] Just how social and just how individual Oakeshott imagines human beings to be has been a source of considerable debate in the Oakeshott literature. The debate has centered on how Hobbesian (liberal individualism) versus how Hegelian (culturally and historically embedded) Oakeshott views the individual. See Paul Franco, *The Political Philosophy of Michael Oakeshott* (New Haven: Yale Univ. Press, 1990), esp. chap. 5, for a more Hegelian reading of Oakeshott; and Steven Gerencser, *The Skeptic's Oakeshott* (New York: St. Martin's Press, 2000) for a very skeptical Hobbesian account. For

Nevertheless, as we have seen, Oakeshott is following Hegel in his criticism of Plato's failure to recognize the significance, however dependent on society, of the individual. However, Oakeshott has an implicit critique of Hegel as not being concrete and historical enough in his treatment of Plato. If we return to Oakeshott's third essay in *On Human Conduct*, the idea of individuality Hegel is concerned with may not have been available to Plato. As Oakeshott traces the development of the modern state, the modern individual appears on the scene in sufficient numbers when the recognition that human beings are reflective intelligences comes to be viewed as 'the emblem of human dignity and as a condition for each individual to explore, to cultivate, to make the most of, and to enjoy as an opportunity rather than suffer as a burden' (*OHC*, 236). This can only happen when an increasing number of activities are not directed by the political regime, are not put in the service of the regime, but left to individuals to decide upon. Only then can the practice of deliberating and choosing develop into a disposition 'to recognize imagining, deliberating, wanting, choosing, and acting not as costs incurred in seeking enjoyments but as themselves enjoyments, the exercise of a gratifying self-determination or personal autonomy' (*OHC*, 236).

It would be hard to imagine the individualism Hegel describes as available, in practice, in the Greek world and thus available as something to theorize. The *polis* remained the central locus of one's identity both in the imaginings of someone like Pericles, where the glory, victory, and autonomy of the city is what is most significant[34], in the Platonic city in speech where each contributes to the justice and good of the city by tending to their own business, or in Aristotle's insistence that one is more fully actualizing one's human potential when exercising *phronesis* over that which is more complete and self-sufficient (i.e., the *polis* or public thing).

Though Plato may rightly be criticized for his lack of appreciation of the subjective freedom involved in one's obligations to the city, it

---

an account of the individual as more culturally and morally situated see John Wendell Coats, *Oakeshott and His Contemporaries: Montaigne, St. Augustine, Hegel, et al.* (Selinsgrove: Susquehanna University Press, and London: Associated University Presses, 2000), esp. chap. 3. Oakeshott's reading of Plato may shed some light on this debate by revealing the nature of Oakeshott's early idealism.

[34] See Pericles' 'Funeral Oration' in Thucydides, *The Peloponnesian War*, trans. Richard Crawley, rev. T.E. Wick (New York: The Modern Library, 1982), 2.35-46.

could hardly be the fault of Plato that he is unable to theorize an individuality barely intimated in the Greek experience (except perhaps
in a nascent form in Socrates). It would be difficult, if not impossible,
to put it slightly differently, for Plato to theorize something other
than a teleocracy. To imagine, with Hegel, that the unity of human
society can only be obtained *through* individualized diversity and
the greater 'the differentiation the greater the unity', would be to
expect too much of Plato given the Greek *sittlichkeit* (*Rep I*, 29v). If the
state is a reflection of the disposition of the individuals who make up
the state and these individuals are not disposed to individualism let
alone to celebrate it as the emblem of their humanity, it is easy to see
why Plato would not have theorized the state in these terms.

IV

This brings us back to the modern European state as Oakeshott theo-
rizes it and to a final Platonic theme in Oakeshott's thinking and a
final critique of Plato. If one of the things Oakeshott shared with
Plato was a belief that the state is a reflection of the disposition of
those who make-up the state, the tension in Plato's disposition has
an analogy in the tension of dispositions reflected in the modern
European state. One disposition Plato has, as we have seen, is that of
a reformer. Out of this disposition comes Plato's desire for system, a
vision of the ultimate *telos* upon which society might finally be rationally organized. This vision would be and has been appealing to a
modern individual (or, rather, individual *manqué*), recently
deprived of the comfort of a defined identity and thrown back upon
himself to construct his own. If the Good could finally be settled, this
disposition might turn into the intolerance of difference characterized by Oakeshott's anti-individual (*OHC*, 278).

Plato's other disposition, however is a philosophic one. This side
of Plato has its roots in the 'sceptical, enquiring spirit' of Socrates and
is an irreconcilable counterpoint to Plato's reforming impulse.[35]
While keeping in mind Oakeshott's published argument in *On
Human Conduct* that Plato erred in thinking the philosopher had any-

---

[35] It is interesting to note here that Oakeshott thought Socrates to combine,
       without necessarily being able to resolve, a social conservatism with a
       philosophical radicalism. 'Socrates was a conservative in that he equated
       the just and the legal. A real loyalty and love of law' (*EGP*, 12). He also
       'taught men to think and to question everything. He refused to cease his
       teaching in spite of prohibition. All except conscience must be under the
       control of the State' (*EGP*, 12).

thing useful to say to those in the cave and that they were perfectly capable of getting on in the cave without the philosopher, Oakeshott is much less severe on Plato in the notebooks. Early on and without question, Oakeshott thought it an error to make the philosopher of direct service to the political realm (*Rep I*, 78, 79, 71v). Yet, Oakeshott sees Plato's philosophical impulse as strong. He has a profound 'sense of the immensity of knowledge' akin to that of 'Pascal's scepticism' (*Rep I*, 78). In his treatment of Plato's discussion of the Good, Oakeshott remarks, 'All through the *Republic* you feel the true humbleness of Socrates. We do not know all things. Life is very great, and not easily to be understood' (*Rep I*, 74).

Oakeshott's understanding of Plato's argument on the sovereignty of philosophy reflects the dual disposition of Plato. The philosopher must be in the service of the state. However, Oakeshott interprets this service the philosopher may give to the state as much broader than that involved in actually ruling or directly influencing the rulers in a particular regime. 'The relation between society and great men should be one of mutual recognition and service' (*Rep I*, 79). We must recall, Oakeshott notes in this series of notes, 'We are not God's, nor children, but men among men' (*Rep I*, 79).[36] Next to this quote Oakeshott references the *Laws* (739b). The suggestion seems to be that given the limitations of human beings, a second best city is what is required as a practical alternative.[37] Nevertheless, 'The great man must remember that he owes a tremendous amount of his greatness and character to society; and he will willingly serve society in return' (*Rep I*, 78v). But, what is this service? Is it for philosophers to be kings? Oakeshott does not focus on this 'service' being directly political in nature and one might usefully compare his essay 'The

---

[36] Bosanquet, in his *Companion*, has an illuminating reading of Socrates' answer to the question of the practicability of the city in speech and philosophers becoming kings. Plato doesn't avoid the question, but 'in perfect logical order, when he turns to the question of possibility begins by explaining that between this abstraction and its realization in historical fact there is undoubtedly a condition interposed; he then proceeds to state this condition (viz., a scientific treatment of politics), and subsequently to show, from the connection both of the ideal and of its condition with the central realities of life and mind, that the degree in which the condition is fulfilled will also be the degree in which the essentials of his "illustration" will become historic fact' (*Companion*, 200-1).

[37] This is the reading Nettleship gives to this section of the *Republic*. In the *Laws* Plato 'proceeds to show what he thinks the nearest practicable approximation to the institutions' of the *Republic* are (*Philosophical Lectures*, 185 n. 1).

Claims of Politics' where one's service may be to abstain *from* engaging in politics.[38] The comparison to Socrates' argument that his private way of life has been a gift to the city is unmistakable.

This disposition in Plato — the more detached, humble, philosophically inquisitive side — has a strong parallel in the disposition of the *socius* in a modern civil association. It is the skeptical disposition to imagine, not that the Good does not exist, but that it may be exceedingly difficult if not impossible to fully know the Good let alone use it as a guide for political arrangements. Absent a clear roadmap for human beings, bereft of a comprehensive agreement about our ends to which we might all direct our energies, life might alternatively be viewed as an adventure, and our relationship to others as a

> *civitas peregrina*: an association, not of pilgrims travelling to a common destination, but of adventurers each responding as best he can to the ordeal of consciousness in a world composed of others of his kind, each the inheritor of the imaginative achievements (moral and intellectual) of those who have gone before and joined in a variety of prudential practices, but here partners in a practice of civility the rules of which are not devices for satisfying substantive wants and whose obligations create no symbiotic relationship. (*OHC*, 243)

To modern individuals with a strong historical sensibility and a Socratic humility about the limits and possibilities of human beings, both in action and in thought, the state as a *societas* would be more appealing. It establishes an authority to lay down rules of civility while maintaining a sphere for individual self-expression and activity. To a modern individual drawn to the comfort of a comprehensive roadmap that provides relief from the burden of making often very difficult choices, the state as a *universitas* may be more appropriate. 'It may be true,' Oakeshott suggests, 'that, hidden in human character, there are two powerful and contrary dispositions, neither strong enough to defeat or to put to flight the other' (*OHC*, 323). These two dispositions find an early expression in Plato and account for the ambivalent character of the activities of the modern European state.

---

[38] Oakeshott, *Religion, Politics and the Moral Life*, ed. Timothy Fuller (New Haven: Yale Univ. Press, 1993), 94. Hereafter: *RPML*.

3

Corey Abel

Appropriating Aristotle

To seek everywhere the element of utility is least of all fitting for those who are magnanimous and free.   *Politics*, 8.3.12

In the preface to *On Human Conduct* Oakeshott says, 'The themes explored here have been with me nearly as long as I can remember.'[1] He is not only adverting to his age in a charmingly indirect way, but disclosing that this work revisits questions that have occupied him since the 1920s. During those years, he studied Plato and Aristotle's political philosophy with some care. Drawing on notebooks from this early period, I would like to explore how he appropriated Aristotle throughout his career.[2] However, there were many authors he studied early and long remembered. As his notebooks reveal, Oakeshott's sympathies were wide-ranging; his full intellectual biography would include Plotinus, Spinoza, Pascal, Epicurus, Confucius and others, including his 'contemporaries.'[3] So I am not interested in pegging him as 'Aristotelian.' In any event, the adjective, having been claimed by, or for, such diverse thinkers as Arendt, MacIntyre, Nussbaum, and Gadamer, would be as harmless as it would be uninformative if applied to Oakeshott — one more figure

---

[1] Oakeshott, *On Human Conduct* (Oxford: Clarendon Press, 1975), vii. Hereafter: *OHC*.

[2] Oakeshott, Notebooks titled *Republic I*, and *Republic II*, July 1923, LSE Files 2/2/1 (*Rep I*), and 2/2/2 (*Rep II*); Oakeshott, Notebooks titled *Aristotle I*, November 1923, LSE File 2/3/1 (*Nic I*); *Aristotle II*, December 1923, LSE File 2/3/2 (*Nic II*); *Aristotle III*, January 1924, LSE File 2/3/3 (*Nic III*); and *Aristotle IV and V*, n.d., LSE File 2/3/4 (*Pol I* and *Pol II*); Oakeshott, Notebook titled *Early Greek Philosophy*, October [1923] 1925, LSE File 2/4/1 (*EGP*). I shall cite the notebooks with the abbreviations just indicated followed by the page number and a 'v' for verso pages.

[3] See Wendell John Coats Jr., *Oakeshott and His Contemporaries: Montaigne, St. Augustine, Hegel, et. al.* (Selinsgrove, PA: Susquehanna Univ. Press, 2000). Besides those in the title, Coats examines Hobbes, Constant, Rousseau, and Hume.

sheltered under the broad cloak of Aristotle's authority. What I would like to show is simply that Aristotle's political thought represents more than an early fascination later abandoned. Since Oakeshott is usually seen in a modern context,[4] noticing his lifelong engagement with Aristotle may help to clarify his achievements in political philosophy.

Reading the notebooks, one discovers that Oakeshott plays with ideas for decades: In a 1924 notebook on the *Ethics*, there is a cross-reference to Aristotle saying, in the *Metaphysics*, 'what is man in comparison to the heavens?' Oakeshott comments, 'The idea of the littleness of man has occurred to most of the world's greatest men. It seems they feel their own littleness more acutely than smaller men do' (*Nic II*, 81-2). An entry in a 1936 notebook says that Augustine's view was 'that pride and sensuality are the two extremes to be avoided in [a] life to be lived in accord with reason and nature.'[5] In 1947, Oakeshott writes that Hobbes reconfigured the Augustinian myth of pride and sensuality, and 'recalls man to his littleness.'[6] This example shows not only the persistence, but the migratory character of ideas in the mind of Michael Oakeshott — he begins with a reflection on Aristotle's character (not his doctrines) gleaned from a remark in the *Metaphysics*, then joins this with an observation on St. Augustine to describe the achievement of Hobbes.

Another such resurfacing occurs when, in *On Human Conduct*, as an example of moral relationships hardening into rules, he writes, 'loyalty becomes legality,' and later says the 'idea of *societas*' involves a tie of 'loyalty to one another . . . which may achieve the formality denoted by the kindred word "legality"' (*OHC*, 67, 201). In 1964 he notes, '"Loyal" is an innovation on "legal".'[7] Much earlier, he saw in Socrates 'A real loyalty and love of law' (*EGP*, 12).

Yet another example of long-lasting concerns is Oakeshott's distinction between the authority of a government, its offices and activ-

---

[4]   Paul Franco, *The Political Philosophy of Michael Oakeshott* (New Haven: Yale Univ. Press, 1990), treats Oakeshott as 'thoroughly Hegelian;' Steven A. Gerencser, *The Skeptic's Oakeshott* (New York: St. Martin's Press, 2000), argues that Oakeshott's idealism gave way to a later Hobbesian skepticism; Robert Orr, 'A Double Agent in the Dream of Michael Oakeshott,' *Political Science Reviewer* 21 (Spring 1992) sees Oakeshott as migrating from Montaigne and Hume to a later Kantian position.
[5]   Oakeshott, Notebook XIII, April 1936, LSE File 2/1/13, 33v.
[6]   Oakeshott, 'Leviathan: A Myth,' in *Hobbes on Civil Association* (Indianapolis: Liberty Fund, 2000), 163. Hereafter: *HCA*.
[7]   Oakeshott, Notebook XVIII, LSE File 2/1/18, 34.

ities, and its mode of association, a distinction he uses to clarify the scope of political reflection.[8] He observes that Aristotle's political vocabulary distinguished:

(i) (*politeuma*): the government, i.e., the administrative officers;

(ii) (*politeia*): gov.: administering and being administered, i.e., the constitution,

(iii) (*polis*): the state, which includes everything.

He adds, 'These meanings, are, however, fluid, and constantly pass into one another' (*Pol I*, 41).[9] In *On Human Conduct* he devotes a lengthy footnote to the fluid meanings of *politeia*. 'It stands for that in terms of which a *polites* is related to his fellows (with perhaps an emphasis upon rules in their character as rules of recognition)' [i.e., the mode of association]; 'it denotes the rule of a *politikos* distinguished from that of a master' [i.e., the activity of government]; and 'it designates the constitution of a particular kind of ruling authority, namely, one which is a mean between democratic and oligarchic rule, "polity"' [i.e., the authority of government] (*OHC*, 166-7, n. 1).

Such similarities abound; but to discern Aristotle's place in Oakeshott's thought, I first survey Oakeshott's critique of Rationalism, then look at his treatment of happiness and human excellence, and then explore the end of civil association. Oakeshott says it pursues no common substantive purpose, and many critics have said either that there are purposes that Oakeshott did not recognize, or that civil association, to the extent it is purposeless, is an incoherent theory of the state. Let me repeat: Oakeshott composed from many sources, and other notes can certainly be heard. For Oakeshott, to philosophize meant, among other things, to transcend the authority of mere books,[10] to seek self-understanding. He took what he could use, and left the rest to the antiquarians.

---

[8]   Oakeshott, *Rationalism in Politics and other essays, new and expanded edition*, ed. Timothy Fuller (Indianapolis: Liberty Press, 1991). Hereafter: *RIP*. Oakeshott, *Morality and Politics in Modern Europe: The Harvard Lectures*, ed. Shirley Robin Letwin, (New Haven: Yale Univ. Press, 1993). Hereafter: *MPME*.

[9]   Also, 'Some (e.g. Congreve, and Laski) have (erroneously) concluded from [the fluidity of Aristotle's political vocabulary] that the state is the government. This is neither true nor Aristotlelian.' I have transliterated Oakeshott's Greek here and below.

[10]   Oakeshott, *Experience and its Modes* (Cambridge: Cambridge Univ. Press, 1933), 7. Hereafter: *EM*.

Rationalism

Oakeshott's critique of Rationalism is a critique of an abstract conception of reason as independent of tradition, of knowledge severed from the activities in which it is meaningful. Merely technical knowledge, Oakeshott says, can never be complete without practical knowledge; what can be formulated in explicit rules is never the whole of a practitioner's knowledge. However, a no less important theme in Oakeshott's critique has to do with politics, not epistemology. Oakeshott uses 'politics' casually in *Rationalism in Politics*, but later, in *On Human Conduct*, narrowly specifies its meaning, and this helps us look back at the critique of Rationalism with fresh eyes. Political activity, he says, has 'none but a distant analogue elsewhere than in civil association,' (*OHC*, 161, 159). Oakeshott is defining two modes of association: civil and enterprise. The former, 'nomocracy,' is association in terms of law and has no extrinsic purpose, while the latter conceives the state as 'teleocratic' (*OHC*, 203, 205), ruled by ends pursued in common. By saying politics is 'unique to civil association,' he is saying that a discourse devoted to the pursuit of common substantive ends is not political but managerial.

'Politics,' he writes, 'is a deliberative and argumentative engagement designed to persuade...[and]...there is nothing in the engagement itself to suggest a profession and much eloquently to deny it' (*OHC*, 165). Politics is not only open to anyone, it is not limited to particular times or places: '[W]hen Aristotle identified it as an *agora* activity it was not to give it an exclusive venue but to distinguish it from the discussion of the affairs of a tribe and from the management of an estate' (*OHC*, 166). For Oakeshott, politics, properly speaking, is first intimated, first enjoyed, and explored, in ancient Greece, and Oakeshott's two ideal regime types distantly recall the Aristotle's separation of political rule from household management and other 'despotic' relations of mastery. Still, the historical connections between politics in civil association and politics in ancient Athens are indirect, complicated by the Greek city-states' emergence from 'tribal' life, as well as Europe's on-going balancing of its pagan and Biblical inheritances, so Oakeshott avoids any suggestion of direct lessons to be learned from the ancient polity.[11] This is why Oakeshott

---

[11] Oakeshott notes the importance of religion in the life of the polity, and the differences between a *cultus* and a universal church (*Pol I*, 27v, 57v; *Pol II*, 3v, 4); and in a rare moment, defends Plato against the charge of totalitarianism, on both historical and rhetorical grounds (*Nic II*, 51).

both repeatedly insists that the modern European state arose out of medieval circumstances, and nearly as often alludes to more ancient sources of the state.[12]

In the posthumously published essay 'Political Discourse,' Oakeshott discusses two types of argumentative discourse — demonstrative or *apodeictic*, and persuasive, or *enthymemic*. He cites Aristotle's *Rhetoric* as his guide, and calls persuasive argument 'both the commonest and most difficult to describe' (*RIP*, 77), and says it is 'the design of all political speeches which have come down to us from the ancient world' (*RIP*, 81). True to the form of his subject matter, he begins with an example — Pericles' speech advising the Athenians to make their stand against Sparta.[13]

Following Aristotle's *Rhetoric*, Oakeshott says persuasive arguments are composed of probabilities, signs, and examples. If the argument is syllogistic, it will be an *enthymeme* in which the major premise is a maxim concerning what is 'usually expected in human affairs' or what is 'normally agreed to be desirable' (*RIP*, 79). Because such arguments do not pretend to certainty being shown to reach uncertain conclusions cannot refute them. They can only be 'resisted by arguments of the same sort which, on balance, are found to be more convincing' (*RIP*, 79).

Oakeshott adds that this kind of political discourse is designed not only to persuade to decision and action, but to convince an audience about the good or harm expected to follow the action. Thus, 'Like all

---

[12] He allows, '[P]olitical activity . . . in ancient Greece . . . was a comparatively narrow activity' (*MPME*, 8-9); 'Some features of modern politics . . . have their counterpart in the ancient world . . . But it is a shadowy counterpart.' Oakeshott, *The Politics of Faith and the Politics of Scepticism*, ed. Timothy Fuller (New Haven: Yale Univ. Press, 1996), 1-2. Hereafter: *FS*. He also differentiates the 'politics of faith' from the city-state: The politics of faith 'seems to have some . . . affinity to the political style of an ancient Greek city state, but it is an affinity which ceases to be convincing as soon as we leave generality for concrete detail' (*FS*, 68). However, when dealing with political *thought*, including his own view of theorizing (*OHC*, 3 n.1, 27-31), he broadens his context: (*FS*, 39-41, 115); (*RIP*, 9 n. 2, 13 n. 6, 14 n. 7, 20, 58, 64, 68), etc. While distinguishing three phases of the Western tradition (*RIP*, 226-7), he links theorists from Plato to Hobbes when examining the end of 'civil association' (*RIP*, 292), and curiously links Hobbes and Aristotle's views of the individual's freedom in relation to law (*RIP*, 282 n. 116). Finally, his vocabulary includes both out-of-date terms such as 'statesman', 'tyrant', '*technē*', '*scholē*', '*theoria*', and neologisms like 'nomocracy' and 'teleocracy' along with borrowings from Rome.

[13] For Oakeshott, Plato saw Sparta 'organized for a purpose — war,' a useful analogy for the reform of Athens (*Rep I*, 3v). He later counts war among the causes for and analogies of the state as an enterprise.

advice, political advice is concerned with *eudaimonia*, human happiness' (*RIP*, 80). Having started by saying, 'in this matter we cannot do better than to listen to Aristotle, whose *Rhetoric* is the classic treatment of this subject' (*RIP*, 78), this Hobbesian skeptic lets Aristotle's view stand without comment or qualification. He next claims that for Aristotle '*eudaimonia* is not understood to be a simple, universal, unchanging condition…but to be composed of the complex, changing, condition of things, often circumstantially discrepant…which we are usually disposed to agree to be desirable' (*RIP*, 80). Happiness is not an achieved condition of things, but an on-going activity.

In his abbreviated discussion of Aristotle's *Rhetoric*, Oakeshott passes over the rest of Aristotle's thoughts on the different species of rhetoric, the topics appropriate to each kind, and so on. His concern seems to be not solely with rhetoric or even with the logical status of the *enthymeme*, his announced topic. Another purpose of this essay becomes clear when, after criticizing an array of thinkers who have seen political argument as demonstrative — including Plato, Rousseau, Merlin, Jeanne d'Arc, and Marx — he says that while his aim has been explanatory, he will end on a practical note.

Here, one of the few times he explicitly addresses the practical concerns of theory, he recognizes that political life is 'important enough for it to be impossible not to wish' for a demonstrative end to our political reflections. However, yearning to end all political argument is corrupting. It may lead us to believe we do not have to make choices 'sometimes on little more than the courage of our convictions;' it may suggest to us an escape from responsibility for our choices; it may lead us to believe that the only form of reasoning appropriate to political affairs is really unreason; and it may dissuade us from taking political discourse seriously enough to sustain

> the effort to understand our 'principles' and our 'admitted goods' . . . in such a way that each is given its due and none becomes a tyrant; the effort to address ourselves to real and not imaginary situations; and the effort to support our proposals with relevant arguments in which conjectures are not confused with certainties nor opinion with demonstrable truth. (*RIP*, 95)

Oakeshott's view of political discourse is one thread in his critique of Rationalism, which includes a view of mind, conduct, and practices as inextricably linked (which has ties to Aristotle plain enough not to need close examination here: habit, a traditional 'ethical' life, skillful engagement in activities, practical judgment as a cultivated perception of the mean, and so on).[14] This critique stands or falls on philosophical grounds, but it is also animated by a deep moral concern, which must partly account for the intensity of admiration and opposition it has evoked. Although 'Political Discourse' was not published in Oakeshott's lifetime, it fits the contours of his critique of Rationalism and his later discussion of politics in civil association as a deliberative and persuasive engagement. In both his critique of Rationalism and his view of political discourse Oakeshott draws directly from Aristotle. In addition to addressing political discourse, Oakeshott's critique of Rationalism also implicitly points to an idea of harmonious and prudent conduct.

Without suggesting that Oakeshott shared Aristotle's idea of virtue, there are certain features of Aristotle's view of noble conduct that are picked up by the early Oakeshott, and recollected by the aged theorist of civil association. The gracefulness of action in the excellent character is very much a concern in Oakeshott's early notebooks, and also in his essays on Rationalism, which complain of Rationalism 'desiccating' tradition, and breaking up its 'flow of sympathy,' while defining *rational* conduct as coherent 'activities of desiring' that form a person's 'character' (*RIP*, 41; 59, 130, 515; 125, 127). In his late treatise, he speaks of morality as 'a continuously extemporized dance' (*OHC*, 63), and extols 'the singleness and spontaneity of all morally educated conduct' (*OHC*, 70). A *morally educated spontaneity* seems closer to the mood of an Aristotle than to a Romantic like Goethe's Werther.

Oakeshott also remarks that the understanding exercised by agents in human conduct is 'akin to the Aristotelian *phronesis*' (*OHC*, 89). He adds, 'whereas the *aisthesis* of the *phronimos* was, primarily, his understanding of how to act rightly (his *sophronein*), I am primarily concerned with the understanding implicit in both acting and acting rightly' (*OHC*, 89). He makes the point that his focus is more generally theoretic than Aristotle's — the postulates of virtuous conduct are difficult to specify beyond the postulates of conduct as such.[15] In any case, he includes alongside the concern with acting rightly, his *additional* concern with 'acting' simply.

---

[14] Timothy Fuller, 'Introduction' to *FS*, notes that in his discussion of the goal of politics 'striking a mean between extremes he identifies here as the "politics of faith", and the "politics of scepticism",' we find Oakeshott 'at his most Aristotelian' (*FS*, x).

[15] 'There is no one principle or categorical imperative of "virtuous" conduct when we go beyond *the postulate that it is not virtuous unless it is chosen*'

In 'Rationalism in Politics,' Oakeshott alludes directly to the opening of the *Nicomachean Ethics*, and here, too, his concern is 'the understanding implicit in both acting and acting rightly.' The allusion begins his discussion of technical and practical knowledge:

> Every science, every art, every practical activity requiring skill of any sort, indeed every human activity whatsoever, involves knowledge. (*RIP*, 12)

Aristotle's version, of course, introduces the ideas of purpose, goods, and the good:

> Every art, and every investigation, and likewise every practical pursuit or undertaking, seems to aim at some good: hence it has been well said that the Good is that at which all things aim.[16]

Despite the differences implied by Oakeshott's omission of 'the good,' his notebooks show certain continuities in his meditations on human conduct, from his early studies onward. Again, there is no question of Oakeshott's slavishly following Aristotle's every move. Consider these selections from his *Ethics* notebooks where he contrasts 'available' and 'acquired' knowledge, analogues of his later 'practical' and 'technical' knowledge:

> VII, ii, 7: The idea of 'self-control' is too rigid — it lack (sic) the wisdom, judgement, the constant moral choice added to perfected habit which is found in perfected self-mastery. Self-control . . . cannot adapt itself — it is mere machinery.
> Cf. . . . the idea of <u>Freedom</u>.
>
> VII, iii, 5: The relations of acquired knowledge to a man's life and action.
> Cf. Plato's 'Theatetus' 197-198.
> Knowledge is not available simply when it has been acquired — a new process has to be put into operation for this end
> Cf. Newman 'Grammar of Assent' — his treatment of Real and Formal assent.
>
> VII, iii, 6. A man may have knowledge which is in abeyance because he does not apply a minor premiss (sic) to his general principle.
> A universal proposition has to go through a long process before it can be brought into immediate relation to a practical situation. There are no rules which can be slavishly applied.
> Cf. Bradley, 'Ethical Studies' (*Nic III*, 12-4)

We find these themes recollected in the view that 'acting cannot be "implementing" or "applying" [moral theorems] to contingent situ-

---

(*OHC*, 75, italics added); cf. 'Aristotle insists . . . if goodness is voluntary, vice must be so also . . . [T]he individual is the originating cause of his actions' (*Nic II*, 5).

[16] Aristotle, *Nicomachean Ethics*, trans. H. Rackham (Cambridge: Harvard Univ. Press, 1934), 3. Hereafter: *NE*.

ations because they are unable to specify actions' (*OHC*, 90). Oakeshott recognizes that general principles are both unavoidable and useful, but hardens the distinction between 'a universal proposition' and its 'relation to a practical situation.' Rather than 'a long process' needed to bring a 'general principle' to bear on a contingent situation, he suggests the relation between 'theorems' and action by saying that 'the agent needs to know . . . how to *illustrate* them in actions' (*OHC*, 90). 'Illustration' is interesting because it suggests a *performance*, while remaining within the *perceptual* — mainly visual — ambit of traditional moral vocabulary. While emphasizing the agent's *pro-* or *re-creative* action, 'illustration' also highlights the gap between something perceived and the conduct that makes it actual. The emphasis is clearly on the doing, not the seeing, but it is a doing that makes something seen.

Some of Oakeshott's glosses on Aristotle's virtues are also reflected in his own theory of human conduct. Let me notice one important connection before turning to *eudaimonia*, and the end of civil association.

> IV, ii, 9: 'This [magnificence] is the great principle of both Platonic and Aristotelian Ethics — A thing should be well done, and it should be the sole aim of the doer to do it well. Excellence is the *porro unum necessarium*. Expense, time, trouble, and the rest are not to be considered at all.
>
> The modern world has deserted this. (*Nic II*, 32-4)

This neglect of 'expense, time, [and] trouble' resonates with Oakeshott's later discussion of self-disclosure and self-enactment. Self-disclosure concerns outward and visible success, and corresponds with what Oakeshott calls, in his writings on religion, a worldly disposition. In achieving substantive ends, expense, time, and trouble are naturally considered. Self-enactment concerns motives, the 'sentiments in which a man permits himself to act' (*OHC*, 72), or the 'demands an agent makes upon himself in which he requires of himself a *delicatesse* of conduct' (*OHC*, 77). In his notes, 'the great-souled man does not avoid vice because it is "wrong," but because it is unworthy of him' (*Nic II*, 34). Whatever an agent achieves (or loses) is distinct from the motive in which he acts, which he controls, unlike the externals of worldly existence.[17] The inherent disinterestedness of self-enactment, where expense, time, and trouble are neglected, corresponds to the religious disposition. In self-enactment, 'doing is delivered...from the deadliness of doing, a

---

[17] Motive 'has an important place in both the Stoic and Epicurean understanding of conduct' (*OHC*, 73 n. 1).

deliverance gracefully enjoyed in the quiet of a religious faith' (*OHC*, 74).[18]

Again we see Oakeshott's ideas migrating — the magnificent man's nonchalance slides into a characterization of the religious temperament. But then, Oakeshott's discussion of religion concludes with Aristotle's injunction 'to live "so far as possible as an immortal"' (*OHC*, 86). Aristotle's great-souled man may be a variant, for Oakeshott, of the religious man, or the religious man a refinement or abandonment of an earlier reading of the importance of motive — it would depend on whether *delicatesse* coheres with greatness of soul.[19]

In his studies of Aristotle Oakeshott encountered ideas he later used in his critique of Rationalism and his account of human conduct. Oakeshott's uses of Aristotle, show, as T.S. Eliot said of Dante, 'he knew how to pillage right and left.'[20] So, when he gets hold of happiness, it may be feared he has ransacked the temple.

Happiness and Human Excellence

For Oakeshott's Aristotle *eudaimonia* is 'not understood to be a simple, universal, unchanging condition... but to be composed of [a] complex, changing, condition of things' (*RIP*, 80).[21] If happiness is 'complex and changing,' then how can it be the aim of conduct, much less of particular actions?

Oakeshott tells us, 'A morality is . . . the practice of practices; the practice of agency without further specification' (*OHC*, 60). He takes up the view that morality promotes a 'superordinate purpose of human life,' namely, '"human excellence," the purpose of all purposes . . . the good life.' Moral relationships, on this view, are 'instruments for procuring a substantive state of things called "the common good"' (*OHC*, 61). I should point out that Oakeshott does

---

[18] Cf. Kant and Aristotle (*Nic III*, 75), and later (*OHC*, 71).

[19] Cf. *Nic II*, 33v. See also, 'the grandeur of devilry' (*OHC*, 84) — another echo from the notebooks where Aristotle was 'always down on petty meanness — sin boldly if you are going to sin at all' (*Nic II*, 64).

[20] T. S. Eliot, 'The Possibility of A Poetic Drama,' in *The Sacred Wood and Major Early Essays* (Minneola, NY: Dover, 1998), 34.

[21] Plato's view seems precisely opposed: 'What is desirable must be simple, universal, and unchanging' (*RIP*, 83). It emerges, though, that Plato, who wished political discourse to be demonstrative, knew that contingent situations could not be understood in the same way as ideals, so 'He does not attempt to deduce the details of the life and education of the Guardians from the axiom of 'justice' (*RIP*, 84). Cf. *RIP*, 9, 20.

not mention Aristotle here, even though the topic clearly relates to how he is normally understood.

Oakeshott's rejection of the pursuit of the 'common good' is qualified: First, '"human excellence" or "the human good" is not a substantive purpose to be achieved as the outcome of performances,' and second, 'it is not a purpose which an agent might choose to pursue in preference to the satisfaction of some other want or in terms of which he might or might not choose to be related with others in achieving (and then, perhaps, deliberately revoke the choice)' (*OHC*, 61).

The point is that 'human excellence' is not achieved in particular actions satisfying wants, and so cannot be among an agent's choices in conduct, for these always involve particular 'performances' within practices.[22] Since 'human excellence' cannot be chosen as the aim of an action, it cannot be pursued individually or in common; and, if it cannot be chosen as a common pursuit, it cannot be revocable, as other common pursuits are, such as 'joining an expedition to climb Mount Everest' (*OHC*, 61-2). Simply put, 'the "common good" is not a substantive satisfaction ... [and] a morality may be identified as a practice without any extrinsic purpose' (*OHC*, p. 60-61). On this view, he began by saying, morality is 'procuring a substantive state of things.' Can happiness or excellence be *procured*?

If a morality is 'a practice without any extrinsic purpose,' can it have an intrinsic purpose; or, does 'purpose' mean only what is *extrinsic* and *substantive* — *procurable*? Whether Oakeshott has established that the good cannot be pursued because it is not a purpose, or that certain kinds of purposes — extrinsic, substantive — are not or should not be called 'the good,' the question of whether there *is* a final good has been left to one side, as his skepticism requires.

Recalling the distinction between ends external to the activities that produce them, and activities that have their ends in themselves,

---

[22] Perhaps the good is not a choice because, implicitly, we always seek the good. This would explain why 'revocability' is invoked in *the moral realm* where no authority is *sovereign*. Revocability should only be relevant where the compulsory character of *the state* makes participation in common enterprises a near guarantee that agents' freedom is infringed, especially if they seek their own happiness. Incidentally, our seeking the good fits Oakeshott's view of religion as the 'completion' of the moral life. *Religion, Politics and the Moral Life*, ed. Timothy Fuller (New Haven: Yale Univ. Press, 1993), 41-2, 44-5. Hereafter: *RPML*. In respect to religion, the good, and sociality, Oakeshott links Plato, Aristotle, and St. Paul (*RPML*, 58-9) In *On Human Conduct*, Oakeshott 'adds' a profound meditation on religion to his treatment of conduct.

and which are 'free' and characteristic of man's higher pursuits, we might wonder if Oakeshott speaks of intrinsic, non-substantive purposes. Not exactly. Instead, we find that self-enactment 'endow[s] human conduct with a formality in which its contingency is somewhat abated' (*OHC*, 74). 'Formality' is also juxtaposed to 'substantive' in respect of moral rules, and law in civil association, which Oakeshott also describes as formal, not instrumental to the achievement of substantive satisfactions. But being formal is not something we do in the same sense as eating a pudding, filing a lawsuit or climbing a hill.[23]

Oakeshott quietly discards the term 'purpose,' except for extrinsic, substantive ends. He defined a morality as '*the practice of all practices.*' The phrase oddly echoes the very 'Aristotelian' thing he rejects — *the purpose of all purposes* (*OHC*, 60-1, italics added). But a practice is an activity, an on-going stream of idiomatically related performances. If there can be no 'superordinate purpose,' because purposes are limited to the substantive ends pursued by agents, this leaves open the relation between 'human excellence' and 'the practice of practices,' which he also calls 'the practice of agency without further specification' (*OHC*, 60). Oakeshott seems to have thought that the terms 'ends' and 'purposes' were ill-suited for describing both the products of action and things enjoyed as inherently worthy and internal to the actions themselves, for identifying cabinets and conversations alike.[24] This may be how we should take his cryptic remark that 'There is no need to quarrel with such an expression as the "human good", and the teleological suggestion it contains may be neglected' (*OHC*, 61).

Although Oakeshott discusses 'excellence', and 'the good', he does not discuss *eudaimonia* in the passages I have been examining. Perhaps he was not hopeful that the good life and the happy life could be reconciled (Cf. *Nic III*, 61). In any case, he later mentions 'happiness' in connection with a view of moral rules understood as abridgements of 'alleged calculations of the tendency of actions to

[23]   Though character is less an aim than the by-product of innumerable actions, it may loosely be spoken of as an aim, and an achievement. In his notes, Oakeshott writes, 'Aristotle bids us not pray for things, but for a better state of ourselves' (*Nic II*, 49). Character as an achievement appears in both 'Rational Conduct' (*RIP*, 125), and his later work (*OHC*, 74-7, 89-91).

[24]   Re: *NE*, 8.3.6: 'Aristotle here puts "usefulness" and "pleasure" in their right places — they are results, incidental to some extent, and not ends to be aimed at. The same process of distinction must be applied to "The State" — but this many fail to do' (*Nic III*, 30).

promote a suppositious "happiness",' and he also denies that justification is concerned to 'show that [an act] conduced to a suppositious condition of "happiness"' (*OHC*, 66, 69). What is 'suppositious' is not happiness, but a view of happiness as the calculable outcome of instrumental conduct, and a related view that mere success could justify a course of action.

Since happiness could be achieved — *enjoyed*, rather — only if it is neither substantive nor extrinsic, the 'end' of conduct must be fulfilled in the *activities* of self-disclosure and especially self-enactment. But this is not a common pursuit. In another (earlier) passage of *On Human Conduct*, Oakeshott also denies that 'actions in respect of their meanings' have a common end. If actions have no common end

> it does not follow that agents and their actions are mere particulars, . . . [but] . . . that the words . . . used to denote a suppositious common substantive end pursued in all conduct, or . . . a suppositious universal reason for the performance of all actions (words . . . such as 'survival', 'pleasure', 'happiness', 'the desirable', 'the good', etc.) must be taken to refer . . . to the formal character of actions. . . . [P]roperly speaking, . . . they refer . . . to the ideal condition, impossible to be made the substantive outcome sought in conduct. (*OHC*, 54)[25]

This ideal, formal condition he goes on to describe as 'each [agent] exercising his own *potestas vivendi ut velis* . . . thus winning their way through to their own existences, whatever these may be; and 'happiness' is not a substantive condition of things aimed at, but merely not to be thwarted in this engagement' (*OHC*, 54). It seems we have migrated from Aristotle (*via* Cicero) to Hobbes. Let me suggest that the *Nicomachean Ethics* remains in play.

Throughout Oakeshott's works one finds discussions of activities with inherently worthy implicit ends, like conversation, poetic contemplation, love and friendship, 'play', and various theoretical inquiries, and on several such occasions he cites Aristotle.[26] One of Oakeshott's greatest values is that he takes seriously these forms of experience and makes them central to his understanding of society.

---

[25] 'Mere particulars' *might* refer to Hobbes, a nominalist (Cf. *RIP*, 280). 'The particulars of nominalism and the universals of realism are equally foreign to the character of experience' (*EM*, 46). Cf. *RIP*, 512; *OHC*, 6.

[26] Cf. 'The Voice of Poetry in the Conversation of Mankind' (*RIP*, 514, passim); 'On Being Conservative' (*RIP*, 416-18); 'The Tower of Babel' (*RIP*, 479, 485); 'Work and Play,' in Luke O'Sullivan, ed. *What is History? and other essays* (Exeter: Imprint Academic, 2004), 310-14, hereafter: *WH*; 'The Voice of Conversation in the Education of Mankind' (*WH*, 185-99); 'On Arriving at A University' (*WH*, 335); 'The Character of a University Education' (*WH*, 388); and throughout *The Voice of Liberal Learning*.

However, one also finds 'Hobbesian' ideas on law and authority, and approval of Hobbes' individualism. So it may help to look at Oakeshott's views of nature and convention, and habitual functioning, which lay behind the notion of 'not being thwarted' in the exercise of one's capacities.[27]

Although Oakeshott says that an agent 'has a "history", but no "nature"; he is what in conduct he becomes' (*OHC*, 41), his rejection of 'human nature' is qualified.[28] He continues:

> This 'history' is . . . what he enacts for himself in a diurnal engagement. . . . [A]lthough he may imagine an 'ideal' human character and may *use this character to direct his self-enactments*, there is no ultimate or perfect man hidden in the womb of time or prefigured in the characters who now walk the earth. (*OHC*, 41, italics added)

'[T]here is no . . . perfect man;' yet we may direct the enactment of our 'histories' by reference to an imagined ideal human character. It matters that Oakeshott refers only to *enactment* here, first, because this aspect of action is less what we do than the manner in which we do it. In respect to self-disclosure an ideal human character is of little help — unless we know how to illustrate it; but even then, such an ideal can be only a very general outline. Second, other than this brief reference, Oakeshott's only discussion of human nature concerns *explaining* an agent's *substantive performances* 'by relating them to an ideal character called "human nature".' In other words he switches to the disclosive aspect of conduct; and he switches to explanation rather than doing — the issue now is not what we think of ourselves, but how to explain what others have done. He examines not whether there is a human nature, but whether the idea is a useful explanatory device. 'The virtue of this understanding,' Oakeshott says, is to have recognized human nature as 'the outcome of learning and education in which the supposed organic needs . . . of the species are wholly transformed and superseded . . . as a practice to be subscribed to' (*OHC*, 93).

Characters, or dispositions, such as 'the Miser, the "Stoic," the Magnanimous,' and others have been elaborated in our tradition, and for Oakeshott this idea of ideal characters '*is one of the great achievements of human self-understanding; we call upon it in all our*

---

[27] Will is 'an aspect of mind' (*EM*, 258; cf. 25, 251-2); or, 'intelligence in doing' (*OHC*, 39). He denies that conduct arises from a faculty of 'will' (*OHC*, 37, 52).

[28] Cf., *OHC*, 37, 81, 107.

attempts to interpret actions and utterances' (*OHC*, 93-4, italics added).[29] Yet it is not a useful explanatory device.[30] His reason is simple, and recalls his rejection of 'human excellence' as a purpose. Just as we 'cannot want happiness,' but only 'to idle in Avignon or hear Caruso sing' (*OHC*, 53), a dispositional capacity cannot account for the concreteness of action: 'It is only the meanness of an action which may become intelligible when an agent is recognized to have a mean disposition; and no action is merely mean' (*OHC*, 95).

Since Oakeshott admits no natural *telos* for human conduct he appears deeply un-Aristotelian. However, Oakeshott can give the impression, not unlike his Hobbes, of a greater disagreement with Aristotle than appears upon closer examination (Cf. *RIP*, 232). His differences usually involve sticking to a path of theoretical explanation made tight and narrow by the intensity of his skepticism. He also, like Hegel (and later, Michael Foster), saw both Plato and Aristotle as intimating things that they did not fully explore.[31]

In at least one area though, Oakeshott's claim does not hinge on the limits or usefulness of concepts, but concerns the definition of an experience; and moreover, he thinks of himself as agreeing with Aristotle. His claim is that Aristotle's *eudaimonia* is a formal condition in which agents continuously disclose and enact themselves.

I have mentioned this above, but I should also notice some places where this claim is first developed. Oakeshott reads Aristotle as showing 'how the conceptions of nature and convention interpenetrate' (*Nic II*, 63). In an entry headed: 'Nature (*physis*) and Convention (*nomos*)':

> Society requires mutual understanding and adjustment between individuals, i.e., Convention . . . Laws, etc.: are conventions, but nonetheless natural. Man's nature issues in all that he does — and conventions are his handi-

---

[29] He is known for such 'ideal characters' as: the historian, scientist, poet, theorist; the Rationalist, the conservative, the individualist, anti-individualist, the individual-*manqué*, the leader, the gardener, the teacher, etc. In his notes we find 'Human Relationships: Friend, Comrade, Partner, Ally, Companion, Accomplice, Convive.' Oakeshott, Notebook XVIII, LSE, File 2/1/18, 132. Elsewhere he outlined a dialogue between 'the soldier, the philosopher, the doctrinaire, the Poet, the man of the world, the politician/public man, the scientist, the religious man, the visitor.' Oakeshott, Notebook titled 'Conversation,' LSE File 2/4/3, title page, verso.

[30] A substantive performance is made intelligible by being 'put into a story.' Agents may 'use' stories for purposes ranging from crass to consolatory — this is not story telling, but myth making (*OHC*, 105).

[31] See M. B. Foster, *The Political Philosophies of Plato and Hegel* (Oxford: Oxford Univ. Press, 1935).

work.... Debates as to what is conventional and what is not arise from the difference of opinion about what is still of use in man's rules and regulations. If injustice were really best, and if man thought so, it is clear society would never have come into existence. Its existence shows that man judges law and convention as better than individual independence. (*Rep I*, 24v)[32]

The *de facto* superiority of justice and its identification with society is, of course, oversimplified.[33] What is intriguing, though, is that while Oakeshott wrote 'It was the melancholy achievement of Plato to have imposed the analogy of craftsmanship upon government' (*WH*, 297), he nevertheless comes close, in his comments on nature and convention, to seeing in Plato and Aristotle an almost Hegelian insight: 'politics in the full sense' is found only where law and government are recognized to be shaped by human choice and will, as historical (*MPME*, 9). In agreement with Foster, Oakeshott's 'Introduction to *Leviathan*' argues that the lack of the concept of creative activity introduced by 'the Judaic-Christian conception of will and creation' (*RIP*, 277-8) is decisive. Without this conception, the creative freedom of human conduct would have to be elicited from the 'interpenetration' of nature and convention implicit in the peculiarities of man's intellectual nature.

Following Ferrier's *Lectures on Greek Philosophy*, Oakeshott identifies the difference between human and other natures as a difference between 'an absolute *dynamis*' like the famed rock that never 'falls upward,' and a *dynamis* that allows for activity to flow off in opposite directions, allows for choice — virtue is not automatic. In addition, 'instead of the practice of virtue (*energeia*) arising out of the capacity or *dynamis* of virtue, it is rather the *dynamis* arises out of the *energeia*. And a *dynamis* acquired by practice is called by Aristotle a habit, *hexis*' (*Nic III*, 74-5). Thus, energetic functioning is connected with character, freedom and individuality. 'Free,' according to Oakeshott's Aristotle, means 'caused immediately by character' (*Nic I*, 76), and virtues are described as 'an inward individual energy,' or 'energy of the individual soul' (*Nic II*, 27, 14). Oakeshott records a passage (from Grant, not cited) that says, 'The principle of individuality, a sense of life, and free action (*energeia*) are, with Aristotle, the basis of morality' (*Nic II*, 26). This recognition of individuality points to an important philosophical issue.

---

[32] 'Law and convention, almost *sittlichkeit*' is appended to the heading.
[33] Cf. Oakeshott's conception of the 'inner meaning' of law, and the *jus* inherent in *res publica* (*OHC*, 153, passim). See also 'The Rule of Law,' in *On History and Other Essays* (Oxford: Basil Blackwell, 1983).

First, Oakeshott says that Aristotle assumes 'man is an *archē* of his own action. In what sense, and how, the individual is an *archē* is the point where Aristotle stops short in the enquiry' (*Nic I*, 76). His reading echoes Hegel's, though he sees the principle of freedom as being associated with Aristotle's view of human character and therefore as a positive if incomplete achievement, rather than with Socrates and with threats to an 'objective' social order. Second, 'individuality' here is merely Aristotle's acknowledgement of everyday conditions. It is not grounded in 'Free Will,' but identifies acts caused by character as the locus of responsibility. This is important because Oakeshott balances Aristotle against the Idealists.

> Aristotle seems to admit the existence of an individual apart and separate from all social relations. Justice exists . . . because men are not one in aim and life, for were they one indivisible and complete whole there could be no justice — 'for no man chooses to hurt himself'.

He continues:

> Later idealists' theories seem to hold that, in fact the individual is an abstraction, that society — or the State — is a single whole and that 'each individual is not only himself but also the State' (Bosanquet, 'Phil. Th. Of State' p. lvii), but that man has an evil, individual, selfish inclination or 'will' which must be converted into a good, social, real, or general will. From the conflict of these two wills . . . arises the necessity of law, justice, punishment, etc.' (*Nic II*, 61-2).

Although neither Oakeshott nor Bosanquet use the term here, the idealists' account of will is Pauline, divided against itself. These views of how injustice arises are significant because they imply two kinds of individuality, one Greek, one Biblical. Both hold promise and peril for liberty — the former will tend to constrict the choice of targets to be aimed at, the latter will insist on overcoming one's separateness, losing oneself in the (cosmic or social) whole.

As many have noticed, the 'early Oakeshott' seems decisively idealist. One finds Rousseau, Hegel, and Bosanquet addressing Hobbes' inadequate theory of volition (*HCA*, 157). One sees his hostility toward Locke's bourgeois individualism,[34] his social monism and attack on the doctrine of consent,[35] his assertion that 'the private individual is an institution, a social, indeed, for the most part a legal, creation.'[36]

---

[34] Oakeshott, 'John Locke,' *The Cambridge Review* 54 (1932-3): 72-4.
[35] Oakeshott, 'The Authority of the State' (*RPML*, 74-90).
[36] Oakeshott, Review of *The State and the Citizen*, by J.D. Mabbott, *Mind* 58 (1949): 385.

Nevertheless, we see him complaining of the idealist's theory of the state, saying, 'it has yet to receive a satisfactory statement.'[37] Oakeshott does not elaborate. One clue, as Franco has observed, is that he 'reject[s] the substantive theory of human nature which seems to lurk in the idealist doctrine of self-realization and of the "real will." And he rejects the substantive or purposive character this doctrine . . . seems to impose on the state.'[38] In other words, if the Judaic-Christian doctrine of creative will complicates the legacy of Greece in respect to our understanding of ruling, then it does so also at the level of the ruled — at the level of the individuals who make up the state, and whose characters are reflected in the character of the association. If a man 'does what he would not do,' *and* 'each individual is also the State,' then correcting the will by bringing it into conformity with a correct social order might be dangerously appealing for any but Pauline political theorists able to sustain intense skepticism about the offerings of the earthly city.

Oakeshott's early idealism has been much debated, with varying assessments of how thoroughly and quickly he abandoned or tempered it through his reading of Hobbes. It seems, however, that this tension between idealism and a more skeptical individualism was present from the start, and involved Aristotle as well as Hobbes. Indeed, Oakeshott links the two in a review published just one year before *On Human Conduct*.[39] In it, he de-emphasizes the differences between Aristotle's teleological and Hobbes' inertial motion, saying that neither drew conclusions about human conduct from 'cosmological' principles. Instead, 'both these writers regard human conduct as an intelligent engagement' (*RIP*, 353). While Aristotle's recognition of man as an *archē* was incomplete,

> Human conduct, for Aristotle, displayed *logos* in virtue of being deliberate, of being in terms of educated and understood choices and not on account of being (like all activity) teleological...human excellence was not the outcome of a process like that in which an acorn (barring accidents) matured into an oak tree; it was the outcome of a procedure that had to be learned. Not only was the condition itself unique to human beings as the excellence of anything is unique to its kind, but it was sought in a unique engagement of self-conscious self-enactment. (*RIP*, 354)

---

[37] Oakeshott, Review of *Bernard Bosanquet's Philosophy of the State: A Historical and Systematical Study*, by B. Pfannenstill, *Philosophy*, 11 (1936): 482.
[38] Franco, *The Political Philosophy of Michael Oakeshott*, 102.
[39] '*Logos* and *Telos*' (*RIP*, 351-9).

I have contoured the hillsides rather than follow a *direttisima*, but I have not lost sight of *eudaimonia* as 'not being thwarted.' If human nature issues in conventions, if man is 'an *archē* of his actions,' whose energetic functioning is the basis of his character (virtuous or vicious), which is inseparable from his freedom, then when Oakeshott says we have only a history he is indeed overthrowing, in Franco's phrase, the 'substantive theory of human nature,' and its teleological suggestions.[40] Yet he may plausibly be read as addressing the excesses of idealism by offering an account of conduct as intelligent, purged of notions appropriate to the natures of non-intelligent beings, and this purging clears the way for a view of the excellence of human things as unique to their kind — the excellence of intelligent or rational beings. Since intelligent means chosen, a measured individualism is implied.[41] Without exploring it in detail, Oakeshott's view of the self is notable for rejecting 'free will,' indeed, all 'faculties' (*EM*, 56-7, 60-1, 72), along with subjectivity, and egocentrism (*OHC*, 36, 39-41, 51-3; cf. *OH*, 11, 16, 146), so that none of the familiar modern categories — or criticisms — apply. Agents are not selfish, do not 'will' independently of thinking, do not have merely 'subjective' opinions; but they *'may care for one another because they can think of one another'* (*OHC*, 53, italics added). The passage on conduct displaying *logos* can be applied almost *verbatim* to Oakeshott. Despite the fact that Oakeshott read Aristotle in the light of idealist philosophy, he could find in him, unlike in Hobbes, an angle of vision on agency and excellence from the other side of the politico-theological divide.

Finally, Oakeshott doubted whether

> human excellence (the 'purpose' human beings are joined in seeking) was, for Aristotle, anything more substantial than ... deliberative self-enactment, and whether the good *polis* was anything more than that which had the constitution best disposed for deliberating and reaching genuinely common decisions about what to do in contingent situations. (*RIP*, 355)

Polis Association

Opening part 2 of *On Human Conduct*, Oakeshott says that what Aristotle called the *polis* corresponds with what he calls *civitas*, and notes that Aristotle identified four key features of civil association —

[40]   Cf. 'Rational Conduct,' where Oakeshott defines conduct as 'energy' (*RIP*, 125).

[41]   Despite his celebrating those like Montaigne, whom he called 'besotted with liberty.'

that it is a relationship of human beings, a relationship of equals, a constituted condition, and a self-sufficient relationship (*OHC*, 109). Oakeshott's interpretation of the first feature sharpens Aristotle's distinction between human and animal (or insect) sociality, though without reference, as in the *Politics*, to humans' use of language. Instead, human conduct is defined as exhibitions of intelligence in subscribing to language-like practices, rather than an autonomic process. Second, the relation of *polites* to one another, not a functional or hierarchical relationship, so political life, or civil association, is a moral rather than instrumental practice. Third, differentiating political life from the 'fellowship of the bread-bin,' connects civil association and the *polis* as 'constituted', not 'organic' conditions. Household rule is despotic — concerned with mastery rather than equality, necessity rather than nobility, and command rather than persuasion. The state conceived as an enterprise association, Oakeshott says, is made plausible by the emergence of some European states from feudal estates, where the distinction between management and political rule failed to appear (*OHC*, 219, cf. 198, 219, 253 n. 1).

Noting Aristotle's 'imaginative *tour de force*' in discerning the features of civil association in 'the Athenian *polis*' (*OHC*, 181), Oakeshott points out that he 'recognizes only indistinctly what is perhaps its most important feature . . . a system of rules' (*OHC*, 111).[42] This raises some interesting problems. In Oakeshott's notes, Aristotle's comments on law are said to have a generality akin to the formality of law in civil association. For example, Oakeshott remarks, 'Law is a "general statement" — a statement "in outline" and so can never contain the whole of justice. Equity supplies this deficiency' (*Nic II*, 68-9; cf. *Nic III*, 70).

Aristotle's ruler, though, was also engaged in educating citizens. Oakeshott, glossing the *Ethics*, 10.9.8: 'The supreme task of the education of the young. Upon this everything depends — and so, it should be made a matter for legislation, or rather, the laws that gov-

---

[42] Aristotle, says Oakeshott, achieved 'a very sketchy delineation of civil association,' and while this 'may be . . . an invitation to improve upon it,' it has only a 'propaedeutic' value for the theorist, who wants to understand its postulates (*OHC*, 111). However, not only are Aristotle's 'features' and Oakeshott's 'postulates' of conduct and civil association similar, but Oakeshott says that Aristotle's 'consideration of features, is...*preliminary to his investigation of polis in terms of its postulates*' (*OHC*, 110 n. 2, italics added). Oakeshott may be understood as accepting this 'invitation.'

ern the lives of men (especially the young) must be good ones.' He comments, 'The reformer in Aristotle is far less evident than in Plato, but here he shows just that ardour which fell in love with Spartanism' (*Nic III*, 69).[43] However, Aristotle's 'Platonic' moments of Spartanism were rare and out of character; Oakeshott was not convinced that Aristotle saw the *polis* as an enterprise association.

The fourth feature of civil association and the *polis* is self-sufficiency, or *autarkeia*, which Oakeshott defines as 'self-completeness in the sense of having no extrinsic substantive purpose' (*OHC*, 110). Again, 'extrinsic' and 'substantive' are key adjectives. This seems to do violence to Aristotle's understanding of *autarkeia*, in part by categorically distinguishing between the *polis'* material basis and genesis and its ideal character more sharply than Aristotle does, in part by rejecting the purposive character of political life. Oakeshott is alert to this; he clarifies, saying the *polis'* self-sufficiency is 'a mark of great importance' for Aristotle, but 'has escaped the attention it deserves . . . perhaps because in Book VII it is obscured by the trivialities of trade' (*OHC*, 110 n. 1).

Oakeshott identifies the *polis'* self-sufficiency in exactly the terms used to describe the inability of 'the good' to be pursued in common. The *polis* is both self-sufficient and lacks extrinsic and substantive ends. It is precisely the lack of extrinsic and substantive ends (its apparent purposelessness) that allows it to be self-sufficient. As Aristotle recognized, activities pursued for the sake of an external end are inherently less worthy than the ends, done only by necessity. Paradoxically, ascribing a purpose to political life devalues it, makes it something we would do without if we could.

Critics have claimed that Oakeshott's concept of civil association as non-instrumental and non-purposive fails, because it must have at least basic purposes such as peace, or security; or, because laws have impacts, content, or purposes.[44] Oakeshott rejects any attempt

---

[43] Oakeshott, in a posthumously published paper, identified this educational analogy of government — mentioning not Aristotle or Plato, but Christianity (*WH*, 293-4). Cf. *OHC*, 220-5, 279-86.

[44] Cf. D.D. Raphael, 'Review of *On Human Conduct*,' *Political Quarterly* 46 (October 1975): 450-4; Judith Shklar, 'Purposes and Procedures, A Review of *On Human Conduct*,' *Times Literary Supplement* (12 September 1975): 1018; David Mapel, 'Purpose and Politics: Can There Be a Non-Instrumental Civil Association?' *The Political Science Reviewer* 21 (Spring 1992): 63-80. For one of the best explications of Oakeshott's view of law see Richard B. Friedman, 'What is Non-Instrumental Law?' *The Political Science Reviewer* 21 (Spring 1992): 81-98.

to define civil association in terms of enterprises to secure a common good. In a footnote in his discussion of enterprise association, he says that the view of civil association as an enterprise to procure substantive goods 'is often attributed to Aristotle' mistakenly. The footnote would seem gratuitous unless we suppose that Oakeshott wished to amplify the correspondence between Aristotle's theory and his own. Suppose the view of the *polis* as an enterprise association for the pursuit of the good life *has* been attributed to Aristotle, rightly or wrongly — so what? Why would a Hobbesian care? This note is worth quoting at length, and is remarkable for its assimilation of Oakeshottian terminology and Aristotelian ideas.

> While [Aristotle] speaks of *polis* association as having and (sic) 'end' and as having the same 'end' as human conduct in general, namely, 'the good life' or 'human excellence', this is not for him a substantial purpose but a formal condition. He appears to have thought that *eudaimonia* was difficult if not impossible of attainment in the absence of certain substantive conditions (e.g. good health and adequate material means) but it is not itself a substantive condition of things. It is an agent continuously disclosing and enacting himself in his own chosen actions while subscribing adequately to considerations of moral propriety or worth. (*OHC*, 118-19 n. 1)

Oakeshott's use — the only time I can recall — of '*polis* association' is extraordinary, since he develops a 'civil' vocabulary to avoid the ambiguities bequeathed to us by the Greeks. Not only is '*polis*' substituted for 'civil,' but by rendering '*polis*' an adjective, Aristotle's focus, his noun, becomes 'association,' which suggests optative adventurers acknowledging the authority of *res publica*, rather than tribesmen recently emancipated from 'kingly' rule. And, as we have seen above, the formality of *eudaimonia* echoes the formality of law and moral rules, while the *energeia* is that of individuals.

This view of *eudaimonia* and of the *polis'* end is debatable, but the merits aside what matters is that Oakeshott's view of happiness corresponds with what he takes Aristotle to be saying and thinks others have misconstrued. As I noted, Oakeshott does not mention *eudaimonia* when he discusses 'human excellence' and 'the good,' but he does so here (making it synonymous with these terms), in the section of the book on *our common life in 'polis association'*. If civil association is a formal condition in which agents disclose and enact themselves continuously, then is the happiness of *cives* supported by this mode of being associated, by being 'not thwarted' in their self-chosen conduct? Aristotle is usually not invoked in support of quite so 'individualistic' positions.[45]

Would Aristotle agree that we cannot *want* happiness because it is not a substantive outcome of particular actions, but that we can want to 'idle in Avignon or hear Caruso sing' (*OHC*, 53)? Perhaps, if he had ever been to Avignon or heard the tenor sing. But, speculating on Aristotle's tastes and pastimes would take us far afield, so let me suggest another question: Is there any sense in which civil association, like Aristotle's *polis*, has an 'end' related to the practices of civil association not as a result, but as an inner meaning, enjoyed, and neither procured nor exhausted in the world of practical desiring? This may be answered with a strongly qualified affirmative. First, to speak of an 'end' of civil association opens several possibilities of disastrous misunderstandings in which Oakeshott could be seen as a more common and therefore vulgarly appealing theorist. Second, it is all too easy to forget Aristotle's political skepticism. While political life provides the nursery in which essential human faculties are developed and the stage on which they may be displayed, it is the philosophic life that allows the fullest, least qualified realization of what is highest in human nature. Oakeshott remarks on the similarity between the perfect friendship of virtuous individuals in Aristotle's *Ethics* and 'Plato's idea that in the conversation (*dialektike*) between friends the truth alone can be grasped' (*Nic III*, 26). Political life involves only *watery* friendship (*OHC*, 110).

These considerations should make us answer the question, 'does civil association have a *eudaimonaic* end analogous to the *polis*?' with a less strongly qualified negative. When Oakeshott clarifies Aristotle's view of political ends, he raises no objection to understanding '*polis* association,' mingling his and Aristotle's terms, as an association in terms of *eudaimonia rightly understood*, as a formal condition of energetic functioning — 'an agent continuously disclosing and enacting himself in his own chosen actions while subscribing adequately to considerations of moral propriety or worth' (*OHC*, 118-19 n. 1). Again, the description of *eudaimonia* is given in the same terms Oakeshott uses to define human conduct (Cf. *OHC*, 74-8).

The non-instrumentality of civil association gives it a somewhat conversational character. It may be said therefore to intimate and

---

[45] Oakeshott is an individualist who junks nearly every piece of the conceptual equipment used to prop up the isolated and exiguous self. Yet he is no communitarian if this means thinking of human beings as 'capital'.

perhaps prepare the way for the higher life of reason found in conversation.[46] However, the focus of attention in civil discourse is narrowly proscribed to the desirability of changes to the legal system, and such narrowness is not conversational. While political deliberation is not geared to the achievement of substantive purposes, and can therefore be expected to be less argumentative than the board meetings of some great enterprise, the concern is still with the 'desirability' of changes to the legal system, and this must necessarily stir the passions. And if Oakeshott articulates a strong view of political discourse as essentially deliberative and persuasive, he is no less clear that this style of reasoning is not the only one available to human beings. He does not make politics king. Deliberation is for equals to figure out what to do in contingent situations under conditions of uncertainty, and to give deliberation — or politics — a substantive, extrinsic end paradoxically devalues politics itself.

While we exercise choice in our friendships, we most commonly find ourselves, by chance, born into a political community that is made up of strangers — not our clansmen, nor our tribe, but fellow citizens, related by a common recognition of the authority of the laws. Civil association allows, at best, for the exercise of a narrow range of human capacities in its specifically political domain. This is not to forget the whole range of human flourishing the rule of law makes possible, but its gift, as Oakeshott might say, is negative (*RIP*, 292-3). Civil association is a relationship of different sorts of people — thus far, Aristotle would agree (*OHC*, 217; cf. 223, 235). But to imagine *cives* as porcupines, as Oakeshott does, appropriating a metaphor of Schopenhauer (*RIP*, 460-1), suggests a coolness that results from Oakeshott's clarity about the limits and scope of politics that is not shared by Aristotle. If Aristotle 'recognizes only indistinctly' the most important feature of civil association, its system of rules, Oakeshott's concentration upon this feature, and his exploration of its postulates, leads to civil association being more sharply distinguished, not only from the household, but also from the pursuit of the best way of life.

---

[46]   Despite important differences in his understanding of the nature and scope of philosophy, Oakeshott shares this dialectical ideal with Plato and Aristotle. Conversation, for him, is true society. We must also keep in mind the activities in which, Aristotle says, 'the activity of practicing the art is itself the end' (*NE*, 1.1.1). For Oakeshott, these include civil association, friendship, gardening, fishing, hill walking, conversation and aesthetic delight.

II

Oakeshott and the
Moderns

4

Douglas J. Den Uyl

Spinoza and Oakeshott

The mind must pass from knower to unknower and engage itself always with particular things.

Michael Oakeshott, interpreting
Spinoza's *Tractatus de Intellectus Emendatione* (1923)

The only sustained comment on Spinoza I know of in Oakeshott is his notebook (unpublished) on the *Tractatus de Intellectus Emendatione* (TdIE). This is a notebook completed very early in Oakeshott's career.[1] It would seem to be of marginal value, since the kind of rationalism and universalism so characteristic of Spinoza might have been an enthusiasm of Oakeshott's in his early years, but was hardly the case for him in his mature thought.[2] Still the notebook exists, so it is worth at least a moment's reflection, if for no other reason than to satisfy our curiosity about whether any of the later Oakeshott appears in the early one.

The Spinoza Notebook

Although it is clear that Oakeshott read Spinoza's *Ethica*, the only writing we have of his which contains systematic comments on Spinoza is the notebook on the *Tractatus* (TdIE).[3] Oakeshott asserts

---

[1] Oakeshott, Notebook titled *Spinoza I*, June 1923, LSE File 2/4/2. Hereafter: *Spinoza I*.

[2] I originally owe this insight to Luke O'Sullivan — both the insight into how Oakeshott may later reject Spinozism and the early influence of Spinoza upon Oakeshott.

[3] I do not know which version of the *Tractatus* (TdIE) Oakeshott studied, but I will be using *The Collected Works of Spinoza*, ed. Edwin Curley (Princeton, N.J.: Princeton Univ. Press, 1985), vol. 1. References to the *Tractatus Politicus* and the *Tractatus Theologico-Politicus* will use 'TP' and 'TTP,' respectively, followed by a chapter number and paragraph number if applicable. A.G.

that the *Tractatus* (TdIE) is to be preferred as a better introduction to Spinoza's *Ethica* than the *Short Treatise on God, Man, and Well-being*. This opinion is quite plausible, though Oakeshott does not make it clear why he drew this conclusion. More pressing is, why do we have a commentary on this work of Spinoza's and not on the *Ethica* itself, or at least some commentary on part of the *Ethica*? Oakeshott, for example, cites Joachim's great study of Spinoza[4] throughout his notebook, and Joachim's work is devoted to Spinoza's philosophy as a whole, the *Ethica* in particular. This suggests an interest in understanding Spinoza generally and not just the *Tractatus* (TdIE). Indeed, Oakeshott takes notes as if he wishes to understand Spinoza generally. I say this because there are numerous citations of the *Ethica* in this notebook, as well as general statements of principle. Why then not comment on the *Ethica* directly? I have no guess to make other than perhaps the *Tractatus* (TdIE) was known to Oakeshott through Joachim who had already written his commentary of the *Tractatus* (TdIE), even though it was not published until after his death in 1940.[5] Joachim was himself part of the idealist movement in Britain to which I understand Oakeshott belonged in his early years. Perhaps the appearance of this great study of Spinoza was an inspiration to Oakeshott, and he somehow had access to or awareness of Joachim's reflections on the *Tractatus* (TdIE). Still, that would not answer why the *Tractatus* (TdIE) rather than the *Ethica* would be chosen unless its length and lack of sustained metaphysical reflection made it more convenient for Oakeshott.

In some of Oakeshott's other references to Spinoza where the *Ethica* is clearly intended as the point of reference (e.g., his reference to Spinoza in 'The Voice of Poetry in the Conversation of Mankind' to which we will refer later), Oakeshott often wishes to distance himself from Spinoza. It may be that the *Tractatus* (TdIE) was a work more to Oakeshott's liking than the *Ethica*. The latter appears to be a massive universalistic, foundationalistic, rationalistic, and wholly naturalistic account of things. By contrast, what is remarkable about Oakeshott's commentary on the *Tractatus* (TdIE) is that he appears to

Wernham edition, *The Political Works* (Oxford: Clarendon Press, 1965), for both the *Tractatus Politicus* and *Tractatus Theologico-Politicus*.

[4] Harold H. Joachim, *A Study of the* Ethics *of Spinoza* (Oxford: Clarendon Press, 1901).

[5] J. Thomas Cook, 'Spinoza's Place in This Century's Anglo-American Philosophy,' paper presented at *Vereniging Het Spinozahuis in Amsterdam*, 16 May 16 1997.

find few of these characteristics in the argument of the *Tractatus* (TdIE). It may be, then, that the *Tractatus* (TdIE) sparked an early enthusiasm on Oakeshott's part for Spinoza, and that as he read on (e.g., into the *Ethica*) he grew less and less enchanted with what he found. The point is that what I expected to discover, and did not, was evidence in this notebook of an original attraction on Oakeshott's part to the universalism, rationalism, foundationalism, and natural- ism that he certainly came later to reject. I did not find it there. Indeed, quite the opposite. Perhaps the extent to which Oakeshott embraced idealism early on could itself be qualified. Still, none of this successfully answers why one would turn to a good *introduction* to the *Ethica*, rather than the main source itself?

Oakeshott's commentary on the *Tractatus* (TdIE) contains little or no reference to metaphysics and ontology. Neither to a large extent does the *Tractatus* (TdIE) itself. Instead, as the title suggests, the focus is on the improvement of the mind or understanding. Why then consider this work as the precursor to the *Ethica*? After all, the *Ethica* opens with the big metaphysical concepts of substance, attrib- ute, mode, self-causation and the like. The mind hardly gets men- tioned until books 2 and 3, and by books 3 and 4 Spinoza seems more interested in the emotions than the intellect, returning to the intellect at the end of 4 and 5. In any case, can we really understand Spinoza without focusing extensively on the ontological and metaphysical components of his thought? If Spinoza really did proceed *more geometrico* wouldn't the ontological and metaphysical categories be primary, leaving us once again to wonder why Oakeshott chose to give such a careful reading to the *Tractatus* (TdIE) alone?

A couple of answers suggest themselves here. One is that Oakeshott sees the *Ethica* as *essentially* ethical. Despite it's title, the *Ethica* is most often read in a metaphysical, ontological, and epistemological vein. And when ethics is the focus, commentators discuss ethical theory, not practice. But by 'essentially ethical' I mean that it is possible to take the *Ethica* as a guide to life, that is, as a guide to living well in some way. We live well or rightly by improv- ing our minds, the very title of the *Tractatus* (TdIE).[6] It is not implau- sible to argue for this as a central aspect of Spinoza's intention, as I

---

[6]   Commenting on section 34, Oakeshott links Spinoza's doctrine of truth to Aristotle's notion of the good (cf. *Spinoza I*, 15v).

have done elsewhere.[7] Looked at in this light, the *Tractatus* (TdIE) could plausibly be seen as more than a mere introduction to the *Ethica*, but as capturing its essence.

The second possibility — one by no means exclusive of the first — is consistent with Oakeshott's idealistic early period.[8] What has traditionally interested idealists, and continued to do so in Oakeshott's time, was the proper ordering of the mind. If an idealist is one who holds that at root the substance of being is mind, then both accounting for error in our ideas and ordering those ideas towards a grasping of the deepest truths would certainly be a priority. Just as the empiricist must show why every impression is not veridical, so the idealist must show why every idea is not true. And just as the empiricist must come to grips with the question of whether anything lies behind the impressions, so the idealist must wonder whether any ordering of ideas is as revealing of the structure of reality as the next. A youthful enthusiasm for idealism would have certainly led one to look at works such as Descartes' *Discourse on Method* or his *Rules for the Direction of the Mind* when thinking about such issues.

While still not answering completely the choice of the *Tractatus* (TdIE) over the *Ethica*, the foregoing argument would gain convincing plausibility if one knew that the *Tractatus* (TdIE) was one among a number of works on this issue that Oakeshott was examining. Perhaps that is the case. A number of the 'links' in the notebook — that is, references to the works of other authors — are indeed connected to the proper ways to order the mind. But a surprising number of these links are to political or ethical writings that are not so obviously connected to this project or to the specific texts in the *Tractatus* (TdIE) itself. Were this a full study of the notebook, I would want to follow up all such references. For our purposes, to see the political/ethical nature of many of these links is not only to support our earlier claim that Oakeshott read Spinoza as an ethicist, but also this lends support to the speculations below concerning what Oakeshott might think of Spinoza as a political philosopher.

Before closing this section, I would like to offer one other impression of this notebook that struck me. I believe it is fair to say of Oakeshott as a philosopher that although he was prone to arche-

---

[7] Douglas J. Den Uyl and Lee Rice, 'Spinoza and Hume on Individuals,' *Reason Papers* no. 15 (1990), 91–117.

[8] Professor Marina Barabas of Charles University verbally suggested this possibility to me.

types, he was very much tied to the concrete and particular. To my
mind, Oakeshott's 'conservatism' comes not just with respect to his
'essentialism' regarding his archetypes (modernity, the state, individualism, rationalism, etc.) which gives those archetypes a 'nature'
that determines what is or is not accordant or divergent with them;
but also his conservatism comes with his Burkean-like rootedness in
the concrete, the particular, and experiential, rather than the abstract
and universal. What is remarkable is that Oakeshott reads Spinoza
this way in this notebook, even in this period of Oakeshott's life.
Consider a couple of examples. Here's what Spinoza says in
Tractatus (TdIE) paragraphs 39 and 40:

> [39] From this you will easily understand how the mind, as it understands
> more things, at the same time acquires other tools, with which it proceeds to
> understand more easily. For, as may be inferred from what has been said,
> before all else there must be a true idea in us, as an inborn tool; once this true
> idea is understood, we understand the difference between that kind of per-
> ception and all the rest. Understanding that difference constitutes one part of
> the Method.
>
> And since it is clear through itself that the mind understands itself the
> better, the more it understands of Nature, it is evident from that that this part
> of the Method will be more perfect as the mind understands more things, and
> will be most perfect when the mind attends to, or reflects on, knowledge of
> the most perfect Being.
>
> [40] Next, the more the mind knows, the better it understands its own powers
> and the order of Nature. The better the mind understands its own powers, the
> more easily it can direct itself and propose rules to itself; the better it under-
> stands the order of Nature, the more easily it can restrain itself from useless
> pursuits. In these things, as we have said, the whole of the Method consists.

Here is part of Oakeshott's gloss on these paragraphs:

> [39] . . . All knowledge depends upon the background of experience we bring
> to our study. The more we learn, the more we are able to learn. 'Tis the taught
> already that profit by teaching.' Browning 'Easter Day' . . . Verges on the third
> form of perception — §19[9] — but does not go nearly so far as Descartes' 'in-
> nate ideas' or Leibnitz's 'Preestablished harmony.' . . . Spinoza rejects —
> implicitly — all thought of scepticism. "It never occurs here or elsewhere in
> Spinoza that all is vanity, and his freedom from doubt and mental paralysis is
> the more singular, seeing that he was without any of the customary supports
> provided by religion, and was also very nearly solitary in his denial of them."
> [Hale White, preface p. xi] (*Spinoza I*, 19–20)
>
> [40] The direct relation between knowledge and will is again asserted. . . .

---

[9]   Spinoza says in paragraph 19: 'Perception arising when the essence of one
       thing is inferred from another thing, but not adequately; this comes from
       some effect we gather its cause, or when it is inferred from some general
       proposition that some property is always present.'

> True knowledge is knowledge of the totality of a thing's relations. We must know its 'place in Nature' before we can understand it. [knowing the] place in Nature we can best live to fulfil the 'Duties of our station' — to keep ourselves from useless things. The mind that understands is undistracted. (*Spinoza I*, 20-1)

While I quite approve of Oakeshott's reading, it is clear that we have before us an interpretation — one that it less idealistic than it needs to be. Spinoza does not speak of experience, or of perception, even of the third kind. The 'objects of nature' could very well be interpreted in terms of the second or third levels of knowledge as described in the *Ethica*[10] rather than the third level of perception as Oakeshott interprets it here.[11] Indeed, it is hard to see how the third level of perception could even give us the sort of knowledge of relations which Spinoza seems to be calling for. In addition, the comment about 'vanity' on Oakeshott's part is an interesting point to make in this context. Already it would suggest some possible skepticism about idealism and a turn towards the Oakeshott of later years. Finally, the comment about the 'duties of our station' is wildly unspinozistic, though undoubtedly Oakeshott was speaking loosely. Still, there is no evidence whatsoever that Spinoza understood the basic moral project as one of having people fit themselves into some pre-existing moral or social structure and defining their roles accordingly. Indeed, I would suggest more the opposite is true of Spinoza.

We might also make a similar point if we look to abstraction and particularity. Oakeshott says the following of Spinoza's paragraphs 74, 75, and 76:

> Regard abstractions and generalities with suspicion, build on particulars . . . [12] A knowledge of the whole will clarify our ideas of the particular. . . . God's knowledge of the world is a knowledge of particulars. . . .

---

[10] E2P40Schol.2. I adopt the convention referencing of Spinoza's *Ethica* with 'E' being the work, followed by the book number (book 1, 2, 3, 4, or 5), then the 'P' for proposition number and any further components that may fall under that proposition.

[11] Oakeshott actually interprets the third and fourth levels of perception as equivalent to the second and third levels of knowledge in the *Ethica*. This is not the case. The third level of perception is like Humean associationism and fits the first level of knowledge. The fourth level of perception is like the second level of knowledge. I would argue that there is no analogue here in the *Tractatus* (TdIE) to the third level of knowledge.

[12] I have left out references Oakeshott makes to other paragraphs. They do not affect my argument; indeed they support it. In all Oakeshott refers to

Here now is Spinoza speaking:

> [75] . . . Moreover, such a deception arises from the fact that they conceive things too abstractly. For it is sufficiently clear through itself that I cannot apply what I conceive in its true object to something else. Finally, it arises also from the fact that they do not understand the first elements of the whole of nature; so proceeding without order, and confusing Nature with abstractions (although they are true axioms), they confuse themselves and overturn the order of Nature. But we shall not need to fear any such deception, if we proceed as far as we can in a manner that is not abstract, and begin as soon as possible from the first elements, i.e., from the source and origin of Nature.
>
> [76] . . . But since, as we shall see later, the origin of Nature can neither be conceived abstractly, or universally, nor be extended more widely in the intellect than it really is, and since it has no likeness to changeable things, we need fear no confusion concerning its idea, provided that we have the standard of truth (which we have already shown). For it is a unique and infinite being, beyond which there is no being.

In some ways Oakeshott does not get the point; while in others he is right on. Spinoza is not involved in appreciating particulars through an understanding of the whole, or the whole by grasping particulars. Rather, following Descartes, he is arguing that a pure 'particular' idea — one that has no reference to anything but itself (similar to Descartes' 'clear and distinct' ideas) and thus is 'substance' of the *Ethica*[13] — is the basis for any sound inference about the nature of true ideas. He is not, Platonic style, trying to understand particulars by means of the universal or the universal by means of the particular. Something like that might come in due course, but that is not the drift of these passages. But Oakeshott is clearly correct to note that abstractions and generalizations are of doubtful contribution to truth — something that likely attracted him to Spinoza and which he carried with him much later.

We might characterize some of the last point about both Oakeshott and Spinoza by saying that they both rejected *a priorism*. This is essentially how Oakeshott opens up his interpretation of the *Tractatus* (TdIE). He says the following: 'Spinoza was not the man to reject a priori any source of good. He had contempt for nothing until he had found it contemptable (*sic*). If happiness <u>were</u> to be found in riches Spinoza would not have been "shocked"' (*Spinoza I*, 5).

---

paragraphs 55, 62, 38, 41, 42, and 65. (Cf. *Spinoza I*, 25–6, 27–8, 18–19, 21–2, and 28–9).

[13]   Cf. E1Def.1.

Although this is not exactly what Spinoza says in *Tractatus* (TdIE) paragraph 2,[14] it is in fact a plausible and true interpretation of him. In any case, the statement itself is rather 'Oakeshottian' in its nature and implies the deeper insight that there might be 'idealism' in Spinoza without *a priorism*. How this is possible since the advent of Kant is hard for us to imagine, for even the *a priori* synthetic does not cover what Spinoza is doing here and in the ethics. The reason is that for Spinoza there is no ultimate dichotomy between experience and intellection whereas there seems to be in Kant.[15] For Spinoza there are only various degrees of perfection in our comprehension of the same reality. What is '*a priori*' is built into the structure of our confusion as knowers while at the same time being the object of knowledge. What this means is that experience is open to a wide variety of modes, because nothing is given going in, except the reality that underlies them. Perhaps Oakeshott, among others, grew skeptical of there being an underlying reality or did not see the need for it. For our purposes here it is enough to note the similarity between Oakeshott and Spinoza in that both see the variety of modes of experience as paths of intellectual exploration, not as more or less subjective approximations of universalizable truths.[16] There is a degree of endless openness in Spinoza that is also found in Oakeshott, though I think not found in Kant, precisely because there is no *a priori* ordering of experience.

I would like to note one final interpretative move in Oakeshott. In interpreting paragraph 14 of Spinoza, Oakeshott makes the following claims:

---

[14] 'I say "I finally resolved," for at first sight it seemed unwise willingly to lose hold on what was sure for the sake of something then uncertain. I could see the benefits which are acquired through fame and riches, and that I should be obliged to abandon the quest of such objects, if I seriously devoted myself to the search for something different and new. [3] I perceived that if true happiness chanced to be placed in the former I should necessarily miss it; while if, on the other hand, it were not so placed, and I gave them my whole attention, I should equally fail.'

[15] The *a priori* is paradigmatically analytic while experience is paradigmatically synthetic. The problem then is to find the *a priori* synthetic. By contrast in Spinoza it is almost as if all propositions were *a posteriori* analytic because we come to a recognition of the inherently linked structure of reality by degrees of imperfection in our knowledge which gives virtually everything a synthetic character until it is understood. A lot here has to do with the fact that Spinoza is a realist and Kant is not.

[16] Recall in this connection Spinoza's infinite number of attributes and modes, E1P11,P16.

> The 'good life' is essentially social. The principle of Fraternity — bound together by an unseen chain of desire and enlightenment. The object of the State. The State is a society formed for the purpose of enabling the greatest number to acquire this new nature, which is wisdom. (*Spinoza I*, 10)

What Spinoza says[17] here is not dissimilar to Oakeshott's interpretation. But there is not, contrary to the impression given by Oakeshott, any deep-seated sociality in this paragraph in Spinoza. We seek to help others become like those of us who are wise, but that is some distance from suggesting that sociality is itself a constitutive factor in attaining wisdom. Secondly, Oakeshott's way of speaking of the purpose of the state suggests an enterprise association engaged in perfectionist politics. While it cannot be denied that there are strong overtones of this in Spinoza's own passage, it is quite contrary to Spinoza's mature position on the nature of politics, and actually not quite logically implied by what is said in the *Tractatus* (TdIE) passage anyway. The important point, though, is that such a politics would have had to be contrary to Oakeshott's long-term considered position. Noting this invites us to explore the question of Spinoza as a political philosopher, for I think in some form Oakeshott never abandons this understanding of Spinoza as a (modest) advocate of the state as an enterprise association, as he should have.

Spinoza and Hobbes

It would seem methodologically fitting to tackle the question of political philosophy in Spinoza and Oakeshott by looking at Oakeshott on Hobbes. The assumption here is that Oakeshott is favorably disposed towards Hobbes' political philosophy and that in looking at what Oakeshott has to say about Hobbes' political thought, we will gain some insight into Oakeshott's distance or proximity to Spinoza as a political thinker. Theoretically, we could do the same with any political philosopher Oakeshott admired (e.g., Aristotle or Hegel), but Hobbes was a virtual contemporary of Spinoza's, so it seems more likely that our comparison to Hobbes would reap the benefit of context, certainly an Oakeshottian value!

---

[17] '[I]t is part of my happiness to lend a helping hand, that many others may understand even as I do, so that their understanding and desire may entirely agree with my own.' [3] Spinoza says: '[14] In order to bring this about, it is necessary to understand as much of nature as will enable us to attain to the aforesaid character, and also to form a social order such as is most conducive to the attainment of this character by the greatest number with the least difficulty and danger.'

Of course, our comparison is not so much to Hobbes, but to Oakeshott's Hobbes. They may be the same, but our concern is not with how well or accurately Oakeshott interprets Hobbes, but how similar the Hobbes Oakeshott sees is to Spinoza. And it should be predictable at this stage that our main concentration here will be upon Oakeshott's great and insightful introduction to Hobbes' *Leviathan* and other related essays.[18]

In that introduction one finds numerous statements that arrest the Spinozist and call forth comparisons between the two thinkers.[19] Consider, for example, these two statements by Oakeshott:

> for Hobbes philosophy is, in all its parts, preeminently a philosophy of *power* precisely because philosophy is reasoning, reasoning the elucidation of mechanism, and mechanism essentially the combination, transfer, and resolution of forces. The end of philosophy itself is power — *scientia propter potentiam.* (*HCA*, 19)[20]

And additionally,

> It is a false reading of his [Hobbes'] intention and his achievement which finds in his civil philosophy the beginning of sociology or a science of politics, the beginning of that movement of thought that came to regard 'the methods of physical science as the proper models for political.'(*HCA*, 21)

With respect to the second of these statements, it would be fair to say that it would *not* be a misinterpretation of Spinoza to think of the physical sciences as models for the social. Spinoza tells us, for example, that,

> Thus my object in applying my mind to [political science](*ad politicam*) is not to make any new or unheard of suggestions, but to establish by sound and conclusive reasoning, and to deduce from the real nature of man, nothing save the principles and institutions which accord best with practice. Moreover, in order to investigate the topics pertaining to this branch of knowledge with the same objectivity as we generally show in mathematical inquiries, ... I have therefore regarded human passions like love, hate, anger, envy, pride, pity, and the other feelings that agitate the mind, not as vices of human nature, but as properties which belong to it in the same as heat, cold, storm, and thunder and like belong to the nature of the atmosphere. Inconvenient

---

[18] We find some of these essays (including the Introduction) in Oakeshott, *Hobbes on Civil Association*, (Indianapolis: Liberty Fund, 2000). Hereafter: *HCA*.

[19] I shall now refer to Oakeshott's Hobbes as just 'Hobbes.'

[20] 'Introduction to Leviathan,' in *HCA*. Unless otherwise noted, all references will come from the Liberty Fund edition and page numbers listed in the text above.

though they be, such things are necessary properties; they have definite causes through which we try to understand their nature.[21]

Here, as elsewhere, we find that the reading of Hobbes Oakeshott wants us to avoid is not far from the correct reading of Spinoza. We shall come back to this point momentarily, but in general I find that doctrines objectionable to Oakeshott when attributed to Hobbes may very well be ones Spinoza would embrace.

With respect to the first citation from Oakeshott above, this looks very much like a statement attributable to Spinoza as well. I have argued elsewhere[22] that Spinoza has the only purely power-based political philosophy — as opposed to a rights-based theory like Locke's (and ostensibly Hobbes') — with Hobbes fitting somewhere in between Locke and Spinoza. Though Oakeshott's statement is about philosophy in general, the power orientation is nonetheless also true of Spinoza with respect to more than just politics. That, in a way, is the whole point of the *Ethica*.[23] If anything, what Oakeshott says here about Hobbes' philosophy seems less accurate about Hobbes than Spinoza, at least when applied back to politics. Hobbes is much more concerned with constraining power, whereas Spinoza by contrast wants its complete expansion. But we may be getting a bit ahead of ourselves. Our first task should be to say something about the respective understandings of the nature of political philosophy.

In Oakeshott's 'Introduction to *Leviathan*' we are told early on that political philosophy

> may be understood to be what occurs when this movement of reflection takes a certain direction and achieves a certain level, its characteristic being the relation of political life, and the values and purposes pertaining to it, to the entire conception of the world that belongs to a civilization. (*HCA*, 4)

A few pages later Oakeshott claims that the true political philosopher faces a 'predicament' of having to draw a connection between the eternal and the specific context of political life the thinker sees in front of him. Indeed, the thinker discovers that 'the link between politics and eternity is the contribution the political order is conceived as making to the deliverance of mankind' (*HCA*, 6). Moreover, 'every masterpiece of political philosophy springs from a new vision of the

---

[21] TP1,4.
[22] See Douglas J. Den Uyl, *Power, State and Freedom: An Interpretation of Spinoza's Political Thought* (Netherlands: van Gorcum, 1983).
[23] E5P42Schol.

predicament; each is the glimpse of a deliverance or the suggestion of a remedy'(*HCA*, 6).

For Oakeshott what motivates Hobbes in the concrete is a grief for the 'calamities of my country' which involves trying to find a way to reconcile the exaggerated claims for liberty on the one hand and authority on the other. In doing this, Hobbes links himself to eternity by seeing how the political is reflective of, and upon, the nature of man and man's aspirations generally understood.

These reflections are consistent with what we find elsewhere in Oakeshott. In *Religion, Politics and the Moral Life*, two essays are devoted to the subject of political philosophy.[24] In one of the essays, we are told that political philosophy is 'an explanation or view of political life and activity from the standpoint of the totality of experience'(*RPML*, 126). In the second of these essays we are told that

> Political philosophy, then, may be said to be the genuine, unhindered impulse of reflection, setting out from a political experience, and keeping faith with the original experience, not by continuous conformity to it, but by reason of an unbroken descent. (*RPML*, 153)[25]

All these characterizations of political philosophy agree on two points: 1) political philosophy is rooted in actual political events and experience which must be then related to and transformed by universal philosophical reflection, and 2) political philosophy is not a guide to action, but a way of reflecting, the practical consequences of which are completely immaterial to what it is.

Is Spinoza a political philosopher in Oakeshott's sense? Does he do political philosophy? Oakeshott says he does in numerous places, though it is not always clear why he thinks so. One way of getting a handle on this issue is through the following passage from Oakeshott:

> It must be expected that a philosophy will conflict at every point with what appears to be the commonsense view, because the merely commonsense view must be expected to be incomplete. Indeed, the whole point of philosophy is to get at something more coherent than commonsense gives us. . . . And a philosophy of politics must also be expected to conflict with many of the

---

[24]   Oakeshott, *Religion, Politics and the Moral Life*, ed. Timothy Fuller (New Haven: Yale Univ. Press, 1993). Hereafter: *RPML*. See 'The Concept of a Philosophy of Politics' (*RPML*, 119-37) and 'Political Philosophy' (*RPML*, 138-55).

[25]   This essay begins with an idea very much like the epigram for this paper drawn from Oakeshott's notebook on Spinoza: 'We begin with knowledge which is nevertheless assumed to be ignorance'(*RPML*, 138).

refinements which the merely commonsense view suffers from in the course of redefinition. (*RPML*, 135-6)

Political philosophy in some way transforms the ordinary commonsense political experience without abandoning it.[26] Political philosophy tells us in a way what we are 'really' doing, however we may understand our experience of it at the moment.[27] How is that possible? How is it possible to both reflect what is found in experience, and at the same time to describe it in terms that the very actors in that experience would not themselves use, or perhaps even understand?

In Spinoza's case we see this clearly once we understand that however ordinary experience may appear, in the end we have nothing more in politics than modalities of power. So, in other words, while one might obey the law because it is the right thing to do, or one might go to the polls to help determine the course of political events, what is 'really' going on for Spinoza are various configurations of, and adjustments to, power relations among individuals in society. In this way the 'eternal' or 'wider experience' of universal *conatus* pulsating through the individual modalities of being is linked to the particular station or context of political life one finds oneself within. Oakeshott himself recognizes that Spinoza is a philosopher in the way just described. We are told, for example, that Spinoza (unlike Hobbes)[28] 'presents us with a universe composed of metaphysical individualities' (*HCA*, 84). This perspective coupled with the idea that a defect cannot apply to nature in itself gives Spinoza the project of 'deducing civil society from the "very condition of human nature"' (*HCA*, 63). These are clearly efforts to relate the political to that wider experience that encompasses the eternal.

In saying these things about Spinoza as a political philosopher, we are reminded of our opening citation on Hobbes' philosophy being a philosophy of power. That both thinkers saw philosophy in this way, we shall take as given. Moreover, that some of this truth spills over into political philosophy shall not be doubted as well. Yet it is

---

[26] Oakeshott says, for example, that a philosophy of politics has as its task 'to transform the concepts involved in political life by relating them to a concept of right' (*RPML*, 134).

[27] Cf. 'The Activity of Governing,' in Oakeshott, *Morality and Politics in Modern Europe*, ed. Shirley Robin Letwin (New Haven: Yale Univ. Press, 1993), 14. Hereafter: *MPME*.

[28] 'The Moral Life in the Writings of Thomas Hobbes' (*HCA*, 84). Hobbes, in contrast to Spinoza, offers us 'unique *human* individuality.'

also precisely on this point of power that Hobbes and Spinoza differ. The difference seems to me to turn on two main pillars: 1) an optimism or perfectionism in politics found in Hobbes but not Spinoza, and 2) the place reason has in politics for Hobbes but not Spinoza. In discussing both these pillars I shall be assuming that Oakeshott himself is in sympathy with Hobbes rather than Spinoza in cases where the thinkers diverge.

The gateway into both our pillars of difference is to be found in a passage that comes at the very end of Oakeshott's 'Introduction to *Leviathan*':

> Spinoza, who perhaps more completely than any other writer adheres to the conception of human life as a predicament from which salvation is sought, finds in civil association no more than a second-best deliverance, giving a freedom that cannot easily be dispensed with, but one not to be compared with that which belongs to him who is delivered from the power of necessity by his knowledge of the necessary workings of the universe (*HCA*, 78).[29]

It should be noted before we proceed, that for both Hobbes and Spinoza civil society gives us only a 'negative gift' of providing peace and not felicity. But despite this agreement, the fact remains that for Spinoza civil association is not a second best deliverance, but no deliverance at all. Spinoza was not a state of nature theorist, so we are not delivered from that condition by the state.[30] Civil association is ever present for Spinoza, so the issue is one of resource efficacy in organizing the civil association, not one of deliverance. Even when civil society is well organized, one is not necessarily delivered from anything. Our most likely condition in any civil order is one of 'unfreedom' in Spinoza's technical ethical sense, rather than salvation. For unlike Hobbes for whom civil association delivers us from war into peace,[31] for Spinoza what civil society can provide is but varying degrees of freedom. It is tempting to say that Spinoza's freedom is the same as Hobbes' peace — a form of enabling offering a 'deliverance' from the predicament of weakness in which we naturally find ourselves.[32] But this sort of 'deliverance' for Spinoza comes outside of politics, that is, outside of any social structuring provided

---

[29] I am ignoring here the technical mistake of being delivered from the power of necessity, which is not possible for Spinoza. But Oakeshott's sense here is not mistaken.

[30] See Den Uyl, *Power, State and Freedom*, chap. 3.

[31] See the last paragraph of 'Introduction to Leviathan' (*HCA*, 79).

[32] Indeed, in *Power, State and Freedom* I argue that the terms 'freedom,' 'peace,' and 'reason' are virtual synonyms in Spinoza's political theory.

by Leviathan. Leviathan is the occasion, not the cause of the benefits we receive from living together in society. At best Leviathan would facilitate by failing to hinder, but there would be no loss if it were not needed. For Hobbes, by contrast, Leviathan alters our very state of being by delivering us from the state of nature. For Spinoza, the state of nature is always with us,[33] so the task at hand is one of more efficient coordination of pre-existing forces, a task in which Spinoza's Leviathan plays only an indirect and limited (though necessary) role. Spinoza's Leviathan can frustrate and obscure, but it cannot deliver or enhance.

Of course, one could argue that Oakeshott means here by 'deliverance' only the move away from conflict and barbarism that would be present without the peace-keeping arbitrator that is Leviathan. Spinoza's point is that with the state of nature being ever present, so are conflict and barbarism to some degree. Leviathan does not remove them. Indeed, Leviathan is often its very instrument. The hope instead is that whatever forces there are within society — including peace-keepers and arbitrators — that can mitigate the conflict and barbarism to which human beings are often prone be allowed to exert their influence.[34] This is not deliverance by politics. Politics at best facilitates for Spinoza, it does not deliver. It does not deliver because politics is nothing more than a re-orientation of some forces so that others may find their efficient exercise. It is less a change of condition, than a condition of change.

When speaking of the absence at any level of political deliverance, there is, ironically, also the fact that for Spinoza, unlike Hobbes, there is a substantive notion of salvation built into his ethics — one which Oakeshott himself cites, at least in general terms, in a footnote within the very passage we cited above. For Spinoza 'blessedness' was conceivable and possible, and Oakeshott's general claim about Spinoza being a thinker concerned with salvation from the human predicament is on the mark. That is precisely why Spinoza needs a

---

[33] TP2,15;3,3.

[34] Notice that in saying this we see the roots of a sensibility exploited by later authors. For Spinoza there seems to be an inherent notion of progress — the idea of the rudiments of improvement are in society already and will, if given a chance, come to the fore. Hobbes, by contrast, is 'conservative.' There's no sense that things will get better or that human nature is the source of its own improvement. The paradox here is that Spinoza has progress without perfectionist politics, whereas Hobbes has perfectionism to some degree without progress.

substantive concept of salvation. But Oakeshott's Hobbes has nothing similar. There are only procedural acts of living without overall felicity. Leviathan for Hobbes ensures the continuity of procedural acts and thus 'delivers' us from their interruption — the *best* we can do in this life. By contrast, as I've argued elsewhere, politics for Spinoza contributes absolutely nothing to what is best for us ('blessedness').[35] Indeed, given its essentially affective nature leading men to seek glory, honor, and riches, politics is probably a significant distraction from what is best for us, rather than a mitigated form of it.

That politics facilitates in some way what is best for us is the modest perfectionist element in Oakeshott's Hobbes, and thus perhaps his overall political theory. Ironically, the politics without an ethical *summum bonun* (Hobbes') retains some perfectionism, whereas Spinoza's politics coupled as it is to a perfectionist ethics with a clear conception of 'blessedness,' does not. While both thinkers leave politics primarily to the task of negative liberty, the sensibilities are quite different. With Spinoza, there is a more market-like spontaneous order approach, whereas Hobbes is, in Hayekean language, more constructivistic.

Indeed 'constructivistic' seems to me the correct word to move us to our next topic and further appreciate the last one. This topic is the role of reason. Though Hobbes and Spinoza often sound the same — for example, chapter 16 of Spinoza's *Tractate Theologico-Politicus* can often seem like a paraphrase of many of the early chapters of *Leviathan* — they are quite different. Leviathan, as both Hobbes and Oakeshott tell us, is a construct, an artifice that is the result of human reason. In Spinoza, politics is not a construct of human reason, but an outcome of the interplay of the passions that accords with reason. Politics is virtually devoid of reason for Spinoza; it is strangely filled with it for Hobbes and Oakeshott. Civil society is actually 'civil' for Oakeshott and Hobbes, that is to say, it is pervaded by rational agents who recognize the need for an artifice to mediate their mutual associations. But that recognition is itself a kind of civil quality that exists among those agents, a sort of gentlemanly recognition that rules are needed and we should play by them. There may be none of that in Spinoza's politics. Rules are themselves the outcomes of evolutionary struggles among interacting agents whose adherence to those rules is tied more to their relative power positions at any given

---

[35] Den Uyl, 'Autonomous Autonomy,' *Social Philosophy and Policy* 20, no.2 (Summer 2003), 30–69.

point, than it is to their recognition of the need for rules and obedience to them. The effect is the same. Whether we obey because we recognize the utility of a rule or because our passions move us to do so produces the same actions or results. But in the one case the outcome is a function of the use of reason; in the other we have at best what accords with it.[36]

Politics does deliver us for Oakeshott's Hobbes — not because it brings us closer to a *summum bonum*, but because in its very nature it is humanizing. To associate on the basis of reason is a distinctively human activity. As Oakeshott clearly tells us, 'the civil condition is an artifact'(*HCA*, 49). And since human beings are a 'race condemned to seek its perfection in the flying moment and always in the one to come, whose highest virtue is to cultivate a clear-sighted vision of the consequences of its actions'(*HCA*, 79) it constructs the artifice to facilitate its motions. Without reason, or the clear-sighted vision of consequences, we would be lost.[37] Aristotle was right to think of politics as the arena in which we humanize ourselves, though not as the communitarians often interpret this. The act of creating Leviathan is symbolic of our need to come together to consider consequences that jointly affect us, so that we might pursue our disparate felicities. Awakening to this need for civil association is a human awakening. It is one rooted in an act of introspection and reason on the part of each of us (*HCA*, 31).

What we have just said about Hobbes seems inapplicable to Spinoza. There is, first of all, no creature less introspective than Spinoza's political man. He tells us, for example,

> But men are led more by blind desire than by reason; and so their natural power, or natural right, must not be defined in terms of reason, but must be held to cover every possible appetite by which they are determined to act, and by which they try to preserve themselves.[38]

---

[36] Specifics for these claims in Spinoza can be found in the sources already cited of arguments made elsewhere. Many authors make arguments that at least support part of what I say here (e.g., Negri, Rice, Matheron, Barbone).

[37] Oakeshott wants to make it clear that for Hobbes man is not primarily a reasoning creature, but an affective one (*HCA*, 27), though he does allow that 'hypothetical reasoning' distinguishes us from animals. I find this vacillation between the affective and the rational to be a tension in both Hobbes and Oakeshott.

[38] TP2,5.

That politics humanizes is, then, the perfectionist element to Hobbes and Oakeshott's politics.[39] Its absence in Spinoza perhaps marks the first manifestation of the tension between constructivist and non-constructivist approaches to modern political and social theory. We see the appeal of both sides. On the one hand, the 'spontaneous order' market-like arguments that would characterize Spinoza's non-constructivist side carry with them a certain realism and validity. On the other, it could be argued that at some point our planning or injection of an order based upon envisioned consequences is inescapable — even for markets — and thus is at root the most essential component of the political. I suspect for Hobbes, and thus for Oakeshott as well, the Spinozistic story was simply too arational to accept. It seems likely to me that Oakeshott sensed something of this in his relative neglect of Spinoza as a political thinker. And this alternative hypothesis (that Oakeshott saw something 'unhuman' about Spinoza's politics) is significantly more appealing to me, on the basis of textual evidence, than supposing the usual opinion about Spinoza and Hobbes that Spinoza is relatively neglected because he is simply a footnote to Hobbes.

Before leaving this topic, a brief word is in order about individualism. Oakeshott speaks quite favorably about individualism and attributes the origins of that philosophy to both Spinoza and Hobbes. Hobbes is 'the first moralist of the modern world to take candid account of the current experience of individuality. But it is clear also in Spinoza.'[40] Oakeshott also notes, however (lending some support to our argument above about the seamless quality of Spinoza's view of nature) that 'unlike Spinoza, who presents us with a universe composed of metaphysical individualities (man being only a special case of a universal condition), Hobbes' starting point as a moralist was the unique *human* individuality'(*HCA*, 84). Although Oakeshott here mixes categories (the metaphysical and the moral), the more significant issue is what he might mean by 'human individuality.' The answer seems to me to come in the following passages:

---

[39]   Oakeshott cites Hobbes' own introduction to the Latin edition of *Leviathan*: 'This great Leviathan, which is called the State, is a work of art; it is an artificial man made for the protection and salvation of the natural man, to whom it is superior in grandeur and power'(*HCA*, 77).

[40]   See 'The Activity of Governing' (*MPME*, 22).

> In the morality of individuality…human beings are recognized (because they
> have come to recognize themselves in this character) as separate and sover-
> eign individuals, associated with one another, not in the pursuit of a single
> common enterprise, but in an enterprise of give and take, and accommodat-
> ing themselves to one another as best they can: it is the morality of self and
> other selves….Moral conduct is recognized as consisting in determinate rela-
> tionships between these individuals, and the conduct approved is that which
> reflects the independent individuality understood to be characteristic of
> human beings. Morality is the art of mutual accommodation. (*HCA*, 82)

And again:

> By the morality of individuality I mean, in the first place the disposition to
> make choices for oneself to the maximum possible extent, choices concerning
> activities, occupations, beliefs, opinions, duties and responsibilities. And fur-
> ther to approve of this sort of conduct — self-determined conduct — as con-
> duct proper to a human being, and to seek the conditions in which it may be
> enjoyed most fully. It is this approval — not merely on one's own account but
> in respect of others also — that the impulse towards individuality becomes a
> moral disposition. This is how human beings ought to live, and to be
> deprived of this exercise of individuality is recognized not only as the great-
> est unhappiness but also as the diminution of moral stature. (*MPME*, 20-1)

What Oakeshott is apparently denying to Spinoza, and what also
answers our question of what it means to be human, is the idea that
individuals recognize themselves as such, both when reflecting
upon themselves and when thinking of their relations with others.
Are Spinoza and Hobbes/Oakeshott really at odds on this point?

First it is important to correct the misleading attribution by
Oakeshott concerning Spinoza's metaphysical holism. In one sense,
of course, Oakeshott is quite correct — individuals are simply
modalities of a greater whole. But the conclusion usually inferred
from this — that somehow individuals are therefore fundamentally
illusory — is quite mistaken. Especially in the political writings, the
building blocks of Spinoza's political theory are individuals and not
some ephemeral metaphysical surrogates.[41] Oakeshott's other intuition, that Spinoza *was* indeed one of the first theorists of a real individualism, is quite correct. The problem, and thus the difference
between the two thinkers, then, goes back to the issue we have
already raised — namely, the place of perfectionism.

---

[41] Spinoza says that nature as a whole 'is nothing other than the power of all
      individuals taken together,' *Tractatus Theologico-Politicus* (TTP), chap. 16.
      See also, Lee C. Rice, 'Spinoza on Individuation,' *The Monist* 55, no. 4
      (October 1971).

For Hobbes, politics begins with individuals. They are self-contained choosers who are self-aware of their own individuality as units of moral value and moral worth. However perverse, weakened, and combative, the parties to the social contract for Hobbes see themselves as individual agents in the 'human' sense given by Oakeshott above. They contract as moral equals, one among others, for the partial relief of their condition. They have no *a priori* expectation that they are inferior to anyone else, though they take their own desires more seriously than they do those of others. And it would be hard to make sense of the 'sufficient signs' needed for a social contract to take root unless there was some mutual recognition of autonomous agency — that is, individuality.

For Spinoza, by contrast, individuals in something close to Oakeshott's sense only exist insofar as they are the adequate causes of their own conduct, which is to say insofar as they live by reason alone. Prior to that, they are pushed and pulled by forces outside their control and understanding. Consequently, it is more accurate to say that individuals do not exist in politics for Spinoza in the human or moral sense Oakeshott gives them in his account of Hobbes. That is to say, there is no individuality. Spinoza's individuals have ontological status as *foci* of behavior, but their moral status as individuals, their individuality, comes only when they are living the life of reason.[42] That life, as we have noted, is well outside the political. It is best then not to think of politics as the interaction of independent rational moral agents, but rather as the impassioned exertions and repulsions of individuals responding to stimuli in their social environment.

The difference here is significant, though the message at first sight appears ambiguous, because Oakeshott's descriptions are somewhat mixed. Oakeshott will describe Hobbes' individuals in terms I have just used to describe Spinoza's. But we are here speaking of individuality not individuals; and however Spinoza-like Hobbes' individuals are in many circumstances, at some point that is both critical to and necessary for the formation of civil society, they recognize and depend upon their individuality. An individual in the Oakeshott/Hobbes sense may be present in Spinoza's civil society, but that individual is so statistically insignificant as to warrant no place whatsoever in theorizing about that society. As a consequence, it is correct to say of Hobbes that by grounding politics in the moral

[42] E4P66Schol., and P73Schol.

centrality of the individual, Hobbes generates a form of political theory exhibited in later thinkers such as Locke and Kant. Individuals for these thinkers have moral rights against each other, and make claims upon one another in light of these moral rights. Individuality foreshadows notions of autonomy that are so central to much of liberal politics. Political theory has, in this tradition, a moral core and purpose.

But since there is no individuality in Spinoza's politics — only individuals moved by various forces outside of themselves — there is in fact no moral core to the theory. The theory borders more closely upon the descriptive or what is better captured under the heading of 'social science' than 'political philosophy.' There is no moral standard circumscribing the theory and giving events a moral significance. Cooperation may be the essence of politics for both Hobbes and Spinoza, but for Hobbes discrete moral units recognize the value of cooperation in light of their own awareness of themselves as centers of moral authority. In Spinoza, to the contrary, cooperation is achieved as an expression of an equilibrium of interactive forces. There is no real moral value to it, because the result is not necessarily the product of moral design or moral agency. What is striking about politics for Spinoza is its amorality. Individuals must make themselves for Spinoza, and thus individuality cannot be at the core of politics. So for Spinoza, politics ends when we have the sort of individuals alluded to by Oakeshott above. For Hobbes/Oakeshott, individuality is where politics begins.

Oakeshott may have appreciated this difference in his metaphysical dismissal of Spinoza cited earlier. If we cannot stand out as anything but instances of some greater whole or force, we will never have the individuality so necessary to Oakeshott's civil association. And in saying this we have again witnessed the non-perfectionist politics and perfectionist ethics of Spinoza, as contrasted with the perfectionist politics of Hobbes/Oakeshott and their non-perfectionist ethics. Individuality, nonetheless, is to be found in both.

Conclusion: Which Conversation?

If nothing else, we have discovered a remarkable absence of commentary by Oakeshott on Spinoza given Spinoza's proximity to things Oakeshott does care about (both historically and philosophically). I would speculate that this omission is deliberate. Spinoza, by Oakeshott's own admission, is too great a thinker to be ignored without reason. I believe that many of the components of Spinoza's thought were quite attractive to Oakeshott, but that something fundamental and general never allowed Oakeshott to embrace Spinoza as an ally in Oakeshott's cause. The key to the problem lies in the most critical comments about Spinoza I could find:

> Some writers (whose manner of thinking has impressed itself deeply upon our intellectual habits) understand contemplation as an experience in which the self is partnered, not by a world of unique but transitory images, but by a world of permanent essences: to contemplate is to 'behold' the 'universals' of which the images of sense, emotion, and thought are mere copies. . . . Spinoza appears to have attributed this character to what he calls *scientia intuitiva*.[43]

And elsewhere he says:

> First, there has been a laudable conviction that mental honesty, disinterestedness, absence of prejudice, are intellectual virtues of the highest value. But this conviction has unfortunately been combined, in a strange confusion of mind, with the belief that disinterestedness is possible only to a mind which is wholly self-moved — that is, a mind devoid of acquired disposition. It would be difficult to find a more persuasive account of this doctrine than that contained in Spinoza's *Ethics*. (*RIP*, 112)

What we have in these passages is a view of Spinoza that I would label the 'one conversation' problem. Whether one is reflecting on politics, science, or art there is only one way to do so as Oakeshott sees Spinoza. For the sake of simplicity, let us call this one way the *more geometrico*. All discourse that seeks truth must proceed *more geometrico* as Oakeshott understands Spinoza, because the very clarity of mind that attracted Oakeshott in the first place to Spinoza's *Tractatus* (TdIE) is, given Spinoza's parallelism, necessarily a reflection of reality itself. And this unity of purified thought and reality is itself a sign of Spinoza's holism, since ultimately, *sub specie aeternitatis*, all is tied together in the one substance. Metaphysically, then, it looks like one thing, one story.

But this is precisely what Oakeshott wants to avoid. There is no special single reality that a certain specialized mode of thinking or rationality brings one to discover. The realities are diverse; the modes of thought rooted in actual practice with rationality, in an acceptable sense, being never too distant from that experience. For Oakeshott the one path, one conversation idea is anathema. To see what, if anything, Spinoza might say in response to this interpreta-

---

[43] 'The Voice of Poetry in the Conversation of Mankind,' in *Rationalism in Politics and other essays, new and expanded edition*, ed. Timothy Fuller (Indianapolis: Liberty Press, 1991), 511. Hereafter: *RIP*.

tion of his thought would be another paper. Aside from what we said about multiple conversations early on, I would only note in passing that in metaphysics the attributes are infinite in number as are modes,[44] allowing for multiple 'conversations' in principle; that the human mind is but the idea of the body whose diversity is a function of the diversity of the 'experiences' of the body;[45] and that in politics experience is the better guide than the ruminations of philosophers.[46]

Yet Oakeshott's characterization of Spinoza is not implausible, since clearly for Spinoza there is both a reality and a particular way of grasping it that would seem to be a version of the one conversation problem. In this we are saying something that is little more than what might be recognized with only a superficial understanding of both thinkers — namely, that if Spinoza is a rationalist in the standard Enlightenment mode, Oakeshott is opposed to it and abandons whatever early attraction such rationalism may have held for him. Having said this, we have seen above that if we set aside some of the grander metaphysical theses of Spinoza, some definite commonalities exist between Oakeshott and Spinoza, as well as some interesting points of contention that do not depend upon a misguided form of rationalism. The real question would then seem to be how is it possible for someone like Spinoza to have so many correct inclinations in some specific areas of politics and ethics with such a faulty (from Oakeshott's perspective) metaphysical framework? In other words, how could such individualistic and experiential sympathies arise from a doctrine so holistic and rationalistic? It would have benefited us greatly if Oakeshott had sought to answer these questions himself, for to simply slide Spinoza into a Western tradition in philosophy prone to reducing all to 'one conversation' is to fail to account for the inconsistency. This is especially true in Spinoza's case, since he, perhaps above all others, was never afraid to face the implications of his thought clearly, openly, completely, and without reserve. How could a man who reputedly went where Hobbes himself dared not to go be so blind to the inconsistency between his metaphysics and actual practice?

I suspect that in the end the problem is really, after all, not one of rationalism. Spinoza would have no trouble accepting that rational

[44]   E1P11,16.
[45]   E2P11,14-16.
[46]   TP1,2.

action 'springs up within an already existing idiom of activity,' though he would be uncomfortable with holding that rationality in science, for example, is to be determined by the scientist's 'faithfulness to the traditions of scientific inquiry' (*RIP*, 121, 123). The problem, however, is not rationalism, because rationalism — that is, the rationalism that Oakeshott repudiates — is very much dependent on a premise Spinoza explicitly rejects, namely the separation of will and intellect.[47] That separation is in essence what Oakeshott rails against in the opening pages of 'Rational Conduct' and which prevents the deepest integration of reason and practice that Oakeshott so desires. If we separate intellect from will, then it is in principle possible for an abstract model to pre-exist the practical activity that may wish to implement it. This divorce of reason from practice is the source of all the pathologies of rationalism for both Oakeshott and Spinoza. In Spinoza's case, the idea of a set of pre-existing Liebnizian possible worlds waiting for practical implementation was the metaphysical source of error. It is in correcting that metaphysical mistake that keeps Spinoza from being a rationalist in Oakeshott's sense. In this connection, it is interesting to note that while Oakeshott may believe we can only account for the integration of reason and practice within a metaphysics of skeptical empiricism, Spinoza could be worth some attention precisely because he gets so much of what Oakeshott wants out of an alternative metaphysical framework.

Be that as it may, what is, I believe, truly troublesome to Oakeshott about Spinoza in the end is not Spinoza's adherence to a faulty rationalism, but rather that there is ultimately in Spinoza no meaningful sense of history or artifice. There is for Spinoza nothing radically created, because Spinoza's world is quite contrary to 'a world composed wholly of contingencies and in which contingencies are intelligible, not because they have been resolved, but on account of the circumstantial relations which have been established between them.'[48] A world of contingency allows for radical artifice and history. It allows for something to exist now that is not strictly a determinate function of causal chains. Spinoza, in contrast, tells us simply, 'Nothing in nature is contingent.'[49]

---

[47]   E2P49&Cor.
[48]   'The Activity of Being an Historian' (*RIP*, 182).
[49]   E1P29.

5

Josiah Lee Auspitz

Modality and Compossibility

Pour bien savoir les choses, il en faut savoir le détail; et comme il est presque infini, nos Connoissances sont toujours superficielles et imparfaites.   La Rochefoucauld (*Maxime* 106, marked
                  by Oakeshott in a copy presented to a friend).

[To know things well, one must know them in detail, and as detail is virtually infinite, our understandings are always superficial and imperfect.]

I should like to lay the ground here for a fresh view of modality initially prompted both by the power and by the inadequacy of the use of the concept in Michael Oakeshott's *Experience and Its Modes.*[1] Oakeshott, too, was concerned to resolve anomalies in this first treatise. He reported his successes four decades later in *On Human Conduct,*[2] and at several stopping points along the way. One test of the view to be developed is that it should illuminate Oakeshott's achievement against the background of his modern precursors and show why, on his own terms, Oakeshott had to revise the grounds of his earlier work. We shall also see that the full course of revision has not yet been run, even within the lines that Oakeshott laid out.

It will be a further test, to be pursued in a sequel, to see how well the fresh view proposed — which we shall call a 'sign-modal' or more loosely, a semiotic approach — can stand on its own, providing a ground for, among other inquiries, a philosophical critique of institutions, including the institutional aspects of philosophy itself.

[1] Oakeshott, *Experience and its Modes* (Cambridge: Cambridge Univ. Press, 1933). Hereafter: *EM.*
[2] Oakeshott, *On Human Conduct* (Oxford: Clarendon Press, 1975). Hereafter: *OHC.*

While a sign-modal approach may be presented as a response to Oakeshott and to two of his predecessors — Spinoza and Hegel — it will also draw upon a second strand of modern reflection beginning with Locke, pausing at Kant and culminating but not completed in the late letters and notebooks of C. S. Peirce. From Oakeshott we get a view of modality writ large, addressing the great divides of our experience — modes of explanation and of association; but this large view presents, in Oakeshott's phrase 'an invitation to further inquiry' into a view of modality writ small, focusing on sign modalities that mark infinitesimal variations and *possibilia*.

The completed view of modality will knit these two strands into a single fabric. It will enable us to glimpse a world at once variegated and unified, forever settling into convention and yet exploding with new possibilities. Within this unfolding world, we can then place ourselves: we can address the sense in which philosophy and other varieties of theorizing may be viewed and may view themselves under the category of modality.

Modality and Compossibility in Brief

A mode, as used here, is a principle of differentiation defined by human judgment. It modifies a substrate, which must be unified and homogeneous with respect to it (otherwise, the mode could not be a principle but merely an attributed property of a given individual). To speak of a mode is to accept necessarily, at least with respect to that modification, an underlying unity and homogeneity in the substrate modified.

From the underlying unity of the substrate it follows that alternate principles of modification, even when one excludes another, need not be contradictory. Rather they are compossible — that is, they may coexist as modifiers of the self-same substrate without depending upon each other for definition or validation.

Well-worked examples of the application of 'modes' may be found in Western music, and in grammar, rhetoric and logic, the three foundational subjects, or *trivium*, of medieval liberal education.

In music the underlying substrate is tonal or rhythmical and the modes are different patternings of the predefined tonal and rhythmical elements: for example, the Dorian mode, the *tribrachic* mode.

In grammar, the substrate is discourse and the moods (an early form of modes) are self consistent manners of discourse: the indicative, imperative, subjunctive, interrogative.

In logic an early application was to modes or 'figures' of the syllogism, where the syllogistic elements were the substrate. In later logic, modes were applied to assertion (necessary, possible, actual). In the past century, as academic logic has tried to give a formal account of the full range of human judgment, we see the proliferation of 'modal logics', each carrying through a principled differentiation in formal notation.

In rhetoric, which Aristotle early distinguished from logic, modally, by observing that it employed enthymemes rather than syllogisms, the topic was also further differentiated internally by the purposes the rhetor might serve — deliberative, forensic, epideictic — and these modes of rhetoric, in turn, were rooted in social occasions: an assembly convened to discuss ways and means (deliberative rhetoric), an assembly convened as a trial court (forensic rhetoric), an assembly convened for ceremonial rites (epideictic rhetoric).

If music and the *trivium* provide age-old applications of modality, the concept has been given a new twist with the advent of digital devices, where each re-purposing of an underlying body of data is loosely but quite properly called a 'mode': user mode, programmer mode, read-only mode, safe mode, display mode, and so on. In children's video games the term now appears frequently: two-player mode, shooter mode, racing mode, jumping mode, diving mode, character improvement mode, analysis mode. Thus a term central in philosophy is now tolerably well understood by every nine year-old.

The philosophical importance of modality is not trivialized, replaced, exhausted or outdated by these applications. Whether or not the term 'mode' is used, the notion of a principled, patterned or self-consistent differentiation of a substrate is indispensable to human thought. Any inquiry into first philosophy must address the categories that recur necessarily in our thinking. Since categorization entails differentiation, the category of modality in some form is always present in the problem of the categories as such. And the companion notion of compossibility — that multiple differentiations may coexist, variously configuring the selfsame substrate without necessarily competing with each other — lies at the very core of our grasp of such ideas as plurality, variety, potentiality and hypothetical possibility.

Modality Writ Large in Oakeshott and Two Precursors

Oakeshott's treatment of 'modes of experience' in his first treatise signaled a departure, and as he would have said, a journey. The very title of *Experience and Its Modes* announced a small revolution. It set forth as ambitious a use of the concept of modality as had been seen in a major philosophical treatise since Spinoza's *Ethics*. And yet in doing so, it left itself open to a line of criticism that Hegel had made of Spinoza's modes.

Though Oakeshott's first philosophical treatise has been seen, on the authority of his own acknowledgement, against the backdrop of Hegel, Bradley and the Idealists, the concept of modality that gives *Experience and Its Modes* its élan has stronger echoes of Spinoza. As we shall see, the tension of placing a Spinozistic modal apparatus within a Hegelian framework animates the movement of Oakeshott's thought from *Experience and Its Modes* to *On Human Conduct* forty years later. The very sorts of arguments that Hegel makes against Spinoza, Oakeshott begins to make against himself.

Even if Oakeshott had never read a word of Spinoza, the *Ethics* would be the obvious *locus classicus* for the strong modal device that structures *Experience and Its Modes*. And even if he had encountered Hegel only through the British Idealists, that author would be the place to look for a critique of the device. It happens, however, that Oakeshott was a close student both of Spinoza and of Hegel, and of works relying and commenting upon them. There is thus a scholarly as well as a philosophical interest in comparing their thought with his on the topic of modality. We shall stick here to the philosophical parallels (raising a piquant question of direct historical influence only in an archival note at the end of the article). But in an age when the practice, history and criticism of philosophy lean upon each other for mutual support, the philosophical argument may also cast light on the growing scholarly attention to Oakeshott's sources and self-critique, and itself be open to refinement and elaboration as new findings in this literature take shape.

Spinoza's Example

Spinoza's use of modality is remarkable not for the mere appearance of the term, which he takes up and revises from Descartes, but for its centrality in his system. Spinoza deploys modality as the indispensable device against what he, Hegel and Oakeshott all saw as the grave and recurring error of philosophy: a 'vicious dualism,' as Oakeshott put it.

The uncompromising monism of Spinoza's philosophy rests logically on the postulate of a necessarily unified, self-consistent, self-aware and eternal substance, which he calls alternatively God and Nature ('*Deus sive Natura*'). God has attributes that are, like Him, eternal, in the many-sided sense of being timeless, infinite and unchanging. Two of these Divine attributes have been grasped by human beings: thought and extension. Those modifications (or 'affections') of substance that follow from these two attributes are what Spinoza defines as the modes of substance. As he puts it at the outset, in definition 5 of part 1 of the *Ethics*:

By mode I mean the affections of substance; that is, that which is in something else and is conceived through something else.[3]

Spinoza further defines the term 'mode' (in part 1, proposition 23) in a way that makes it his operative concept for all differentiation of substance. He introduces it less formally earlier (in proposition 16) in a way that makes clear that modes possess an infinity of possibilities. The modes of thought and extension, he makes clear, cannot exhaust the attributes of God; they are merely those ways in which we grasp Divine attributes to achieve our views of multiplicity and variety. They are the philosopher's substitute for revelation. In all, substance and mode are the organizing categories of Spinoza's metaphysics.

To carry the burden Spinoza places upon it, his notion of modality has to be versatile. It has to cover all apparent variegation in the unity of substance. For subsequent philosophy Spinoza's notion of modality thus serves as a kind of storehouse for permutations of the modal idea. In Spinoza modes may be finite and infinite, immediate and mediate. They may, as in finite modes like color and measure, exist independently of each other, combining in complex patterns to form individuals. Or, as in motion-rest, the infinite modes of extension, they may be conjugate — yoked together in dyadic patterns that exclude any other modes at the same level. Or they may be presented in tandem but open-endedly.

In the deep logical structure of the *Ethics* thought and extension appear in tandem but not as correlatives, nor as complementary *yin-yang* divisions of the world. Thought and extension cannot con-

---

[3]   Spinoza, *Ethics*, trans. Samuel Shirley, (Indianapolis: Hackett, 1992), 31.

tradict each other or other possible modes without denying the unknowable infinity of God's attributes. Modes may operate upon modes at all levels to achieve an inexhaustible variegation of substance, but thought and extension define worlds that must be kept distinct.

Being infinite they are the context in which we can apprehend finite objects. Each of these two modes defines its own finite objects. As Spinoza puts it in definition 2:

A thing is said to be finite in its own kind (in suo genera finita) when it can be limited by another thing of the same nature. For example, a body is said to be finite because we can always conceive of another body greater than it. So, too, a thought is limited by another thought. But body is not limited by thought nor thought by body.[4]

Axiom 5 further lays the logical ground for the distinctness of the modes:

Things which have nothing in common with each other cannot be understood through each other; that is, the conception of the one does not involve the conception of the other.[5]

In Spinoza's usage, then, there are two modes writ large and lesser modes that operate within them. This enables him to embrace with appropriate adaptation both physical and ideal explanations, to keep them distinct, and yet to see them ultimately reunited in a common substrate or Nature. Spinoza's notion of modality easily covers the ground of substance and attribute of the Aristotelians as well as of the 'attributes of body' in the new philosophy of the seventeenth century. Whether primary or secondary, attributes of body refer to bodies limited by bodies. They therefore reside within the mode of extension. Similarly, the uses within traditional logic of 'modes' to denote figures of the syllogism or modalities of assertion refer to objects of thought limited by other thoughts; therefore, each is a thing *in suo genera finita* within the mode of thought. From Spinoza's fifth axiom it follows that it is a gross error to mix the modes of thought and extension. He ridicules, for example, Descartes' attempt to explain acts of volition by locating the faculty of will in the pineal gland.

---

[4]   Spinoza, *Ethics*, 31.
[5]   Spinoza, *Ethics*, 32.

For the subsequent practice of philosophy, in sum, Spinoza lays the maximal ground for modality, develops a range of devices proceeding from it, and preserves the analytic distinctness of thought and extension without compromising the unity and homogeneity of their common substrate. For a canonical view of modality Spinoza's philosophy remains the strongest available statement of the monistic undergirding of any modal view.

This applies even when modal categories might seem to pay lip service to a dualism. When, to repeat the most far-reaching example, Spinoza portrays thought and extension as modes he is in effect denying, not accepting a Cartesian mind-body dualism. This is because Spinoza, unlike Descartes, replaces the notion of God as Creator *ex nihilo* with a notion of Nature as continuously self-generating (*natura naturans*). God does not create the modes as divisions of the world with their own separate careers. To the contrary, God is immanent in them and manifested through them. The on-going, self-generating nature of God, *natura naturans*, assures that the manifestations of His Nature, as seen in the modes, *natura naturata*, have a common, continuing and inexhaustible cause. Modes can have no career independent of God, because, being modes, they are 'in something else and conceived through [that] something else.' No finite thought or body can be adequately understood unless it is related to the whole of substance, namely *Deus/Natura*. No particular or individual can be understood in its full degree of reality if we prescind from it the Divine Nature immanent in it. Quite literally, then, Spinoza presents the apotheosis of the proposition that the category of modality entails an underlying unity and homogeneity in a substrate with reference to which it must be understood.

On the same metaphysical level, Spinoza also provides the ultimate warrant for the compossibility of the modes. With regard to the modes of thought and extension, the entire unity of substance may be approached under one or the other of these without compromising the integrity of either mode. The possibility of one is fully consistent with the possibility of the other, even though their definitions do not depend upon each other. Moreover, as we have noted, Spinoza takes care in proposition 16 to provide for an infinite number of other modes at the same level, each deriving from one of God's infinite attributes. It happens that the human mind has not yet settled on any but these two, but it is not to be ruled out that thought and extension, in addition to their mutual compossibility, are also compossible with other modes that may achieve cogency.

The enduring power of Spinoza's modal system is most quickly grasped at its quasi-religious core. Often accused of atheism, Spinoza claims in an undated response to a 15 November 1675 letter of Oldenburg that his view of God as 'cause immanent' echoes St. Paul ('In Him we live and move and have our being,' *Acts* 17:28). More strikingly, he suggests that his God retrieves in uncorrupted form a view he attributes to 'all the ancient Hebrews.'[6] Since God as 'cause immanent' entails for Spinoza the denial of God as 'cause transient' — that is, the denial of God as Creator — few of Spinoza's critics have credited his claim to a Biblically compatible monotheism.

Yet a point of Hebrew grammar more familiar to Spinoza than to his readers makes precise why he could assert that his *Deus sive Natura* recaptures the immediacy of the God of the Hebrew Bible. Hebrew has no present tense conjugation of the verb 'to be'. It commonly relies on juxtaposition rather than a verbal connective to denote the relation 'is'. For example, asserting 'the boy' in juxtaposition to 'little' is equivalent to 'the boy is little.' Or as a logician might now say, the existential quantifier is entailed in the act of assertion (an economy of notation employed in Peirce's existential graphs).

Later Hebrew grammar does have a term of art for the present tense: HVH (pronounced 'hoveh'). A grammatically sophisticated reader of the Hebrew Bible like Spinoza (whose *Hebrew Grammar* along with his *Ethics* was published posthumously) cannot fail to see that the ineffable, four-letter name of God, the YHVH, is compounded of what the present tense of the verb 'to be' might look like if Hebrew had one. YHVH (pronounced in ordinary English 'Jehovah' or in scholarspeak 'Yahweh') really should be translated as 'The Is' or 'The All-Present' or 'The Eternal' in Spinoza's atemporal usage of the term.

After YHVH became ineffable, it was piously read Adonai by Jews at prayer, and a similar substitute was translated through the Septuagint and Vulgate into modern European languages as Lord, *Seigneur, Herr, Heer,* etc. But the metaphor of mastership embodied in

[6] Spinoza to Oldenburg, undated, *The Chief Works of Benedict de Spinoza,* vol. 2, trans. and comp., R. H. M. Elwes, (1883; New York: Dover, 1951), letter 21, 298; also in *The Correspondence of Spinoza,* trans. and ed., A. Wolf, (New York: Lincoln MacVeagh, 1927; London: George Allen and Unwin, 1928; London: Frank Cass, 1966), letter 73, 343.

these anthropomorphisms is utterly absent from the original. All that is connoted in the Proper Name of God is a ubiquitous presence. If we limit God's modes and attributes (Hebrew: *Midot*) only to what can be inferred from the literal force of God's Proper Name, YHVH, we have precisely Spinoza's *Deus sive Natura* — a God whose essence is necessarily His existence, an all-pervasive Presence distributed throughout Nature and immanent in every thing, whether animate or inanimate, whether of mind or body, thought or deed. It is in this sense that Spinoza could see his notion of universal substance as retrieving what was rationally acceptable in the pristine conception of a monotheistic deity.[7]

Beyond time and place, *Deus sive Natura* is the infinite self-causing cause of whatever there is, a unified and universal substance without reference to which no understanding can be complete. Control of the emotions to focus on this ever-present in all phenomena, is the self control that Spinoza calls *amor dei intellectualis*, the intellectual love of God; it is his equivalent to 'the love of wisdom' embodied in the word philosophy.

Spinoza's notion of philosophy and the topics flowing from it — the whole as criterion for the parts, degrees of truth, the limited reality of time, the rejection of the dualisms of subject-object, mind-body — would be taken up in other guises by those writing in the British Idealist tradition more than two centuries later. So much so that the leading British commentator on Spinoza's work could assert with some justice that its theme is summarized in a paragraph from Bradley:

For me every kind of process between the Many is a state of the Whole in and through which the Many subsist. The process of the Many and the total being of the Many themselves, are mere aspects of the one Reality which

---

[7]   This writer has had more to say on this theme in an unpublished paper, 'I Am That I Am', delivered at a conference on 'Metaphor in the Hebrew Bible' co-sponsored by the Departments of Linguistics and Theology, at the Catholic University of Leuven, Belgium, July 2000. The paper, along with the further parts of this essay, will be available at the Philosophy of Institutions website under construction at www.sabre.org. See also Warren Z. Harvey's 'Spinoza's Metaphysical Hebraism' in *Jewish Themes in Spinoza's Philosophy*, ed. Heidi M. Ravven and Lenn E. Goodman (Albany: SUNY Press, 2002), 107-14.

*moves and knows itself within them, and apart from which all things and
their changes and every knower and every known is absolutely nothing.*[8]

Bradley could take for granted the replacement of Spinoza's
quasi-religious terms — God, His Attributes and Modes — with a
vocabulary of the One and the Many, because the ground for this
had been prepared earlier, in Hegel's response to Spinoza's modes.

Hegel's Response

Hegel acknowledged: 'To be a follower of Spinoza is the essential
commencement of all philosophy.'[9] And he did mean 'commencement.' Hegel saw in Spinoza, as in so many philosophers previous to
himself, defects that his own system would overcome. But he also
treated Spinoza with great respect. In Hegel's lectures on modern
philosophy only Kant received comparable treatment. Hegel credits
Spinoza with the view that all definition is negation — a crucial element in Hegel's own thought — and he takes over, in new clothing,
Spinoza's doctrine of a unifying immanence.

As Hegel is the second major precursor for Oakeshott's reworking
of the modal idea, we shall select from Hegel's two explicit critiques
of Spinoza the issue that further prepares the ground for Oakeshott:
what Hegel took to be the one-sidedness of Spinoza's view, and his
well-known corrective — the dialectical unfolding of the Absolute
Idea.

Between Hegel's two passages on Spinoza — the first in the early
Lectures on the History of Philosophy (vol. 3: A, 2), the second in the *Science of Logic* (vol. I, bk. 2, sec. 3, chap. 1) — his reading became more
precise and profound. In both passages, as elsewhere in Hegel's
writing, Spinoza is a pole of reference for Hegel's own philosophy.
So it is not wrong to cite Hegel's most distinctive philosophical
moves in restating his case against Spinoza.

Hegel saw Spinoza's system as not permitting a sufficiently rich
and ramified view of the individual. He traced this failing to a logical
flaw. As Hegel saw it, Spinoza did not implant in the unity of substance the seeds of its individuation. Spinoza's substance lacked a

---

[8] The passage is from F. H. Bradley's Explanatory Notes to *Appearance and
Reality*, intro. Richard Wollheim, 2d ed. (1897; reprinted, Oxford: Clarendon
Press, 1969), 550; as quoted in Harold H. Joachim *A Study of the Ethics of
Spinoza* (Oxford: Clarendon Press, 1901), 102 n. 1.

[9] E. S. Haldane and Frances H. Simson, trans., *Hegel's Lectures on the History of
Philosophy*, vol. 3 (Atlantic Highlands, NJ: Humanities Press, 1983), 257.

principle of self-enfolding. It left us without logical tools to explain variety and multiplicity. Spinoza, according to Hegel, did not show how the unity of substance necessarily contains within it the basis for all becoming. Spinoza had succeeded in showing that the Many necessarily reduced to the One but not how the One necessarily generated the Many.

The problem lay in Spinoza's modes. His positing of thought and extension lacked for Hegel the cogency of an objectively true emanation from God. If (as Hegel first misread Spinoza to say) thought and extension were to be seen as exhaustive, they must be proven to be final and parallel, which Spinoza declines to do. They must be rooted in the essence of God rather than added on adventitiously. If, on the other hand (as Hegel later and more accurately read Spinoza to say), the two modes were not exhaustive and not defined in terms of each other, the validation of each was merely empirical. They merely happened to be categories currently imposed upon substance by human judgment. There could be no objective guarantee that they flowed from the deepest essence of substance. This latter critique does indeed correctly state Spinoza's position, though it does not credit the selfless humility in the face of God's Nature that animates it. (Such humility struck Hegel as alien — he called it 'oriental' in Spinoza, derided Newton's scientific version of it in physics and optics as 'barbarian' and 'English'.) Spinoza flatly denied, for example, that we could have any *a priori* knowledge of extension that would enable us to explain the physical universe.[10]

To dramatize his own resolution of the problem of the modes Hegel set Spinoza's substance against Leibniz's monads. Leibniz suffered from a converse one-sidedness. His monads, on Hegel's reading, built in a dynamically unfolding principle of individuation, an *entelechy*, without adequate grounding of the multiplicity of monads in a unified and irreducible substance. Hegel's aim was to combine a monism as uncompromising as that of Spinoza with a principle of individuation as fecund as that of Leibniz. To do this he added a principle of consciousness that became for him a master key to both philosophical and historical inquiry.

The first move in his solution was to take thought as the unifying substrate for philosophy. Relative to Spinoza's account, the underlying argument for Hegel's position would go something like this: It is given in Spinoza's philosophy that the attributes of God are known

[10]   Wolf, *Correspondence of Spinoza*, letter 83; 365.

only through human thought — that is, they are attributed to God by human judgment; it is further given that the modes of thought and extension follow immediately (or a Cartesian might say intuitively) from the attributes; it then follows that the only verifiable basis for the modes is thought. Anything else can be neither more nor less than a construction of thought and is therefore not reducible to anything but thought. Extension must, then, be subordinated to thought as a philosophical category. But if this is done, thought — or in Hegelese, the Idea — takes the place of substance/God/Nature as the unified substrate.

A second move in Hegel's solution is to posit within thought the dynamic of its own unfolding: the method of critical reason that he calls dialectical. The central logical operator in the dialectic is negation, in a newly contextualized sense. A dialectical negation is not a mere canceling out but the discerning of a lack or deficiency with respect to which an idea is negated. This is why Hegel can say that dialectical negation retains the idea negated, and why he can say that the negation of a negation retains both the idea negated and a new transforming element that supplies its deficiency. A lack, as opposed to mere nothingness, presupposes a context in which a deficiency has been noted. Negating the lack means to supply it, hence a move toward greater completion. When Hegel says that the negation of a negation is positive and sublating, he means that it contains the idea negated while transforming it with a previously neglected principle of completion.

A third move is to observe that thought in this dialectical sense has its own forward movement or *entelechy*, which Hegel calls the in-itself-for-itself. The in-itself-for-itself is so essential to thinking as to be a logical necessity independent of individual psychology. The whole thrust of dialectical thought is toward ever greater completeness. Critical thought implicitly invokes a condition in which no deficiency will remain unremarked and uncorrected. This ultimate, completed condition is what Hegel calls the Absolute Idea — literally *ab-solus*, because it is capable of standing alone unified and self-sufficient. It embraces all ideas that can be discerned as incomplete along with those supplying their deficiencies — the theoretical idea along with the practical idea, the objective along with the subjective, the moments of being, the very consciousness of thinking as being thought — all together seen as distinguishable within a larger totality. The Absolute Idea is thus the self-conscious standard by which we judge, limit and define anything that falls short of completeness. It is the ultimate basis of our critical capacity, the logical ground from which we discern deficiency, define limitations, supply correctives, relate opposites, correlatives, complements and moments.

A fourth Hegelian move is to use this criterion to show why three fundamental technical terms — the universal, the particular and the individual — must be mutually implicative. Generality and particularity cannot be defined except in relation to each other and cannot be illustrated except as embodied in an individual. General-particular-individual supply deficiencies in each other. Taken together they mark the moments of any conception (*Begriff*) that can have traction in reality. If we focus on any one in the absence of the others we lose a certain grip (again, *Begriff*) on the real. Universality is not something that exists independently of particulars, and the particulars are never found in isolation from other particulars that form an individual. Under Hegel's Absolute, universality can never be completed until it is concretized in individuals, first through instantiation in the particulars that define them, and second in the singular character of the finite individual itself. This is Hegel's doctrine of the concrete universal. It replaces Spinoza's view of the individual as defined by the conjunction of modes.

These four logical moves, compacted here from a much richer argument, support Hegel's supersession both of Spinoza's modes and of Leibniz's monads. Hegel shifts Spinoza's monistic substrate from God/Nature/substance to thought, implants in it a dialectical movement, shows how the dialectic necessarily entails an ultimate criterion, and uses this criterion to develop a theoretical apparatus that accounts for complex individuals in terms that reaffirm the underlying unity of the substrate. The modal device under its Latinate terms (*Modus, Modalität*) can now be returned by Hegel to its traditional role in syllogistic and to its revived importance in the Kantian table of judgments.[11] The Absolute has replaced Spinoza's substance; the interplay of universal-particular-individual has replaced individuation as conceived through Spinoza's modes; and dialectical relatedness has replaced Spinoza's looser compossibility of the modes.

---

[11]   For Hegel's dialectical critique of Kant's notion of logical modality see A. V. Miller, trans., *Hegel's Science of Logic* (London: Allen and Unwin, 1969), vol. 2, sec. 1, chap. 2(d), 657-63.

At the same time, the doctrine of the concrete universal opens the door to a new career for modality under common German terms (*Geist, Weise*). The concrete universal provides the logical warrant for Hegel's most distinctive contribution: his elucidation of the gradations of knowledge evident in history and philosophy, including the history of philosophy and the philosophy of history. For if we see concrete universality in historical entities — whether they be events, acts, actors, institutions or identities at whatever level — we can, by varying permutations and degrees of abstraction, pursue the general, particular and individual aspects of them in multiple directions. The Absolute Idea can in one aspect be seen as the repository of historical experience and in another aspect as a timeless philosophical standard. As a repository, the various contributions to its development can be stamped with dates and names, and placed in their contingent relations. As a standard, it provides a systematization of these contributions such that taken together they become an ultimate and universal criterion for reasoning in all the special disciplines. Through self-critique of its own historical experience Mind can take wing from its concrete instantiations to arrive at a unified logical criterion, the Absolute Idea, which can then be reintroduced into experience as a key to knowledge. Hegel's logical innovations can thus serve, on the one hand, as tools to trace the contingent patterns of becoming in history, and on the other, as elements toward a timeless and placeless criterion, a master science opening new vistas for inquiry.

Hegel proclaimed as much at the conclusion of his first major treatise: 'The goal, which is Absolute Knowledge, or Spirit knowing itself as Spirit, finds its pathway in the recollection of spiritual forms (*Geister*) as they are in themselves and as they accomplish the organization of their spiritual kingdom. Their conservation, looked at from the side of their free existence appearing in the form of contingency is **History** [Hegel's emphasis]; looked at from the side of their intellectually comprehended organization, it is the **Science** [Hegel's emphasis] of the ways in which knowledge appears (*die Wissenschaft des erscheinenden Wissens*).'[12]

---

[12]   G. W. F. Hegel, *The Phenomenology of Mind*, J. R. Baillie, trans. (New York: Harper, 1967), 808.

Oakeshott's Innovation

The stage is now set for Michael Oakeshott. In *Experience and Its Modes* Oakeshott responds precisely to the Hegelian call for a philosophical *Wissenschaft des erscheinenden Wissens*, 'science of the ways in which knowledge appears.' Oakeshott calls these phenomenological forms modes. He delineates three of them from what Hegel calls 'the side of their intellectually comprehended organization', or what Oakeshott would later call, more simply, their 'ideal character'. In so doing, Oakeshott accepts the four Hegelian moves we have just traced, while taking care to distance himself from neo-Hegelian jargon that he sees as open to superstitious excess: he accepts thought as the unified substrate for philosophy, definition as limitation and negation of the substrate ('arrests' in experience), a philosophical criterion seeking completion (without, however, much talk of an Absolute or an in-itself-for-itself), and a view of the concrete both as developing in time ('experience') and as falling under the timeless gaze of philosophy ('*sub specie aeternitatis*'). And with Collingwood, his immediate 'idealist' English predecessor, he provides a philosophical conspectus of forms of the spirit (without, however, any attempt to rank them or prescribe for them).

But there are marked changes from Hegel and his followers, both in logic and in tone. For Oakeshott revives a modal apparatus that has the very features which Hegel found unacceptable in Spinoza. The modes Oakeshott discusses — history, science, practice — have no 'objective' connection with each other or with their substrate. They merely happen to be those modes upon which human judgment has settled. They are not defined in terms of each other. Neither do they contradict each other. They are fully compossible in the very kind of loose construction that Hegel criticized in Spinoza. As with Spinoza's modes they lack a tight logical or organic tie to their substrate — a tie that would explain why, rather than merely that, they must be as they are. No ranking of them or systematic relation between them is warranted. Their limitations are not defined by each other but by the ways in which they fall short of experience taken as a whole. Moreover, as in Spinoza the number of modes remains open. The modes of science, history and practice are currently the best developed, but there might be others. And as with Spinoza, Oakeshott's refusal to rank compossible modalities bespeaks a certain humility about the capacity of human intellect.

Experience in Oakeshott, like God's Nature in Spinoza, is inexhaustible, so that the number of its modes cannot be limited.

There is also in Oakeshott, as in Spinoza, a bifurcation of the modal principle, though to very different ends. In Spinoza we have infinite and finite modes, in Oakeshott determinate and indeterminate modification. But whereas the thrust of Spinoza's modal devices is to assert a pervasive role for philosophy, the *amor dei intellectualis*, in the critical examination of each particular, Oakeshott's elucidation of the 'determinate' character of the modes has exactly the opposite effect. His view of the limitations of philosophy is so unflinching and original as to leave behind any suggestion that what is distinctive in *Experience and its Modes* is merely combinatorial.

Science, history and practice are 'determinate' in the sense of defining internally coherent worlds of their own. Like all modification in Oakeshott they take place against the homogenous substrate of concrete experience. But they also create a homogeneous substrate of their own that is abstracted from experience: '[S]ince all are modifications of a single concrete whole, they have a general character in common; but as specific and abstract worlds they are independent of one another' (*EM*, 327).

The homogeneous world of one determinate mode is unassimilable to another because their organizing categories differ. Science, history and practice have different standards of fact, of relevance, of validity:

[W]hat belongs to one such world would necessarily disrupt the homogeneity of every other. Between these worlds . . . there can be neither dispute nor agreement; they are wholly irrelevant to one another. And an argument or an inference which pretended to pass from one world to another would be the pattern of all forms of ignoratio elenchi. An idea cannot serve two worlds. And although it may be difficult, or even impossible to determine the exact degree of coherence attained in each or any of these modes of experience, the fact that two worlds are distinguished by different explicit principles of homogeneity indicates that they are arrests in experience at different points and that they are consequently exclusive of one another. (EM, 327)

Thus far, the notion of modal distinctness follows that of Spinoza's second definition and fifth axiom. But the role of philosophy in representing the common substrate is radically different. So long as the determinate modes stay within their own abstractly defined bounds, they are also immune to internal philosophical critique. Philosophy has no more to say to history, science and practice on their own terms than any of them has to say to the others. These modes can never be integrated by philosophy as branches of a master science, nor even much enlightened by it. By remarking the abstractness of a mode philosophy does not thereby gain command of its contents. It does not even add a completing or advisory element. A philosophical science, a philosophical history, a philosophy of life — all these are 'monstrosities' to the early Oakeshott, every bit as chimerical as the cross-modal political rationalisms he later deplored.

There will, to be sure, always be a role for philosophy, since determinate modes can be relied upon to exceed their bounds. Precisely because a determinate mode has created its own abstract world it is unaware of its incompleteness from the point of view of the totality of experience. Philosophical critique will always have its work in limiting the pretensions of the determinate modes, reminding them that though they are worlds, they are not the entire world.

For 'indeterminate' modifications the situation is otherwise. These are botched or inadvertent attempts to create an abstract and homogeneous world of ideas. They typically fail by mixing elements of practice with philosophy and the other modes. Thus whereas science is a determinate mode, scientology is founded on indeterminate modifications. Philosophy can point this out expeditiously. Indeterminate modes simply do not work. They are pseudo-philosophies. The field of study called 'Ethics' abounds in such fodder for philosophical critique.

The critical role of philosophy in exposing the pseudo-philosophical character of indeterminate modification is all that remains in *Experience and Its Modes* of Hegel's notion of sublation or *Aufhebung*, the capacity of mind to supersede a deficient idea in a more complete one. Philosophy can supersede pseudo-philosophy in respect to its incompletely philosophical character. It cannot do the same with the determinate modes because they are not attempting to be philosophical. They seek coherence not with respect to the totality of experience but within abstract worlds of their own construction. The only things that are *aufgehoben* in a true philosophy are false philosophical claims.

Experience and Its Modes, in sum, presents a view of modality that, while drawing upon devices traceable to Spinoza and Hegel, goes well beyond them. Spinoza's compossible modal apparatus reappears, but without even a gesture toward its grounding in logical necessity or Divine being. If Hegel's critique of the overly 'empirical' character of the Modes holds for Spinoza, it holds even more strongly for Oakeshott. Spinoza's Modi, after all, were immediately apprehended by human thought from Divine attributes. This did not satisfy Hegel but it is still far stronger a warrant for them than anything claimed for the determinate modes by Oakeshott. The most that Oakeshott claims for any of his modes is reserved to the 'practical', which he sees as necessary to human survival. But even here there is no claim that human survival is an adequate philosophical standard. Quite to the contrary: a life devoted to practice — including its culmination in religion — is a philosophically unacceptable arrest in experience.

But if Oakeshott, in presenting his modes purely as a falling away from the totality of a unified substrate, is wide open to Hegel's critique of one-sidedness, his view of philosophy makes a virtue of this. Philosophy, as it appears in *Experience and Its Modes*, is unabashedly one-sided on Hegel's terms. It can only criticize the modes from the side of showing that they fall short of the totality of experience. It has no capacity for showing how the determinate modes unfold, why they must be what they are, or even to what degree they fall short of completeness. In *Experience and Its Modes*, then, we have the construction of compossible modes without Spinoza's groundedness in Divine attributes, set against experience seen as an unfolding world of ideas without Hegel's dialectical method — or indeed any philosophical method — to account for its unfolding. Is this a philosophically tenable result?

In defense of *Experience and Its Modes* one can say that it carries through a coherent vision of philosophy that is of a piece with its definition of the determinate modes. Philosophy can only define the modes as falling short, as abstract. Its method of doing so is to state for each mode the leading (and limiting) abstractions and to show how these function as organizing categories. And since that is how philosophy knows whatever it can know, it can never be in command of detailed knowledge. Its aim is not to explain how the modes unfold but how they fall short. The notion that philosophy can provide a master science is for Oakeshott a delusion.

In further defense of *Experience and Its Modes* one should note that it launches a rich program of inquiry. From the treatise a fivefold program takes shape. First, there is the question of whether we can find in experience other worlds in addition to those of science, history and practice that meet the conditions of a determinate mode; second, the affirmative task of exploring each of the determinate modes in greater detail; third, a wide field for applying the modal device critically, both in exploding indeterminate modifications as pseudo-philosophical, and in limiting the inevitable pretensions of determinate modes; fourth and fifth, the modal device can be used as an instrument both for recommendation and for inquiry outside a strictly philosophical domain.

Oakeshott in fact carried through such a program. He found two other modifications of experience that meet the conditions of a determinate mode: poetry, as the generic term for aesthetic experience, and the rule of law, as a self-consistent, self-completing world within practice. He enriched his analysis of the organizing categories of history. He carried through an exposé of the consequences of mixing up the modes: Rationalism. He showed how the determinate modes could give meaning to the liberal character of university education generally and to the study of politics specifically. And as a teacher, he imparted to others the use of the modes as a tool of inquiry, in discerning what is genuinely philosophical from what is practical and historical in his lectures and seminars on the History of Political Thought.

In final defense of Oakeshott's modes, one should note that strictly speaking, the old Hegelian criticism of Spinoza's *Modi* really does not apply. What is distinctive about Oakeshott's modes is already post-Hegelian. Unlike Spinoza's *Modi*, Oakeshott's modes are presented frankly as contingent historical achievements. Their emergence with a tightly reasoned character did not have to happen. Even the emergence of the practical from mytho-poetic thinking is a civilized achievement. To analyze the logical structure that defines and determines each mode does not require a theory of necessary emergence. The organizing categories of a mode can be necessary *to it* without having an *a priori* basis in the substrate of experience. The project undertaken in *Experience and Its Modes* has, in sum, the integrity of a classic philosophical definition: It elucidates the *differentia specifica* of the modes in terms that proceed from and carry through a consistent, passionately self-limiting view of philosophical inquiry.

But all this was not in the end satisfactory to Oakeshott, nor can it be to us. For there remain tensions within *Experience and Its Modes* that should prompt us, as it prompted him, to revise its initial modal grounds.

Oakeshott's Self-Critique

As we have seen, *Experience and Its Modes* stipulated that 'an idea cannot serve two worlds' but also that 'since all [worlds] are modifications of a single concrete whole, they have a general character in common.' The tension within *Experience and Its Modes* between the particularity of an idea to a given mode and the rootedness of all ideas in the concrete whole of experience prompted Oakeshott to make changes in his initial modal approach.

As a definitional enterprise, *Experience and Its Modes* depends crucially on what distinguishes each abstract world from the concrete whole. It can succeed on its own terms only if it finds a precise and adequate basis of intelligibility to separate each of the modes from the experience that is the common substrate of them all. Yet about this 'general character' that is shared by the modes *Experience and Its Modes* has little to say, except — and this is its far-reaching point — that it is founded in consciousness, a concrete world of ideas in relation to which all the modes are 'abstract.' *Experience and Its Modes* avoids a detailed anatomy of the attributes of experience because what it seeks to establish is exactly the opposite: that experience is a unified and homogeneous world of thought, with no priority given to that which purports to be less than thought (notably, sensation) or more than thought (intuition), or some antidote or complement to thought (volition, feeling). The important discussion of experience with which *Experience and Its Modes* begins is aimed not to endow consciousness with structures that will explain the modes but rather to rescue 'the philosophy of experience' from the false subdivisions, hierarchies, and dualities that had plagued the discussion of it since Locke, who gave a special place to sensation, and Descartes, who gave priority to intuition.

For science, history and practice, Oakeshott's strategy in *Experience and Its Modes* is to portray each world in terms of a salient organizing category and concepts proceeding from it. Thus, science is an abstract world seen under the category of quantity, history under the category of the past, practice under the category of volition. But one need not go far in *Experience and Its Modes* to notice that these categories cannot bear the weight of the Spinozistic modal apparatus that Oakeshott employs. Spinoza was able to sustain a strong, mutually independent system of modes, because each of his modes, thought and extension, rested on a single master category traceable to a Divine Attribute. The leading categories of Oakeshott's modes, by contrast, bear a much weaker relation both to the substrate they modify and to the worlds they define.

With respect to the world defined, each leading category is evocative rather than fully definitive of the mode associated with it. Quantity, for example, may be used to define an abstract and homogeneous world (mathematics?) but it does not happen to be the world of science as Oakeshott portrays it; science on Oakeshott's view entails additional presuppositions — about fact and theory, among others. Quantity is not really used to define science in *Experience and Its Modes*, but rather to stand for a more complex composition of ideas that do so. *Experience and Its Modes'* reliance on a leading category to define a mode is a rhetorically compelling device but not logically sufficient. In contrast to Spinoza's usage, Oakeshott's modes are not uni-categorial.

With respect to the common substrate — concrete experience seen as an ever-unfolding totality of ideas — each leading category is inevitably a specialized version of a more general idea, which may appear in some lesser role in other Oakeshottian modes. Volition, for example, may dominate the world of practice, but it is not wholly absent from the worlds of science and history. Similarly, though the 'past' is salient in history, there is, as Oakeshott discusses at some length, a 'practical past.' Each of Oakeshott's modes is a complex of ideas, many of which are reconfigured in other modes. Thus, though the modes may indeed be exclusive in the sense of determining their own worlds, *Experience and Its Modes* overstates the case to suggest that 'what belongs to one would necessarily disrupt the homogeneity of every other.' For the ultimate basis of homogeneity comes not from within the worlds of the modes but from the concrete substrate in and through which they must be understood: experience.

Put another way, each mode has the appearance of being 'homogeneous' not by virtue of being a world but by virtue of being a world of ideas, abstracted from the larger world of experience in which ideas are the sole common currency. It is ideas as such without rankings or orderings that are the ultimate basis of homogeneity and unity. The organizing ideas that constitute a modal arrest — by virtue of having priority within their respective Oakeshottian modes — are themselves a sign that each determinate mode falls short of the complete homogeneity we find in concrete experience. Quantity, volition, the past and their associated concepts may rank high in this or that determinate mode, but there are no such priorities or rankings in experience as a whole.

Two of the modes of *Experience and Its Modes* — Science and History — are mainly about varieties of knowing, and the third, Practice, is primarily about doing. Philosophy itself is about understanding these modes in their relation to a concrete whole. Poetry, introduced in a 1959 essay, is about enjoying, a concept which embraces a range of ideas from delight to contemplation.[13] Understanding, knowing, doing, enjoying — these are not exclusive to a given mode, but rather ideas drawn from general experience which each of the modes arrests and configures in its distinctive, abstract and determinate way. It is by virtue of their rootedness in a commonly shared human experience that Oakeshott could in due course portray the modes as 'voices' in 'the conversation of mankind.'

Such reflection on the commonality of experience led Oakeshott to alter the initial terms of *Experience and Its Modes*, even as he pursued the program of inquiry arising from it. His changes did not come all at once. They began to appear piecemeal in his essays and reviews. Finally in *On Human Conduct* a well-developed revision takes shape. We learn on the very first page that 'understanding' is inseparable from the human condition. It is a pervasive and continuing engagement with three characteristic resting points: first, 'recognition' of 'goings-on' in terms of characteristics; second, 'identification' of them in terms of an 'ideal character;' third, 'theorizing' of them in terms of their 'postulates.' We learn that all goings-on exhibit 'an imperfectly resolved tension between particularity and genericity' (*OHC*, 5). To resolve this tension, understanding renders 'verdicts' culminating in 'facts' and 'theorems.' It avails itself of well-worn methods that become increasingly systematic as it moves from recognition to identification to theorizing. There is in all this an interpenetration of concepts relating to understanding (explaining, describing, recognizing, and so on) and doing (performing, enacting, disclosing): 'Doing is an understanding, and undeniably, in all understanding there is doing' (*OHC*, 34). The hermetically sealed character of the modes of *Experience and Its Modes* has given way to a

[13] Oakeshott, *The Voice of Poetry in the Conversation of Mankind* (London: Bowles and Bowles, 1959).

minutely graded and differentiated scheme permitting the interpenetration of concepts drawn from common experience.

History and science are no longer called modes but 'orders of
inquiry' and 'conditional platforms' for theorizing, and there are
important changes in the accounts of each. The term 'practice' no
longer denotes a mode but a 'postulate' of 'conduct *inter homines.*'
The critique of Rationalism is now qualified to recognize 'practical
theorem-making.' The term mode in its strong sense is replaced by
the notion of theorizing an 'ideal character' in terms of its 'postulates,' more precisely representing the complex of ideas that
Oakeshott had in mind in the first place. The only use of the term
'mode' in something like its previous sense now marks two poles of
European thought about the modern state — the modes of association Oakeshott calls civil association and enterprise association —
and these, far from having independent careers, are always linked as
'sweet enemies' (*OHC*, 147) in undying conjugacy. These and other
changes can be read (and were so read by this writer when *On
Human Conduct* was published)[14] as the admirable result of four
decades of self-critique.

The revisions follow a common line. Oakeshott keeps reaching
into the substrate of experience to bring forth new distinctions, in
effect mining a ground shared by all the modes to provide a more
supple view of them, until in the end his previous notion of modality
recedes, much as Spinoza's *Modi* receded for Hegel once he found a
way of impregnating the Idea with a principle of dynamic movement and variegation.

But whereas Hegel's dialectical principle was explicit and
all-encompassing, Oakeshott enriches his picture of experience only
as required to meet the two tasks at hand in *On Human Conduct*: the
theorizing of human conduct, and within it, of the civil condition. He
does not attempt a master system. But he does proceed magisteri-
ally. Where a conventional distinction will serve, he uses it. Where
technical jargon can be avoided, he shuns it ('anticipatory guessing,'
for example, replaces 'hypothesis'). His language, labored in its syn-
tax yet fresh in its choice of terms, evinces an effort to rethink his
work anew.

To lay the ground for understanding as an engagement he reformulates Hegel's notion of the mutually implicative character of the

[14]   Josiah Lee Auspitz, 'Individuality, Civility, Theory: The philosophical
        imagination of Michael Oakeshott,' *Political Theory* 4 (August 1976), 261–300.

particular, the general and the individual. Oakeshott sees a 'unity of particularity and genericity' in any given identity. Every datum of experience thus poses a problem to be understood in its particular and generic aspects. Every 'going on' becomes an *explicandum*.

To lay the ground for a carefully balanced discussion of the conduct of theorizing and the theorizing of conduct, he distinguishes gradations of understanding and doing, so that he can address the kinds of doing entailed in understanding and of understanding entailed in doing. Oakeshott is now able to recognize and discuss varieties of understanding, knowing and explaining relevant to doing (*phronesis*, practical theorem-making, practical explanation, the discipline of rhetoric, knowledge of 'performances' within the 'languages' of a practice) and the kinds of doing relevant to understanding (constructive theorizing, scientific experiment, historical narrative).

Earlier, *The Voice of Poetry in the Conversations of Mankind* drew from the common substrate of experience the further category of enjoying, which helped to account for the 'mutual affection' that keeps human beings in friendly converse even when they speak in voices riven by the modes. One can infer that understanding-doing-enjoying are common to all experience and configured kaleidoscopically in various human activities. Once modes are seen in and through common experience, there is a greater interpenetration of concepts in them than Oakeshott first used the term mode to signify.

Without anything so grand as a dialectical method, then, Oakeshott progressively marks elements of a common character shared in differing degrees by the modes in *Experience and Its Modes*, by the voices of mankind in 'The Voice of Poetry,' and by theorizing and deliberated conduct in *On Human Conduct*. But what undergirds this common character if not the notion of modality writ small? Understanding-doing-enjoying are really compossible modes of ultimate interpretation of any human experience. The proof is that if they be applied to the selfsame object, a conversation can take place:

A: <u>I can get $60 a dozen for those roses.</u>

B: **Did you know that they were first bred by gardeners to the Queen Mother?**

C: *And that the color is affected by the acidity of the soil?*

D: HOW FRAGRANT THEY ARE!

E: *<u>THERE IS A $50 FINE FOR PICKING THEM.</u>*

Here we have ostensibly the same object interpreted through five modes derived from Oakeshott's work: practice as enterprise, history, science, poetry, practice as law. I have set them off with five different typographical conventions to acknowledge that they come from different worlds and to give graphic force to the dictum that 'no idea can serve in two worlds.' From this standpoint a <u>rose</u> is not a **rose** is not a *rose* is not a ROSE is not a <u>*ROSE*</u>. But common experience tells us that there exists an object, represented by the four-letter symbol 'rose', which may be interpreted variously in accordance with whether and how we mean to enjoy, use or understand it. That is, 'rose', or indeed any object and its sign, may be interpreted in modally distinct ways without invoking the larger considerabilities of an Oakeshottian 'world.' Though each interpretive modality may have its *ultimate* or most salient meaning within a larger, complex of ideas in which it represents the dominant idiom, it may also be meaningful in contexts in which it plays an incidental role.

Thus, should a florist refer to the history, botany, beauty, or legal regulations of breeding hybrid roses, we need not rap his knuckles for the sin of *ignoratio elenchi*, but cheerfully observe that he is enriching the disciplined enterprise of selling flowers. If we remember that modes must be viewed in and through their substrate, as compossibilities rather than as self-sufficient things, there is no obstacle to their working with and upon each other. We have all experienced the enjoying of doing, the enjoying of understanding, the understanding of enjoying (which in one aspect we call connoisseurship), understanding of doing ('knowing how'), and so on. Oakeshott's later terms make place for these finer shadings.

Nor are these three, understanding-doing-enjoying, the only set of micro-modes implicit in his later work. The 'unity of genericity and particularity' is, as we shall see in the sequel, a not quite completed modal assertion about identity. Oakeshott's three levels of understanding — recognizing-identifying-theorizing — may be also read as compossible modes marking arrests in a continuous substrate.

Similarly, the two macro-modes that survive in *On Human Conduct* — civil and enterprise association — can be brought down to the level of modality writ small. As such, they need not be limited to the modern state. They suggest that all conduct may be governed compossibly by rule and purpose. Elsewhere, in his scattered remarks on friendship, Oakeshott suggests that conduct may be governed by affection, with no rule or purpose other than one's enjoyment of another. Rule-purpose-affection may be taken as another micro-modal division — a *nomic-telic-philic* aspect, if you will, in all human association. In *On Human Conduct* the *philic* element is subsumed in 'civility', the 'watery fidelity' among citizens under the rule of law. But in a broader theory of institutions, the affective element deserves independent weight. The *philic* element directs attention to a second non-purposive mode in institutions, of the kind Aristotle addressed when he described the varieties of friendship in the several political regimes, or that Hegel noticed in discussing the family as an institution.

To summarize: The movement of Oakeshott's thought from *Experience and Its Modes* involved finding in common experience a richer fabric replicated in differing patterns in the various activities of human life. The contingent variations of this fabric may be explained by reference to human conduct — deliberated choices of performances within practices. The logical patterns of variation may be explained by reference to modal compossibilities impregnated in experience. Making these compossibilities explicit and systematic enables us both to extend and question Oakeshott's line of thought.

One extension, from a philosophy of law and the modern state to a philosophy of institutions, can draw on a *nomic-telic-philic* division implicit in his work, but not needed in *On Human Conduct*. A second line of work, not adumbrated in Oakeshott, is to pursue radically the notion of modality writ small. These two are really part of the same task. We cannot broaden a modal theory of the state to a theory of institutions without a more systematic conspectus of variegation. A conventionalism in marking distinctions, of the kind upon which Oakeshott relies in *On Human Conduct*, may do for this or that theoretical task. But if our aim is to view 'experience and its modes' as broadly as possible, we shall need something more comprehensive.

What if we take each and every datum of experience as an occasion for modality writ small? What if we see every moment as exploding with possibility? What if each representation of experience — each sign — were seen as open to a multiplicity of compossible and interpenetrating modes? Could we then give a unified modal account both of the small gradations in experience and of the larger forms embodying our habits, traditions and institutions?

To answer these questions it will be useful to trace a second, 'semiotic' strand of reflection on the topic of modality, beginning with Locke, who introduced this term into modern philosophy.

Archival Note

Oakeshott, Spinoza and Joachim

The philosophical relevance of Spinoza's modal scheme to Oakeshott's is of course quite independent — modally distinct, one might say — from any historical argument about sources. But interest in the philosophical parallels has led to the uncovering of archival materials that bear on the topic. (A similar exploration of what Oakeshott learned directly from Hegel would begin with the extensive notes Oakeshott made on his German editions of Hegel's *Phänomenologie des Geistes* and *Philosophie des Rechts* in the 1920s.)

1. Though not cited in *Experience and Its Modes*, Spinoza appears to have been Oakeshott's starting point for the modal apparatus that gives the work its philosophical force. The collection of notebooks in the Oakeshott archive at The London School of Economics shows that Oakeshott began a close reading of Spinoza in October 1923. Having received a Cambridge first class honors degree in the History Tripos the previous June, Oakeshott was elected to a Studentship that enabled him to stay on at Gonville and Caius College for graduate work. The Spinoza notebook thus contains some of his first systematic philosophical readings in the Michaelmas term after his graduation.[1]

Oakeshott concentrated mainly on Spinoza's *Tractatus de Intellectus Emendatione*, but with cross references to the *Ethics* in the W. Hale White translation and to the turn-of-the-century commentaries of Sir Frederick Pollock[2] and Harold H. Joachim's *A Study of the Ethics of Spinoza*. Oakeshott's reading notes twice make reference (*Spinoza I*, 5, 12) to the opening definitions of the *Ethics*, which lay out the conceptions of God, substance, mode, attribute, eternity and infinity that set up Spinoza's modal framework. Oakeshott remarks that Spinoza's definition of eternity does not conform to the vulgar

---

[1] Oakeshott, Notebook titled *Spinoza I*, June 1923, LSE File 2/4/2. Hereafter: *Spinoza I*.

[2] Sir Frederick Pollock, *Spinoza: His Life and Philosophy*, 2d ed. (London: Duckworth and Co., 1899).

notion of that concept — evidence that the a-temporal logical structure of the *Ethics* did not escape him. He also grasped, following
Pollock, that the core of Spinoza's method was to acquire clear and
distinct knowledge of particulars against a view of the universe as
'all of a piece': 'we can understand the parts only in the whole and
the whole only through the parts,' he noted (*Spinoza I*, 32, 36).

2. Oakeshott's use of Joachim's 1901 commentary on Spinoza's
Ethics (Joachim's companion commentary on the *Tractatus* was published posthumously in 1940) bears closer attention. Joachim's acute
discussion of the relation between Substance and Mode, upon which
the entire metaphysical structure of the *Ethics* depends, is resonant
with Oakeshott's later approach to modality in *Experience and Its
Modes*. Joachim was alert both to the anti-Cartesian thrust of the
dependency of Mode upon Substance in Spinoza[3] and to its anticipation of Bradley's holistic view of Reality.[4] Joachim gives prominence
to what he calls 'Spinoza's modal system' in discussing Spinoza's
positions on metaphysical issues of interest to the 'British Idealists':
his arguments against mind-body dualism, his theory of degrees of
reality, and his views on the limited reality of time. Many passages in
Joachim's explication of the relation between Substance and Mode in
Spinoza now read as remarkably evocative of the relation between
experience and mode in *Experience and Its Modes*, and even his (to me,
not convincing) criticism of Spinoza as having given too much play
to God's Attributes over the Modes[5] finds a remedy in Oakeshott's
exclusive reliance on modality as the category of differentiation in
Experience and Its Modes.

Oakeshott sought out Joachim in Oxford in 1924 and appears, as
we shall see in the next item, to have made a lasting impression upon
him.

3. There is archival evidence, supporting the prominent acknowledgement in the Preface to *Experience and Its Modes* itself, that 'copi-
ous criticisms' from Joachim influenced the year-long final revisions
of the manuscript of *Experience and Its Modes*. As Oxford doyen of the
British Idealists, Joachim appears to have been, administratively, the
key reader upon whose opinion the syndics of Cambridge University Press relied in speeding the manuscript to acceptance. Joachim
was recruited to this role by W. R. Sorley, Oakeshott's continuing

[3]   Joachim, *A Study*, 21 n. 1, 30 n. 1, 61 n. 3.
[4]   Joachim, *A Study*, 102 n. 1.
[5]   Joachim, *A Study*, 105.

supporter and advisor at Cambridge University. He responded with detailed comments of some fifty handwritten pages, which Oakeshott used in revising the original manuscript.

In a letter to W. R. Sorley, Joachim recalled having met with Oakeshott for about twenty minutes in 1924 and remembered him well enough eight years later to have asked about his doings a few days before receiving a request from Professor Sorley in October 1932 to review the manuscript of *Experience and Its Modes* for Cambridge University Press. He responded promptly and graciously. Joachim's four-page hand-written covering letter and three-page hand-written *Report to the Syndics of Cambridge University Press on 'Experience and Its Modes' by M. J. Oakeshott* may be found in the Cambridge University Press archive,[6] along with six shorter pieces of related hand-written correspondence from Oakeshott and Joachim.[7]

Both in his covering letter dated 12 November 1932 and the accompanying *Report to the Syndics* Joachim strongly recommends publication: 'Mr. Oakeshott, while he fully acknowledges his indebtedness both to Hegel and to Bradley, develops in this work, and defends, a theory which is undoubtedly 'original' in the best sense of the term. He has thought out anew and independently the leading principles of the Idealist position; and the result is a vigorous re-formulation of them…which amounts to a new philosophical theory.'

At the same time, Joachim proposes that 'the author should be urged to regard his present manuscript as the <u>penultimate</u> draft of his book, and to subject it to a detailed and thorough revision.' He believes that a rewriting would be in the author's own interests. To assist Oakeshott in this Joachim included a much longer set of comments entitled *Notice and Suggestions* that he asks the Secretary of the Cambridge University Press to pass on to Oakeshott with his compliments '<u>after the Syndics have made their decision</u>' (Joachim's emphasis). These lengthier comments — 'not anything like so formidable as their bulk may suggest,' Joachim tells the Secretary — cover both 'small slips…which [the author] will correct the moment he sees them' and 'a good many criticisms and suggestions of a more important sort, in regard to many of [which] the author's view is quite as likely to be right as mine — and after considering what I have to say he may decide (perhaps rightly) to make no alteration.'

---

[6]   Cambridge Univ. Library, CUA Pa.O.4, [items 5a and b].
[7]   Cambridge Univ. Library, CUA Pa.O.4, [items 1-4 and 6-7].

4. The chronology of the processing of the manuscript provides a vignette of a simpler age of peer review, when a single manuscript copy could be passed from author to press to reader to reader and back to press and author in an approval process lasting exactly eight weeks from submission to acceptance. Oakeshott formally submitted the draft manuscript of *Experience and Its Modes* to the Cambridge University Press in letters dated 28 and 29 September 1932.[8] The actual handwritten manuscript was then in the hands of Professor Sorley, who asked Joachim if he would be the second reader. Joachim agreed to review it in letters to Sorley and the Secretary of the Press dated 4 and 7 October, with advance apologies that blindness in one eye might delay his response.[9] He returned the manuscript by registered parcel post on 12 November and mailed his comments, also dated 12 November the following Monday, 14 November. The very next week the Syndics approved the publication of *Experience and Its Modes*, and transmitted the *Notice and Suggestions* to Oakeshott as Joachim had requested.

In a letter to the Secretary of the Press dated 23 November 1932 Oakeshott acknowledged and accepted the favorable decision of the Syndics, adding, 'I am very grateful indeed for Joachim's notes. I have not yet had time to more than glance through them, but as soon as I can I shall get on with a revision of my MS with their help. And I will let you know when that is completed and the MS ready for press.'[10] Oakeshott transmitted the final item to the press, probably the index, a year later, on 24 November 1933.[11] The book was published in 1933.

5. The content of Joachim's comments remains unknown. In conversation, Oakeshott described Joachim's *Notes and Suggestions* as running fifty pages and as having been very helpful to him. [Geoffrey Thomas, for example, has reported in a written communication to Leslie Marsh an interview with Oakeshott that took place on Tuesday, 9 July 1968, in which Oakeshott referred to having received a fifty-page commentary from Joachim and expressed, in Thomas' phrase, 'enormous intellectual respect' for him.] But as Joachim's comments and the original 1932 manuscript submitted to

---

[8]   Cambridge Univ. Library, CUA Pa.O.4, [items 1 and 2].
[9]   Cambridge Univ. Library, CUA Pa.O.4, [items 3 and 4].
[10] Cambridge Univ. Library, CUA Pa.O.4, [item 6].
[11] Cambridge Univ. Library, CUA Pa.O.4, [item 7].

the syndics are both unavailable, Joachim's precise influence on the final version cannot be ascertained.

Oakeshott's habit of composition was to recopy manuscripts entirely, making changes along the way. The final manuscript submitted to Cambridge University Press[12] includes a few scattered pages from what would appear to be the 1932 draft written in stubbed pen, and easily distinguishable from the pages written in Oakeshott's more characteristic finepoint. These stubbed-pen pages, cannibalized for the final version, appear to be the only ones surviving from the original 1932 submission. In the absence of the actual text of Joachim's *Notice and Suggestions* — the original has not been located in the LSE Oakeshott archive or in the possession of Simon Oakeshott, and if there was a copy, which is unlikely given Joachim's partial blindness, it is not to be found in the Cambridge Press archive or in the several repositories of Joachim's papers at Oxford — one cannot speculate on how dutifully Oakeshott followed Joachim's suggestions, except to take at face value both Joachim's own generous verdict that the original manuscript was 'well planned and, in the main, brilliantly executed' prior to the revisions he proposed and Oakeshott's generous acknowledgment of Joachim's assistance in the preface to *Experience and Its Modes*, and in conversations decades later.

It would be an important 'find' for Oakeshott studies to locate the original Joachim comments.

---

[12]   LSE File 1/1/9.

6

Paul Franco

Oakeshott's Relationship to Hegel

Hegel is one of the two philosophers that Oakeshott consistently refers to throughout his career as offering a 'genuine philosophy of politics' and a profound interpretation of modern political life; the other, of course, is Hobbes.[1] Unlike he did with Hobbes, however, Oakeshott never wrote at length about Hegel, apart from the seven brilliant pages devoted to the *Philosophy of Right* in *On Human Conduct*. There is a story that Isaiah Berlin once suggested, during a lunch at Oxford, that Oakeshott should write a book on Hegel, exclaiming that 'the need for such a book was so great that better one written by a charlatan than by no one at all.'[2] Not surprisingly — but sadly — Oakeshott did not leap at this left-handed invitation.

Though he wrote comparatively little on Hegel over the course of his career, Oakeshott never concealed the degree to which his philosophy had been influenced by Hegel's. The frankest acknowledgement of this influence appears in the introduction to *Experience and Its Modes*, where Oakeshott remarks that the philosophical works from which he is 'conscious of having learnt most are Hegel's *Phänomenologie des Geistes* and Bradley's *Appearance and Reality*.'[3] In many ways, it is the influence of Bradley that predominates in *Experience and Its Modes*; but both Bradley and Oakeshott take from Hegel the fundamental anti-empiricist insight that in experience or knowl-

---

[1] See, for example, the posthumously published manuscript 'A Philosophy of Politics,' in Oakeshott, *Religion, Politics and the Moral Life*, ed. Timothy Fuller (New Haven: Yale Univ. Press, 1993), 137. Hereafter: *RPML*.

[2] This story is told by Noel Annan in *Our Age: English Intellectuals Between the Wars — A Group Portrait* (New York: Random House, 1990), 401.

[3] Oakeshott, *Experience and Its Modes* (Cambridge: Cambridge Univ. Press, 1933), 6. Hereafter: *EM*.

edge we do not begin with separate and independent particulars but with meanings or universals, and it is only on the basis of such meanings or universals that inference can take place. The brute and atomistic datum from which the empiricist supposes thought and induction take their start simply does not exist. Oakeshott sums up the radically idealist standpoint of his philosophy by saying 'perhaps the only satisfactory view would be one which grasped, even more thoroughly than Hegel's, the fact that what we have, and all we have, is a world of "meanings"'(*EM*, 61). Though he later jettisons much of the absolute idealism that characterizes the argument of *Experience and Its Modes* — for example, the monistic belief in an absolutely coherent and presuppositionless world of experience — Oakeshott never abandons the idealist thesis that the world we inhabit is not one of physical objects or 'things' but a world of meanings, a *geistige Welt*.

I do not intend to focus on Hegel's influence on Oakeshott's epistemology in this paper; rather, I confine myself to his influence on Oakeshott's political philosophy. Though there is ample evidence that Oakeshott's early political philosophy was heavily influenced by Hegel and his British idealist followers, this influence becomes more complicated to trace in his later political philosophy, which contains a substantial Hobbesian component. After tracing the way in which Oakeshott understands and appropriates Hegel's political philosophy over the course of his career, I address two fundamental questions: First, what of Hegel survives in the final articulation of Oakeshott's political philosophy? And second, does Oakeshott's selective appropriation of Hegel in his theory of civil association ultimately refine or betray the fundamental insights of Hegel's political philosophy?

I

In his earliest writings on political philosophy, we find the young Oakeshott heavily under the influence of Hegel and the British idealists. This influence is chiefly reflected in Oakeshott's understanding of the interdependence of self and society. In the 1925 essay on 'The Nature and Meaning of Sociality,' for example, he criticizes utilitarianism for failing to grasp this interdependence and treating society as an aggregate of isolated selves instead of as a genuine social whole (*RPML*, 50). And in the unpublished manuscript 'A Discussion of Some Matters Preliminary to the Study of Political Philosophy,' again from 1925, he denies that the self is something opposed to society; rather, the self requires society for its fullest development. In his rejection of traditional liberal individualism here, Oakeshott uses the most extravagant idealist language, claiming that a 'self not only requires its society, but in the fullest sense *is* its society.' And: 'The self is the State; the State is the self.' And finally: '"Man *versus* the State" is sheer nonsense.'[4]

Similar statements about the inadequacy of liberalism's 'crude and negative individualism'[5] and the superiority of the idealist theory of the self can be found in Oakeshott's writings from the 1930s and even the 1940s. In a 1937 review of Leo Strauss's book on *The Political Philosophy of Hobbes*, for example, he claims that Hobbes lacked a satisfactory theory of volition and that this lack has to some extent been remedied by Rousseau's notion of the general will, Hegel's notion of the rational will, and Bosanquet's notion of the real will. Such idealist reflection represents 'the most profound movement in political philosophy.'[6] Oakeshott reinforces this view in a 1936 review of a book on Bosanquet, writing that the 'so-called Idealist theory of the State is the only theory which has paid thoroughgoing attention to all the problems which must be considered by a theory of the State.' He claims that Bosanquet's *Philosophical Theory of the State* remains 'the most comprehensive account' of this idealist theory of the state and picks out for special commendation Bosanquet's 'philosophy of the self,' which is far superior to 'so-called "individualistic" theories, which are inclined to treat the self as something too important to be examined.'[7]

Though clearly sympathetic to the idealist theory of the state, Oakeshott is not uncritical of it. In the same review that he praises the idealist theory as 'the only theory which has paid thoroughgoing attention to all the problems which must be considered by a theory of the State,' he also writes that it is a 'theory that has yet to receive a satisfactory statement.' The study of Bosanquet's *Philosophical The-*

[4]   Oakeshott, 'A Discussion of Some Matters Preliminary to the Study of Political Philosophy,' LSE File 1/1/2, 131, 133, 137. Hereafter: *DSM*.

[5]   Oakeshott, *Social and Political Doctrines of Contemporary Europe* (Cambridge: Cambridge Univ. Press, 1939), xvii. Hereafter: *SPD*.

[6]   Oakeshott, *Hobbes on Civil Association* (Indianapolis: Liberty Fund, 2000), 157. Hereafter: *HCA*.

[7]   Oakeshott, Review of *Bernard Bosanquet's Philosophy of the State: A Historical and Systematical Study*, by B. Pfannenstil, in *Philosophy* 11 (1936), 482.

ory of the State is only a 'useful preliminary' to such a restatement.[8] Oakeshott is no less cryptically critical of Bosanquet in a review of J.D. Mabbott's *The State and the Citizen*, written more than a decade later. There he remarks that, since the publication of *The Philosophical Theory of the State*, 'no general work on political philosophy by an English writer has impressed those interested in the subject as being of first-class importance.' This he finds remarkable 'because Bosanquet's work did not leave the subject in so firm a state of equilibrium that it was difficult to know in what direction advance was to be made: the book was recognized to have grave defects, though its most important shortcomings were not those which its contemporary critics fastened on.'[9]

One wishes Oakeshott were a little more explicit about the 'grave defects' and more profitable direction alluded to in this passage. Bringing to bear the direction in which Oakeshott's own political philosophy was to develop, I would suggest two possible objections he would have to the idealist theory of the state as expounded by Green and Bosanquet. First, I think Oakeshott would have profound reservations about their Kantian doctrine of the limits of state action. This doctrine rests on the double thesis that the moral value of an action lies exclusively in its motive and that state action, operating through force and fear of punishment, inevitably compromises the purity of our motives. Such a doctrine seems to reinstitute at the level of moral motivation the very individualism that the idealist theory seeks to overcome. It is not clear that the law, concretely understood, always operates through force or fear of punishment, or that it inevitably compromises the purity of our motives (whatever that might mean). Mabbott, in the book alluded to earlier, is very good on this, and Oakeshott seems to endorse his argument.[10] Unfortunately, in his own attempt to determine the limits of state action, Mabbott falls prey to a similar type of individualism by drawing lines around the 'private individual' and invoking a distinction between social and non-social goods. Oakeshott speaks in full Hegelian voice when he counters:

> The 'private individual' as I understand him is an institution, a social, indeed
> for the most part a legal, creation, whose desires, emotions, ideas, intelli-

---

[8]   Review of Pfannenstil, 482.
[9]   Oakeshott, Review of *The State and the Citizen*, by J. D. Mabbott, in *Mind* 58 (1949), 378-9.
[10] J. D. Mabbott, *The State and the Citizen* (London: Hutchinson and Co., 1948), chap. 8.

gence, are social in their constitution. Nothing, I take it, is more certain than that this individual would collapse, like a body placed in a vacuum, if he were removed from the 'external' social world which is the condition of his existence.[11]

The second difficulty I think Oakeshott would have with Green and Bosanquet's idealist theory of the state involves their teleological conception of human nature and of human self-realization. In Green especially, there is a clear sense of the sort of character we ought to realize and of the 'higher self' the state ought to promote. His whole ethical and political philosophy is suffused by the Kantian dualism between duty and inclination; and his identification of self-sacrifice for the sake of the common good with self-realization seems not only excessively ascetic but also to obscure the very real conflicts that can arise between the claims of the individual and the claims of society. Bosanquet is less ascetic than Green and more authentically Hegelian, but he too assumes that there is a 'real will,' a true human nature, that we ought to realize and that the state ought to promote. He also assumes that the state is in many respects wiser than we are in articulating our 'real will' and guiding us to genuine self-realization.

Though Oakeshott does not explicitly reject Bosanquet's and Green's teleological conception of human nature and the purposive character it imposes upon the state in his writings from the 1930s, his divergence from them is implicit in his admiration for Hobbes. Though in his review of Strauss Oakeshott saw the idealists as redressing the lack of a coherent theory of volition in Hobbes' political philosophy, there is a sense in which Oakeshott himself uses Hobbes' skeptical Epicurean outlook to correct the teleological and rationalistic tendencies of the idealist theory of the state. For Oakeshott, Hobbes (along with Montaigne) embodies the radical, Epicurean individualism that forms the deepest current in modern liberalism. In his 1935 article on Hobbes, for example, he calls Hobbes 'the most profound philosophical individualist in the history of political theory.' And he claims that, far from being the enemy of liberalism, as he is often portrayed (by Green and Bosanquet, for example), Hobbes 'had more of the ground of liberalism in him than even Locke.'[12]

---

[11] Oakeshott, Review of Mabbott, 386.
[12] Oakeshott, 'Thomas Hobbes,' *Scrutiny* 4 (1935-6), 272.

The impact of Hobbes on Oakeshott's political philosophy receives its most direct expression in his 1946 Introduction to *Leviathan*. Once again, Oakeshott celebrates Hobbes' individualism, which, he says, 'is far too strong to allow even the briefest appearance of anything like a general will.' And he denies that Hobbes' robust doctrine of civil authority is in any way incompatible with individual liberty. Hobbes' positive conception of law 'as the command of the Sovereign,' he argues, 'holds within itself a freedom absent from "the classical, Platonic conception of law" as Reason or custom: it is Reason, not Authority, that is destructive of individuality.' Oakeshott puts this point in the most provocative way possible: 'Hobbes is not an absolutist precisely because he is an authoritarian. His scepticism about the power of reasoning . . . together with the rest of his individualism, separate him from the rationalist dictators of his or any other age' (*HCA*, 66-7). Here one can see how Hobbes' skeptical doctrine of authority serves as an antidote to the teleological and rationalistic tendencies of Green and Bosanquet.

And what about Hegel? To what extent does he fall prey to the rationalism from which Oakeshott argues Hobbes can rescue us? In his 1935 book, *The Political Philosophies of Plato and Hegel*, Michael Foster argued that Hegel failed to grasp the Hobbesian insight into the positivity of law — failed to differentiate law from reason and custom — and thereby failed to recognize the radical freedom of the human will that can ultimately be traced back to the biblical notion of creation.[13] Oakeshott wrote an admiring review of Foster's book, but he studiously avoided endorsing Foster's thesis about Hegel's rationalism and failure to do justice to the 'subjective element' of modern political life.[14] Indeed, his references to Hegel during this period are generally quite positive, and his later political philosophy (as we shall soon see) does not involve the abandonment of Hegel for Hobbes but an original synthesis of the two thinkers. The exact nature of this synthesis and the degree to which it does justice to Hegel's political philosophy are the questions we must now take up.

---

[13] Michael Foster, *The Political Philosophies of Plato and Hegel*, (Oxford: Clarendon Press, 1935), esp. chap. 4.

[14] Oakeshott, Review of *The Political Philosophies of Plato and Hegel*, by Michael Foster, in *The Cambridge Review* 57 (1935-6): 74. Wendell John Coats, Jr. pursues the comparison between Foster and Oakeshott at some length in his chapter on 'Oakeshott and Hegel,' in *Oakeshott and His Contemporaries: Montaigne, St. Augustine, Hegel, et al.* (Selinsgrove, PA: Susquehanna Univ. Press, 2000).

II

In Oakeshott's postwar rationalism writings, the contours of his synthesis of Hobbes and Hegel begin to be visible. From Hobbes he takes the ethical idea of 'the individual' as the primary subject of moral and political theory. The modern 'individual' is characterized by the desire to make her own choices and to find happiness in doing so. To this modern disposition of individuality there corresponds a certain understanding of the office of government, which Hobbes also correctly delineated. Governing cannot involve the imposition of choices on individuals, nor can it consist in making them more virtuous. Rather, governing is a specific and limited activity designed to prevent individuals who are engaged in a vast variety of self-chosen activities from colliding with one another. The end or purpose of government, as Hobbes made clear 450 years ago, is simply peace.

What, then, does the postwar Oakeshott take from Hegel? In keeping with his earlier comments about the inadequacy of liberalism's 'crude and negative individualism' and the superiority of the idealist theory of the self, Oakeshott looks to Hegel for a more philosophically satisfying account of the Hobbesian 'individual.' While he accepts Hobbes' radical conception of individuality as an ethical idea, he does not subscribe to the ontological atomism that underpins it. The individual is not to be understood as a self-contained substance, cut off from its environment, and standing in a purely external relationship to others. The modern 'individual' is, above all, a social construction (to use a fashionable phrase), an historic achievement. The 'private individual' of much liberal theory that serves as a 'limit' to state activity is a myth. As Oakeshott puts it in a passage from which I have quoted already: 'The "private individual" as I understand him is an institution, a social, indeed for the most part a legal, creation, whose desires, emotions, ideas, intelligence, are social in their constitution.'

Oakeshott's Hegelian understanding of the self and critique of liberal atomism appear most clearly in his consistent hostility to the doctrine of natural rights. Though this doctrine is associated more with Locke than with Hobbes, the seeds of it can be found in Hobbes' contention that the natural right to preserve oneself remains operative in civil society, allowing an individual to resist

arrest and execution and to run away in the heat of battle.[15] Against
the doctrine that natural rights serve as the only secure barrier
against the overweening power of government — a doctrine that
descends from Locke to present-day conservative libertarians —
Oakeshott writes in his 1948 essay 'Contemporary British Politics':
'The truth is . . . that we do not begin by being free; the structure of
our freedom is the rights and duties which, by long and painful
effort, have been established in our society. Individuality is not natural; it is a great human achievement. The conditions of individuality
are not limitations; there is nothing to limit.' And he goes on to add
that 'so simple a doctrine of natural law cannot be held to survive the
criticism (not of Bentham, which is negligible) but of Burke and
Hegel.'[16]

'Contemporary British Politics' is interesting not only for its
Hegelian critique of the doctrine of natural rights but also for the
Hegelian mode of social organization that it holds out as an alternative. Criticizing the idea of central social planning espoused by
Labour socialists, Oakeshott distinguishes between two different
modes of integration or organization of society. The mode of integration that belongs to a centrally planned society is of a simple and
external sort. All power is concentrated in the hands of the government, and the government imposes order on society from the
outside, as it were. In contrast to this mode of integration is another
of a more complex sort, based on the rule of law. This integration is in
terms of rights and duties, which are not, again, to be conceived of as
'natural' or absolute. This latter mode of social integration provides
the basis for a Hegelian understanding of liberal democracy as a
tradition or way of living. We must not, Oakeshott urges, think of
liberal democracy as an abstract idea or a fixed body of abstract
rights but, rather, as a 'living method of social integration, the most

---

[15] Interestingly, Oakeshott sees Hobbes as avoiding the 'individualism' of
traditional liberal theory: '[T]he seventeenth century notion that when man
entered political society he surrendered, not the whole, but a part of his
natural rights . . . is a notion from which Hobbes might have rescued us if we
had listened to him.' Review of *Natural Law and the Theory of Society*, by Otto
Gierke, trans. with an introduction by Ernest Barker, in *The Cambridge
Review* 56 (1934-5), 11.

[16] Oakeshott, 'Contemporary British Politics,' *The Cambridge Journal* 1
(1947-8): 488, 475.

civilized and the most effective method ever invented by mankind.'[17]

It is just such a Hegelian understanding of liberal democracy as a 'living method of social integration' that Oakeshott devoted himself to theorizing over the next twenty-five years or so, culminating with his theory of civil association in *On Human Conduct*. Before addressing myself to that work, I would like to briefly consider a review Oakeshott wrote in 1955 of Herbert Marcuse's *Reason and Revolution* because it contains his most sustained discussion of Hegel prior to *On Human Conduct*. At the heart of Hegel's political philosophy, Oakeshott argues in this review, is the modern 'individual,' which Hegel recognized 'as a great achievement but one difficult to manage' because of the individual's propensity 'to collide with others in his efforts to enjoy the world.' Whereas some of Hegel's contemporaries 'dreamed of a human association from which collision had been excluded by the destruction of the "individual," ' Hegel himself 'held fast to the view . . . that the "individual" is an achievement not to be surrendered' and 'recognized government (not a comprehensively managerial activity, but a sovereign activity in which men exercised their power to make rational laws for themselves) as the *tertium quid* required by the situation.'[18] Here we see clearly not only how Oakeshott understands Hegel but how this understanding coincides with the animating concerns of his own political philosophy.

Oakeshott concludes his review of Marcuse by commenting that, while the latter's correction of various misunderstandings of Hegel is valuable, 'there remains something more to be done. Hegel is so profound and stimulating a thinker that he deserves not only to be not misunderstood, but also to be learned from.'[19] One could hardly formulate a better description of what Oakeshott does with Hegel in *On Human Conduct*, a work that does not slavishly follow Hegel's political philosophy but learns from it while creatively transforming it into something that is distinctively Oakeshottian.

---

[17] Oakeshott, 'Contemporary British Politics,' 489-90.
[18] Oakeshott, Review of *Reason and Revolution*, by Herbert Marcuse, in *Spectator* 194 (1955), 404-5.
[19] Oakeshott, Review of Marcuse, 405.

III

In the first essay of *On Human Conduct*, Oakeshott elaborates a teaching about human freedom that serves as the basis of his theory of civil association. This teaching can be understood as Oakeshott's own original contribution to the idealist effort mentioned earlier to overcome the lack of a coherent theory of volition in Hobbes' political philosophy. With it he attempts to overcome the atomism of traditional liberal theory by conceiving of human freedom or agency in such a way that its qualification by morality and law need not entail its being compromised.

The crux of this teaching on human freedom lies in Oakeshott's controversial distinction between the substance and form of conduct. What he calls the 'freedom inherent in agency' consists in conduct's being substantively undetermined. Human beings are formally free insofar as they are able to choose their own specific actions and the specific sentiments in which those actions are performed. Freedom thus understood is not compromised by the qualification of conduct by prudential and moral considerations, provided that these considerations do not determine the substantive choices and performances of agents. This is precisely the point Oakeshott makes with respect to prudential, moral, and intellectual 'practices': they adverbially qualify but do not determine the substantive choices or performances of agents; the 'practical' is only an aspect of any action and must always be accompanied by a substantive action chosen by an agent. It is precisely on account of this adverbial character of practices that they do not compromise the freedom inherent in agency.

Oakeshott goes on to distinguish moral practices from prudential practices on the basis that the latter are instrumental to substantive purposes, while the former are not instrumental to any particular purpose or enterprise. The basic intuition here seems to be the Kantian one that there must be a distinction between moral and prudential conduct. In the end, though, Oakeshott's conception of morality is more Hegelian than Kantian. This becomes clear when he analogizes a moral practice to a language. What this analogy highlights more than anything else is the wholly colloquial or vernacular character of a morality. A morality is not something above our daily existence that we bring to bear on our actions through an act of reflective effort; rather, it is a medium for conduct without which no action or utterance could take place. A morality does not somehow supervene on the more primary or natural activity of desiring or instinctual gratification, thus inaugurating a titanic battle between duty and inclination; it is a language within which the pursuit of any satisfaction takes place, a knowledge we are never without. Oakeshott sums up this Hegelian dimension of his thought by saying that 'human conduct is not first having unconditional wants . . . and then allowing prudential reason and moral sensibility to indicate or to determine the choice of the actions in which their satisfaction is sought: it is wanting intelligently.'[20]

It is, of course, in terms of the idea of a moral, non-instrumental practice that Oakeshott fundamentally understands civil association. By defining civil association in this way, he is able to overcome some of the atomism that has dogged liberal theory from Locke to Mill. Like his idealist predecessors from Hegel to Bosanquet, he shows that freedom and law, self and society, individual and government, are not necessarily opposed to one another. As a moral practice, civil association does not compromise the freedom inherent in agency because it does not determine the substantive choices of agents but only prescribes procedural or adverbial conditions to be taken into account when choosing and acting. Far from being an external limit on agency, civil association is indispensable to it, serving as a vernacular language of intercourse by which agents enact and disclose themselves.

In addition to this Hegelian dimension, there is a strong Hobbesian component to Oakeshott's conception of civil association. This component can be most clearly discerned in what Oakeshott has to say about civil authority. Like Hobbes, he argues that civil authority has nothing to do with the desirability — utility, wisdom, rationality, or justice — of the conditions of civil association. Recognizing the authority of civil association is simply accepting its conditions as binding regardless of whether one approves of them or not. Such a doctrine of authority may be thought to pose a threat to the moral autonomy of human beings, but Oakeshott argues that this is not so for two reasons: first, civil law does not specify substantive actions but only adverbial considerations to be taken into account when choosing and acting; and second, precisely because recognizing the authority of civil association does not involve approval of its conditions, 'the link between belief and con-

---

[20] Oakeshott, *On Human Conduct* (Oxford: Clarendon Press, 1975), 79-80. Hereafter: *OHC*.

duct' that constitutes free agency is not compromised. Oakeshott
puts the latter point in this way: 'in acknowledging civil authority
cives have given no hostages to a future in which, their approvals and
choices no longer being what they were, they can remain free only in
an act of dissociation' (*OHC*, 157-8).

Oakeshott's reflections on the intimate connection between freedom and authority here recall his comment on Hobbes that I quoted
earlier: 'Hobbes is not an absolutist precisely because he is an authoritarian'; 'it is Reason, not Authority, that is destructive of individuality.' They also point to an important difference between Oakeshott
and his idealist predecessors. The core of the idealist project consisted in the attempt to reconcile the authority of the state with individual freedom by basing that authority, not on the consent of the
individual, but on her 'real' or 'rational' will. While Oakeshott certainly follows Hegel, Green, and Bosanquet in rejecting individual
consent as the basis of authority, he nevertheless does not identify
authority with the 'real' or 'rational' will of the individual, at least
not when this will is conceived of teleologically. His reconciliation of
freedom and authority depends instead (as we have seen) on showing that civil authority does not compromise the formal freedom
inherent in agency. In this regard, he diverges most sharply from his
British Hegelian predecessors, whose doctrine of the 'real will' does
seem to point to a substantial and teleological doctrine of human
nature, and whose doctrine of authority therefore does not clearly
distinguish between authority and wisdom.

And what about Hegel? In the third essay of *On Human Conduct*,
Oakeshott provides a magisterial reconstruction of Hegel's political
philosophy that largely assimilates it to his own conception of
non-purposive civil association. He begins by summarizing Hegel's
argument concerning *das abstracte Recht*, showing how it breaks
down because it does not bind the subjectivity of individuals. It is
only after *das Recht* has been (inter)subjectively recognized that it
becomes a concrete and *sittlich* form of human relationship. This
subjective dimension of *das Recht*, however, can be taken too far.
Echoing his own argument about how civil association does not violate the freedom inherent in agency, Oakeshott writes:

> The necessary characteristic of *das Recht* is not that the Subject must himself
> have chosen or approved what it requires him to subscribe to, but that it
> comes to him as a product of reflective intelligence and exhibiting its title to
> recognition, and that it enjoins not a substantive action but the acknowledge-

ment of a condition which can be satisfied only in a self-chosen action. (*OHC*, 260)

Oakeshott also assimilates Hegel's distinction between *bürgerliche Gesellschaft* and *der Staat* to his own distinction between an instrumental and a moral practice. In *der Staat*, he argues, *das Recht* consists of non-instrumental rules of law (*Gesetze*) whose authority does not rest on 'approval of what they prescribe' (*OHC*, 261).

Needless to say, Oakeshott provides what might be called a 'strong' reading of Hegel here. Though his interpretation serves as a useful corrective to excessively metaphysical and communitarian readings of Hegel, it is ultimately too formalistic, neglecting Hegel's critique of the atomism and narrow self-interest of traditional liberal theory and his attempt to provide the liberal state with a more exalted purpose than mere security of life, liberty, and property. What is important about the Hegelian state is not merely that it does not violate the formal freedom inherent in agency but that it realizes and embodies human freedom understood as rational self-direction and autonomy. In the course of the *Philosophy of Right*, Hegel delineates the institutions and associations — including the family, civil society, and the corporations — that lift individuals out of their particular self-interest and lead them to identify with a more universal purpose. The 'destiny of individuals is to lead a universal life,'[21] and this destiny is fulfilled only in the political institutions of the state. There, citizens enjoy not only the subjective freedom to choose and find satisfaction in their own actions but also the more important freedom that consists in willing the universal — freedom — itself.[22]

The deficiencies of Oakeshott's interpretation of Hegel's political philosophy point to the differences between his formal conception of civil association and Hegel's more substantial conception of *der Staat*. The freedom that civil association enables and protects is not the positive, rational, or substantial freedom that Hegel attributes to the state; rather, it is the negative or subjective freedom of individuals 'to make choices for themselves and to find happiness in doing so.'[23] In this regard, civil association is far more continuous with traditional liberal political thought from Locke to Mill than is the

---

[21] G. W. F. Hegel, *Elements of the Philosophy of Right*, ed. Allen Wood, (Cambridge: Cambridge Univ. Press, 1991), §258R.

[22] See my *Hegel's Philosophy of Freedom*, (New Haven: Yale Univ. Press, 1999) for a complete development of this reading of Hegel's political philosophy.

[23] Oakeshott, *Morality and Politics in Modern Europe*, ed. Shirley Letwin, (New Haven: Yale Univ. Press, 1993), 85. Hereafter: *MPME*.

Hegelian state. It is true (as I have argued) that Oakeshott rejects the kind of liberal individualism that opposes the individual to the state and tries to set limits on the latter by invoking natural rights or non-social goods. Nevertheless, he does not abandon the core liberal belief that the individual qua individual is of supreme value and the state is merely a means by which the individual can more safely and securely pursue his or her own particular ends or purposes. For Hegel, on the other hand, this liberal understanding of the state, in which 'its determination is equated with the security and protection of property and personal freedom, [and] *the interest of individuals as such* becomes the ultimate end for which they are united,' involves a confusion of the state with *bürgerliche Gesellschaft*. A truer understanding of the relationship of the state to the individual recognizes that 'it is only through being a member of the state that the individual himself has objectivity, truth, and ethical life. *Union* as such is itself the true content and end, and the destiny of individuals is to lead a universal life.'[24]

That Oakeshott's political philosophy differs in important ways from Hegel's does not necessarily mean that it is less compelling. One obvious advantage it has over Hegel's political philosophy is that it does not invoke controversial metaphysical hypotheses. In one place, Oakeshott writes that he believes 'it to be a virtue in any [political] theory that it avoids calling upon unnecessary hypotheses,' and he goes on to criticize political thinkers who have 'invoked metaphysical theories of personality' or 'elaborated theories of human nature in general' (*MPME*, 83-4). Hegel's conception of the state as the realization of rational freedom certainly falls into this latter category. The most satisfying liberal theory, according to Oakeshott, need not involve anything more than 'the simple recognition of subjects who have acquired (perhaps only temporarily) a disposition to make choices for themselves and to find happiness in doing so; subjects, that is, who have acquired, and are intent upon exercising, a high degree of individuality,' and constructs a theory of government appropriate to this historical circumstance (*MPME*, 85). It is on this metaphysically parsimonious foundation that he constructs his own theory of civil association.

From another point of view, though, Oakeshott's metaphysical parsimony can appear excessive and prevent him from adequately addressing the problems of liberal society and culture that moti-

---

[24] Hegel, *Philosophy of Right*, §258R.

vated Hegel's political philosophy. It is not clear, for example, how civil association combats the atomism that Hegel associated with liberal *bürgerliche Gesellschaft*, the problem Tocqueville, shortly after Hegel, would designate by the term 'individualism': the problem of individuals in a liberal democracy retreating into the private circle of their family and friends without connection or a sense of responsibility to the larger community around them. Unlike Hegel (and Tocqueville), Oakeshott has little to say about the crucial role that the intermediate institutions of civil society play in lifting individuals out of their isolation and identifying them with the political whole. It is not that he is unaware of the pathologies of modern liberal life, but his austere conception of philosophy forbids him from considering these contingent 'sociological' issues.

Hegel's conception of the state as the realization of rational freedom is also, in many ways, more attractive than Oakeshott's conception of civil association as a means for individuals to pursue self-chosen ends, a necessary condition for the exercise of their arbitrary will. It is true that Hegel's positive conception of freedom as rational self-determination rests on controversial metaphysical premises; but it also brings out more clearly than other, negative conceptions just what we understand by freedom and why we find it valuable. Our deepest intuitions about freedom suggest that it does not involve simply doing what we please but, rather, self-mastery, cultivation of capacities, and fulfillment of significant purposes. It is this account of freedom as rational self-determination that enables Hegel to conceive of the state as not merely instrumental to individual freedom but as the very realization and embodiment of freedom. By conceiving of the political community in this positive — one might say Aristotelian — way, Hegel endows it with a moral dignity that is missing from typical liberal accounts, including Oakeshott's, and he is able to generate the sort of allegiance and identification that is necessary to sustain it.

7

George Feaver

Regimes of Liberty

Michael Oakeshott on Representative Democracy

During Michael Oakeshott's life, 'democracy' changed from being largely a fringe doctrine to one at center stage in the deliberations of the western world and beyond. The outcome of the unprecedented global conflicts of the twentieth century, especially since 1945 and the eventual end of the Cold War, favored the fortunes of democracy. At the same time, so-called 'nation states' carved out of the remnants of European and Asian Imperialism (Oakeshott called them 'imitation states')[1] sought somehow to manufacture instant authority out of their newly-concocted but only formally 'democratic' constitutions. A recent estimate suggests that '118 of the world's 193 countries are democratic, encompassing a majority of its people.'[2] Though tyranny survived, its practitioners had learned to pay propagandistic lip-service to democracy.

---

[1] Oakeshott, *On Human Conduct* (Oxford: Clarendon Press, 1975), 188. Hereafter: *OHC*. Emoting over this large and still controversial topic has yielded much rhetorical fog. But in the precincts of the LSE during Oakeshott's tenure of his Chair, he was not lacking in sympathetic company for his more skeptical view of such matters. I have in mind among others, Elie Kedourie's *England and the Middle East: The Destruction of the Ottoman Empire, 1914-1921* (London: Bower and Bower, 1956). The 1978 and 1987 editions contain an 'Introduction' setting out Kedourie's rejection of what he regarded with some cause as the dogmatic liberalism of his Oxford D.Phil. Examiner, H. A. R. Gibb. Also, Peter Bauer's *Equality, The Third World and Economic Development* (Cambridge: Harvard Univ. Press, 1981); the writings of Leonard Shapiro on the Soviet Union, and, in some of his wide-ranging intellectual product, Ernest Gellner.

[2] Cf. Fareed Zakaria, 'The Rise of Illiberal Democracy,' *Foreign Affairs* (November/December 1997), 23.

Michael Oakeshott had a good deal to say about democracy. He
had read Bentham and J.S. Mill and the so-called 'Victorian critics of
democracy' — Carlyle, Ruskin, Arnold, J.F. Stephen, Maine and
Lecky — as an undergraduate, and their texts apparently formed a
central part of his teaching materials when he was a history don at
Gonville and Caius College, Cambridge in the interwar years. From
that time onward, however, his many insights and asides about the
character of democracy were typically uttered in an idiom that was
exploratory, tentative or ironic, rather than definitive in tone. In
elaborating his philosophical positions he could also be at once
demanding and reticent and not a few of his readers were discon-
certed by an obliqueness that seemed to belie his literary prowess.
His critics labeled Oakeshott a 'conservative' who was impatient
with the tentacular reach of 'liberalism.' All this has meant that his
many important insights about democratic regimes have been
ignored, misunderstood, or plainly misrepresented.

I

It is not widely known that Oakeshott compiled 'a book of documents'[3] intended to serve in schools as well as in universities as a
rough textual guide to 'the social and political doctrines of contemporary Europe'. Revisiting the *Social and Political Doctrines* with the
benefit of hindsight, one finds evidence of a characteristic approach
to political doctrines, particularly democracy, that Oakeshott elaborated in the decades to come. We now live, he began, in an age of
'self-conscious communities' (*SPD*, xi), though it would be mistaken
to suppose that the value of a regime depends on the intellectual
competence of its apologists: 'indeed, in most cases, practice is more
coherent than doctrine and its superiority should be recognized'
(*SPD*, xv). The task of the intellectual critic of a doctrine was to detect
incoherence, but this criticism was unlikely to influence practical
affairs. Oakeshott focused on five contemporary European social
and political doctrines: Representative Democracy, Catholicism,
Communism, Fascism and National Socialism, each of which had
what he termed 'a universal aspect' (*SPD*, xiii), and each chosen on
the grounds that it was, to some degree, realized in the life of a
nation. These doctrines signified 'five separate and distinct ways of

[3]   Oakeshott, *The Social and Political Doctrines of Contemporary Europe*
(Cambridge: Cambridge Univ. Press, 1939), 'Introduction,' xvii–xviii.
Hereafter: *SPD*.

conceiving the fundamental character of society, and by implication, five separate and distinct ways of conceiving the nature and earthly destiny of man' (*SPD*, xiv). It follows that Oakeshott thought the common view that Representative Democracy was merely a method of government was untenable.

Their intellectual defects as doctrines aside, all of them had successfully 'subjugat[ed] whole communities' (*SPD*, xxiii). To Oakeshott, the second best of them was Catholicism, even though it was by 1939 widely regarded as 'a harmless museum piece' (*SPD*, xvi). Because of its formalization by St. Thomas Aquinas, it was more systematic and philosophical than the others, as well as being the sole contemporary representative of the Natural Law theory so central to the European tradition.[4] In England, besides, Catholicism was the source of 'many of the principles which belong to the historic doctrine of Conservatism' (*SPD*, xx). Communism, despite its self-contradictions and 'a quaint mediaeval jargon,' was at least imaginative, proposing 'a type of society, and indeed a type of man more unlike what the world has hitherto seen than any of the other doctrines' (*SPD*, xx). Next there was Fascism, which 'asserts as fundamental principles what anyone might be excused for believing for a short time and in unfortunate circumstances,' but 'few can desire war more than anything else' (*SPD*, xxi). The most disagreeable of the lot for Oakeshott, was, by inference, National Socialism. This youngest of the new regimes in Europe, like all the others, claimed a universal character; but more than any of the others, he alleged, 'it came into being in order to put a specific policy in operation' (*SPD*, xxii). In its tone of self-righteousness, as in the zealotry of its doctrines of race, blood and leadership, its nationalism was more fierce even than that of Fascism, and it was socialistic only in the sense of its obsession with a planned society.

It was the extracts concerned with 'Representative Democracy' that Oakeshott chose to place first in order. He regarded it, despite its muddle, as on balance the most important and protean of the contemporary doctrines of European social and political life. Catholicism rejected the secularism of modernity, but 'Each of these newer doctrines is an express reaction from the Democratic doctrine as a whole or from some specific elements of it' (*SPD*, xvii). There was no denying the force of Fascism's critique of abstract individualism in

---

[4]   Even though Oakeshott makes clear that he does not himself subscribe to the philosophical assumptions of the Natural Law tradition.

Liberal Democracy, and there was much to learn from Communism's radical criticism as well. But each of these newer doctrines was importantly *derived from* aspects of Representative Democracy. For Oakeshott, democracy was 'the parent of these ungracious children'(*SPD*, xvii) and it 'lives on' in their denunciations of it — from the materialism of Fascism and National Socialism, to the reappearance of the democratic moral ideal of productivity in Communism.

Oakeshott then explained that he had chosen the term 'Representative Democracy' and rejected 'Liberal Democracy' to avoid confusion with what he termed 'the crude and negative individualism' of much current 'Liberalism.' What he wanted to convey by 'Representative Democracy,' he mused,

> is something both older and younger than Liberalism, something of which Liberalism was an expression but an incomplete expression. Liberalism in that sense is perhaps dead; the doctrine of Representative Democracy has survived that death. . . . Liberalism in England is still understood as the creed of a party and to be contrasted with Conservatism and Socialism, whereas the doctrine I wished to find some statement of, the doctrine of Representative or Parliamentary Democracy, is a tradition expressed, so far as this country is concerned, in the spirit of our laws rather than in the programme of any one party. Nevertheless, it is a Liberal doctrine...the social and political beliefs of Representative Democracy are more in the nature of a tradition and a tendency than a well-knit doctrine, and are, in consequence, more difficult to express precisely and completely (*SPD*, xvii).

And he said that representative democracy was 'a more comprehensive expression of our civilization than all the others...and its adaptability is a sign of vitality rather than mere vagueness' (*SPD*, xviii).

Oakeshott described the principles of representative democracy as principles of which he plainly approved: '*that a society must not be so unified as to abolish vital and valuable differences, nor so extravagantly diversified as to make an intelligently co-ordinated and civilized social life impossible, and that the imposition of a universal plan of life on a society is at once stupid and immoral*' (*SPD*, xix, italics added). So emphatic was he about this point that he later reiterated it in a footnote on the cleavage separating the moral ideals of the five doctrines he had now passed in review, '*between those which hand over to the arbitrary will of a society's self-appointed leaders the planning of its entire life, and those which not only refuse to hand over the destiny of a society to any set of officials but also consider the whole notion of planning the destiny of a society to be both stupid and immoral*' (*SPD*, xxii, italics added). On one side stood three modern authoritarian doctrines, and on the other, Catholicism and Liberalism. 'To the Liberal and the Catholic mind alike,' he declared, 'the notion that men can authoritatively plan and impose a way of life upon a society appears to be a piece of pretentious ignorance; it can be entertained only by men who have no respect for human beings and are willing to make them the means to the realization of their own ambitions.'[5] In drawing attention to these bifurcating moral tendencies of European political doctrines, Oakeshott planted the seed of his later analyses of the character of politics in a modern European state.

While Oakeshott advised the reader that his collection offered no particular conclusion, he acknowledged that his most remarkable discovery had been 'the comparatively small amount of damage' which the doctrine of Representative Government has suffered from 'the bombardment' of criticism leveled against it by the authoritarian doctrines of contemporary Europe. 'It is difficult to see that anything relevant has been said against the doctrine which, for example, Matthew Arnold did not say half a century ago, and said much better'(*SPD*, xxiii).[6] But Oakeshott sought, not a rejection of Representative Democracy, but a radical restatement of its principles — addressing especially the 'inadequate foundations of Mill's individualism'(*SPD*, xvi). With the benefit of hindsight, we can detect in this prewar collection of documents an implied alignment between 'Representative Democracy' and Oakeshott's subsequent discussions of the 'politics of skepticism,' and then 'the politics of individualism,' and ultimately, of 'civil association.' This task of further elaborating contemporary Europe's political doctrines thus begun in 1939 was one to which Oakeshott would remain drawn all his life.

II

We have witnessed Oakeshott's early insistence that Representative Democracy was something 'both older and younger than Liberalism.' It seems that, by the time he set to work on *The Social and Political Doctrines of Contemporary Europe*, he had thus assigned himself the

[5]   In the 'Editor's Introduction' to Oakeshott's *The Politics of Faith and the Politics of Skepticism* (New Haven and London: Yale Univ. Press, 1996), viii-ix, Timothy Fuller draws the reader's attention to the anticipation of that work's central theme in the same footnote from *SPD* I have cited here. Hereafter: *FS*.

[6]   He must have had in mind Arnold's denunciation of the 'philistinism' of popular or democratic culture.

task of rethinking the premises of modern European politics. But just after that collection appeared, his scholarly pursuits were interrupted for the duration of World War Two, during which he served in the British Army.[7] With an epochal war finally in the past tense, he returned to his abiding philosophical interests by preparing for publication his bravura edition of Hobbes' *Leviathan* in 1946. In these postwar years some of Oakeshott's most polemical writing appeared, motivated in part by his distaste for the apparent all-party drift of British politics towards the 'Welfare State' (most pronounced in the Labour Party's hope of final arrival at a social and political 'New Jerusalem'), and by an insidious postwar preoccupation of assorted enthusiasts for educational reform with demoting liberal education in Great Britain and promoting in its place a trendy species of vocational training.[8]

Oakeshott had completed, apparently in 1952, a lengthy typescript concerned with the dialectical movement of modern European political thought, posthumously published as *The Politics of Faith and the Politics of Skepticism*. For nearly five centuries, he suggests, the political vocabulary of modern Europe has been marked by an ambiguity resulting from its service to two masters, which he proposes to call the politics of faith and the politics of skepticism. In an ideal characterization of the 'abstract extreme' of the politics of faith, the business of governing is nothing less than the perfection of mankind. Human power is deemed sufficient to procure such salvation by imposing a single, comprehensive condition of human circumstances. Governing is an unlimited activity and government is omnicompetent, if not necessarily absolute. Such a style of politics welcomes power rather than being embarrassed by it, and govern-

---

[7]   Robert Grant has astutely commented that Oakeshott's military experience strengthened his convictions about the awesome and unprecedented capacity of the modern state to marshal resources and exercise power. See Robert Grant, *Thinkers of Our Time: Oakeshott* (London: Claridge Press, 1990), 16-17. In Grant's view, war convinced Oakeshott of the inadequacy of mere technical knowledge, and moreover, that military organization, necessarily directed to a single overriding goal, is the worst of all possible models for peacetime society. War made a deep impression on him; but 'it was by no means an altogether romantic one.'

[8]   See, for instance, Oakeshott, 'Contemporary British Politics', *Cambridge Journal* 1 (1947-8): 474-90; and his 'The Universities,' *Cambridge Journal* 2 (1948-9): 212-29, the same issue of which carried his first version of 'The Tower of Babel,' subsequently republished in Oakeshott, *Rationalism in Politics and other essays, new and expanded edition*, ed. Timothy Fuller (Indianapolis: Liberty Press, 1991), 465-87. Hereafter: *RIP*.

ment is viewed 'as the representative of the society in an enterprise of communal self-assertion' (*FS*, 29). In such circumstances, governing is seen as a 'godlike adventure' in which strict attention to the proper constitution and authorization of government will be less important than pursuing *raison d'etat*. The present will be more important than the past and the future more important than either. The activity of governing in the politics of faith will require not only obedience, but express approval and even love; dissent and disobedience will be punished as error and sin. The task of education will be to induce enthusiasm and the moral elevation of the office of government in accordance with which the politician and his associates will be regarded as at once the servants, the leaders, and the saviors of society.

The roots of skeptical politics in the modern world, on the other hand, are traceable to an outlook of prudent diffidence that requires that the activity of governing be detached from the pursuit of perfection. In the abstract ideal of skeptical politics, the first object of government is to sustain peace and order, the second to seek out improvements to the existing system of duties, rights and means of redress. The activity of governing is but one of a complex of activities, superior to the whole only in respect of its guardianship of public order, and 'moral approval and disapproval are no part of the office of government, which is not at all concerned with the souls of men' (*FS*, 35). The politics of skepticism display 'a certain nervousness' (*FS*, 36) about the exercise of power, and thus, a tendency to procedural formality, a respect for precedent, and a higher regard for institutional arrangements that diminish the damage done by ambitious men than for those designed for the more efficient dispatch of business. Individual punishment is viewed as preferable to prevention since it requires the exercise of less intrusive power, and consequently avoids 'turning civil society into a badly managed classroom in which every lesson is preceded by a search for catapults, cribs and chess sets, a search which makes pupils and teachers equally miserable and anxious for the holidays' (*FS*, 37). In short, the activity of governing in a politics of skepticism is 'manifestly nothing to be enthusiastic about' (*FS*, 38).

In considering the broad fortunes of these contending advocacies in the political life of modern Europe over the course of the past four or five centuries, Oakeshott leaves no doubt (unlike an assortment of 'deliberative' democrats, republicans and so-called communi-

tarians) that he holds no great expectations of politics save its vital
contribution to the maintenance of peace and order:

> Politics at any time are an unpleasing spectacle. The obscurity, the muddle,
> the excess, the compromise, the indelible appearance of dishonesty, the coun-
> terfeit piety, the moralism and the immorality, the corruption, the intrigue,
> the negligence, the meddlesomeness, the vanity, the self-deception . . . offend
> most of our rational and all our artistic sensibilities. For so far as political
> activity succeeds in modifying the reign of arbitrary violence in human
> affairs, there is clearly something to be said for it, and it may even be thought
> to be worth the cost. But, at the best of times, political activity seems to
> encourage many of the less agreeable traits in human character (*FS*, 19).

Yet he makes equally clear, late in the book, that there was a time,
especially in British politics during the late seventeenth and early
eighteenth centuries, when a mean between these two extremities of
faith and skepticism seemed closer than at any other to realization.
There momentarily appeared in view the concrete character of a
complex manner of politics — at a time when 'enthusiasm was not so
much decried as put in its proper place' (*FS*, 122). Oakeshott provides an exquisitely English image to conjure up what was then, on
an admittedly sympathetic appreciation, evidently afoot:

> Faith had knocked up an impressive score, and its innings ended characteris-
> tically in hit-wicket. (The scorers, unaware of what had happened, went on
> chalking up the runs: faith, particularly in France, was believed to have 'a
> splendid future behind it'.) In the situation, however, it looked as if skepti-
> cism would take a mighty revenge. But not at all; the contest was adjourned
> for tea. And in the conversation that ensued, the political principle of the
> mean in action made its appearance. Many voices were heard in this conver-
> sation, but among the more notable participants were Locke, Berkeley,
> Shaftesbury, Halifax, Boyle, St. Evremond, Fontenelle and Hume, and there
> were wits (like de Mandeville) on the circumference who provided the com-
> edy. (*FS*, 122)

They did not compose a political party, or belong to a single
nation, their conversation drew from the thoughts of others who had
gone before; nor was their conversation confined to politics but
ranged over the entire field of human conduct.

Oakeshott's elliptical remarks on republicanism and democracy
also call for comment. Now, the American constitution was in his
view 'the most profoundly skeptical constitution of the modern
world' (*FS*, 80). It was an achievement attributable to the foresight of
the Founding Fathers in wishing, not to eradicate the monarchical
inheritance of the American colonists, but to modify it by adapting a
derivatively British institutional framework in such a manner as to

forestall its potential degeneration into despotism. But it would be a mistake, in Oakeshott's judgment, to infer from the celebrated skeptical prudence of the Founders that there is in consequence any exclusive historical affinity between republicanism and the politics of skepticism. On the contrary, he insists: 'Of all the follies of the politics of skepticism, the strangest is that which appears in the history of modern republicanism' (*FS*, 83). What he has in mind is that not a few well-intentioned republicans, yearning for a certainty that belongs properly to the politics of faith, have been drawn to the deluded idea that we somehow have it in our power to fix irrevocably the means to divide, check and balance the power of government.[9]

He closes his book by reiterating his views on the irremediable ambiguity of our political vocabulary, which, like so much in the modern world, turns out to be a mixed blessing.[10] There are dangers as well as practical benefits; political language provides a means of self-serving obfuscation but it is also a highly useful tool of mollification. Besides, awareness of the ambiguity of political language ought to help to deprive it of some of its power to confuse.

'Democracy,' for instance, is an inherently ambiguous word. Strictly, it signifies a manner of authorizing or constituting government, but more loosely, it stands for 'the activity of governing turned in a certain direction' (*FS*, 131). Confusion abounds because *both* the politics of faith and the politics of skepticism have been adroit at appropriating the word to foster their fortunes. If the manner of governing is faith, then popular institutions are celebrated solely with respect to the amount of power with which they are able to endow government; but in skeptical politics, popular institutions chiefly recommend themselves as a means to control government. In the politics of faith, democracy is preferable to monarchy because it delivers greater quantities of power; in skeptical politics is it deemed superior to monarchy because it provides a continuous control over

[9]   In Oakeshott's later years, theorizing republicanism was to become a vogue topic, traceable in part to the influence of Quentin Skinner and the so-called 'Cambridge school' of historiography and political theory. See James Tully, ed., *Meaning and Context: Quentin Skinner and His Critics* (Princeton: Princeton Univ. Press, 1988). See also, Oakeshott, 'The Foundations of Modern Political Thought,' *The Historical Journal* 23, 2 (1980): 449-53 and Wendell John Coats Jr., *A Theory of Republican Character and Other Essays* (Selinsgrove, PA: Susquehanna Univ. Press, 1994), 45-8, 63-77.

[10] He also discusses in some detail the historic ambiguities of the expression *'salus populi, suprema lex esto,'* and the term 'rights.'

government, and the broader the franchise the broader the authority behind this control. Of course, the whole point of his book had been to suggest that the governments of the modern world represent a range of positions across a spectrum embracing two conceptual extremes. Oakeshott concludes that merely to defend or attack democracy is pointless. Popular institutions are amenable to the purposes of *both* current styles of politics. For him, the question whether democratic institutions can be made to work is ill-considered; what is really being asked, he suggests, 'is whether "popular" institutions can be prevented, in contemporary circumstances, from selling themselves entirely to the politics of faith' (*FS*, 132).

III

The chapters that make up another of Oakeshott's posthumously published works were originally delivered as lectures in April, 1958,[11] some six years after the completion of the typescript of *The Politics of Faith and the Politics of Skepticism*. They succinctly summarize Oakeshott's approach to the study of modern political life and represent a further installment of the ongoing project to which he repeatedly returned over the years. Like the successive entries in an artist's sketchbook, these Harvard lectures record in preliminary drafts what would find masterful expression on the figurative canvas of part 3 of *On Human Conduct*, 'On the Character of a Modern European State.' He begins by drawing attention to some distinctions to be borne in mind in any inquiry into the 'activity of governing.' The most rudimentary distinction is between *the activity of ruling*, or government, and *political activity itself*, which is 'an activity, not of governing, but of determining the manner and matter of government' (*MPME*, 8). Whenever the topic of 'government' arises, these two separate concerns are brought into play: thought about what government *actually is* — its constitution and authorization — and about *what it does* — its engagements and pursuits. He differentiates these because they are conceptually 'independent of one another,' and because their relative importance has varied considerably at different times and in different circumstances.

Oakeshott claims that 'political activity' is European in origin but that it is now found elsewhere in the world; moreover, at least in the 'intensity' in which it now exists, it is 'a comparatively modern invention' (*MPME*, 8). In mediaeval Europe, for instance, interest was directed mainly to questions about the authorization of ruling authorities, and the activity of governing was limited mainly to the provision of peace and order and to guarding the laws and customs of the community. Oakeshott observes: 'the main circumstance that prevented the activity of governing's being, or being thought proper to be, an activity of enterprise was not any abstract principle, but the conspicuous lack of power to be enterprising' (*MPME*, 10). This situation continued into early modernity; but over the past four hundred years, the power at the disposal of modern governments has become immense.

This has encouraged the appearance of a different center of gravity for political reflections: preoccupation with the office of government has now become pre-eminent, and reflection on the constitution and authorization of government has been subordinated. What is surprising, Oakeshott suggests, is that what had been tantamount to a sea change in our habitual manner of perceiving the activity of governing has remained generally unobserved. He offers several possible reasons for this perceptual nonchalance. First, while respect for the authorization and constitution of governments has remained strong, it is now routinely proffered for the wrong reason. He says pointedly:

> The case for that sort of constitution and authorization of government we call 'democracy' has been argued, whether or not correctly, very largely on the observation of the power at the disposal of modern governments; where it was not argued that a democratic constitution would increase the power of government, it was argued that it is intolerable that governments disposing of such immense power should not be democratically constituted. (*MPME*, 11)

Second, in the epochal struggles for political ascendancy pitting royal against aristocratic claims in the early modern world, constitutional issues were rhetorically at center stage. This fostered a misleading but highly influential belief that the pursuits of government derive from their constitutions, which attained a 'fictitious pre-eminence' even though the main concern all along had been with the activities of governments 'disguised as a concern with the constitutions of governments' (*MPME*, 12). And third, this shift of emphasis has tended to remain concealed from us because the political vocabulary of modern Europe, inherited from a mediaeval past in which it had been elaborated largely in relation to questions concerning constitutions and authorizations of government, is still substantially the same vocabulary but it is now used to articulate concerns centered upon the activity of governments. It is worth quoting the example that Oakeshott again chooses, somewhat reprovingly, to illustrate his point:

> [T]he word 'democracy' stood originally for a government constituted and authorized in a certain manner, but has now commonly come to be used to indicate a government active in a certain manner; and similarly the word 'freedom', which stood for a condition of human circumstance recognized to be the concomitant of government authorized in a certain manner (Rousseau, for instance, contrasts 'free' with 'monarchical' governments), now commonly refers to a condition of human circumstance springing from what a government has or has not done. (*MPME*, 12)

Commonly and erroneously these distinct components — the activity of ruling and political activity — have been made interchangeable, and this has fostered a ruinous transposition in which power is wrongly regarded as tantamount to authority itself.

In his remaining lectures, Oakeshott proposes that there have been three more or less mutually opposed moralities current in European societies during the modern period. Each reflective person, he guesses, 'has felt the pull of each of these moralities,' since modern European moral character is 'a composite…prey to many internal stresses' (*MPME*, 18). He labeled the first and oldest of these moralities, a mediaeval inheritance, *the morality of communal ties*. This morality was superseded in the modern era by *the morality of individuality*, which in turn provoked *the morality of collectivism*. Oakeshott went on to offer a rather pithy retracing of the lineage of the political theory of individuality, from Locke through Kant, Adam Smith, Burke and Bentham, to J.S. Mill. He concluded this review by suggesting that what these writers were concerned with was 'the elucidation of a view of the office of government appropriate to certain circumstances' — chiefly, 'the appearance of subjects who desire to make choices for themselves, who find happiness in doing so and who are frustrated in having choices imposed upon them' (*MPME*, 84).

He then turned to the political theory of collectivism and its attendant disposition. This disposition arose out of subjects' distress at the collapse of the mediaeval communal order and their inability or unwillingness to embrace the new individualism. This was a perfectionist morality that recognized 'a "common good" or a "communal good" to which one's own and others' activities are subordinated and government is understood as the custodian and promoter of this "common good"' (*MPME*, 90). There have been three primary versions of the political theory of collectivism. In its religious idiom, its aim is righteousness or moral virtue; in its productivist rendering, a condition of prosperity or abundance is the goal; and in its distributionist depiction, security or welfare take pride of place. Calvin, the *philosophes*, Francis Bacon, Robert Owen, St. Simon and Marx — all have contributed to different versions of collectivism.

Up to now, we have set to one side Oakeshott's concise, but suggestive outline, of the 'character' of modern politics. He draws on Montesquieu's discussion of political regimes in *De L'Esprit des Lois*. For Oakeshott, the salient characteristics of the new political conditions that Montesquieu scrutinized were that the activity of governing had become generally recognized as a 'sovereign' activity, and that governments enjoyed powers so much greater than at any earlier period. At the same time, the moralities of individualism and collectivism had grown out of the old feudal order. The union of sovereignty and power on one side, and individualism and collectivism on the other, bred new modes of political and moral life that called for a new theoretical ordering. Montesquieu elaborated three ideal models to depict the various dispositions of what was, as yet, only a partly revealed character. His genius, in Oakeshott's estimation, was his determination to go beyond the mere formal composition of government and investigate the principle or 'spirit' of their respective regimes. Montesquieu wanted to examine not only the constitution and authorization of governments, but the activities of government in despotism, monarchy and aristocratic republicanism, and democracy — and to show how these were related to the character of their subjects. Each of these different manners of governing, says Oakeshott, 'discloses itself in a characteristic attitude towards law and the administration of justice, towards liberty, towards the dispositions and conditions of life of its subjects, and towards their political education' (*MPME*, 37).

The principle of despotism is fear. The despot rules in his own interest and the activity of governing is understood to be an activity of exploitation in which there will be few if any rules, and no courts of law. Offences will be regarded as offences against the despot himself or his agents, and severely punished. The activity of subjects, because life is uncertain, is unenterprising, marked by both indolence and excess; their condition is one of servitude and a shared equality of insecurity. Under despotism there will be little room for friendship or trust, and the object of political education will be to foster servility and blind obedience to the despot.

In a novel representation of Montesquieu's second model, Oakeshott takes the liberty of treating as one monarchy and aristocratic republicanism, even though they are separated in the original text. While Montesquieu regarded them as differently constituted, he also made clear that they are quite similar in the manner in which they are disposed to be active — sharing, in Oakeshott's terms, a single understanding of the office of government. The principle of this regime is honor. Here, government does not exploit but simply rules by means of laws, which are few, precise, and administered in independent courts. Offences are regarded as not against the society but against other subjects, whose condition is one of freedom and equality of status. Since the activities of these subjects of monarchy spring from individual choice, they are multifarious, and subjects may be thought of as associates. Social intercourse is free; and the object of political education is to inculcate the virtues of honor and moderation fitting for membership in such an association.

The principle of the third model, democracy, is virtue, in the sense of care for the public or common good. Here we are in the presence, not of association but of a genuine community. Governing is neither exploitation nor ruling, but leadership, managing the affairs of a concern. Laws in this regime are wide-ranging, and tend not to distinguish between crime and sin. *Salus populi* is the supreme law informing all laws, even, where necessary, overriding the administration of particular laws. The judicial apparatus will display the traits of 'people's courts' concerned less with the letter of the law than with pursuing the common good. Offences will be recognized as against the community, and there will be a tendency to believe that prevention is better than punishment. Private law relationships will be fewer. In the democratic model, subjects enjoy equality — meaning each is alike a servant of the community and has a right to an equal share of the products of communal activity. These subjects' activities spring, not primarily from individual choice, but from a shared desire to pursue the common good. Here, individuality arouses suspicion, there is a common mediocrity of ability and fortune, and the object of political education is to inculcate subservience to the common good and acquiescent conduct, which has love of the republic as its motive.

As Oakeshott interprets him, Montesquieu thus displays the range of dispositions that make up the modern European character in respect of the pursuits and engagements of government. Of course, the actual regimes of modern Europe do not manifest any one of these dispositions to the exclusion of the others, but contain all three, while tending to one or other of the poles. In the Europe of his day, Montesquieu thought that despotism was the weakest, almost falling outside the capabilities of the modern European character. Among the realistic alternatives, monarchy or aristocratic republicanism, and democracy were capable of being good or bad of their kind. If monarchy has a tendency to degenerate into despotism, democracy has a tendency to generate into a sort of monarchy that springs from distrust of the constituted rulers, 'and the desire of every man to have a finger in government' (*MPME*, 41). Despotism, in Montesquieu's view, sets in whenever a regime abandons its principle — when monarchy deserts honor and when in democracy equality becomes 'either extinct or extreme' (*MPME*, 42). Otherwise, given the appropriate circumstances — of geographical situation, size, history, and the religion and principal occupations of the subjects — either of the two, monarchy and democracy, may be viable and apt regimes.

Oakeshott reminds his audience that Montesquieu was also disposed to draw a second conclusion from his enquiry. Following Aristotle, who had argued that the best must entail a mean between extremes, Montesquieu thought that monarchy was the best of the dispositions available in modern Europe because it represented a mean between despotism and democracy. What is of interest, for present purposes, is that Oakeshott goes on to propose that Montesquieu's 'monarchy' and 'democracy' be regarded as reflecting the two dispositions he has characterized as the 'individual' and the 'anti-individual' respectively. In Oakeshott's version of Montesquieu's theory, European political life is depicted as a constant dispositional struggle for ascendancy —' "monarchy" being the manner of governing appropriate to "individuality" and "democracy" to "anti-individuality"' (*MPME*, 42-3). Compared to the favorable view of 'representative democracy' in his 1939 study of the political doctrines of contemporary Europe, Oakeshott appears to have substituted a preference for monarchy. But we need to bear in mind that the ostensible form of government was less important in his eyes than its mode of authorization or character. And in renovating Montesquieu's eighteenth century vocabulary, Oakeshott merely extended to 'monarchical or aristocratic republicanism' characteristics he had earlier indicated one might expect to find in desirable versions of twentieth century democracy.

IV

Several early occasional papers relate tangentially to Oakeshott's attitude to democratic politics and the character of the modern state. We have seen the rather acerbic regard in which he held politics and politicians in the contemporary scheme of things by the 1950s, but his postwar outlook merely corroborated a position he had set out in a short essay published in the year that World War Two erupted and *The Social and Political Doctrines of Contemporary Europe* appeared. In this paper he insisted that the benefits of everyone's taking an active part in politics were greatly exaggerated. 'Political activity,' he ventured, 'is neither the only adequate expression, nor the overwhelmingly most important expression of a sensibility for the communal interests of a society or of mankind...I do not think that there is a duty for everyone to take part in it.'[12] Even in a world replete with loosely liberal and participatory-democratic belief, he averred, politics rightly remains a specialized form of activity conducted largely on the surface of the life of a society. Its proper purpose is the maintenance of a legal and social order. Political activity generated 'Magna Carta' and the 'Bill of Rights,' but the contents of these documents derive from 'a stratum of social thought far too deep to be influenced by the actions of politicians. A political system presupposes a civilization' (*RPML*, 93). We must not, though, equate the narrow activity of governing with creating and recreating the values of a society. 'Societies . . . are led from behind' (*RPML*, 96) by their artists, poets and philosophers, and this is true, Oakeshott concludes, with a pointed reference to the imminence of war, no less in times of crisis than in others.

In a much earlier paper, Oakeshott identifies 'true sociality' as the basis of 'political life' or the 'good life.' 'Sociality' is the metaphoric law of life for a society; it cannot be captured by either naturalistic or utilitarian means. Nor is it a merely biological sociableness. Only in friendship, as Aristotle saw, can we achieve the unity of life and

---

[12] Oakeshott, *Religion, Politics and the Moral Life*, ed. Timothy Fuller (New Haven: Yale Univ. Press, 1993), 94. Hereafter: *RPML*.

mind that points to the principle of the good. The deepest insights into the nature of love and friendship derive from the large, difficult, and untimely subject of religion. It is worth noting that this reference to religion, a lifetime interest of Oakeshott's, should have led him directly to some heartfelt reflections on patriotism — 'a subject much on our minds during these years' (*RPML*, 60). He regarded patriotism as 'the basis of all morality... the greatest emotional and intellectual effort of which we are capable.... We cannot refuse to acknowledge something real in the impulsive love of country and countryside which plays so great a part in the life of most of us' (*RPML*, 61).[13] The account he has attempted to provide of the character of social life, he concluded, is one in which, like finite selves in the philosophy of Plotinus, 'all move round a single conception, but do not always fix their gaze upon it. They are like a choir of singers standing round the conductor, who do not always sing in time because their attention is diverted from him. But when they look at him they sing well' (*RPML*, 62). Looked at from a somewhat different angle, in Oakeshott's conception of sociability associates know how to play and not merely to work.[14] Oakeshott is adamant that only individuals are capable of love and friendship and that only between individuals is true sociality possible. The social whole never swallows up 'finite selves.' If his use of this Plotinian image might appear to some to carry an anti-democratic implication, we must remember that, for Oakeshott, his preferred sense of democracy is ultimately linked to the attributes of non-purposive, 'civil association.'

In a third early paper, 'The Authority of the State,' Oakeshott set out to examine the notion of finite selves moving round a single conception of sociality from another perspective. Here he displays a philosophical debt not only to Hegel, but to Hobbes. Rejecting alternative, allegedly more 'factual' notions of the state as a piece of territory, a collection of persons, the secular or the political whole, he asserted that the state is 'the social whole which is correlative to individuals who are complete and living persons . . . the totality of an

---

[13] He said, years later in 'On Being Conservative,' of friendship, patriotism and conversation, that 'each . . . demands a conservative disposition as a condition of its enjoyment' (*RIP*, 417).

[14] Cf. Oakeshott's posthumous 'Work and Play,' *First Things*, 54 (June/July 1995): 29-33; and *FS*, 110 passim. 'Work and Play' has also been published in Luke O'Sullivan, ed. *What is History? and other essays* (Exeter: Imprint Academic, 2004), 303-14. Hereafter: *WH*.

actual community which satisfies the whole mind of the individuals who comprise it . . . Government and law, economics, religious, intellectual and every other activity and aspect of social life find their explanation in this totality' (*RPML*, 83). It does not follow that this entails investing the noun 'society' with a life of its own, or reifying the adjective 'social.' Oakeshott is clear that a state is nothing other than its members. But, he cautions, before we can grasp this in philosophical terms, we must first abandon 'the moral and legal conception of the individual as that which is isolated, for a more concrete conception which takes him to be that which is complete' (*RPML*, 85). For Oakeshott, it was at this point that the centrality of the authority of the state revealed itself:

> The authority of the state is not mere government and law, nor is it founded upon a contract or any other form of the consent of the people, but resides solely in the completeness of the satisfaction which the state itself affords to the needs of concrete persons. Apart from its completeness, the state has no authority, for that only is authoritative, in the full sense, which is itself complete. Of this authority, and of no other, can it be said: *Non est potestas super terram quae comparetur ei* (*RPML*, 87).[15]

As background to his subsequent ruminations about the history of modern political thought and modern moral characters, then, Oakeshott had early insisted that the guardianship of civilization, individuality, and sociability, requires acceptance of the completeness of the authority of the modern state, as well as a political education appropriate to nurturing in rising generations of associates a patriot's appreciation, both heart-felt and reasoned, of the obligations of subjects in the everyday life of a people deserving of the enjoyment of liberty. As a political philosopher of *liberal* inclination, J.S. Mill had correctly intuited in the political life of modern Europe deep tensions in the competing claims to figurative 'sovereignty' of the individual, the political powers that be, and society at large. In some of his early papers, Oakeshott can be seen struggling with the challenge of devising a philosophical account in which these ostensibly competing individual, political and social advocacies might be more satisfactorily reconciled.

---

[15] The Latin phrase deployed by Oakeshott here is, of course, taken from the famed frontispiece to the 1651 Andrew Crooke edition of Hobbes' *Leviathan* depicting a figure made up, on close inspection, of numberless discrete individuals. Above his crown is written the inscription in Latin, from *Job* 41: 24 Vulg.; 41:33 AV, signifying that there is no comparable earthly power.

V

For Oakeshott, certain societies, by dint of chance, circumstance and
resourcefulness more than conscious design — the Romans and
Normans,[16] for instance — have displayed greater success than others in the activities of governing and being governed. Cultivation of
the manners and institutions amenable to the flourishing of freedom
has been far from universal in the complex history of modern
Europe, let alone the world beyond. 'Freedom,' as he once put it,
'like a recipe for game pie, is not a bright idea'; the freedom of an
Englishman is not an ideal premeditated independently of political
experience, but 'what is already intimated in that experience' (*RIP*,
54). Oakeshott esteemed what he sometimes called British parliamentary democracy, 'not as an approximation to some "ideally"
democratic system of government, but an instrument of remarkable
refinement and responsiveness, thrown up in the course of our political history, [and] capable of digesting the enterprises of zealots.'[17]

Oakeshott tended to regard the British and the Americans as figurative family members sharing a common inheritance, even if on
occasion, what he regarded as a particularly egregious American foi-
ble might elicit from him a mild scolding — the tendency, for
instance, to miss historical nuance and to swallow whole the unreflective notion that practice derives from theory, which he described
as 'the shortened American way of thinking in which a manner of
conducting affairs is inconceivable without an architect and without
a premeditated "dedication to a proposition"' (*RPML*, 117).[18]

Whatever their differences, America and Britain were societies
alike enjoying the blessings of what he once called 'The Political
Economy of Freedom' (*RIP*, 384-406). Their histories had been
marked by 'old-fashioned liberal' traditions in which the practice of
politics was notable for the absence from it of overwhelming concen-
trations of power. Under such conditions, authority was diffused

---

[16] Oakeshott, 'The Rule of Law,' in *On History and Other Essays* (Oxford: Basil
      Blackwell, 1983), 164. Hereafter: *OH*.
[17] Oakeshott, 'Introduction' to Reginald Bassett, *The Essentials of Parliamentary
      Democracy*, 2d ed. (London: Frank Cass, 1964), xxi-xxiv.
[18] The Englishmen who first came to America's shores had no choice but to try
      to make appropriate responses to the novel circumstances in which they
      found themselves and did so by applying ingenuity and adaptability
      derived from their inheritance of British civilization to the prodigious task
      at hand (Cf. *RIP*, 55). Continuity and innovation yielded a New World
      civilization now less tied to its British inheritance but neither inferior nor
      superior to its overseas original.

between past, present and future. A multitude of interests and organizations comprised society. The conduct of government was a shared affair involving both administration and opposition. The rule of law secured freedom of association for all, as well as private property rights and freedom of speech.[19] Monopoly and near monopoly were contained. Restraint of trade was regarded as a major crime. The burden of proof lay with those who would transfer to the public domain undertakings otherwise subject to the discipline of competition. Economic policy aimed first of all at a stable currency. Now, since these societies did not spring up overnight but had endured by consistently recognizing human fallibility, when any matter thought to require change arose, it would, as a matter of course, invoke familiar principles of continuity and prudential consensus in preference to the pursuit of any preconceived purpose. In the political economy of freedom, thus, reforms were deemed appropriate only when their necessity had already begun to manifest itself in the ever-changing goings-on of society.

What is striking for present purposes about Oakeshott's account of the political economy of freedom is the absence from it of any direct reference to democracy. Indeed, in a broadside in the later pages of the essay clearly aimed at the direction of British politics in the immediate postwar years, he protested at the manner in which '[w]ith eyes focused upon distant horizons and minds clouded with foreign clap-trap, the impatient and sophisticated generation now in the saddle has dissolved its partnership with its past and is careful of everything except its liberty' (*RIP*, 397). A magnanimous politics that concentrated on matters of fundamental importance — say, the right to life, liberty and happiness — had been dislodged by mawkish concern over such mundane welfare matters as the 'right' of a pregnant mom to a glass of orange juice.

---

[19]   But Oakeshott is of the view that we currently tend to exaggerate the importance of free speech, which, while certainly a significant form of liberty, has not historically been nearly as essential as freedom of association and private property rights. 'The major part of mankind has nothing to say; the lives of most men do not revolve around a felt necessity to speak' (*RIP*, 391). That said, free speech is for him at least a *bone fide* freedom, unlike some other more supposititious rights, such as 'freedom from want'.

The postwar erosion of liberal education had only made a bad situation worse.[20] By diminishing our regard for history it has encouraged the ignorant, the gullible, and the ambitious in a self-satisfied belief that the flourishing of liberty has been virtually synonymous with the ascendancy of democracy. So the absence of democracy from Oakeshott's discussion of the political economy of freedom serves to remind us of his submission elsewhere that liberty and individuality can thrive at least as well in a constitutional monarchy or aristocratic republic as in a democracy, when these terms are understood in the sense of Montesquieu's preferred types of regimes. Democracy, Oakeshott thought, with its enormous command of power and its temptation to confuse it with its formal authority, actually posed the greater immediate threat. The danger of so disregarding the historical record is that by removing from our store of knowledge acceptable alternatives or modifications to democracy, we are left without criteria for distinguishing good democracy from bad, left devoid of the wherewithal with which to halt, even in an otherwise ostensibly good democracy, an unthinking drift to collectivism. The unquestioned moral prestige and political authority of 'democracy' in the postwar world had only exacerbated these dangers.

Oakeshott acutely observes that 'the real spring of collectivism is not a love of liberty, but war. The anticipation of war is the great incentive, and the conduct of war is the great collectivizing process' (*RIP*, 400). The moral authority of 'democracy' in the political rhetoric of the decades following the Second World War was invoked in two spheres, the domestic life of the western societies, and the so-called democracies of the Soviet Union and China. In 'The Masses in Representative Democracy,' Oakeshott delineated more fully than he had in the Harvard lectures the threat of collectivism posed by the rise of 'the mass man' within the liberal democracies. While retaining his belief that the individualist disposition is the more substantial part of the character of moral and political life in modern Europe, he emphasized that the individualist character was shadowed by an antipathetic disposition, 'the individual *manqué*' (*RIP*, 371). The individual, for his part, saw that what was appropriate to his purposes was a manner of governing and being governed capa-

---

[20]   See Oakeshott, *The Voice of Liberal Learning: Michael Oakeshott on Education*, ed. Timothy Fuller (New Haven: Yale University Press, 1989). Hereafter: *VLL*.

ble of transforming the interests of individuality into rights and
duties. The pursuit of that condition culminated in the parliamentary governments of the late eighteenth and early nineteenth centuries, passed on as an inheritance that we have come to speak of
loosely as 'representative democracy.'

The individual *manqué* was the product of the same subsidence of
communal ties as the individual, but seeing in individuality a burden as much as an opportunity, sought refuge from it in a protector,
the government. His initial trepidation turned to despair when a
moral revolution began to sweep aside the relics of the old communal morality. At this juncture, Oakeshott speculates, from the individual *manqué* there first sprang up a more militant version — 'the
anti-individual' — who recognized himself as 'the mass man,' 'disposed to assimilate the world to his own character by deposing the
individual and destroying his moral prestige' (*RIP*, 372). This
anti-individual had comrades rather than associates or friends, feelings rather than thoughts, impulses rather than opinions; and
because he had inabilities rather than passions and was only dimly
aware of his power, he required a leader who could tell him what to
think. 'From one point of view' says Oakeshott, ' "the masses" must
be regarded as the invention of their leaders' (*RIP*, 373). And there
was already around a character ready and willing to occupy this
office — the frustrated antihero, the individual *manqué*, who was
'enough of an individual to seek a personal satisfaction in the exercise of individuality, but too little to seek it anywhere but in com-
manding others' (*RIP*, 374).

The emergent morality of the anti-individual, Oakeshott continued, was a morality not of liberty and self-determination but of
equality and solidarity, its nucleus the notion of a substantive condition of human circumstance represented by the common good and
love of the community. The corresponding view of the proper office
of government was one in which the leader was recognized, not as
the referee of the collisions of individuals, but as a sort of moral
leader and managing director of 'the community.' The 'rights'
demanded by the anti-individual were rights that entailed the aboli-
tion of the rights appropriate to individuality. Against the long-rec-
ognized individual right to *pursue* happiness through one's own
choices, he asserted the anti-individual's 'right' to *enjoy* happiness.
Oakeshott went on to identify some of the great enterprises of 'popular government' lately taken up on behalf of 'the mass man' — pro-

jects aimed at a modification of parliamentary government so that it might better impose upon all activities a substantive condition regarded as 'the public good' (*RIP*, 378). One of these enterprises was the establishment of universal adult suffrage, another, diverse stratagems to transform parliamentary representatives into mere delegates, a third, the *plebiscite* (*RIP*, 379-80).

In this, one of Oakeshott's bleakest pieces, he nonetheless managed to conclude on a somewhat brighter note. As he put it, an exploration of modern European political life in terms of the tension between the moralities of the individual and the ant-individual, with their contrasting notions of government and politics, might help us to come to grips with a complex situation. But beyond that, he assured the reader, there was no evidence either that the morality of individuality and its implications for government had ever been decisively routed on the field of doctrinal battle, or that we now actually live in a world in which 'the anti-individual' known to us collectively as 'the mass man' has attained a position of undisputed sovereignty.

Oakeshott's allusion here to the establishment of universal adult suffrage as a pet project of 'the mass man,' and his seemingly disparaging reference elsewhere to 'Votes for Women' (*RIP*, 11), require comment. It was his view that, strictly, neither *universal* adult suffrage nor the notion of representatives as 'delegates' had been directly intimated in the historical practice of parliamentary government, which, generally-speaking, had kept the peace and protected private liberties for centuries without them. His point was to urge friends of liberty to insist that the boundaries of *the constitution* of government and its authorization be kept conceptually clear from those of *the office* of government. For Oakeshott, whether everyone has the vote or not is beside the point; this is a matter of what Walter Bagehot once called the 'dignified' or formal part of the constitution. He suspected that the real motive of 'the mass man' was to deploy universal adult suffrage as a battering ram to increase government's power to *lead* rather than *rule*. Universal adult suffrage thus motivated is, in his estimation, tantamount to an elaborate ruse deployed to further legitimate popular sovereignty.

If Oakeshott's aim in 'The Masses in Representative Democracy' was to warn that the bad type of democracy could undermine freedom in Western Europe, in another piece from this period he turned to the blatant abuse of the trappings of democracy in the Soviet

Union and elsewhere. In the prewar period Oakeshott had depicted communism as a doctrinal adaptation of some elements of liberal democracy, in particular, its notion of 'the plausible ethics of productivity' (*SPD*, xx). Here he combined that insight with his recent ideas on the anti-individual or 'mass man.' To a disconcerting extent, the time-honored appreciation of the art of governing as making appropriate responses to 'emergent political situations,' had given way to a new style of governing as the mobilization of the entire resources of the community in pursuit of a premeditated 'public good.' In the circumstances of mass society, this has had the result of reducing the perceived efficacy of genuine political activity and increasing the value of techniques of mass persuasion.

Moreover, the insidious influence of modern rationalism meant that the mass man inexperienced in genuine political activity looked to political leaders for 'proofs' of the correctness of political decisions. Reliance on figurative proofs is a very old rhetorical trick. But the great significance of Marxism for the mass man was its claim to have provided 'proofs' based on scientific 'laws' of social change. Oakeshott insisted that the immense power of a regime like the Soviet Union to manipulate and to render captive its audience rested on the masses' naive belief in these 'laws' of social change. Nurturing this belief gave politicians a seemingly infallible method of defending their leadership, and relieved them of personal responsibility for their actions. As the sordid political history of twentieth century reminds us (as he wrote, the Hungarian uprising was close to hand, Czechoslovakia still to come):

> [I]f the audience begins to be skeptical, or if the 'laws' of social change seem to be an inadequate or misleading guide on certain important occasions, then, what is interesting to observe are the occasions on which such a politician amends the book, revises the laws, or adds to the vocabulary, when he improves a little on what he has read there, and the great occasions when he shuts the book.[21]

VI

I have tried to establish Oakeshott's lifelong interest in democracy, which usually appeared as the shadowy background of his wider philosophical essaying into the character of government and politics in modern Europe. This interest is explained, first by an important

[21]   Oakeshott, 'Political Laws and Captive Audiences,' in George Urban ed., *Talking to Eastern Europe* (London: Eyre and Spottiswoode, 1964), 291-301.

feature of his intellectual biography that is now largely taken for granted: only in his lifetime did the doctrine and practice of so-called 'Liberal Democracy' gain its historically unprecedented ascendancy. Far from wishing ill-will upon democracy or liberty or the rule of law, Oakeshott attempted a defense that he believed might succeed better, by abandoning the problematic rubric 'liberal democracy' itself in favor of what he reluctantly called, for want of a better expression, 'representative democracy.' He thought that this approach improved our ability to sustain in the present the spirit of an inheritance of ideas and practices that are crucial to the practice of the good type of democracy, which historically long predated democracy naively understood as an exclusive product of liberalism.

Of course, Oakeshott was reflective enough to see that someone might ask of his 'representative democracy' — representative of what or whom? Oakeshott's implied response appears to have been: representative of the interest of subjects, but not the determiner of their choices as associates engaged in the myriad goings-on of people in the enjoyment of freedom. Representative democracy for Oakeshott involved sustaining in rising generations of associates an understanding of the proper office of government as restricted largely to maintaining peace and public order, conditions the gullible seemed to assume were achievable through some rhetorical act of Immaculate Conception. The practices of representative democracy are a legacy hard-won by those who have gone before, though adaptable as circumstances might require to the vicissitudes of everyday political life. Political education in representative democracy provides an introduction to liberal learning appropriate to the cultivation of the moral virtues of individuality.[22] In the restricted but important world of politics, this entails the ready acceptance from below by associates as subjects of the authority of government, and from above, self-restraint in the exercise of power.

Democratic regimes of liberty appropriate to the circumstances of our time are then a species of mixed regime, where democratic virtue is tempered by an individuality that is as much monarchical and aristocratically republican in point of pedigree as democratic, and

[22] Shirley Robin Letwin, *The Gentleman in Trollope: Individuality and Moral Conduct* (Cambridge: Harvard Univ. Press, 1982); and, from a somewhat different angle, her *The Anatomy of Thatcherism* (London: Fontana, 1992), chap. 2, 'The Vigorous Virtues,' 26-48.

where democratic power is mitigated by the presence of a restrained authority that is closer in spirit to constitutional monarchies or aristocratic republics than to the inverted form of absolute monarchy that is liable to result from unlimited popular sovereignty. What we call 'democracy' in the loose sense approximates to a regime of liberty as long as the constitution of government and its authorization are grounded in the principles of what Oakeshott calls 'representative democracy,' and the activities of its offices of government are not over-stimulated by the mutual encouragements of leaders and the masses. The authority of democracy may thus be celebrated at the same time that its power is constrained. For Oakeshott, in sum, a good type of democracy is one that presupposes a certain civilization in which sociability flourishes; that embraces the final authority of the state and practices a self-restraining politics; that steadily aims at a mean between monarchy or aristocratic republicanism and democracy; and that leans more to political skepticism and individuality than to faith and collectivism.

VII

The fullest rendition that Oakeshott has left us of this quest, connecting in three separate essays his abiding interests in philosophy, political theory and history, is to be found in *On Human Conduct*. Part 3 of this work expanded the themes he had explored in *The Politics of Faith and the Politics of Skepticism* and *Morality and Politics in Modern Europe*. He absorbed their ambiance while largely jettisoning their detailed frame of reference. Here, as in earlier undertakings, he set out an account of contending notions of the character of a modern European state. One of these is now rendered as civil association, or *societas*, wherein ruling is seen not as an unconditional engagement but as the exercise of authority in accordance with a rule of law which 'bakes no bread' (*OHC*, 164). The other rests on the notion of enterprise association, or *universitas*, an engagement to pursue a common substantive purpose. And the character of the modern European state discloses 'an unresolved tension between the two irreconcilable dispositions represented by the words *societas* and *universitas*' (*OHC*, 200-1).

What is interesting is that in *On Human Conduct* democracy is, as elsewhere, discernible in the background. Some misled souls, Oakeshott mused, have thought of democracy as a necessary feature of the civil condition (*OHC*, 181), but what he is after, he says, is the pursuit of something that is more general and philosophical, above and beyond democracy. Again he protests that 'democracy' properly signifies a manner of constituting a government and of authorizing it to rule, but that by his later years had become one habitually used to signify 'particular acts of policies of a government or even certain kinds of private relationships and certain motives for acting' (*OHC*, 193). But this has only served to encourage the characteristic political subterfuges of our time:

> [C]onfident of the approval evoked when 'democracy' is used in its proper constitutional meaning, the word is made to qualify a performance or a policy with the [expectation] of evoking the same approval...many would think (incorrectly) that they had said something significant if they said that non-contributory old-age pensions, or legal aid for the poor, or compulsory 'comprehensive' education was 'democratic'. (*OHC*, 193)

Oakeshott is clear that civil association and enterprise association are ideal types and that neither is finally separable from the other; they are the poles of a continuum weighted in one direction or the other in any given circumstance. And these poles, for him, surpass in importance all the usual 'democratic' divisions of political life:

> Travellers have not always been scrupulous in reporting where their intellectual journeys have led them...And the confusion has been increased by jokers of both persuasions who, in deference to the vulgar, have altered the signposts to read: Right, Left; Reaction, Progress; Stagnation, Development; Poverty, Affluence; Conservative, Liberal; Cul-de-Sac, Open Country; Liberty, Security; Authority, Liberty; Conflict, Peace; Competition, Co-operation; Unconcern, Responsibility; Indifference, Compassion; Apathy, Brotherly Love; Hell, Heaven or Heaven, Hell, etc. And even totally irrelevant designations have been posted, such as: Democracy, Authoritarianism, Capitalism, Bureaucracy, Pluralism, Centralism, etc. And before now a whole generation of would-be travellers has awakened to find that one of these jokers has posted both the paths with the same inviting sign: Freedom, Jerusalem, or Cockaigne. (*OHC*, 318)

Now, what might appear to be the outright dismissal of democracy (and much else) in this vividly Oakeshottian passage is really a plea to look beyond the deep muddle of contemporary 'democratic' rhetoric to an exploration of the character of political activity itself and to the contemplation of its place in a wider world of conduct where mortals have always had to make their way as best they can. Oakeshott aims not to dismiss democracy but to find appropriate grounds for depicting it as a tangible feature of contemporary civilization in the changed historical circumstances of an ongoing human adventure.

Like Schopenhauer's colony of porcupines, huddled together in communal warmth on a winter's day only to have to draw away from the pricks of each other's quills, and who, as Oakeshott had elsewhere suggested (*RIP*, 460-1), unknowingly invented civil association, the predicament of associates in the goings-on of a modern state is that there can be no final resolution of their plight. There can be no pristine 'liberal democracy,' no unipolar regime of liberty or equality. The adventure is, as always in the human estate, more a matter of Box and Cox, in which liberty requires authority. Notably, Michael Oakeshott closed the last book published in his life with a recreated essay on the theme of 'The Tower of Babel' (*OH*, 165-9) that is by turns funny and mordant, a barely concealed parody of those who yearn to dwell in Elysian fields of 'democracy,' led there by the politics of faith, or collectivism, or enterprise association.

8

Richard Friedman

Michael Oakeshott and the Elusive Identity of the Rule of Law

Introduction: Some Issues

This paper is concerned with Michael Oakeshott's treatment of law in *On Human Conduct* (1975) and 'The Rule Of Law' (1983) in *On History and Other Essays*.[1] The discussions of law in these two books are the longest and most comprehensive that Oakeshott published. There are two earlier publications of considerable significance for recovering the issues and context from which Oakeshott's later ideas about law emerged: 'The Concept of a Philosophical Jurisprudence' (1938) and *The Social and Political Doctrines of Contemporary Europe*.[2] However, the former is devoted to what jurisprudence should and should not be, and never gets around to a direct discussion of law. The latter book contains some profound statements by Oakeshott about the rule of law and its fate in relation to various political doctrines of the nineteenth and early twentieth centuries, but these statements are dispersed about a long compilation of documents and do not form a sustained argument.

[1]   Oakeshott, *On Human Conduct* (Oxford: Clarendon Press, 1975). Hereafter: *OHC*; and, 'The Rule of Law,' in *On History and 0ther Essays* (Oxford: Basil Blackwell, 1983). Hereafter: *OH*.
[2]   Oakeshott, 'The Concept of A Philosophical Jurisprudence,' *Politica* 3 (1938): 203-22, 345-60; and, *The Social and Political Doctrines of Contemporary Europe* (Cambridge: Cambridge Univ. Press, 1939). Hereafter: *SPD*.

On Human Conduct and 'The Rule of Law' provide the fullest statements of Oakeshott's legal philosophy, and there is no fundamental difference between them as to core-ideas. Nevertheless, there is an obvious formal difference between them. 'The Rule of Law' plunges directly into an analysis of law in the opening paragraph where Oakeshott announces his intention 'to begin as near to the bottom as I can and confine myself to what it ['the rule of law'] *must* mean.' By contrast, in *On Human Conduct*, Oakeshott does not reach an account of law until the second part of a three-part work, in which the discussion of law is placed between the presentation of a philosophical theory of human understanding and action and an analysis of the ambiguous character of the modern state and the vexed question of the doctrinal roots of modern politics.

This textual difference poses an interpretive issue about Oakeshott's approach to law: namely, whether his legal philosophy is fully intelligible outside the broader framework of *On Human Conduct*, and accordingly, whether the attempt to reach an understanding of Oakeshott's legal philosophy can be isolated from an examination of his theory of action and his views about the modern state and modern politics. More specifically, is Oakeshott's treatment of law in 'The Rule of Law' dependent for its meaning and validity on the larger philosophy of *On Human Conduct*? Or does it stand on its own as it was published as an independent essay?

This interpretive question about Oakeshott's writings on law points on to a philosophical question: whether legal philosophy is or can become an autonomous theoretical enterprise, freed from both a philosophical theory of human nature and a general account of political affairs. Certainly one of the most striking and unprecedented characteristics of legal philosophy in the twentieth century was its repeated attempts to establish and cultivate an autonomous jurisprudence, attempts that continue to go on at the present time and that have become increasingly intricate and technical, and studiously indifferent to the historic languages and issues of political thought. Of course the various attempts to create an autonomous jurisprudence have also been the object of intense criticism, and the law-politics nexus never ceases to stir up controversy. The result is that even before entering directly into a discussion of Oakeshott's writings on law, there are lots of compelling questions about jurisprudence and its presentation.

In addition, there are also questions about the rule of law, an expression surrounded by controversy in recent thought. In legal philosophy, there is a striking division of opinion about how the rule of law fits into the interminable debate between legal positivism and natural law theory over the question of what law is. Paradoxically, the rule of law has been associated with both adversaries in this debate — with positivism because of the 'formal-procedural' character of the rule of law and with natural law theory because the rule of law appears to offer an independent moral standard of legality.[3] The rule of law has also been the target of bitter attacks in recent years — sometimes criticized as a mystification of law, sometimes openly renounced in favor of a vision of an extra-legal method of social cohesion. It is also obvious that such expressions as 'the rule of law,' 'the empire of law,' 'a government of laws and not of men' and the like, have been used with different meanings in the context of different theories and disputes.

The fortunes of the rule of law in the twentieth century were rough, and the various debates and their relationship to one another complicated. These debates took place on and off in several languages throughout the first half of the twentieth century in England, continental Europe and the United States. A variety of basic issues in political theory were drawn into these debates, including issues about the foundation and legitimacy of the state, the nature of sovereignty, the role of government, the liberty of the individual, the relation of law to justice, and the obligation to obey law. These debates also constitute one of the contexts in which a variety of revisionary interpretations of the ancient–modern polarity took place, and the adjective 'liberal' came to be used to qualify civilization or society as a whole and not merely a political party or a particular school of thought. It is also one of the contexts in which Thomas Hobbes came to be reconsidered and rehabilitated as indispensable to understanding the modern state and modern political thought.

Michael Oakeshott's discussion of law in *On Human Conduct* and 'The Rule of Law' invites examination in relation to these debates. Oakeshott alludes to aspects of these various debates at several points. He refers (favorably) to the '"inner morality" of a legal system' (*OHC*, 153), an expression Lon Fuller coined in his dispute with

---

[3] See the controversy over the interpretation of Lon Fuller's principles of legality as both procedural principles and natural law, a controversy that has only intensified in jurisprudence as time has passed.

H.L.A. Hart and legal positivism over the question whether the rule of law provides an independent moral standard of legality. Oakeshott also alludes to Hans Kelsen in several places, as for example when he mentions the idea of law 'governing its own creation' (*OH*, 139), a famous Kelsenian formula,[4] which was central to the dispute in Weimar jurisprudence over the modern trinity sovereignty, law, state. Oakeshott also invokes the famous emblem of natural law theory '*lex injusta non est lex*' which figures in almost every recent dispute about the idea of law (although it should be noted that the Latin sentence given in modern discussions is not an exact quotation from the Latin of Augustine or Aquinas).

A full-scale study of Oakeshott's legal philosophy might welcome the opportunity to see what happens when Oakeshott's writings are examined in relation to the recurrent twentieth century debates over the rule of law, both in continental Europe and in the English speaking world. (One potential advantage of this approach is the help it might give in identifying the problem-context that mediated Oakeshott's transition in political theory from his early neo-Hegelianism to his later emphasis on Hobbes.) In any case, some limited attempts have been made in this direction, and Oakeshott's views about the rule of law have been compared to those of several other thinkers. In this connection, some readers have been induced to associate his conception of the rule of law with legal positivism because of the so-called 'content-independent' and 'formal-procedural' character of his conception.[5] Perhaps Oakeshott himself tends to encourage such an interpretation in that he repeatedly speaks in a critical voice about natural law ideas,[6] and again by the remark that the 'vision' of a state ruled by law 'hovers over the reflections of many so-called "positivist" modern jurists' (*OH*, 162).

---

[4] See Hans Kelsen, *Introduction to Problems of Legal Theory* (Oxford: Oxford Univ. Press, 1992), a translation of *Reine Rechtslehre* (1934). See also the allusion to Kelsen (*OHC*, 137): '*lex* necessarily sets its own jurisdiction,' and Oakeshott's statement that 'Hans Kelsen, for example, has shown how the concept of the state may be reduced to that of law, and I think he has shown it fairly satisfactorily,' in *Religion, Politics and the Moral Life*, ed. Timothy Fuller (New Haven: Yale Univ. Press, 1993), 131. Hereafter: *RPML*.

[5] See Ronald Cass, *The Rule of Law in America* (Baltimore: Johns Hopkins Univ. Press, 2001), 1, 154 n. 2. Cass cites Oakeshott's conception of the rule of law as 'starkly positivist' and classifies him under this category with Hart, Hobbes, and Holmes. See also, D. Neil MacCormick, 'Spontaneous Order and the Rule of Law: Some Problems,' *Ratio Juris* 2 (March 1989): 41-54.

[6] Cf. *OHC*, 230; and 'The Rule of Law' (*OH* 150).

An historical inquiry into Oakeshott's legal philosophy in relation to twentieth century legal thought might turn out to be illuminating — and not only for what it says about Oakeshott. However, such a large-scale inquiry can hardly be undertaken here. This paper must be restricted in scope and will therefore concentrate on Oakeshott's discussions of law in *On Human Conduct* and 'The Rule of Law.' The following analysis will, however, take up the positivist interpretation of Oakeshott. Although this interpretation cannot stand up to a careful scrutiny of Oakeshott's writings, nevertheless, to follow it out will help to lay bare Oakeshott's distinctive views and will also help to bring to light an alteration or supplement to his teaching that Oakeshott introduced into 'The Rule of Law,' differentiating it from *On Human Conduct*. This supplement does not appear to have been recognized in published work on Oakeshott, and although it does not amount to a fundamental change of thought on Oakeshott's part, it will prove to be crucial to the interpretation of his legal thought because it has to do with the classical dispositive question of legal philosophy, the question of the status of unjust law.

The following analysis of Oakeshott's legal thought will proceed in a straightforward manner. The initial purpose will be to establish what Oakeshott's treatments of law in *On Human Conduct* and in 'The Rule of Law' share in common. This procedure will set the stage for identifying the supplement which Oakeshott introduced into 'The Rule of Law' and so in turn provide a perspective on some of the main issues posed by Oakeshott's legal thought.

A Breakdown of Oakeshott on Law

There are two main themes about law running through both *On Human Conduct* and 'The Rule of Law.' The first is the theme of law as authoritative utterance: law as that which is promulgated as law by sovereign authority. The second is the theme of the rule of law as an exclusive species of governance: rule by general, impersonal, and non-instrumental rules of conduct.

The relation between these two themes raises an obvious question. If law is authoritative utterance, then law consists of the entire pool of prescriptions promulgated by sovereign authority under the banner of 'law,' and the rule of law, taken literally, would seem to mean rule by all those prescriptions and by no others. But if the rule of law is conceived to be rule by general non-instrumental precepts of conduct, then the laws integral to rule by law consist at best only of a circumscribed segment of the prescriptions laid down as law by sovereign authority and not everything in 'the heterogeneous collection of rules and rule-like instructions' that pass as law in actual states (*OHC*, 128).

The two principal themes running through Oakeshott's account of law in both texts yield two distinct perspectives on law, with no apparent necessary connection between them. The question thus arises, how do or how can these two themes go together coherently within the same theoretical perspective? If a satisfactory response is to be provided to this question, it must begin with a brief examination of each theme, more precisely by recovering the line of reasoning by which Oakeshott arrived at each of them.

Oakeshott's point of departure in his account of law is crucial to both themes. It is 'epistemological': to be ruled by law, an intelligent agent, in contrast to a non-intelligent entity, must 'know what the laws are' (*OH*, 137). To be ruled by law requires a certain kind of knowledge accessible to those who are to be ruled by it, and for Oakeshott, what is essential to this knowledge is authority. To know that a requirement is law is to know two things about it: that it has been promulgated as law by an author and that this author has the authority to enact law.

This first theme connecting law to authority is explicit in both *On Human Conduct* and 'The Rule of Law,' with Oakeshott presenting his views primarily by means of a series of contrasts. In *On Human Conduct*, Oakeshott distinguishes the authority of law from the desirability of what it prescribes (*OHC*, 148-9), and also from liability to a penalty for non-compliance (*OHC*, 149, 192). These distinctions call for a certain level of institutional differentiation, including impersonal offices and authoritative procedures for enacting and promulgating law (*OHC*, 130, 138). Again, in 'The Rule of Law,' Oakeshott states that 'a law...to be recognized as law...must have ascertainable authority'(*OH*, 138-9), and he distinguishes the authority of law from the desirability of its content and from liability to punishment, which are 'extrinsic'(*OH*, 147). At the outset of 'The Rule of Law,' Oakeshott turns attention to the distinction between legal relation and moral relation. This distinction is specified not in terms of such polarities as changeable/unchangeable or conventional/natural, but rather by reference to the presence or absence of an institutional office and procedure for determining and declaring what the rules of the relation are.

The connection between law and authority is a theme prominent in both texts, and what should be noted here is the kind of argument Oakeshott is employing. This argument is concerned to specify the conditions under which it is possible for intelligent agents to know the same law and therefore associate together in the same legal community. Unless the claim that a rule makes to be observed can be established apart from an assessment of the content of what it requires, the agents to whom it is addressed will be placed in the position of having to make their response to the rule conditional on their own judgments of either the value of the rule or the risk of non-compliance. Agents will have no option except to rely on their own judgment, so that it will be possible for them to have the same law only if there happens to be a convergence of judgment. Each will have to judge the rule rather than judge according to the rule, and reach the same conclusion about the merits of the rule.

Sovereign authority makes it possible for intelligent agents with divergent opinions about law and justice to have the same law, 'of evoking the acceptance of all *cives* without exception' (*OHC*, 154).

This kind of argument joining law to authority and severing law from content–oriented judgment provides the perspective in which Oakeshott takes up and dismisses 'intellectual excursions conducted in the vocabulary of natural law' (*OH*, 159; cf. *OHC*, 230). Oakeshott construed natural law according to the vertical model that dominates recent discussion. Natural law is conceived as a 'higher law' (*OH*, 155), hierarchical and controlling over ordinary man-made law, and Oakeshott proceeds to criticize this higher law notion on the grounds that it fails to satisfy the epistemic requirement that law must be known in order to provide guidance to an intelligent agent. The fact that the content of this higher law consists of universal principles of natural justice or of natural reason cannot make it law since law requires a lawgiver: 'mere rationality or wisdom will not do' (*OHC*, 153). On the other hand, if this higher law is furnished with a lawgiver by being situated in a theological framework, it still cannot satisfy the epistemic requirement because it is not possible to know the precepts promulgated by divine authority. The end result of this criticism is that natural law conceived as a higher law is incoherent: if it is natural, it is not law, and if it is law, it is not natural.

This particular challenge to natural law, centered on the question of its status as law, has a long history which arguably goes back to ancient Greece and which was certainly prominent in legal philosophy from Aquinas to Grotius. For Oakeshott, this challenge to natural law as law crystallized in Hobbes because Hobbes staged the issue and its implications in the starkest possible fashion. Thus in 'The Rule of Law,' Oakeshott introduces Hobbes into his unfolding argument precisely at the point where Oakeshott turns attention to natural law, and Oakeshott goes on to associate his own criticism of natural law with that of Hobbes. Oakeshott states that for Hobbes 'the rule of law requires a known and authentic legislator' (*OH*, 150) and that consequently, for Hobbes, 'this *lex naturalis* turns out not to be composed of genuine law capable of imposing obligations' (*OH*, 150). Natural law cannot, then, provide intelligent agents with a known law that they can share, and the result must be that unless they acknowledge a sovereign authority, they will be 'persons devoid of obligations' (*OH*, 150) and reduced to an 'unconditional state of affairs' (*OH*, 158). It may be noted that this interpretation of Hobbes on the laws of nature in 'The Rule of Law' accords with Oakeshott's scholarship on Hobbes in *Hobbes On Civil Association*, where it is elaborated in detail, especially in 'The Moral Life in the Writings of Thomas Hobbes.'[7]

The first theme in Oakeshott's treatment of law yields a particular criticism of 'intellectual excursions conducted in the vocabulary of natural law.' Two points about Oakeshott's approach need to be mentioned at this juncture.

First, the expression 'natural law' is notoriously controversial and the central tenets of so-called 'natural law theory' have long been and continue to be a matter of dispute. Even today, among the various protagonists of natural law, there are deep disagreements, not the least on the question of the status of natural law as law. Accordingly, it should be kept in mind that the target of Oakeshott's (Hobbesian) criticism of natural law is one particular collocation of nature with law (the vertical model of natural law as a higher law); that the expressions 'natural law,' '*jus naturale*,' '*lex naturalis*,' and the like have been associated with a variety of other possibilities; that even the particular criticism Oakeshott levels against natural law as a higher law is a limited criticism; that what it shows is that if

---

[7]   Oakeshott, *Hobbes on Civil Association* (Indianapolis: Liberty Fund, 2000). Hereafter: *HCA*.

there is to be any limitation on law as something promulgated by sovereign authority which is consistent with the epistemic requirement of a known law, this limit cannot be conceptualized as a higher law but must be conceptualized in some other way. The long history of natural law thinking going back to the ancient Greeks has always proved to be a fertile source of ideas, and without further argument, Oakeshott's particular criticism of natural law should not be assumed to rule out the possibility of a non-conventional component of legal order understood in some other fashion.

Second, Oakeshott's analysis of law is, up to this point, consistent with legal positivism. Legal positivism may here be understood in terms of two connected claims: first, the 'separatist thesis' that the rules that count as law in a society can be identified apart from a moral assessment of their content; and second, the 'source thesis' that the criterion of identification is derivation from authority. Oakeshott, of course, does not employ the language of contemporary analytical jurisprudence (e.g., the 'separatist thesis' or even 'positive law'). But he does maintain that law is to be identified by its derivation from authority and that the authority of a rule is not conditional on an assessment of its content. This is consistent with the two basic claims of positivism. But then again, up to this point, classic natural law theory, as presented, for example, in the writings of Cicero and Aquinas, can also be said to be consistent with legal positivism in that promulgation by authority is explicitly included in the account of law that they give.[8] What distinguishes natural law theory — or the criticism of legal positivism — is not the denial of promulgation by authority as essential to law, but rather the contention that promulgation by authority is not sufficient, that something more is required, and that flagrant violation of this additional factor can deprive a set of human arrangements of their lawfulness. The question is: what more?

The preceding considerations bring this discussion to the second theme in Oakeshott's treatment of law, which does indeed involve a certain kind of limitation on law as a manifestation of sovereign authority. For although Oakeshott holds that law is what is promulgated by authority, he does not go on to equate the rule of law with rule by the entire medley of demands announced as law. Oakeshott presents the rule of law as an exclusive species of rule in which the term 'law' is to be understood to refer to a particular type of prescrip-

---

[8]   Cf. Cicero, *De Legibus*, and Aquinas, *Summa Theologica* 1.2.90.3-4.

tion, namely general non-instrumental rules of human conduct. Accordingly, promulgation by authority, although a necessary condition, is not a sufficient condition of the rule of law for Oakeshott, and accordingly the law issued by authority is not coextensive with the law integral to the rule of law.

This second theme is also prominent in both *On Human Conduct* and 'The Rule of Law,' and receives expression in several ways. In 'The Rule of Law,' Oakeshott explicitly defines the rule of law in terms of non-instrumentality. 'The expression "the rule of law," taken precisely, stands for a mode of moral association exclusively in terms of the recognition of the authority of known, non-instrumental rules (that is, laws) which impose obligations to subscribe to adverbial conditions in the performance of the self-chosen actions of all who fall within their jurisdiction' (*OH*, 136). This definition evidently restricts the pool of promulgated laws that qualify as manifestations of the rule of law to a subset of the pool. As far as *On Human Conduct* is concerned, the non-instrumentality theme pervades the second and third parts. The dichotomy between civil association and enterprise association, together with the distinction between non-instrumental rules of conduct and commands to assignable persons to perform specific actions, are central to Oakeshott's unfolding argument. Oakeshott's interpretation of actual states as ambiguous relationships between their members depends on these dichotomies.[9]

Oakeshott also finds it helpful to have at his disposal an invented vocabulary to convey this second theme. In *On Human Conduct* he maintains that the word 'law' is ambiguous, and so he crafts a special term '*lex*' to pick out the subset of laws promulgated by authority that are general non-instrumental rules, expressly giving as his reason 'so that they may not be confused with the heterogeneous collection of rules and rule-like instructions, instruments, provisions, etc. which constitute the conditions of those ambiguous associations we call states' (*OHC*, 128).

There is another component of this second theme regarding the rule of law shared by both texts, which Oakeshott formulates in various ways. In 'The Rule of Law,' he speaks of 'the formal principles inherent in the character of *lex*' (*OH*, 159), 'the *jus* inherent in genuine law '(*OH*, 159), 'considerations that are in fact inherent in the notion,

---

[9]   *OHC*, 128; see also, *OHC*, 152-3, 181, 187, and 201 on the ambiguity of the word 'law.'

not of a just law, but of law itself' (*OH*, 140), and 'conditions which distinguish a legal order'(*OH*, 140). In *On Human Conduct*, he speaks of 'a justice…which is inherent in *respublica*' (*OHC*, 153), 'all that may be called the "inner morality" of a legal system'(*OHC*, 153 n. 1), and simply 'considerations of *lex*'(*OHC*, 138).

Oakeshott also provides brief lists of these principles in 'The Rule of Law' and *On Human Conduct*, and the content of these lists should be noted. In *On Human Conduct*, the most extensive enumeration occurs at page 153 in the course of his account of civil authority. Oakeshott specifies 'the quality of legal subjects; rules not arbitrary, secret, retroactive or awards to interests; the independence of judicial proceedings (i.e., all claimants or prosecutors, like defendants, are litigants); no so-called "public" or "quasi-public" enterprise or corporation exempt from common liability for wrong; no offence without specific prescription; no penalty without specific offence; no disability or refusal of recognition without established inadequacy of subscription; no outlawry, etc.' This list is not intended to be exhaustive, and elsewhere in *On Human Conduct*, Oakeshott mentions some other items (*OHC*, 128, 137, 230).

In 'The Rule of Law,' the most extensive enumeration occurs at page 140 in the course of an analysis of the meaning of justice and injustice in relation to law. Here Oakeshott names 'rules not secret or retrospective, no obligations save those imposed by law, all associates equally and without exception subject to the obligations imposed by law, no outlawry, and so on.' Elsewhere in 'The Rule of Law' Oakeshott once again mentions some other items (*OH*, 159).

So far then, Oakeshott's account of the rule of law in both texts includes the notion of 'formal principles inherent in the character of *lex*,' and the content of the lists of these principles is similar. Nevertheless, it is here in the discussion surrounding the presentation of these lists that a limited difference appears between *On Human Conduct* and 'The Rule of Law,' and Oakeshott introduces a supplement into his treatment of law. In *On Human Conduct*, he confines himself to speaking of these formal principles as 'inherent' in law as *lex*. But in 'The Rule of Law' he goes further, and in two separate passages (*OH*, 140, 159), he elaborates on the meaning of the idea of law as involving inherent principles as well as authoritative promulgation.[10]

---

[10] Cf. 'The Rule of Law' (OH, 139 n. 4): 'A tyrant . . . does not make genuine law.'

These two passages in 'The Rule of Law' are complex and contain some surprises, and although what Oakeshott says in these two passages may be implicit in the legal philosophy presented in *On Human Conduct*, the two elaborations that he presents in 'The Rule of Law' are worth examining on their own. The two passages will therefore initially be considered separately.

The first passage, in 'The Rule of Law', runs as follows:

> there are some considerations that are often and understandably identified as considerations of *jus* but are in fact inherent in the notion, not of a just law, but of law itself. They are conditions which distinguish a legal order and in default of which whatever purports to be a legal order is not what it purports to be. (*OH*, 140)

Oakeshott then proceeds to provide a list of some of these conditions (previously quoted), adding in conclusion that 'it is only in respect of these considerations and their like that it may perhaps be said that *lex injusta non est lex.*'

Oakeshott's choice of words here is unusual, and a peculiar locution is positioned at the center of this statement: 'in default of which whatever purports to be a legal order is not what it purports to be.' First, there is 'purports', which is to put forward, express a claim, or posit, but not necessarily to achieve, where the purporting agent is sovereign authority and what is purported is a legal order because the rules of conduct that count as law and therefore regulate the relations between those who fall within the jurisdiction of this law are the rules posited as law. Second, there is 'default,' an exceptional word designed to attract attention. The *OED* gives for 'default': 'failure in performance,' adding 'in law, failure to perform some legal requirement or obligation, especially failure (on the part of a defendant) to attend in a court.' Default is, then, apparently, failure to perform on the part of the sovereign and the performance failed at is failure to make known in advance the rules that are to be observed as law and/or to stick to these laws when it comes to the application of law to specific cases, as for example, in imposing punishment without crime, or in attributing offense without violation of antecedent law, or in a declaration of outlawry which deprives those who are outlawed of their status as juridical persons within the legal order, so that conduct toward them which had been previously prohibited by law becomes permissible. And so, third, 'what purports to be a legal order is not what it purports to be' in so far as a gulf opens up between the law purported to intelligent agents and the law to which they are held to be answerable. Thus the difficulty about law to which Oakeshott is calling attention in this distinctive locution is the possibility of extra-legal rule that is nevertheless carried out under the name of law.

In this unusual formulation, Oakeshott is undoubtedly threading his way through a thicket of issues that impinge on the problem he is addressing. There are philosophical issues that have been ceaselessly raised in the long-running dispute over the thought-image of 'law that is not really law,' '*lex* that is not *lex*.' And there are practical questions about the implications for moral and political conduct of the judgment 'law/not law'. In this latter respect, Oakeshott at 'The Rule of Law,' page 140, is not merely subdued but silent. There is no mention of the question of the obligation to obey law, of the loss of authority, of the nullity of law, or the responsibility of a judge confronted by '*unrecht*.' These are matters that other legal theorists might have been waiting anxiously for the opportunity to inject into their treatment of law precisely at this point, but that Oakeshott allows to remain undiscussed. Perhaps this silence may be attributed to Oakeshott's general commitment to the distinction between philosophy and practice. But perhaps it may also be attributed to his more specific effort to identify and reconfigure the issue at stake in the problem of 'law/not law' without incurring the distractions that inevitably arise when the legal theorist comes out swinging on practical issues that are complicated and contentious in their own right. In any case, there are several features of the distinctive perspective on law expressed at 'The Rule of Law,' page 140 that deserve to be noted here.

First and foremost, there is the concept of 'legal order' which constitutes the decisive element in the perspective presented there. The concept of legal order operative at 'The Rule of Law,' page 140, is made up of two components: laws and formal principles inherent in *lex*, i.e., the rules enacted as law plus the principles governing the form and promulgation of these rules (public not secret, prospective not retroactive, general not particular) and the principles governing their application to particular cases (no offense without law, no sanction without offense, no privileges, etc.). Thus attention has been shifted by Oakeshott from the initial question in his treatment of law, how to 'know what the laws are' and distinguish them from norms that do not qualify as law, to the question, how to recognize a legal order and distinguish it from the negation of legal order. And while

Oakeshott's response to the first question is in terms of derivation from authority, his response to the second is in terms of coherence in the legal experience of an intelligent agent seeking 'to know what the laws are' between the law as posited and the law in force. 'What has to be known or ascertainable is not only *lex* as a system of general considerations to be subscribed to in choosing actions, but what will count as an adequate or acceptable subscription in a contingent situation…In short, it belongs to the character of *cives*…to be related as suitors to a judicial court' (*OHC*, 130-1).

Legal order is made up of two components, and this duality in effect allows the categories conventional/non-conventional to reenter legal philosophy. Specifically, the formal principles inherent in legal order are non-conventional in the sense that they are not themselves the creation of authority. The principles governing the promulgation and application of law do not acquire their standing as inhering in legal order because enacted as principles by authority. What sovereign authority determines is which rules count as law, but not which principles qualify as 'inherent in the notion…of law itself.' Oakeshott's restricted use of the vocabulary of authority should be noted here. The words 'authentic,' 'authorized,' 'authoritative,' etc., are prominent wherever Oakeshott discusses law. But these words have a restricted scope in his writings, and are used only of laws and not of principles because principles, in contrast to laws, do not qualify as integral to legal order as the result of an originary deed of enactment.

This dualistic notion of legal order allows Oakeshott to rework the question of the relation of law to justice. More precisely, it enables him to disambiguate two distinct issues embedded in this question. The first, which Oakeshott categorizes as 'extrinsic,' is centered on the first component of legal order, the particular laws issued by authority, and is concerned with the justice or morality of the content of these laws. The second, which is categorized as 'intrinsic,' is centered on the entire legal order and is therefore concerned with the consistency/inconsistency in which the posited law stands to the formal principles of law, that is with the 'performance' by a sovereign government of its own law. From this standpoint, Oakeshott can go on, at the end of the quoted excerpt from 'The Rule of Law,' page 140, to suggest a reinterpretation of the emblematic expression of natural law theory, '*lex injusta non est lex,*' assimilating it to his own notion of a legal order. '*Lex injusta*' that is 'non-*lex*' is therefore to be understood by reference to the gulf that may open up between the purported law and the formal principles of law, rather than by reference to the injustice of the content of positive law, which is the standard view of natural law theory in recent legal thought. The end-result is that Oakeshott does not speak the magic words 'law that is not really law' or '*lex* that is not *lex*,' but instead 'whatever purports to be a legal order is not what it purports to be.'

This same notion of a legal order provides the framework for Oakeshott's approach to what he calls 'the common expression,' 'the rule of law.' That expression is indeed now in circulation in public speech, where it has two aspects: the idea that only the prescriptions enacted as law should rule and the idea that no one is exempt from this rule, neither government nor governed. The puzzle this dualism has always generated is how it is possible to conceive sovereign authority as at once the sole source of law and yet as subject to law. The dualistic notion of a legal order held by Oakeshott furnishes him with a response to this puzzle, as exemplified by 'The Rule of Law,' page 140. If legal order comprehends formal principles governing the promulgation of law and the application of law to specific cases, and these principles are not themselves established by authoritative enactment, then it becomes possible to reach the idea of the author of law as also subject to law: 'all associates equally and without exception subject to the obligations imposed by law.'[11]

The preceding remarks on Oakeshott's conception of a legal order may leave some questions unaddressed. But before going any further, the second passage in 'The Rule of Law,' which also contains a supplement to Oakeshott's treatment of law, needs to be considered.

The second passage at page 159 is unexpected because it enlists Hobbes' perspective on a legal order delineated at 'The Rule of Law,' page 140. More precisely, it is unexpected because it gives Hobbes' laws of nature a new lease on life and draws natural law back into Oakeshott's legal philosophy in a novel way.

The relevant passage, at 'The Rule of Law' page 159, breaks into a lengthy analysis of different possible meanings that might be

[11]   In his lucid account of Oakeshott's philosophy, Terry Nardin states (of Oakeshott), 'The rule of law is a mode of association grounded on recognition of the authority of laws' — a valid statement as long as 'recognition of the authority of laws' is understood to extend to recognition of law by government in the form of adherence to its own law, i.e., adherence to the formal principles of law. See his, *The Philosophy of Michael Oakeshott* (University Park, PA: Pennsylvania State Univ. Press, 2001), 209.

imputed to natural law, *lex naturalis, jus naturale,* etc. in Hobbes' writings, in order to offer the following interpretation:

> And secondly, on inspection it transpires that these maxims of rational con-
> duct are not independent principles which, if followed by legislators, would
> endow their laws with a quality of 'justice'; they are no more than an analytic
> break-down of the intrinsic character of law, what I have called the *jus* inher-
> ent in genuine law which distinguishes it from a command addressed to an
> assignable agent or a managerial instruction concerned with the promotion
> of interests. Thus, in spite of these intellectual excursions conducted in the
> vocabulary of 'natural law', the only 'justice' the rule of law can accommo-
> date is faithfulness to the formal principles inherent in the character of *lex*:
> non-instrumentality, indifference to persons and interests, the exclusion of
> privelege and outlawry, and so on. (*OH*, 159)

This passage, containing Oakeshott's last published discussion of Hobbes, is a startling revision in his interpretation of what natural law is all about in and for Hobbes — not only when compared to Oakeshott's discussions of Hobbes in *On Human Conduct* and 'The Rule of Law,' but also when compared to *Hobbes On Civil Association*, especially 'The Moral Life in the Writings of Thomas Hobbes,' where Oakeshott provides a critical analysis of various modern interpreta-tions of Hobbes' teaching on natural law, but never mentions the interpretation advanced in the preceding quotation from 'The Rule of Law.' Initially, as seen earlier in this paper, natural law was con-strued on the vertical model of a higher law whose function is to pro-vide standards for judging the content of man-made laws; and Oakeshott then proceeded to criticize this model (in an argument associated with Hobbes) on the grounds that it could not satisfy the epistemic requirement of furnishing a known law. Now, however, in this revisionary interpretation at 'The Rule of Law,' page 159, the laws of nature in Hobbes are construed as 'an analytic break-down of the intrinsic character of law,' identified with 'the formal princi-ples inherent in the character of *lex*,' and then employed to distin-guish 'genuine law' from another form of governance.

What is going on in this passage is not easy to characterize in a sin-gular fashion. Is Oakeshott assimilating Hobbes' theory of law, or at any rate a particular strain of Hobbes' theory, to his own perspective on legal order as set out most sharply at 'The Rule of Law,' page 140, and/or is Oakeshott seeking to call attention to a neglected compo-nent of Hobbes' theory? Something can be said in support of both possibilities, or some combination of them. On the one hand, Oakeshott is quite explicit at 'The Rule of Law,' page 159, in referring back to 'what I have called the *jus* inherent in genuine law,' and so he proceeds again to provide a short list of the formal principles inherent in law similar to the lists provided in other places in his writings. These statements by Oakeshott would seem to equate what he calls formal principles of law with what Hobbes calls (uncertainly) the laws of nature, which has the effect of restoring these so-called laws of nature to a critical position within civil society as standards for assessing the performance of civil sovereignty. This feat is accomplished by relocating the zone in which the laws of nature remain operative within civil society from standards for evaluating the content of the laws issued by sovereign authority to principles governing the promulgation and application of law to particular cases. So it looks like Oakeshott is absorbing Hobbes into his own views. But now if, on the other hand, attention is turned to those sections of Hobbes' political treatises dealing with this same zone, e.g., *Leviathan*, chapters 26-8, on civil laws, crimes, and punishments, Hobbes can be found to be explicitly invoking the laws of nature at several places as precepts which the sovereign is supposed to observe, e.g., 'it is against the law of nature to punish the innocent,'[12] thus placing the laws of nature in the very zone in which Oakeshott sites them alias the formal principles of law. Thus, so far as these chapters of *Leviathan* are concerned, the laws of nature are operative inside of civil society; they are presented as standards of the activity of the sovereign power; they serve in this regard as standards not of the content of what the sovereign mandates as law but of the form of law and its application to specific cases; they are designed to proscribe the sovereign from acting outside his law; and they are natural in the sense that they are not made law by a legislative act. So at least in this segment of Hobbes' writings, his theory would appear to possess the same dualistic structure as Oakeshott's conception of a legal order: sovereign authority is the sole source of law and yet subject to independent principles as to the 'performance' of this law. The end result of this reconstruction is to impute to Hobbes the thesis that a civil society may be said to exist among some collection of human beings only if two distinct conditions are met: these humans acknowledge the authority of a sovereign government and this government rules them by law in the manner indicated.

---

[12]   Thomas Hobbes, *Leviathan*, ed. Oakeshott (Oxford: Basil Blackwell, 1955), 181, in chap. 26.

Now there are obviously two sets of issues posed by 'The Rule of Law,' page 159, which should be distinguished. There are historical issues concerned with the validity of the interpretation of Hobbes sketched at page 159. It is beyond the scope of this paper to enter into this matter, other than to point out the unusual character of Oakeshott's interpretation of Hobbes' teaching on natural law at page 159, as compared not only to Oakeshott's earlier views but also to the variety of interpretations in recent scholarship, thus offering an interesting hypothesis for historical inquiry. Secondly, there are issues about the bearing of 'The Rule of Law,' page 159, on the interpretation of Oakeshott's own legal philosophy, and the main consideration here is the convergence of page 159 with page 140 as to the centrality of formal principles inherent in law for the notion of a legal order. So, in turn, Oakeshott is pointing to the same difficulty about law in both places: that a gulf can open up between the purported law and the manner in which government actually rules, and accordingly that the distinct kind of injustice to which a legal order is susceptible is failure to adhere to the principles inherent in law by resorting to extra-legal methods of rule.

To return to the principal contention of this analysis of Oakeshott's treatment of law: there is a basic convergence of thought between *On Human Conduct* and 'The Rule of Law'; but nevertheless the latter offers an elaboration centered on the connected themes of legal order, formal principles of law, and the 'intrinsic' kind of injustice to which law is vulnerable. If it is objected that this supplement is implicit or even present in *On Human Conduct*, there can be no serious quarrel with this claim since the main contention of this paper about 'The Rule of Law' has to do with its capacity to help define the essential features of Oakeshott's distinctive legal philosophy. If the study of *On Human Conduct* can accomplish the same purpose, this only goes to show the power of Oakeshott's writing. Moreover, it now becomes possible to see why his legal philosophy cannot be easily fitted into the agenda of contemporary analytical jurisprudence and identified with either legal positivism or natural law theory as the two mutually exclusive and jointly exhaustive forms of legal philosophy, as they are conceived in recent debate. Oakeshott has been interpreted as a legal positivist on the grounds that his conception of the rule of law is 'formal-procedural' and 'content-independent.' This interpretation can now be recognized to rest on the mistaken assumption that the only aspect of a legal order relevant to moral assessment as just/unjust is the content of the law and that therefore there is no job left over for the formal principles inherent in law to perform. A legal order, however, has two basic features, and consequently can go wrong in two different directions.

Oakeshott's legal philosophy is not, then, positivist inasmuch as the controlling theme of his treatment of law is the notion of legal order, comprising both laws and formal principles inherent in law, a dualistic notion that enables him to maintain that a set of human arrangements may not qualify as a legal order even if it contains posited law. This specific way of taking issue with the interpretation of Oakeshott as positivist does not mean that his approach to law can be easily identified with, or incorporated into, the natural law tradition, although some suggestions have been made about this possibility in the course of this paper.

Some Concluding Remarks on Law, Sovereignty, and State

The preceding section of this paper presents an interpretation of Oakeshott's treatment of law attuned to some major issues of recent legal philosophy. This concluding section will make a brief attempt to show the bearing of that interpretation on two connected themes developed in detail by Oakeshott in the second and third parts of *On Human Conduct* — the dichotomy between non-instrumental and instrumental rule and the analysis of the modern sovereign state as an ambiguous combination of civil and enterprise association. Oakeshott's legal philosophy offers a revealing perspective on these two themes.

First of all, the dualistic conception of a legal order that Oakeshott was shown to be working with suggests a determinant way of understanding the polarity non-instrumental/instrumental rule. This polarity has certainly proved to be contentious in the literature on Oakeshott, with various interpretations on offer, and arguments mounted to demonstrate the impossibility of sustaining the bifurcation of rule into two opposed types. The specific suggestion here is that the notion of non-instrumental rule may be construed as a way of expressing, in summary fashion, the idea of legal order, that is, what it means for a legal order to obtain between government and governed. The point can be roughly formulated as follows: if the prescriptions issued as authoritative law adhere to the principles governing the form of law (general, impersonal, public, etc.) and the principles governing the application of the law to particular cases (no sanction without crime, no outlawry, etc.), then the relation between government and governed cannot be an instrumental relationship. Law cannot take the form of a command to assignable persons to perform specific actions as means to ends set by those who rule. Conversely, if the formal principles of law do not mediate the ruler-ruled relation, then the injunctions posited as law will take the form of directions addressed to designated persons to carry out specific actions as means to the ends of those who issue the directions.

Perhaps the most graphic way in which this non-instrumental/instrumental dichotomy receives expression has to do with the formal principles governing the lawful use of force, e.g., no penalty without established legal offense, no outlawry, etc. Here, recourse to force is subordinated to law in the sense that there must be a prior legal offense committed by a person in violation of a general, antecedent, and public law, in order to legitimate the exercise of force. This requirement is strictly non-instrumental in that the use of force is solely justified by reference to a certain kind of conduct on the part of those who are subject to the law and cannot be justified by reference to any independent purpose of those who exercise force. (Cf. *justum bellum* understood as the extension of the rule of law into the field of international relations. *Justum bellum* is non-instrumental inasmuch as a declaration of war is lawful only if the enemy power commits a legal wrong and not because the declaring power has some independent goal to be achieved by going to war).

The prohibition on outlawry provides a vivid expression of the distinction at stake here. This prohibition appears on all of Oakeshott's lists of the principles inherent in law, and it has a long history, e.g., it may be found in Magna Carta. It is crucial to note what outlawry is and is not. Outlawry is not deportation or exclusion from the territory of a state. It is a total transformation in the legal status of the human who is outlawed, in which he is stripped of juridical personality and reduced to a condition of legal nullity, so that he exists from the point of view of the law only as a physical body and not as a bearer of personality, a condition compatible with his continued physical presence within state territory. Outlawry is delegalization, and the legal effect is removal from the protection of the law, in which force is subordinated to law, and thus banishment into a condition in which the use of force becomes permissible for any purpose. The polarity non-instrumental rule/instrumental rule corresponds to the polarity inside legal order/outside legal order.

The preceding remarks, although incomplete, lead into the second theme to be considered in this conclusion — Oakeshott's interpretation of the modern sovereign state as an ambiguous association. Again, his notion of legal order offers a distinctive perspective on this view of the state. As seen earlier in this paper, the concept of sovereignty is given an indispensable function in Oakeshott's treatment of law, since it proved essential to satisfy the epistemic requirement of providing intelligent agents with known laws and so making possible association together in the same legal order. Yet despite the indispensability of the concept of sovereignty to the definition of the state as an association in law, Oakeshott repeatedly insists that something is missing. The idea of the state as an association of those who acknowledge the same sovereign authority to give them a law that they can share is 'imperfectly specified' and 'a masterpiece of neutrality' (*OHC*, 232, 233). Now from the standpoint of his dualistic notion of legal order, it becomes possible to recognize that the conceptualization of the state at the level of sovereignty is 'imperfectly specified' because it leaves open the question whether the sovereign government adheres to the formal principles of law and so rules its subjects as juridical persons or departs from those principles and so rules extra-legally. The modern concept of the state is 'a masterpiece of neutrality' because association in recognition of sovereign authority is not necessarily association under the rule of law. And it is this imperfect specification that constitutes the opening through which modern doctrines of community as purposive entities in which the rule of law had no part to play could be superimposed on the state.

Part III

Oakeshott Today

9

Kenneth Minogue

Oakeshott: Rationalism Revisited

What 'platform of conditional understanding' does Oakeshott's essay 'Rationalism in Politics' occupy? Asking a question about an early writing in terms of a later version of the Oakeshottian vocabulary is appropriate here because this essay cannot quite be assigned either to philosophy or to the history of ideas. It has elements of the practical about it, and flashes of passion often strike the reader. Rationalism is referred to as an 'infection' and the whole work is unmistakably the diagnosis of something Oakeshott wishes were not there.

People, Samuel Johnson once remarked, need more often to be reminded than to be informed, and the business of a philosophical writer is to make us *realize* something already in one form or another grasped. This kind of writing, we might say, deals with 'realizables', things whose truth becomes evident as we think about them. This happens when we become self-conscious about something we had previously done or thought unreflectively. Getting to know a person often begins as a set of experiences, but some event may lead us to formulate a 'character' for that person, and as it happens Oakeshott did think that some things could be grasped as 'characters.' The thing he called 'rationalism' may thus be understood as delineating a 'character', something he performs, of course, with the most delicate footwork. Sometimes he talks about rationalism's 'character and pedigree' and elsewhere of its 'shape.' With Oakeshott, you seldom encounter anything as brutish as a trend, and you are certainly not encouraged to make a practical response. Yet rationalism is unmistakably presented as a problem, and indeed as practical.

He tells us that the rationalism that began to emerge in the early seventeenth century soon spread into politics and had become recognizably dominant in the nineteenth century. By the time of the Labour government of 1945-51 when Oakeshott was writing, it was ubiquitous, especially in politics. 'That all contemporary politics are deeply infected with Rationalism will be denied only by those who choose to give the infection another name,' he wrote.[1] In other words, however subtle and clever his treatment, he was in the business of 'social critique.' And the names other critics had invoked for what they all recognized as the same kind of phenomenon are indeed legion: some talking of scientism, others of technology, ideology, and even 'the colonization of the *Lebenswelt'*. Hayek talked of 'constructive rationalism.' Rationalism is very largely the same as these things, and it intersects with a variety of other phenomena that Oakeshott himself had discussed, or would later consider, such as the politics of perfection or the character of the anti-individual. Rationalism is the deliberate attempt to catch happiness. In a wiser tradition, writers recognized that happiness was not something to be pursued, but something that might, after patient waiting, drop into one's lap. The Rationalist is supremely the mono-modal bore targeted in *Experience and its Modes* for whom everything is really practical, including philosophy, poetry, history and especially science. Rationalism is merely the name given to this thing as possibly the most precise specification of the cast of mind whose features Oakeshott found both fascinating and repellent throughout his long life.

Further, the infection is progressive. It is 'of a kind which the passage of time must make more rather than less severe,' because it 'amounts to a corruption of the mind' (*RIP*, 36-7). Rationalism goes on entrenching the toxin — the fruitless hope that the latest plan or project will deal with the anomalies mostly resulting from the last big solution. Like Midas, who is doomed to encounter only what he has transformed, the rationalist is characteristically incapable of experiencing anything 'straight' because he turns everything he touches into a doctrine.

It is a further problem that 'a society which has embraced a rationalist idiom of politics will soon find itself either being steered to or

---

[1]   Oakeshott, 'Rationalism in Politics,' in *Rationalism in Politics and other essays, new and expanded edition*, ed. Timothy Fuller (Indianapolis: Liberty Press, 1991), 25. Hereafter: *RIP*.

drifting towards an exclusively rationalist form of education' (*RIP*, 37). Oakeshott's pessimism was merely reinforced by the fact that a common response even to his posing of the problem was the typically rationalist demand to be told what to do about it. The essay 'Rationalism in Politics' is thus a powerful account of the predicament of the West and one that points to continuing problems. It thus constitutes an invitation to consider the evolution of rationalism since 1947. That is clearly a tall order, and I shall merely make some remarks on three questions. I shall consider first education, which Oakeshott thought fundamental, then morality and religion, and finally I shall make one or two remarks about the current 'shape' of rationalism.

I

First, education, and my treatment will be unavoidably local, though not, I hope, untypical of what has been happening in other countries. Oakeshott disliked the Butler Act of 1944, which set up a system of education in which schools funded by the state were distinguished into grammar, secondary modern and technical. Here was legislation in which educational provision was rearranged so as to correspond to what were then thought to be the needs of the economy: the provision of managers, technicians, and workers. It very soon collided with another dominant socio-political ideal in the form of a demand that education should serve democracy. The Butler Act was a further step in the policy that subjected education to the will of a centralizing and masterful Ministry, but nothing compared to what was soon to happen. Butler's tripartism was condemned for reinforcing social division, and replaced, with appropriate legislative brutality, by 'comprehensivisation' in which pupils of all backgrounds and abilities were assigned to neighborhood schools irrespective of tested ability. Indeed, some attempt was made to balance in schools the distributions of A's, B's and C's in ability levels. The aim was to avoid the process of selecting the more academically educable pupils at the age of eleven by examination. It was also predicated on the belief that forcing middle class children with their supportive family life to learn alongside pupils without much interest in learning would raise the general level of culture. Like all plans, it had mixed results, but mostly bad, because the new plan collided with a fatal change in pedagogic theory.

Children were caught between the state imposing an administrative structure upon them, and their own teachers who in large numbers had picked up another version of rationalism. This was the belief, soon to dominate teaching colleges, that 'teaching' children by imparting knowledge to them was coercive and indoctrinating. Pupils should rather be allowed to respond to their own individual need for knowledge, and at their own pace. Teachers became 'resource persons.' The combination of this fashion with comprehensive reorganization of schools led to a collapse of authority and discipline in British schools. A new generation of illiterates began emerging from British schools. They were alienated and unemployable. It did not help that yet another moral and pedagogic fashion had removed corporal punishment and other forms of effective control from the disciplinary repertoire. Classrooms became remarkably 'inclusive,' but the silence necessary for learning was largely lost.

By the 1980s, the consequences of all these reforms were widely recognized as one more crisis in the grim narrative of twentieth century British education, but previous changes had been so institutionally brutal that it was hard to see what might improve things. An end to mixed ability teaching in some schools was merely palliative, but the Ministry of Education, forever growing fatter out of each crisis, soon came up with a solution: a succession of examinations at ages 7, 11, 16 and 18 would test whether pupils were learning anything. The original idea was for relatively casual tests as a specific against the dangers of teacher-induced ignorance, but the idea fell into the hands of experts. A new Education Act hundreds of pages long set out a whole new system that dotted the i's and crossed the t's of what should be taught. It did this by providing for a wholly new thing called a 'national curriculum.' The Continental practice by which Ministers could tell at any given moment what children of any age were doing in schools had long been a joke in England. In the 1980s, the laughter died on our lips.

Nor did the new system immediately produce a harvest of scholarly achievement. A new idea began to emerge: why not publicize how schools were faring in terms of exam results — what later came to be called 'naming and shaming.' Performance indicators were the things at the time, and educational authorities began publishing lists of how many exam results of such-and-such a level each school was achieving. It was hoped that this system would reveal which schools were 'adding value' to pupils, and which were failing in their task. The temptation to cheat about this, in one way or another, obviously became irresistible, and indeed in the most obvious way, some schools did. The main corruption resulting from the long domination of education by government was, however, the collapse of confidence in the tests themselves. Each year, it remarkably turned out, pupils were doing better and better, so that soon Britain was awash with pupils emerging from school with straight A's. Had Britain thus become a nursery of genius? Alas, no. Pupils were merely landing at the doors of universities with less preparation than ever before. They had to be given remedial training in the basics. And now to the rescue came the latest rationalist dodge: command pedagogy. The Minister of Education decreed that each day pupils should have a compulsory hour of maths and English, in one form or another.

British education thus constitutes a form of rationalism, as the irritable tendency to solve problems, in its most degenerative form. An activist government seeks to turn education into an instrument for achieving its own specific ends. It has no patience to wait while people respond to their situation in their own way. Things having an important though minor part in education are elevated into basics, and the whole experience is distorted. Beyond a certain point, those who learn how to pass examinations have merely mastered a narrow formula. They have been, as it were, trained, but not educated.

And that brings us to the conceptual question. What are the ideas that are fused with this decline? The key distinction is between education and training. You educate people, but you train dogs. Training is learning how to perform set tasks in an orderly way. It is largely unreflective, but it is much cheaper; drilling is quicker than discussion any time. Education has unpredictable consequences, but the consequence of specific forms of training are essentially predictable — that is their point. We move thus from education to training, from creativity to the formula. Now the concept underlying training is *power*. Once trained, you have the power to do whatever the training inculcates. In Britain from 1945 onwards (and to some extent earlier) the move has been from education to the pursuit of power, understood in a technological sense. It is a remarkable narrowing of culture to what governments imagine that society needs. Getting an education is currently taken to mean acquiring skills. A skill is the power to do something — what Oakeshott described as 'a training in technique, a training that is, in the half of knowledge which can be learnt from books when they are used as cribs' (*RIP*, 38). Scholars would be replaced by clever chaps who were masters of many if not quite all trades. And government responded to this new evolving insight into how to treat the young. The all-powerful Ministry became the Ministry of Education *and Skills*. We shall soon be able to drop off the 'education' bit.

II

Turning now to morality, we may first note Oakeshott's view that 'moral ideals are a sediment; they have significance only so long as they are suspended in a religious or social tradition, so long as they belong to a religious or a social life' (*RIP*, 41). Religion had been something with which Oakeshott had been deeply preoccupied in earlier days, but it is marginal to the rationalism essays, perhaps because he thought it a lost cause. We need, however, to give it some attention. Oakeshott was, of course, a skeptic, but religion was important to him, at the very least because it varied the tedious one-worldism of pseudo-scientific practicality.

Religion had long been under attack from a specific branch of rationalism, also called 'rationalism' and conspicuous in the early twentieth century in the operations of the 'rationalist press association.' Rationalists in this sense identified religion with superstition and repression. They juxtaposed active reason against supposedly passive revelation. Christianity has, as it were, 'italicized' certain events in sacred history, but rationalists deployed hermeneutics and history to bring the career of Jesus into line with everyday life. What had in Christian terms been identified as the 'Arian heresy' was now a conclusion of scientific history. Religion must be 'demystified'. Here is rationalism going about its business as a great leveler.

The issue is vital, at the very least in cultural terms, and to be clear about it we need to ask: 'What actually *is* religion?' More specifically, we can avoid abstraction by asking, 'What is a religious life?' The answer is that it consists of a practice and a set of rituals founded upon a set of beliefs (for Christianity, belief in the divine mission of Jesus as the son of God) and constituting a morality composed of the habits and attitudes available to believers. Religion is essentially social, and focused on some such institution as church, temple, mosque or synagogue (in the familiar cases). These institutions in turn depend, like all institutions, on recognizing the authority of priests, bishop, rabbi etc. Such a structure is the condition, and the indispensable condition, of piety, consolation, and mystical experiences.

The large question — not only for us, but for any form of liberalism — is whether religion can survive without social circumstances of this kind. In individual and family cases, of course, it certainly can, at least for a generation or two. But one can, I think, confidently say that Christian and other forms of religious belief encountering rationalist criticism will be lucky to escape alive. For consider Oakeshott's characterization of the rationalist:

> [T]he truth of an opinion and the 'rational' ground (not the use) of an institution is all that matters to him. Consequently much of his political activity consists in bringing the social, political, legal and institutional inheritance of his society before the tribunal of his intellect; and the rest is rational administration, 'reason' exercising an uncontrolled jurisdiction over the circumstances of the case.' (*RIP*, 8)

'Reason' here consists in the practical experience of the individual mitigated in some degree by a few popular ideas about science. As it happens, Christianity as a characteristically Western idea is founded upon truth claims. Some of these (such as those relating to Jesus and divine creation) are beyond the reach of rational experience, which can say nothing definitive about them; but many others (relating for example to cosmology, or the origins of life), which were added from the traditions of ancient times and taken as truth claims, clash directly with the current conclusions of science. Rationalist criteria for rational acceptance advance these views right to the center of the stage. To be religious is thus to be wrong-footed as endorsing an implausible cognitive competitor with science, rather than cultivating some specific civilizational practice. For the anti-religious rationalist, such a misunderstanding constitutes a refutation of Christianity, but even for the more cautious rationalist it first lures Christianity out into the arena of empirical explanation, and then forces upon it, at best, a tactical retreat into symbolism and metaphor. Issues of truth in this area turn out to be fatal in sustaining a morality with which they are connected in a highly complex way.

Much might be said about these difficult questions, but my concern must be limited to Oakeshott's characterization of rationalism, and the basic point seems to me to be rationalism's relentless drive towards monism. Oakeshott's European civilization is essentially pluralist, and it is pluralist in a variety of ways. One of these is the

dualism of sacred and secular, which is built into the very foundations of Christianity itself. It led to what has been called the 'de-
divinization' of the state.[2] Another is the Christian world juxtaposed
against the philosophy and mythology of classical times as these
were influentially revived at the Renaissance — what Matthew
Arnold called the Hebraic and Hellenistic strains in our thought.
And a further pluralism is built into Western thought in the manner
Oakeshott himself formalized as the various modes of experience,
and which turns up in the wider world as the gruesome simplicities
of 'science versus religion.'

In the name of a misplaced cognitive consistency, then, the rationalist reduces religion to a flavorless sub-philosophical ecumenism
and creates a secular world in which the mind responds according to
whatever resources it finds (largely journalistic as a rule) to a succession of crises and frustrations in a pursuit of happiness which lacks
even the elementary reflectiveness of the Epicurean.

III

If religion declines, can morality be far behind? About morality,
Oakeshott was especially pessimistic, because he thought that the
rationalist had won a victory that his opponent did not even recognize as a defeat. For Oakeshott, these words are a dramatic foray into
practice, and they deserve attention.

The morality of the rationalist consists in 'the self-conscious pursuit of moral ideals,' while 'the appropriate form of moral education
is by precept, by the presentation and explanation of moral principles' (RIP, 40). 'In morality as in everything else,' Oakeshott goes on,
'the Rationalist aims to begin by getting rid of inherited nescience
and then to fill the blank nothingness of an open mind with the items
of certain knowledge which he abstracts from his personal experience, and which he believes to be approved by the common "reason"
of mankind... unavoidably, the conduct of life, for him, is a jerky,
discontinuous affair, the solution of a stream of problems, the mastery of a succession of crises' (RIP, 40-1).

The problem with ideals is that they are external to the activity of
morality as a flow of sympathy animating our understanding of

---

[2]   Eric Voegelin, *The New Science of Politics* (Chicago: Univ. of Chicago Press,
      1952), esp. chap. 4.

what we ought to do.[3] In the jargon of a later time, Oakeshott is an 'internalist' rather than an 'externalist.' Ideas have been abstracted, and then detached from the flow of activity, leaving the moral agent confused about their place in the coherence of his life. Instead of the moral apprentice learning from those around him, as it were, he becomes a reasoner trying to fit abstract propositions into his world. Ideals, for Oakeshott, are useful probing devices with which philosophers might try to explain morality, but they cannot be used as instruments of moral conduct. The moral life is enmeshed in circumstances, and abstractions and circumstances cannot properly connect. They are the oil and water of the moral world.

The latter day reader of 'Rationalism in Politics' can only feel that what is now happening is rather worse than Oakeshott feared: it is the subversion of the entire understanding of morality in the name of social instrumentalism. Our sensibilities have so changed that 'right' and 'wrong' now have a dogmatic sound in the contemporary ear, and have often been replaced by 'socially acceptable' and 'socially unacceptable.' Moral education in family life now turns out to be 'social capital', in which conduct is judged purely in terms of whether it is instrumental to the current purposes of the state. The morality that once related individuals to each other now relates categories, as in the rise of the thing called 'political correctness' or what we might call the 'morality of identity.' The supposed imperfections of society have been formularized as a schedule of victims, and right conduct consists in the required treatment of these categories — often, indeed, it consists of little more than having the socially acceptable opinions on how they should be treated.

No less remarkable are the ways in which the new commendations and condemnations are being diffused. In eliciting the conservative disposition, Oakeshott had argued that the style of government most appropriate to this disposition would tolerate nothing beyond the enforcement of rules: '[I]t will not countenance government by suggestion or cajolery or by any other means but law; an avuncular Home Secretary or a threatening Chancellor of the Exchequer' ('On Being Conservative,' *RIP*, 433). In contemporary politics, suggestion and cajolery (along with a certain element of

---

[3]   William J. Bennett wrote, 'More than once I've been in schools when they are teaching a "virtue of the week." In one such school, the virtue of the week was honesty. There had been a test on honesty, and the teacher told me that she had had to prepare a second test because she had caught so many students cheating on the first.' *Imprimis* 32, no. 2 (February 2003).

menace) are everywhere.[4] Governments lavish large public relations budgets on everything from diet to how young men should conduct themselves as fathers. Oakeshott thought that moral education came by example, and he was thinking of the adults a child encountered and the exemplars encountered in history. Today the state itself commends and often tries to control the conduct of entertainers and sports champions as things called 'role models' for the young.

These developments are part of something implicit in rationalism from the beginning: its reduction of the variety of the world to a single world of understanding. And that world is to be increasingly animated by the state. The feminist slogan that the personal is the political is a license to treat the moral world as subordinate to the political. Sometimes this is mediated by the project of making society more democratic, meaning more in accordance with what people want, or say they want. Our moral admirations are never still, but they have been changed to an unusual extent in recent times. A movement identifying more and more responsibilities as due to the state has paralleled the increasing dominance of social utility. We have experienced a notable lurch towards emphasizing what might be called 'the compassionate virtues' to the exclusion of those that restrain human emotions.

All of this constitutes a corruption of the moral life, and one that abundantly justifies Oakeshott's view that rationalism in morals has been especially pernicious. The new corruptions of the moral life not only fail to recognize themselves as such, but are full of self-congratulation. Morality was once, they say, narrowly focused on the bedroom, but we have now brought it into the public square and the Cabinet Room.

IV

Rationalism, as Oakeshott presents it, is both a fashion and a doctrine, a cast of mind and a belief about knowledge. But rationalism in politics may be further illuminated by a distinction Oakeshott makes in other writings of the same period. It consists in abstracting from the flow of experience elements that are taken to be independent or

---

[4]   In Britain as I write, the Department of Trade and Industry has just published a glossy work of advice to young men about to become fathers. It is explicitly designed to counter the supposedly prevalent belief that only 'Mums matter.' Another government-backed project is urging teenagers to experiment with oral sex as part of a drive to cut rates of teenage pregnancy.

'independently premeditated.' It issues therefore in plans or projects that have become detached from human life. Oakeshott's argument has the same general character as Nietzsche analyzing morals genealogically as generating distinct agencies out of natural impulses, as when the phenomenon of lightning becomes 'lightning strikes.' Esperanto is a kind of dream in relation to peoples actually speaking and thinking in a language. The United Nations is an instrument for securing world peace divorced from the realization that power corrupts. And so on. In political rationalism, therefore, we find two complementary distortions.

The first results from a failure to recognize the many valuable things accumulated around us by the operation of a long tradition. It suppresses our understanding of these things. Recognizing the value of how we live now came easily to Oakeshott. When he talks of conversation he is thinking of the local pub, not Oscar Wilde at the Café de Paris. And it is a corollary of this first distortion that these unrecognized values will continue unchanged into the reformed era. Thus the provision of welfare to cover the hardships people might suffer is legislated on the assumption that they will continue to be prudent and look to the future and that they will continue to value family support. It hardly needs saying that many of them will not.

The second distortion results from overblown expectations about the benefits that will flow from the proposed change. And here again, the mistake is compounded by imagining that the proposal will have no effect upon the current structure of virtues. As Walter Bagehot once said, no reform can be judged in the same generation in which it was enacted. The history of the modern welfare state is an object lesson in how the acquisition of one benefit may be balanced by the disappearance of one or more virtues. A journalist called Hutber is said to have remarked that every reform makes things worse. This is why.

Such a rationalist structure of life corresponds, of course, to how individuals live now. Urban prosperity has us at the mercy of advertising in which we are offered a stream of chances packaged as images of happier times, so that we live from one unfulfilled promise to the next. The sentimental film 'Brief Encounter' has become an image of the kind of conflict many people face over and over again, sometimes solving it one way, sometime the other. The prospect of distant gold drew thousands of men to uproot themselves from their surroundings and take off for California in 1849. We may contrast this nervous instability with the (possibly fanciful) images of those rooted in a rural past dominated by powerful conventions, or alternatively people rooted in an equally determinate religious context. Society has always contained adventurers; only the modern world has created an entire society of adventurers. Those who can combine the sophistication of an Oakeshott with the stability of rootedness are very rare — and indeed Oakeshott himself was not always one of them.

He did, however, at the end of 'On Being a Conservative,' distinguish between the individual's taste for adventure and the propensity for rationalist politics, which may come from extending to the practice of government forms of conduct common in the individual world. For as Oakeshott wrote, in a puzzling sentence in *Rationalism in Politics*, the rationalist 'is something also of an individualist, finding it difficult to believe that anyone who can think honestly and clearly will think differently from himself' (*RIP*, 6). This is puzzling because such a characteristic sounds more like solipsism than individualism. And the passage from solipsism to megalomania is short. Totalitarian dictators have it as standard-issue psychology. Rulers identify their conclusions with social perfection, and 'from this politics of perfection springs the politics of uniformity; a scheme which does not recognize circumstance can have no place for variety' (*RIP*, 10).[5]

Ultimately, the evaluative difference between Oakeshott and the rationalist is how they located the discontents of their civilization. For Oakeshott, these discontents arose from the transitory character of human life. We are the children of contingency and we shall never grow up into eternity as we yearn (perhaps unrealistically) to do. We must simply come to terms with it, and that involves turning inward to discover the riches we actually possess. For the rationalist, however, discontent responds to the present arrangements of society and changing those arrangements is the project. Earthiness is in love with the transcendent and is futily trying to bring it down to earth.

---

[5] A distinguished professor of economics at the London School of Economics has (in March 2003) been delivering a lecture series arguing that the pursuit of happiness should be 'the prime purpose of public policy.'

10

F. Gerhard Wolmarans

Oakeshott's Characterization of 'Politics' in an African Context

Introduction

Most of the recent work done on Michael Oakeshott has been aimed at dissecting his mind and his ideas[1]. These works focus on the internal logic, essential nature, or the coherence of the understanding he presented us of the human condition and its relation to the political. The impetus behind this paper is slightly different, however. Though brief attention will be paid to the basic vision underlying Oakeshott's body of work, this paper is based on a need for a greater understanding of the political as it manifests and plays itself out on the African continent.

Michael Oakeshott as a political thinker was also critically concerned with the project of an enhanced understanding of the political, and although he never explicitly focused his discerning eye on the African continent, his contribution to our understanding of politics and the state is potentially of great value in the study of the African state. This paper is thus not aimed at an internal critique of

[1] In this regard the following recent works serve as examples: Wendell John Coats, Jr., *Oakeshott and His Contemporaries* (Selinsgrove, PA: Susquehanna Univ. Press, 2000); Steven A. Gerencser, *The Skeptic's Oakeshott* (NY: St. Martin's Press, 2000); Terry Nardin, *The Philosophy of Michael Oakeshott* (University Park, PA: Pennsylvania State Univ. Press, 2001); Roy Tseng, *The Sceptical Idealist: Michael Oakeshott as a Critic of the Enlightenment* (Thorverton: Imprint Academic, 2003).

Oakeshott's ideas, but rather at the consideration of his ideas within a new context, and thus hopefully at a more in-depth comprehension of African politics based on his insights. This paper asks the basic question: Is there anything that can be learned by Africa from Oakeshott's work on politics and government? Or to put it differently, what fresh insights and understanding about politics on the African continent can be gained by looking at it through the perspectives developed by Oakeshott? This paper will be limited to a consideration of two of Oakeshott's best-known views on politics and government, namely concrete politics as being rooted in a tradition of behavior, and his modal understanding of associations. Each will be outlined and then related to an African context.

Oakeshott's Dual Perspective

A prominent feature of his life's work is that Oakeshott was always engaged in considering the human condition from one of two standpoints. Either he was engaged with the way in which we as humans come to understand, or to reflectively imagine, the world in which we live, or he was trying to understand the interactions between human beings on a pragmatic level.[2] In the major work of the final phase of his life, *On Human Conduct*, he affirms this by making a distinction between two levels of engagement, namely those of 'understanding' and 'doing'.[3] Oakeshott thus considers the modern world in which we live from two distinct, though not completely unrelated viewpoints. We can call the one his philosophy of experience, and the other his philosophy of conduct *inter homines*. Linking the two is the idea of radical plurality present in both; in the philosophy of experience there exists plurality because of the fragmentation of knowledge into different spheres or modes, while his philosophy of conduct *inter homines* is largely built around the acknowledgement of the individualization of modern societies.

In Oakeshott's philosophy of experience he basically followed the neo-Kantian line according to which the pre-modern unified and interdependent system of knowledge has been fragmented in the modern world into various, often competing systems of knowledge.

---

[2] See Efraim Podoksik, *In Defence of Modernity: Vision and Philosophy in Michael Oakeshott* (Exeter: Imprint Academic, 2003), for a more comprehensive treatment of this dual perspective present in the work of Oakeshott.

[3] Oakeshott, *On Human Conduct* (Oxford: Clarendon Press, 1975), 130. Hereafter: *OHC*.

Oakeshott identifies four such, what he calls modes of experience; namely, science, history, poetry, and practice.[4] Each of these modes represents an independent and self-contained system of knowledge. He famously referred to these modes as 'voices' that participate in a conversation with one another in which each possesses a characteristic idiom irrelevant to the idioms of the other voices. Thus, the idea of the fragmentation of our way of understanding the world in which we live into several well-established spheres of knowledge forms the basis of Oakeshott's philosophy of experience. Though he accepts fragmentation, he resists the postmodern urge of rejecting any notion of objectivity in any sphere of knowledge. For him each of these spheres is self-contained and homogenous, while enclosing criteria of objectivity that cannot be divided further.

In Oakeshott's philosophy of conduct *inter homines* the focus is not on an intellectual adventure in understanding the world, as is the case in his philosophy of experience, but rather on the perplexing question of human relationships in society. His philosophy of conduct *inter homines* was the product of a long intellectual development and it only received its full articulation towards the end of his career in his work *On Human Conduct*. Oakeshott, however, attained fame as a political philosopher even before the publication of this work and thus for many years the study of his work focused on elements that did not necessarily form the central part of his philosophy. We can note, for example, how the focus on his earlier critique of rationalism led to various problematic interpretations of his thought, and resulted in him being portrayed as a mere conservative defender of tradition.

It would be difficult to speak of an Oakeshottian political philosophy in the narrow sense of the word, since for him 'politics' forms an integral part of the relationship between human beings in modern societies. Politics should thus be considered as a part of a more encompassing philosophy of society. According to Podoksik Oakeshott's thought follows in the line of the nineteenth century tra-

---

[4]   The mode of practice was a problematic mode to deal with. In later works 'practice' was reduced to utilitarian and ethical concerns, while the remaining abstract modes of science, history and poetry had to be defended against the assault of practical concerns, or as he called it against 'the deadliness of doing'. The emancipation of these modes from the controlling influence of practice is seen by Oakeshott as the key moment in the development of modern Western civilization.

dition of human studies[5] according to which questions of morality, laws and institutions were merely part of social theory as a whole in which the focus of the study is on the basic postulates of human relationships. Oakeshott himself pointed out that true political philosophy deals not with institutions but with humans.[6] Institutions should not be the focus, but rather the beliefs and habits of humans that gave rise to these institutions. For him the character of a state and government is intimately linked to the character of the individuals, morals, and society that make up such a state.

With these thoughts on the general tenets of Oakeshott's work as a point of departure, we can now turn our attention to a somewhat more detailed treatment of two of his characterizations of politics and its relation to, and usefulness within, the African context.

Politics and The Pursuit of Intimations in Traditional Knowledge

In his well-known and somewhat polemical essay entitled 'Political Education,' first delivered as his inaugural lecture at The London School of Economics, Oakeshott presents us with a very specific, yet at the same time broad-ranging, characterization of politics. He states that for him politics entails the 'activity of attending to the general arrangements of a set of people whom chance and choice have brought together' and that this activity is 'pre-eminent' in those communities or 'hereditary co-operative groups, many of them of ancient lineage, all of them aware of a past, a present, and a future, which we call "states".'[7] He goes on to state that this activity is generally not based on simply responding to instant desires (it is not an 'empirical activity'), nor can it merely be extrapolated from independently preconceived general principles ('ideology'), but that it springs 'from the existing traditions of behaviour' in the states. These traditions of behavior serve as a guide for the manner in which to attend to the general arrangements of the state. Political activity,

---

[5]   Others in this tradition or following in it would be Montesquieu, Hegel, Tocqueville, Weber, and Jouvenel.

[6]   See Podoksik, *In Defence of Modernity*, 130. Podoksik draws this point from Oakeshott's article 'The Cambridge School of Political Science' (1924). Unpublished at the time of Podoksik's study, this essay now appears in Luke O'Sullivan, ed. *What is History? and other essays* (Exeter: Imprint Academic, 2004). Hereafter. *WII*.

[7]   Oakeshott, *Rationalism in Politics and other essays, new and expanded edition*, ed. Timothy Fuller (Indianapolis: Liberty Press, 1991), 44. Hereafter: *RIP*.

thus, entails the exploration and pursuit of what is intimated, or hinted at, in those traditions of behavior (*RIP*, 56).

In emphasizing the importance of traditional knowledge for political activity, Oakeshott is countering the very prevalent notion that political activity can take its direction from a relatively few and simple ideas determined apart from, and before, the activity of politics. His criticism of this manner of thinking rests on an analysis of what he calls rationalism. Rationalism, for Oakeshott, is a mistaken view of knowledge and of the manner in which knowledge is acquired. He asserts that every actual human activity involves knowledge of two sorts. These two types of knowledge cannot exist separately, but they can be distinguished from one another because there exists some important differences between them (*RIP*, 12). On the one hand there is what he calls technical knowledge. This is knowledge that can be precisely formulated into rules, steps or precepts that can be written down, learned and remembered. Technical knowledge is real knowledge, but it is not complete knowledge; it needs what Oakeshott calls practical knowledge to make it complete and effective. Practical knowledge exists only in use and cannot be formulated into rules or precisely written down. It is acquired only through experience and continuous contact with someone who is actually involved in the specific activity, be it gardening, piano playing, or, importantly for us, politics. Practical knowledge might appear imprecise because it consists of everything that cannot be systematically formulated into rules or prescriptions. It cannot, thus, be learned or taught prior to the activity itself but only imparted and acquired by practice in the activity.[8]

The mistake of Rationalism for Oakeshott consists of the fact that it acknowledges only technical knowledge. It believes that this technical knowledge can be gained by the human mind abstracting itself from the pertinent activity to operate in a neutral and impartial manner when assessing the activity to come up with a rational description or solution. This, for Oakeshott, is a false belief; for what actually happens is that an 'ideology', consisting only of the technical knowledge, is extracted from the activity in which it is appropriate and then applied to other activities. Rationalism, thus, ignores practical knowledge and commits the 'error of mistaking a part for the whole, of endowing a part with the qualities of the whole' (*RIP*,

---

[8]   W. H. Greenleaf, *Oakeshott's Philosophical Politics* (London: Longmans, 1966), 47.

16). Oakeshott thus claims that the belief that technical knowledge alone will provide a sufficient understanding of, and competence within, an activity is illusory. If one ignores practical knowledge, the knowledge one has will only be molded to an abstraction of the activity, and not to the activity itself. If we take the activity to be politics, this leads one to conclude, according to Oakeshott, that knowledge of the activity of politics consists of both technical knowledge of politics (an ideological understanding of politics) and practical knowledge (what Oakeshott also refers to as traditional knowledge) of politics.[9] 'Tradition', is a potentially problematic concept to work with, and it will be noted that Oakeshott in his later works chose to move away from the concept of tradition, in favor of the more general term 'practice'. Be that as it may, the whole notion of traditional knowledge, and a tradition of behavior, stands central to Oakeshott's understanding of the activity of politics.

For Oakeshott a tradition of behavior includes, among other things, customs, institutions, laws, and even particulars such as specific diplomatic decisions, and, therefore, essentially entails the whole range of recognized and historic patterns of behavior and ideas that have attained the status of traditional knowledge. A tradition, or a traditional pattern of behavior, for him is never fixed nor does it ever take on a final form; it has no core or essential feature that defines it very nature, for every feature in a tradition may be only of a temporary nature; it does not aim at a specific purpose nor does it move in a single or set direction; it is never immune from change, but the fact that all parts do not change at the same time ensures that there will always be an element of continuity. This principle of continuity entails that its basis of authority is not the present or the past or the future on its own, but that it is defused between the past, present and the future (*RIP*, 61). The individual is never a mere passive recipient of a tradition, nor is he mechanically 'determined' by it, for it is transformed and extended by his personal contribution.[10] Oakeshott, with his idealist outlook, therefore renders a tradition not as a constraint on individuality but as its precondition, for the mind can never be independent of its objects.

---

[9] When referring to practical knowledge, Oakeshott states 'that it would not... be misleading to speak of it as traditional knowledge' (*RIP*, 12).

[10] Robert Grant, *Thinkers of Our Time: Oakeshott* (London: Claridge Press, 1990), 49.

For Oakeshott tradition clearly applies to politics as an activity. A traditional pattern of behavior not only informs politics, nor does it only serve as the point of departure for political activity in the state, it encompasses the whole of this activity, for according to Oakeshott, 'it can take no other form' (*RIP*, 56). As already mentioned, he makes it clear that other understandings of politics, be it politics as an empirical activity or an ideologically preconceived activity, are either not a concrete manner of activity at all, or they confuse an abstraction of a political tradition or another manner of activity with the activity of politics itself. In his understanding of politics he thus feels it important to lift politics from the mud of mere empirical guidance, while at the same time pulling it down from the rarefied heights of a supposedly neutral and extra-experiential guidance, and to rather firmly root it again in a tradition of behavior and understanding.

The problem with tradition is that it is not always a very clear and coherent guide to action. It usually entails a complex matrix of ideas and practices all of which simply suggests, in a vague pattern, a sympathy for a direction of action. It is the task of political activity to explore this sympathy, to make it explicit in a specific contingent situation, and to demonstrate the appropriateness of recognizing it (*RIP*, 57). This task is made very difficult and disjointed however, if political knowledge becomes separated from its traditional moorings.

Oakeshott referred to the early history of the United States of America as an example of politics based on technical knowledge distilled from the European experience, but detached from its tradition (*RIP*, 31-3). It was a society called upon to exercise political initiative on its own without necessarily possessing the command of a political tradition of its own, while at the same time rejecting, or distancing itself from, the tradition of Europe. Thus, people like Jefferson turned to the work of John Locke, which basically consisted of an ideology (the technical knowledge) extracted from the English political tradition, but which they believed was based on rational principles and therefore untainted by the influence of England. This early history of the United States illustrates a society in which the rationalist or ideological understanding of the political was not a direct reflection of a tradition of behavior out of which it was distilled, but where this understanding was imposed on a different tradition. This point can, however, be even better illustrated in the experience of

Africa, with important manifest disjunctures revealing themselves as a consequence.

The African Disjuncture Between Ideology And Tradition

With this view of Oakeshott on politics in mind, what do we find when we now turn to consider Africa? If we carry through on Oakeshott's views it will follow that a coherent understanding of politics in Africa will have to rest to a large extent on an understanding of Africa's political traditions. These need to be unpacked and carefully considered in terms of their impact on African politics. This is no small endeavor, for it implies that we will have to take into consideration the complete range of human developments and experiences on the African continent over at least a number of centuries if we are to come close to a coherent understanding of politics in Africa.

Those scholars that feel the call to take up this task of developing a coherent understanding of politics in Africa can draw inspiration from Oakeshott's distinguished body of work on politics and the state in Europe in which he considered the emergence of associations of people 'whom chance and choice had brought together' and which had over time developed characters of their own. Oakeshott, when engaged in this task, operated in a tradition he called 'historical coherence' in which he, in line with his discussion of political activity, considered primarily political culture or tradition as a basis for an understanding of more abstract levels of thought concerning politics in Europe.[11] It is not my aim in this paper to carry this through to Africa for as Oakeshott said, this type of knowledge is 'unavoidably knowledge of its detail: to know only the gist is to know nothing' (*RIP*, 62). The aim is more modest, for this paper will only attempt to identify some key features of African politics in light of Oakeshott's general understanding of politics, as well as its correlation with some of the main characteristics of European politics identified by Oakeshott.

Africa's political history is quite distinct from that of Europe and the rest of the Western world. One of its unique features is the impact of the European model of politics on Africa politics. Europe never had to deal with high levels of foreign influence or intervention in

---

[11] Timothy Fuller, 'Introduction' to *Morality and Politics in Modern Europe: The Harvard lectures*, by Oakeshott (New Haven: Yale Univ. Press), ix. Hereafter: *MPME*.

the 400 years during which the modern European state developed its present character, and consequently Oakeshott could focus purely on an internal dynamic in this development. In Africa we find both an internal and an external dynamic to consider, with the external influence often overawing the internal and imposing itself on Africa's process of state formation.

This foreign model of politics is in some important respects alien to the local African tradition of politics that prevailed in the pre-colonial era. Despite its alien character, a series of developments, both global and regional, caused the European model to become the dominant mode of formal African political norms and discourse. Even a brief consideration of politics in Africa will confirm the point that African politics is, and has been, based largely on an importation of political ideas that, although not necessarily incompatible with, or absent from, the African character, received their practical actualization in a context alien to the African continent, mainly in Europe. And it is in the form of an abridgement that these European ideas and practices entered the African continent. This resulted in Africa's political vocabulary and institutions bearing a superficial familiarity to the observer in Europe and the Western world at large, while at the same time leaving the observer perplexed and even saddened by the 'unexpected' problems and difficulties within the African state. This situation is, however, uniquely suited to be unpacked by means of the understanding of politics provided us by Oakeshott. His rich understanding of the political can contribute to our understanding of politics in an African context. Following his lead we have to start with the political tradition in Africa.

The political tradition in Africa consists of an interesting mixture and confluence of widely disparate traditions all forming part of a complex political history. Of specific interest to us is the past 300 years, during which time Africa was shaped in line with political constructs and concepts, all in the image of an 'expanding' and 'conquering' Europe. During the time of colonialism the European understanding of politics was imported to Africa along with European institutions and ideals. The colonial power simply assumed that Africa's political experience would conform to the European model and that governmental organizations and instruments such as a Western civil service, the cabinet system, and the judicial system, among others, along with constructs such as 'rule of law' and 'representative democracy' would be as congruent with Africa as it was with Europe. Even in the post-colonial era these categories, constructs and instruments continued to act as the operative mode for most African politics. These do not, however, represent the whole of the African political tradition. In fact, it initially represented an alien tradition to the continent. It represented, in Oakeshottian language, an abridgement of a foreign political tradition, or the collected technical knowledge of the European continent concerning politics. As Oakeshott makes clear, such an abridgement can never constitute a coherent activity on its own. It needs to be grounded in the traditional knowledge from which it was abstracted for it to be considered as constituting such a concrete activity. Thus, for Oakeshott, it is only to be expected that there will be major disjunctures in African politics since a European political ideology attempts to guide an African political tradition that shows some marked differences from the European tradition of which ideology is an abridgement.

The problem for Africa is that European colonialism was so successful in destroying traditional political institutions and structures on the continent, that it created the belief, even among Africans themselves, that there was no useful, truly African, political tradition to return to in a post-colonial era. Even during the struggle for liberation on the continent most Africans felt that they had little choice but to adopt a European political understanding. As decolonization approached, nationalist movements began to mobilize, leading the colonial authorities to look for ways of transferring power to indigenous governments. In the majority of cases this led to negotiations which eventually resulted in the agreement that imperial authorities would oversee multi-party elections, with the victor of this poll taking up the reigns of power under a new 'liberal democratic' constitution based on some European model. It proved to be one of the ultimate ironies of colonial rule. Imperial powers sought to leave a legacy of constitutional liberal democracy, the same liberties and political representation that imperial administrators had consciously withheld from Africans during their own rule. This European model came both with a specific vocabulary, including essentially non-African terms such as 'parliament,' 'individual freedom,' 'civil rights,' 'democracy,' and 'proletariat,' along with European political ideologies, such as socialism and nationalism, as their paradigm for politics. This essentially alien character of the state in Africa is well illustrated by the way in which the European version of 'the state' itself came to dominate African politics.

Pre-colonial Africa contained many stateless societies; and even where states did exist they were not well defined, as power at the center ebbed and flowed, and none of them contained well-defined boundaries. Thus, pre-colonial Africans had no experience of a hegemonic state.[12] The most obvious legacy of European domination was the division of the whole continent into modern states. The state boundaries created by the European powers gave little consideration to pre-colonial political, social, or economic divisions, but were rather determined by the short-term strategic and economic interests of these powers. This resulted in a very weak link between state and society. There existed no sense of the state growing out of the society, or out of the local traditional understanding of authority and rule, nor of the state serving the needs of the people under it. Initially, these concerns did not matter for the colonial powers, for the government of the colony was seen as only good for maintaining order, balancing budgets, and overseeing the extraction of raw materials for export. In post-colonial times this resulted in the existence of a distance between state and the society under it. The decision of post-colonial African states to accept these boundaries, taken mainly because they were fearful of large scale violence that might accompany attempts to adjust boundaries, resulted in this distance between state and society being carried into the very present. Thus, a distinctly European understanding of politics, encompassing a very specific political vocabulary and an abstracted set of political ideals, along with a set of supposedly proven institutions simply copied and transplanted from Europe,[13] continued to form the context of all formal politics in Africa. However, in spite of this continuing dominance of a European ideology of politics on the continent of Africa there is another current flowing within its politics. Notwithstanding the perceived success of colonialism in destroying most of Africa's traditional political institutions, it fell considerably short of annihilating African traditional political values and ideas, or what we can call African traditional knowledge of politics.

The presence of a different traditional knowledge in Africa is reflected by the way in which Africans' response to European political ideologies differed from those of Europeans. In Africa the

---

[12] See Alex Thomson, *An Introduction to African Politics* (London: Routledge, 2000), 10.

[13] The first Nigerian constitution was largely a simple copy of the Westminster system of the United Kingdom.

response was always more to the socio-cultural ideologies, while in Europe the focus always seemed to be on the socio-economic ideologies. Socio-economic ideologies have been attempted in Africa, such as different varieties of African socialism, and Marxist-Leninism. This usually took the form of a president making his personal ideology the ideology of the state, as was the case with Nkrumah and Nyerere. But when the grassroots have been able to express ideological preferences, it has always been socio-cultural ideologies that have exerted the greatest influence. Behind this phenomenon lies the resilience of certain African values and cultural traditions and habits that have survived all the imperial destruction and disruption of the nineteenth and twentieth centuries. Through colonial rule the organized indigenous instruments of authority and rule did slowly fade away, but traditional *mores* and normative approaches to politics have revealed more resilience than might at first have been thought possible.

What has happened over the course of the past forty to fifty years in post-colonial Africa is that these pre-colonial traditions have continued to influence politics, although they were not directly acknowledged in the formal political practices, institutions and ideals. Concomitantly with this, many of the imported ideas and formal practices have slowly started to inculcate themselves on the African character, to the point were it would be difficult for most Africans to imagine African politics without them. Thus, we find that the constitutive act of the new African Union includes among the key principles of government in Africa the rule of law, democracy and constitutional government, all pivotal elements of the European inheritance.[14] The current African political tradition is thus best viewed as a pre-colonial African culture slowly mixing with and absorbing European political constructs and concepts and in the process transforming them from mere technical knowledge into a more concrete activity in which knowledge of technique is combined with practical knowledge. This is well illustrated by the six major traditions of political thought identified by Ali Mazrui as jointly constituting the current political culture, or what Oakeshott would call the political tradition, of Africa:

(i)   A tribal tradition with an emphasis on continuity rather than change. Deeply rooted in this tradition is the idea of *Ubuntu*,

---

[14]   African Union Constitutive Act, art. 3, 4.

which, up to today, still forms one of the cornerstones of the African character.

  (ii) A dignitarian tradition aimed at the search for dignity for the African race.

 (iii) A nationalist tradition, stressing collective solidarity and opposition to foreign rule and external control.

 (iv) A liberal capitalist tradition with an emphasis on property, production and individualism.

  (v) A socialist tradition, sensitive to a morality of equality and opposed to class-based interests.

 (vi) A democratic tradition with its concern for accountability, participation and openness.[15]

Each of these traditions needs to be fleshed out for a proper understanding of its contribution to contemporary African political tradition. What is important to this paper is that some of these traditions are distinctly *Afrikan* while others were originally the result of an importation of European concepts and constructs. Gradually these imported ideas are digging themselves deeper into the African soil, and as they move from mere technical knowledge to concrete knowledge they acquire a sense that will make them different from their European counterparts, not necessarily in essence, but rather in terms of their practical manifestation.

Of special significance for this paper is the specific nature of the European influence in terms of the African understanding of the role of government, or the activity of governing, for it is in regards to the understanding of this activity, that Oakeshott makes an important contribution through his study of what he calls modes of association. Our understanding of the state in Africa can benefit significantly from the recognition of the modal distinction he makes between what he calls civil and enterprise associations, for it points to two fundamentally different understandings of the role of government within an increasingly complex and plural world.

Modes of Association and African Government

In part 3 of *On Human Conduct*, Oakeshott investigates what he calls the 'character' of the modern European state. He argues that an

---

[15]   Ali Mazrui, 'Ideology and African Political Culture,' in Teodros Kiros, ed., *Explorations in African Political Thought: Identity, Community, Ethics* (NY: Routledge, 2001).

unresolved tension between two irreconcilable dispositions regarding the state, the state as a *societas* and the state as a *universitas*, lies at the heart of the character of the modern state in Europe and the related office of its government (*OHC*, 200-1). The idea of 'character' as mentioned here features prominently in a number of Oakeshott's works. Character, for him, refers to the 'balance of dispositions' present within a person or a government. The character of a person would indicate a pattern of conduct in that person's actions. Similarly, the activity of governing may acquire an identifiable character in that it becomes interesting not because of rapid changes, but because it seems to settle into a kind of groove in which it tends to make use of a certain limited stock of ideas, images, beliefs, desires, projects, practices, etc. In other words, it explores what it already possesses, that is, its current character (*MPME*, 29-31). Oakeshott identifies the character of the modern European state as being the result of a gradual development he traces back to the sixteenth century. Characteristic of this development was the emergence of certain moral dispositions employed to help make intelligible whatever thoughts were uttered concerning government and politics. These different moral dispositions resulted in distinct modes of understanding as far as the office of government was concerned.

In much of what follows in his discussion he illustrates how the European political consciousness has been polarized between two modes of understanding. A state understood as a *societas* he calls a civil association, while an enterprise association reflects the *universitas* understanding. For him European states have displayed tendencies towards both civil and enterprise association. This distinction or duality is much more important for Oakeshott in terms of its contribution to our understanding of the very identity of the modern state in Europe than the more familiar but ideologically tainted and ambiguous labels such as 'liberal', 'collectivist', 'progressive', and 'socially just'. This leads us to the state in Africa. Can the enterprise association/civil association distinction help us understand the state here better? What features concerning the state in Africa are highlighted when viewed through the lens of the *societas*/*universitas* distinction? Does the state in Africa correspond more to an enterprise association or a civil association? Before we can address these questions we first have to take a closer look at what Oakeshott meant by these concepts.

Oakeshott maintains that there is a continuous strand of modern European thought in which the modern state is understood in terms of a mode of association he calls civil association, or as he also states, where it is understood in terms of *societas*.[16] According to this understanding, people so associated (*cives*) 'are not joined in the pursuit of a common substantive purpose or in seeking the satisfaction of their individual wants' (*OHC*, 263). They are simply related in respect of their acknowledgement of the authority of a system of non-instrumental laws, which are 'indifferent (not merely impartial) to the satisfaction of substantive wants' (*OHC*, 243). This law (*lex*) is recognized as a system of prescriptive conditions (*respublica*) to be subscribed to in self-chosen conduct. It is not a 'relationship in terms of any common purpose and the *cives* are not joint enterprisers bound to one another in an agreed choice of wants to be satisfied.' It is, rather, a relationship in terms of a system of law that prescribes, 'not satisfaction to be sought or actions to be performed, but moral conditions to be subscribed to in seeking self-chosen satisfactions and in performing self-chosen actions.' In such an association people are related solely because of their 'acknowledgement of the authority, not the desirability, of these prescribed conditions' (*OHC*, 158).

Oakeshott believed that at the very core of this association stood the desire not to 'threaten the link between belief and conduct,' or what he calls 'free agency' (*OHC*, 158). In acknowledging civil authority *cives* would retain their free agency and would not become hostage to a future independent of, and unrelated to, their choice. The core vision behind this highly individualistic outlook on life and its related formalistic view of rules and traditions (where rules simply set conditions to conduct while never prescribing ends to be achieved), is the belief that formality and formalism can best serve to guard and nourish individual moral autonomy and judgment by granting individuals the opportunity to grow in their moral autonomy through the actual and constant practice thereof.[17] In a state understood in terms of *universitas*, the vision is significantly different, however.

A state understood in terms of *universitas*, that is, as an enterprise association, is, according to Oakeshott, a purposive association and as such is a means to an end. It is an association of many human

---

[16] Oakeshott refers to Hegel, Bodin, Montesquieu, and Constant as examples, among others, of thinkers that gave expression to this understanding.
[17] Coats, *Oakeshott's Contemporaries*, 18-9.

beings united in respect of a common substantive purpose, interest, concern, or 'cause' and in seeking the satisfaction of this common end. The people relate to one another as role-performers in the quest after the common purpose, and not as people of divergent wants and interests which all aim to satisfy simultaneously. This association is necessarily a managerial engagement, with the leaders fulfilling not the role of rulers, but that of managers assigning performances contingently connected with the common purpose or interest. Government thus understood Oakeshott calls teleocratic, that is, government aimed at the management of a purposive concern. The rules or laws of such an association are expressed in the form of prudential managerial conclusions specifying the common purpose and the way in which it is to be contingently pursued. Law thus becomes a set of prescriptive conditions, that should instrumentally contribute to the common purpose, and if it does not it should be amended to come in line with this purpose and to serve its attainment (*OHC*, 114-8; part 3, passim).

In the beginning of part 3 of *On Human Conduct* Oakeshott pays specific attention to the arduous and difficult road that European states had to travel in an attempt to acquire appropriate authority for these new states. The first business of a new ruler in a new state was to acquire authority by getting himself and his new office recognized by his subjects. Oakeshott then goes on to claim that most modern European states have failed in this endeavor. Most governments had to turn to what he calls 'implausible and gimcrack beliefs' (*OHC*, 191) to try to prop up their claims to authority, beliefs such as 'the sovereignty of the people', or 'the nation', or 'democracy', etc. These governments also became inclined to rest their claims to legitimacy on their power and their incidental achievements, and in the process the apparatus of government and its effectiveness in wielding power have become to a large extent a measure of its authority (*OHC*, 189-93). This overlap between the office of government (its power) and the authority and legitimacy of government is even more pronounced in the African state and has contributed to the steering of the state in Africa even more decisively in the direction of an enterprise association.

Africa is characterized by a whole number of weak, corrupt, collapsed, and even so-called failed states. Even in stronger states capable of exerting government control over the complete area delineated by the state boundaries, government authority is often undermined by multiple contenders for allegiance and control in the form of tribal authorities or warlords, international business concerns, local militias, etc. In this competitive environment governments aim at solidifying their authority by referring to their performances, be it in liberating the nation from colonialism, protecting its citizens, defeating an opponent on the battlefield, negotiating an end to a conflict, exposing and dealing with corruption, providing jobs for people, driving development, etc. This performance-based legitimation often undermines the state, for weak performance will then lead to weak state authority. This mentality is reflected in an interesting feature of African politics: the often-expressed need to proclaim a 'fresh start', or 'a new beginning' at each change of government, which in turn implies low levels of continuity in political practice. New governments more often than not feel the need to proclaim a complete break with the past and past practices, be they colonialism, apartheid rule, military rule, neo-patrimonial rule, corruption, autocratic rule, etc. — that is, with the dispensation that prevailed under the previous leadership — and to start afresh with a blank slate. This occurred in most African countries as part of the decolonialization process, but is also often repeated with monotonous consistency in country after country on the continent. Here we can refer to events in the Democratic Republic of the Congo (previously Zaire), Uganda, South Africa, Kenya and Lesotho to mention but a few recent examples. It is also most likely that a similar break with the past and new beginning will be proclaimed in Zimbabwe after the departure of Robert Mugabe. These 'new beginnings' usually entail a completely 'redesigned' constitutional order, in effect, attempting to completely destroy the 'failed' past and to reconstitute the state along lines of 'universally accepted practices of social justice and democracy'. It, however, just serves to illustrate that authority in African politics remains closely linked to government performance and to the desirability of the outcomes of its policies, and illustrates a common perception that the state in Africa has become a highly intentional instrument to be designed for the attainment of some perceived common goals.[18] This makes the enterprise association characterization of the Africa state

---

[18]   This contrasts with the state in Europe of which Oakeshott says, 'since there was no architect, understanding it cannot be an inquiry into an intention' (*OHC*, 198). This in turn serves to highlight the strong level of Rationalism present in African political discourse.

more compelling, for it seems to be a situation where governments feel compelled to manage the whole state in the direction of a common purpose in an effort to ensure its legitimacy.

Oakeshott identifies a number of contingent circumstances that have helped enhance the plausibility of a *universitas* understanding of the state (*OHC*, 267-74). These general European circumstances can and do relate to African circumstances that have enhanced a similar understanding of the state in Africa. He mentions four such circumstances. The first was the gradual and ceaseless extension of a central administrative apparatus that was developed to provide an instrument of rule when a specific substantive purpose was pursued such as the collection of taxes, or the protection of the government against local or foreign threats. This administrative apparatus, although not initially designed as a tool for the management of people, proved invaluable as an instrument to the managerially inclined governments associated with enterprise association.

A second characteristic was an unpurged relic of 'lordship' that remained hidden in the office of modern rulers, and was passed on to their successors. 'Lordship' here refers to ownership of a piece of land or an estate, along with the enterprise of the exploitation of its resources. The relic of lordship has had the effect of influencing the European state in the direction of an enterprise association, in that the state is viewed as an estate to be exploited, 'its laws as rules instrumental to the success of the enterprise, the office of government as estate management, and "subjects" as role-performers in an undertaking' (*OHC*, 268).

Third, Oakeshott points to colonialism and its influence on the European imagination to regard the office of government as an exercise of management. Colonies were usually seen as extensions of the royal domain, the purpose of which was to supply their 'lord' with certain goods and services. The colonies were largely managed like a business venture aimed at the maximum exploitation of the bounty the colony could offer. They were enterprises in which government and management were indistinguishable from one another, again preparing the European mind for the view of their own governments as the managers of an enterprise.

Finally, and most importantly, Oakeshott identifies war as the main circumstance that has pushed Europe in the direction of enterprise association. He refers to the prominence of near continuous war in the past five centuries of European history. The needs of a state facing war, preparing for it, fighting in it, recovering after it, decisively turn a state in the direction of association in terms of a substantive purpose. They entail 'devices for controlling the use of resources' (*OHC*, 273), and result in removing substantive choice from the conduct of subjects as they are mobilized in the quest after the common goal, be it victory, survival, preparation for a conflict, or rebuilding after one. This applies not only during actual wars but also in the intervals between wars, for the successes of this managerial style help it to burrow itself into governments and tempt them to apply the same methods to whatever they confronted in the task of governing. Oakeshott goes so far as to call this the 'chief nourishment' of the state understood as a enterprise association, and that 'War in a modern European state is the enemy of civil association; belligerence is alien to civil association' (*OHC*, 273).

These four factors present in the European context are not unfamiliar to the African context. The impact of colonial government on Africa was already mentioned. The effectiveness of colonial rule in destroying local African authority structure has also already been referred to. This implied that, for the duration of colonial rule, the only form of government known to Africans, and thus the only experience and practical example they had was of a government in the form of a corporate enterprise, comprehensively managing the society aimed at the fulfillment of its self-appointed purpose. This purpose was the maximization of the exploitation of the natural resources of the colony for the benefit of the imperial powers. The effective management of this enterprise required an effective administrative apparatus, which resulted in the establishment of highly bureaucratic and authoritarian rule in the colonies, all of a very interventionist nature, where domination was ensured by coercion. In one of the few passages where Oakeshott mentions Africa, he goes on to make the following statement that underscores this point:

> It was, however, this, the crudest of all the voices of lordship, in which European mentors addressed the emergent so-called states first of South America and later of Africa. Our disposition to recognize what is going on in terms of the constitutions (not the engagements) of governments and of techniques of ruling (not modes of association) has persuaded us that our gifts to these new states have been 'liberal' constitutions and a model for an apparatus of ruling, and we are sometimes surprised at their indifference to them. But what they have learned from us is an understanding of a state as a compulsory corporate association and the notion of ruling as the management of a corporate enterprise, which they call 'nationalism' (*OHC*, 296-7 n. 2).

This example, set by local colonial governments, along with its understanding of the role and functioning of a government, was carried into the post-colonial era. Consequently, the modern African state carries with it, as a result of its torturous birth, a strong inclination in the direction of an enterprise association.

It should be noted at this point, that although imbued with a strong bureaucratic mentality inherited from the time of European rule, few African states were able to carry this mentality through to the actual detailed administrative management of the whole of their countries. The well-trained indigenous corps of administrative officials left by the colonial powers when they withdrew was more often than not insufficient in numbers and capacity to ensure effective governmental control over all the regions of the various states. By the early 1990s, for example, effective government control in Zambia is said to have extended only to about 50 km outside of the capital, Lusaka. This lack of immediate capacity did not, however, seriously undermine the view that the role of the government was essentially a managerial role aimed primarily at the development of the state.

As for the question as to a lingering presence of a 'lordship' understanding of rule in Africa, we have to return to what Mazrui called the 'tribal tradition'. Is there an element of the 'lordship' Oakeshott identified in Europe present in the 'tribal' understanding of leadership? In this tribal tradition we can basically identify four theories of leadership. First, there is the elder tradition, conceding deference to age on the assumption that the older is wiser. Some striking illustrations of this in post-colonial Africa can be found in the rule of President Jomo Kenyatta in Kenya where he was referred to by the title Mzee Kenyatta, meaning 'old gentleman Kenyatta' or 'father-figure Kenyatta.' Then there is the warrior tradition, where leadership is action-orientated, disciplinarian, and based on the skills of force and violent assertion. Idi Amin Dada of Uganda is a good example of this tradition. Thirdly, we find the sage tradition where the relationship between the leader and followers is understood as that of teacher to students. The leader is the instructor to the general population about political virtue and political vice, and sometimes even more. He is the guide to the nation through the intricacies of interpreting the present world and preparing for the national future. Some examples of this can be found in the rule of Julius Nyerere of Tanzania and Gamal Abdel Nasser of Egypt. Finally there also exists a monarchical tradition, which often characterizes all three above-mentioned traditions. Some surviving examples on the continent are the monarchies in Swaziland, Morocco, Ashanti, and the Zulu Royal House in South Africa. These four traditions, although not similar in manifestation to what Oakeshott identifies as 'lordship' or 'seigneurial management', are all very patriarchal in nature and view their subjects as people that need to be 'led' on a specific venture or campaign, 'uplifted', or 'educated'. The relic of these understandings of leadership still manifests themselves daily in African politics and provides a fertile soil for a managerial understanding of government. It is however, in war, conflict, disaster and crisis that we find the main impetus for enterprise association manifestated in Africa.

Africa's recent history is replete with conflicts, wars and military takeovers. In some states it started with prolonged struggles for independence or liberation, as was the case with Mozambique and Zimbabwe, while in many states war has been an almost constant reality in the time after independence. The civil war in Angola raged for almost 30 years while the wars and fighting in Somalia have caused an almost total collapse of the central authority of the state. The recent conflict in the Democratic Republic of the Congo has killed an estimated three million people over the past four years, while the struggles for liberation in South Africa and Namibia have left a deep mark on the respective post-liberation societies. According to a recent World Bank report, there are currently three wars and fourteen violent conflicts on-going in sub-Saharan Africa, while ten countries are at a high risk of an outbreak or resumption of conflict. Some of the states that are currently experiencing conflict, be it internal or external, include Burundi, the Democratic Republic of the Congo, Liberia, Sudan and the Comores, while the simmering or potential conflicts referred to are in states such as Zimbabwe, the Ivory Coast, Sierra Leone, Ethiopia, and Rwanda.

Apart from the terrible toll these conflicts exact in terms of human suffering and misery, they are also bound to influence the understanding of the role of government. As Oakeshott argued (*OHC*, 272-3), the needs of a state confronted by war or conflict decisively push it in the direction of an enterprise association, for a government or movement or party engaged in such a conflict will aim at the maximum mobilization of its people (or its supporters) towards the aim of winning the conflict. A struggle for survival tends to relegate all other aims to the dustbin of insignificance, and thus a government so engaged will view all opposition to its aim of winning the war as treason. [19] The government will direct the affairs of the whole of society towards this aim while the population is required to unify behind this goal. This mentality, born and nurtured under the extreme conditions of war and violent struggle, is all too easily carried over into other areas of life, be it health-care, education, or many others and becomes part of the way government — be it the old victorious one or a new movement or party that has taken over — sees its role. Oakeshott claims that a good indicator of this is that the political vocabulary of such a government will be replete with military or warlike jargon (*OHC*, 274). Of this there are ample examples in African political discourse where phrases such as the 'fight against illiteracy', the 'assault on poverty', and 'the battle against unemployment' fill government documentation and declarations. In the past couple of decades African governments started to express themselves in this regard primarily within the context of the developmental idea.

The so-called 'development imperative' stands at the heart of governments' understanding of their role and task in Africa. The argument is often advanced that Africa is an underdeveloped region of the world and that it needs to develop its people and their circumstances if it is to catch up with the rest of the world, or even simply to survive the future. The destitution, hunger, unemployment, disease, and generally low standards of living on the continent underscore this view. The immediacy of these problems creates the impression that the state in Africa is confronted by a whole number of crises, and that the future depends on these being addressed speedily and with maximum effort; the idea that all the future plans and prospects of the people need first be guaranteed by their short-term survival of the current emergency. The government is tasked with the main responsibility in this fight for development, for there usually exists no other agency or organization within African societies capable of driving this developmental agenda. It is interesting to note that Oakeshott himself identifies certain conditions under which even a civil association might suspend its civil condition in favor of an enterprise association in order to address these crisis conditions (*OHC*, 146). He identifies the threat of destruction or dissolution, or when the '*cives* are deprived of shelter and the amenity of a civil

---

[19] A struggle for survival can also be as a result of a natural disaster such as a widespread famine, as was the case in Ethiopia in the early 1990s and in Southern Africa in 2002-3.

order' as instances of such contingent circumstances. It can be argued that these conditions apply to many an African state. This clearly illustrates the point that such perceived crises will, even in the 'best' of circumstances, push a state decidedly in the direction of an enterprise association; thus it should come as no surprise that the African state, which is greatly lacking in what Oakeshott calls the 'civil condition', should find expression mainly in the form of such enterprise associations.

Development for the African state becomes the purpose of the state and government becomes the agency that is to manage this process. It has to determine the roadmap for the development of the state and its people, and it has to drive society along this road, while the law of the society becomes instrumental in this goal of development. In this, African states closely resemble what Oakeshott called 'development corporations' which he used as a clear manifestation of enterprise association, where the state is an association engaged in the maximum exploitation of a 'corporate property recognized to include the total resources of its territory and the talents of its members' (*OHC*, 295). This mentality is reflected in the focus of many African states. Such is the case in the Nigerian constitution, which maintains that one of the fundamental objectives and principles of state policy is 'to harness the resources of the nation.'[20] In all this Oakeshott sees a strong relic of 'lordship' and he even uses a rare African example to illustrate this point when he quotes an ex-president of Malawi, Hastings Banda, who said 'I don't care what the world calls me, a dictator or what, my job is to develop this country' (*OHC*, 296-7 n. 2).

We can, I believe, conclude that certain circumstances exist on the African continent that decisively pushed, and continue to push, the understanding of the state in the direction of an enterprise association. There is, however, a further consideration we need to take into account in our reckoning of African politics in terms of modes of association. Oakeshott claimed that the character of the associates who comprise the state, nourishes a specific understanding of the state, either in terms of *societas* or *universitas*. Following from this he linked civil association with the character of the individual and its accompanying disposition towards a morality of individualism, and the enterprise association with the character of the anti-individual, or as he called it, the individual *manqué* and its accompanying moral-

---

[20] Constitution of Nigeria, art. 16.

ity of collectivism (*OHC*, 234, 274-5). If we then state that the African state manifests itself primarily in the understanding of an enterprise association, does it follow that the primary character of the associates within the African state is that of the anti-individual, or to put it differently, is the individualist character very weak, or absent in Africa, to such an extent as to make a civil association not feasible for the continent?

A few comments in this regard. First, Oakeshott makes it very clear that the individual/anti-individual distinction he refers to is a post-tribal phenomenon (*OHC*, 265, 275) and that the anti-individual, who prefers the 'substantive satisfactions entailed in an enterprise association to the adventure and risk of self-enactment' entailed in civil association (*OHC*, 276), is responding to the emergence of individualism, and not pre-existent to it. Oakeshott seemed to have felt that these two postulates adequately circumscribe the modern European state and though he acknowledged that there was a feudal communal character type present in European history, he felt that it did not contribute significantly to the understanding of the modern state in Europe. This is not necessarily the case in Africa. We can identify the same two human postulates in the modern African state, but it would not be as easy to ignore the tribal/communal character and the role it plays in the character of the modern African state. If we thus want to consider the human postulates of the African understanding of the state we will have to expound upon not only the individual and anti-individual character type, as Oakeshott did in Europe, but also the communal, tribal character and its influence on the understanding of the office of government.

Africa is historically very communal in terms of its social expression. This can be traced back to the strong communal tribal tradition and the *Ubuntu* worldview that is said to dominate the African character. *Ubuntu* incorporates notions of an African collective consciousness and a universal brotherhood of Africans, and is perhaps best expressed in the saying that 'a person is a person because of other people'.[21] It entails the belief in a universal bond of sharing that connects all humanity. The fundamental *ethos* of such communal societies is, according to Wiredu, the principle of adjustment, where the individual adjusts her interests to the interests of others even at

---

[21] P. H. Coetzee, and A. P. J. Roux, eds., *Philosophy from Africa: A Text with Readings* (Johannesburg: International Thomson Publishing, 1998), 451.

the possible cost of some self-denial.[22] The individual defers to the group or the greater collective, thus creating a strong impetus for solidarity and unity of purpose. Makgoba specifically identifies *ubuntu* as the main reason why Africans have not warmed to the idea of individualism, which is often perceived to be too egotistical and exclusivist.[23] Collective solidarity and a characteristic deference of the individual to the collective, thus also tends to pull Africa if not more in the direction of enterprise association, then specifically away from civil association. Government and the activity of governing tend to be viewed in this idiom of collective solidarity and unity of purpose. As to the possibility of a European-style Renaissance in Africa that would birth a similarly deep sense of individuality in the African character, this is something that needs to be investigated seriously. Will a gradual rise in living standards, link to increased functional diversification in economic life, and industrialization, contribute in this regard, or will it simply enhance the managerial role and responsibilities of the state?

Summary

When the states of Africa are viewed through Oakeshott's lenses certain striking features present themselves to us; features that can go a long way in contributing towards the understanding of the perplexing nature of the African state, both in terms of its uniqueness as well as its self-understanding and the role it sees for itself.

One of the most important features identified is the presence of what we may call a cultural lag in much of African politics in that the political traditions of Africa were, and to a certain extent still are, usually incongruent with the political ideals on the continent. The technical knowledge in Africa concerning politics is not rooted in practical or traditional knowledge, but is rather the result of an external influence. This technical knowledge consists of an abridgement of a distinctly European knowledge of politics, which was then exported to a region whose historic development and cultural experience differed significantly from that of Europe. Despite its alien

[22] Kwasi Wiredu, 'Society and Democracy in Africa,' in *Explorations in African Political Thought: Identity, Community, Ethics*, ed. Teodros Kiros (NY: Routledge, 2001), 172.
[23] Malgapuru William Makgoba, 'Oppositions, Difficulties, and Tensions Between Liberalism and African Thought,' in *Ironic Victory: Liberalism in Post-liberation South Africa*, ed. R. W. Johnson and David Welsh (Cape Town: Oxford Univ. Press, 1998), 272.

origin this European technical understanding of politics served, and continues to serve, as the guide for much of African politics in that it provides the ideals, the institutions, the procedural understandings, etc. entailed in it to African politics, thus resulting in the cultural lag. Since Oakeshott insists that a concrete activity of politics must involve both technical and practical knowledge, we thus have to conclude that Africa's politics consists of an activity in which a European understanding of politics is slowly mixing with local African norms and practices. Some elements of the European technical knowledge are slowly inculcating themselves in Africa, while the African traditional knowledge is also transforming the originally European ideals into uniquely African and local ones.

One of the most important influences of the European understanding of politics on Africa is that of the European disposition not to clearly recognize the difference between what Oakeshott calls the constitution and authority of a state, and its mode of association. This lack of distinction resulted in many African states adopting so-called 'liberal' constitutions and 'democratic' practices, while still operating in the mode of corporate enterprises experienced under colonial rule, and thus operating without regard for what Oakeshott calls the 'civil condition'.

The *universitas* understanding of the role of government, as experienced in Africa, has some roots in the traditional understanding of authority and rule in pre-colonial Africa, but its main impetus in the modern world came from the example of colonial rule in these states. In post-colonial times this understanding was, and still is, being strengthened by wars, conflicts, disasters, disease, and the 'crisis' of underdevelopment. The demands these make on governments result in their continually functioning in the mode of crisis management, thus further enhancing the enterprise association state in Africa.

Oakeshott conceded that a *universitas* understanding of the state is also very prevalent in Europe, but that it is constrained by the strong sense of individualism embedded in the European character. This sense of individualism is, however, not as strong in the African character, which is typified by a more communal understanding, rooted in the tribal tradition and the *ubuntu* worldview. Though this view of the world cannot be fully equated with that of Oakeshott's individual *manqué*, it nonetheless does not provide fertile soil for the civil condition to grow, and thus further underscores the real and potential vitality of an enterprise association state on the African continent.

11

Terry Nardin

Oakeshott's Philosophy of the Social Sciences

An important question in contemporary philosophy is how the social sciences are related to the natural sciences. Reflecting on the study of politics and political thought, Oakeshott arrived at his own answer to this question. In *Experience and Its Modes* he suggests that there can be a genuine science of human behavior, one that, like all science, is concerned with abstract quantitative relationships. Studies of individual objects or events, in contrast, are essentially historical. The social sciences are scientific when they frame general laws. They are historical when they describe and explain individuals. But because science and history are distinct and autonomous universes of discourse, the social sciences lose coherence when they try to do both.

In *On Human Conduct* and other late writings, which are the only ones I discuss in any detail in this paper, Oakeshott reformulates these claims. Some aspects of human activity can be explained scientifically as the unconscious product of natural processes, but such explanations are irrelevant to understanding human activity as intelligent choice and action. In taking this position, Oakeshott in effect disputes the now fashionable postmodern contention that there is no significant distinction between the natural and social sciences because both involve meaning and interpretation. According to this view, which has achieved the status of dogma in the humanities, all theories are systems of meaning and all theorizing interpretive or hermeneutic. Oakeshott, while far from embracing the

---

This paper draws on my book, *The Philosophy of Michael Oakeshott*, copyright © 2001 The Pennsylvania State University.

postmodern humanities on its own terms, would agree that the social sciences, insofar as they are concerned with intelligent human conduct, are in fact hermeneutic disciplines. But he argues that they differ from the natural sciences in being doubly hermeneutic: not only do social scientists bring meanings to the study of experience but the human experience they study is itself composed of meanings.

For Oakeshott, who in this departs from the postmodern consensus, explanations of intelligent conduct are historical as well as hermeneutic. In studying human conduct we refer to practices to make sense of particular human performances. To this extent, our inquiry is hermeneutic. But to explain an individual performance we must go beyond interpreting it as an expression of certain practices to reveal its character as a response to other performances. We must establish that it was the contingent outcome of events that illuminate its individual character. Explanation in the social sciences is, in this sense, 'historical'.

In this paper, I explain how Oakeshott's philosophy of the social sciences springs from nineteenth-century debates about the autonomy of historical inquiry, explicate his hermeneutic conception of these sciences, and show how this conception depends on his theory of historical explanation. Taken together, these ideas constitute a carefully articulated philosophy of the social sciences, one that traces an attractive *via media* between the prevailing and doctrinaire scientific and antiscientific alternatives.

The Problem of the Human Sciences

With the emergence in the nineteenth century of history as a self-conscious discipline, philosophers could consider the epistemological status of historical inquiry and its relationship to science. Their task was complicated, however, by the ill-defined boundaries of these fields. 'History' meant both the study of past events and the study of human activity in general. The word 'science' was also ambiguous: it could mean either the study of nature or any systematic inquiry, whatever its subject. Many thinkers, impressed by the achievements of natural science, regarded it as the model of authentic knowledge. Human behavior, they thought, is explained in the same way that nonhuman phenomena are explained in the natural sciences, that is, by general laws based upon induction from observable facts. The problem for those who rejected this 'positivism' was to show that the study of human activity could be distinguished from the natural sciences and made coherent in its own terms.

An early critic of positivism, the historian J. G. Droysen, defended the autonomy of the emerging discipline of historical studies by arguing that history and nature demand categorially different kinds of inquiry. Following Kant and Hegel, he distinguished the human from the natural, one a realm of freedom, the other of necessity. Both history and nature can be studied empirically, but the methods of history differ from those of the natural sciences. Historical inquiry constructs a coherent body of knowledge on its own presuppositions, correcting and enlarging that knowledge by critically examining historical evidence. It is scientific not because it emulates the natural sciences but because it is a disciplined way of approaching and representing its distinctive subject, the historical past. The historian's task, then, is to proceed by a method that, although it differs from the methods of the natural sciences, is no less scientific.[1] Droysen's formulation of the problem of historical method set the agenda for subsequent debate about the proper study of human affairs.

This debate generated two criteria for distinguishing the social from the natural sciences. According to the first, which I shall call 'the individuality criterion', historical inquiry is defined by its concern with individuals as such and not merely as examples of general laws. It seemed evident to historians that their subject was the deeds of individual persons and the character of individual events, institutions, and nations. According to some philosophers of the period, in contrast to the natural sciences, which frame general laws about recurrent phenomena, the social sciences describe the unique character of individual occurrences. A field like psychology, which seeks to frame general laws about human behavior, therefore belongs not to the social but to the natural sciences.[2] They saw psychology as a discipline concerned with immediate lived experience, not with general laws of behavior, and as fundamental to the social sciences for this reason. But they also argued that experience occurs within an

[1]   Johann Gustav Droysen, *Outline of the Principles of History*, trans. E. Benjamin Andrews (Boston: Ginn, 1893).
[2]   Wilhelm Windelband, 'History and Natural Science,' trans. Guy Oakes, in *History and Theory* 18 (1980): 175; Heinrich Rickert, *Science and History: A Critique of Positivist Epistemology*, trans. George Reisman (Princeton: Van Nostrand and Co., 1962), 57.

objective cultural world. To deal with the objection that psychology, though concerned with mind, resembles the natural sciences, those who defended the autonomy of the social sciences did so by distinguishing the study of mental processes, which are explained by general laws, from the study of mental content — individual ideas — which are not. The required distinction is between psychological and hermeneutic understanding: it is hermeneutics, not psychology that gives us access to ideas.

This brings us to the second criterion of demarcation that emerged in the nineteenth-century debate: that the social sciences are distinguished from the natural sciences in being concerned not with 'nature' but with 'mind' (*Geist*). I shall call this 'the hermeneutic criterion'. The study of mind and its products belongs to the 'human sciences' (*Geisteswissenchaften*). *Geist*, here, is not the inner, private experience of individual consciousness; it is what Hegel had called 'objective mind', the outer, public world of collective consciousness that is expressed in languages, customs, and other cultural practices. In studying texts, for example, the human or social scientist is not concerned, as a psychologist or cognitive scientist would be, with processes in an author or reader's mind. The human scientist (today, we would say the humanities scholar or the scholar in the humanistic social sciences) is concerned with 'a structure created by these processes,' an intellectual object that requires interpretation to be understood.[3] Accordingly, the human sciences investigate mind-created objects. Human behavior becomes the subject of these sciences only when our concern is to interpret its meanings. As a method of the human sciences, hermeneutics involves treating all human expressions as if they were texts. The objects of this interpretation, its texts and text-analogues, include a diversity of actions, artifacts, customs, relationships, and other cultural phenomena. And the methods of interpretation that are required to make sense of these expressions are similarly diverse.

Positivists have responded to these claims in two distinct ways. First, they argue that hermeneutics cannot provide an objective method for studying human activity because it relies on intuition or empathy to understand the meaning of human expressions. But this objection, we can now see, confuses the interpretation of meanings

---

[3]   Wilhelm Dilthey, 'The Construction of the Historical World,' in *W. Dilthey: Selected Writings*, ed. H. P. Rickman (Cambridge: Cambridge Univ. Press 1976), 174-5.

or ideas with other kinds of understanding. Hermeneutic understanding does not rest on empathy, a procedure through which historians or anthropologists recreate in their own minds the thoughts
of those whose expressions they are studying. Hermeneutic understanding is not, like empathy, a psychological concept. It rests on the
premise that thoughts are ideas and that ideas depend on the shared
meanings that constitute linguistic and other cultural practices. Hermeneutic interpretation must therefore be distinguished from imaginative reconstruction. Second, positivists argue that interpretation
is merely a source of hypotheses, not a mode of explanation, and that
to count as knowledge its hypotheses must be confirmed scientifically. But the hermeneutic disciplines verify interpretive hypotheses
according to their own methods of confirmation. These methods are
'scientific' in the nineteenth-century sense, in that they are systematic and objective, but they do not rest on the metaphysical premises
of natural science. The existence of such methods therefore deflates
the charge that the human sciences cannot be objective. Because cultural expressions are public and can be examined by anyone, objectivity according to the canons of systematic historical, philological,
and other kinds of hermeneutic scholarship is possible.[4]

The Social Sciences as Hermeneutic Disciplines

Since Dilthey, philosophers have advanced several versions of the
hermeneutic criterion. One is that the social sciences explain actions
in relation to an agent's 'reasons' for acting, in contrast to the natural
sciences, which seek 'causal' explanations. Another, drawing on the
view that reasons are intelligible only in relation to linguistic practices, is that explanations of action presuppose rules. A theoretical
understanding of human conduct must pay attention to the
self-understanding of those whose conduct is being explained, and
this self-understanding cannot be described except in terms of the
shared meanings expressed in the rules of various communities.[5]
This view, which philosophers attribute to Wittgenstein, is
discernable across a wide swath of the humanities and social sciences and reflects sources far broader than Wittgenstein's auto-

[4]   Georg Henrik Von Wright, *Explanation and Understanding* (Ithaca: Cornell
       Univ. Press, 1971), 5-6; Gurpreet Mahajan, *Explanation and Understanding in
       the Human Sciences*, 2d ed. (Delhi: Oxford Univ. Press, 1997), 57-61.
[5]   Peter Winch, *The Idea of a Social Science and Its Relation to Philosophy* (London:
       Routledge, 1958), 87-9.

didactic reflections. According to yet another version of the hermeneutic criterion, the social sciences study 'intentional phenomena' —
states of mind that, like a belief, are directed at an object and express
propositions about it. Because they involve intentional phenomena,
human actions cannot be explained without referring to this propositional content. Natural processes, in contrast, can be the subjects of
propositions (scientific hypotheses) but they do not themselves contain propositions.[6]

In *On Human Conduct*, Oakeshott develops his own version of the
hermeneutic criterion to distinguish the social from the natural sciences: the former are concerned with intelligent conduct, the latter
with not-intelligent processes. To understand something as an
expression of intelligence is to attribute meaning to it and to invite
investigation of this meaning. The distinction between the intelligent and the not-intelligent is more comprehensive than the classical
distinction between history and science (which Oakeshott had
defended in *Experience and Its Modes*) because though history and science are two among an indefinite number of modes, the categories
'intelligent' and 'not-intelligent' are exhaustive: everything must be
understood under one or the other of these categories.

It follows that the natural sciences are categorially barred from
having anything to say about human activity as an expression of
intelligence. 'Science' includes inquiries in economics and psychology that seek to explain human behavior as the outcome of underlying processes, but these inquiries are not concerned with 'human
conduct' defined as intelligent choice and action. Science, as a mode
of inquiry, is concerned with not-intelligent processes, including
those that affect the behavior of human beings as living organisms,
not with ideas, practices, and actions. The distinction is between 'behavior', which does not depend on an agent's understandings and is
not under the agent's control, and 'conduct', which does involve
such understandings and which implies voluntary choice. Only
inquiries that attend to the character of human actions — interpretive inquiries into the meanings that make an individual performance what it is — can be properly called inquiries into human
conduct. The disciplines that study intelligent human activity,
Oakeshott suggests in *The Voice of Liberal Learning*, are those that

[6]   Franz Brentano, 'The Distinction between Mental and Physical
      Phenomena,' in Roderick M. Chisholm, ed., *Realism and the Background of
      Phenomenology* (Glencoe, IL: Free Press, 1961).

'used to be called the "human sciences" . . . to make clear that their concern is with human beings as self-conscious, intelligent persons,'[7] not with human beings conceived, as they are in the natural sciences, as organisms whose behavior (motion) is determined by biological processes. Paradoxically, the human or social 'sciences' seek an understanding of human conduct that is not a (natural) scientific understanding.[8] Insofar as they study the activity of intelligent agents, Oakeshott suggests, the human sciences belong to the 'humanities,' and distinguishing them from the humanities was 'an unfortunate mistake' (*VLL*, 34).

In his later writings Oakeshott repudiates the expression 'the social sciences', and not only because the word 'sciences' is equivocal and misleading. The word 'social', he suggests, is also confusing when used to designate the subject of an inquiry. This subject may be the residual class of phenomena left behind after those that have been successfully theorized by economics, psychology, and other specialized fields have been removed, but the miscellaneous contents of a residual class cannot be the subject of a coherent inquiry. The word also refers to the sum total of human activities and implies a general science of society that integrates the conclusions of the specialized disciplines. But in this case it identifies a fiction, for nothing coherent corresponds to this all-embracing conception of society. Social relationships are defined by the specific practices in which actual persons are related. They are 'human devices, autonomous manners of being associated, each with its own specified conditions of relationship,' not 'the components of an unspecified, unconditional interdependence or "social" relationship, something called a "society" or "Society"' (*VLL*, 34-5). There is no such thing, Oakeshott insists, as a social relationship that is not a relationship of a specific kind: 'human conduct is continuously and decisively "social" only in respect of agents being associated in terms of their understanding and enjoyment of specific practices.'[9]

Whether we conceive them as being concerned with general laws or with individual meanings, the social sciences, like the natural sci-

[7]   Oakeshott, *The Voice of Liberal Learning: Michael Oakeshott on Education*, ed. Timothy Fuller (New Haven: Yale Univ. Press, 1989), 34. Hereafter: *VLL*.

[8]   Hans-Georg Gadamer, *Truth and Method*, 2d rev. [English language] ed., trans. Joel Weinsheimer and Donald G. Marshall (NY: Crossroad Publishing Co., 1989), xxii.

[9]   Oakeshott, *On Human Conduct* (Oxford: Clarendon Press, 1975) 87. Hereafter: *OHC*.

ences, are for Oakeshott explanatory inquiries. They must always be distinguished from the objects they study. The point can be illustrated by the distinction between the fine arts and art history. The arts themselves are not part of historical inquiry, understood as an explanatory discipline. They do, however, belong to the *geistige Welt* of human meanings and can become the concern of historical or other explanatory inquiries. We must distinguish, in other words, between artistic activity and the study of that activity. As human sciences, the disciplines that study the arts presuppose the existence of cultural objects with which their own conclusions must not be confused.

Oakeshott uses a parallel argument to establish that the social sciences are not necessarily tied to practical concerns — that the oft-asserted 'unity of theory and practice' in the social sciences is no more than inane dogma. Oakeshott's argument identifies a deeply-rooted error in the hermeneutic tradition. By reducing all experience to practical experience (the realm of 'life', 'praxis', 'values', etc.), Dilthey, Collingwood, Heidegger, Habermas, Taylor, Rorty, and many others argue that the human sciences seek a theoretical understanding of human activity that is also (today we would say, 'always already') practical. But if the human sciences are distinguished from the poetic arts, they are equally distinguished from the practical. These sciences study practical experience but they purport to generate knowledge that is detached from the values, interests, and other practical concerns that compose that experience. Of course they fail, but if they do not postulate the possibility of such knowledge, the have no claim to being knowledge, no claim to objectivity (intersubjectivity). One reason that hermeneutic philosophers so often insist on the inherently practical, or as they sometimes say, 'value-laden', character of the social sciences is that in opposing positivism they believe themselves compelled to disagree with the positivist claim that knowledge can be 'value-free'. But positivism might be (and, I believe, is) correct in distinguishing explanatory knowledge from practical concerns even if it mistakenly claims that there is no difference between explaining human and natural events. Although the social sciences have, historically, united theoretical and practical concerns, these concerns are distinct. Combining them is a source of confusion, not an inherent, much less desirable, aspect of inquiry. That reasoning of one kind (say, historical) is affected by reasoning of another (practical) is not inherent to reasoning but incidental. The historian, qua historian, is concerned to work out a distinctive and autonomous historical manner of understanding, which only emerges when false scientific or practical concerns are put aside. The hermeneutic tradition can therefore be accused of failing to question the premises of the sciences it seeks to theorize. A philosophy of the social sciences might begin with the self-understanding of those sciences, but it cannot uncritically accept that understanding.

Orders and Idioms of Inquiry

Because Oakeshott's conception of the human sciences (as he expounds it in *On Human Conduct*) rests on the distinction between the categories 'intelligent' and 'not-intelligent', that distinction calls for further elucidation. Any coherent inquiry must first categorize what it wishes to understand. These categories define what Oakeshott, in that work, calls the 'order' of an inquiry. When we identify something as expressing intelligent conduct, we imply an inquiry different from that implied by identifying it as the product of a not-intelligent process. No inquiry can yield coherent conclusions if the 'identities' it investigates are categorially ambiguous: 'a categorially unambiguous identity is the condition of every significant adventure in theorizing, and the recognition of the category of the identity concerned is the first step in every such adventure' (*OHC*, 15). For Oakeshott, much of what is called 'social science' involves the categorial error of attempting to explain intelligent conduct as the outcome of non-intelligent processes. No significant understanding is possible where 'rules are misidentified as regularities, intelligent winks as physiological blinks, conduct as "behavior" and contingent relationships as causal or systematic connections' (*VLL*, 35).

To see something as an exhibition of intelligence, and therefore as human action or an outcome of human action, implies an inquiry that uses the concepts of thinking and choosing and pays attention to meaning. To see it as not being an expression of intelligence, in contrast, is to search for processes, not involving thinking and choice, that determine it. But the intelligent/not-intelligent distinction, though categorial in that each category excludes the other, is not an ontological one. The claim is not that there are two kinds of things in the universe — mental things and physical things — but that we construct the world differently according to how we categorize whatever it is we are trying to understand. The kind of 'thing' we are dealing with – intelligent or not-intelligent – is chosen, not given in its 'nature'. It springs from 'a distinction within the engagement of understanding' (*OHC*, 14). The inquirer's task is not to discover the uniquely correct description of what is going on, but to be clear about what category a description belongs to and the order of inquiry it implies.

Furthermore, to say that the intelligent/not-intelligent distinction is a categorial one is to say that explanations that reflect these different identifications are mutually incompatible. To see something as the product of intelligent conduct and to regard it as the result of a not-intelligent process is to understand it in mutually exclusive ways. The kind of understanding provided by one order of inquiry cannot be translated into that provided by the other. We can understand an intelligent activity (like writing a book) as involving not-intelligent processes, but the activity is not itself these processes. Propositions about not-intelligent processes cannot explain the ideas an author is expressing or their relationship to other ideas. Such propositions may explain the biochemistry of thinking and writing, but they cannot explain the semantic content – the meaning, importance, or truth – of what is thought or written.

The claim that arguments are nothing more than the outcome of biochemical or other processes is, in fact, self-refuting, for this proposition (which is also an argument) must then be a manifestation of such a process, not a proposition with truth-value. But if this proposition does have truth-value, so do other propositions, and that they are the result of a process is irrelevant to choosing between them on the basis of their truth or falsehood. The process does not invalidate the argument, which is distinct from the process that produced it. It cannot, therefore, be reduced to that process. Each is governed by its own laws – the process by the causal laws that are its mechanism, the argument by the rules that are its standards.

To identify something as either intelligent or not-intelligent determines the 'order' of the inquiry appropriate to it, but it does not determine what Oakeshott calls its 'idiom'. Within each order we can distinguish idioms of inquiry ('sciences') that, although distinct, do not categorially exclude one another. One idiom might conceivably be reducible to another idiom within the same order: the principles of physiology, for example, might be restated in chemical terms, or political theory shown to be an extension of ethics. But an authentic idiom of inquiry is one that avoids the incoherence that exists in a field when the understanding it offers is categorially ambiguous.

Oakeshott's mature view, then, is that the human sciences are distinguishable but not necessarily independent inquiries concerned with the ideas, actions, practices, and institutions of human beings. Each begins by identifying these phenomena as expressions of human intelligence and is therefore an idiom within the order of inquiries determined by this identification. The social sciences as commonly understood and practiced, in contrast, are categorially ambiguous because they seek to combine propositions about intelligent conduct, on the one hand, and not-intelligent processes, on the other.

Interpretation and Individuality

All understanding, Oakeshott maintains, is concerned with meanings. When he defines the categories 'intelligent' and 'not-intelligent', he does not deny this basic idea but simply refines it by distinguishing two kinds of meaning in understanding: that which belongs to the object to be understood and that which the observer brings to the study of the object. Intelligent things have meaning in both senses, not-intelligent things only in the latter.

To make sense of human actions we must pay attention to the self-understandings of those whose actions they are. It is the self-understanding inherent in an action that distinguishes it from a natural event. This self-understanding is not entirely idiosyncratic, however, for it rests on the intersubjective meanings that constitute languages and other human practices. To understand any action we must understand the systems of shared meaning, the practices, on which it draws. The natural sciences generate explanatory theories that are themselves systems of meaning, but these theories ignore the element of meaning that may be present in the objects they seek to explain. If our concern is to understand a not-intelligent process, the choice of an interpretive scheme that excludes meaning at the level of the object to be explained is methodologically necessary and productive. But intelligent conduct, as such, cannot be explained by natural (not-intelligent) processes.

The doubly hermeneutic character of knowledge about what we identify as an expression of intelligence permits us to distinguish Oakeshott's understanding of the relationship between the human and the natural sciences from the view that there is no significant distinction between these sciences. Richard Rorty, for example, dismisses the distinction between the two, together with the mind-nature distinction itself, as arbitrary and insignificant.[10] From the true premise that all knowledge involves meanings and rests on interpretation, he falsely reasons that hermeneutics has the same significance in the natural as in the human sciences.

If this were true, the distinction between the natural sciences and the human sciences would indeed be superfluous. 'Universal hermeneutics' takes Vico's dictum — that we can know the human world because we have constructed it — and extends it to the natural world, for to say that everything is experienced in terms of human categories is to make nature itself a product of mind. The *geistige Welt*, the inherited world of meanings into which every human being is born, is a world composed not of physical objects but of ideas. But if, as Oakeshott suggests (*VLL*, 45), both the natural and the human worlds are human achievements belonging to the same *geistige Welt*, how can we distinguish between the natural and the human sciences? As Robert Grant puts it, 'if the world is really a unity, why does it require two distinct kinds of study?'[11] And the answer, it should now be clear, is that although all understanding involves meanings and is therefore 'hermeneutic', to understand human conduct we must pay attention to two levels of meaning. Understanding human activity requires a second level of interpretation, beyond that needed in the natural sciences viewed as systems of ideas, because in the human sciences the object of inquiry as well as the inquiry itself is composed of meanings.

There is a connection between understanding something as an expression of intelligence and understanding its individuality — a connection that illuminates the relationship between the two criteria identified by nineteenth-century philosophers to distinguish the study of human activity from the study of nature. To understand something as an expression of intelligence is to see it as an individual object having its own distinct character and significance. To understand what is categorized as a natural object, in contrast, is to understand the properties of the class to which it belongs. In scientific understanding we are concerned not with an individual object but

---

[10] Richard Rorty, *Philosophy and the Mirror of Nature* (Princeton: Princeton Univ. Press, 1979), 343-56.
[11] Robert Grant, *Thinkers of Our Time: Oakeshott* (London: Claridge Press, 1990), 42-3.

with the class of things it represents. But the human sciences — the humanities and humanistic social sciences — are concerned to understand individual human performances and practices — individual acts and texts, rituals and genres, and so forth — not the class 'human actions'. Human activity, construed as expressing intelligence, consists of the actions performed by actual persons at particular moments. Because a performance is an individual event, it can be understood as the unique outcome of other events. When understood in this manner, individual performances are connected in a kind of relationship that Oakeshott explores, in *On Human Conduct* and more thoroughly in *On History*, under the label 'contingency'. And the kind of inquiry that establishes such connections is historical inquiry. The same can be said for practices, which are individual at another level.

Because there are many possible contexts in which an action can be understood, there are many ways of elucidating its meaning. Every performance presupposes practices that are part of its context and are therefore relevant to understanding it. But the meaning of a performance is not exhausted by its relation to the various practices it may illustrate. It is also an intelligent act whose meaning depends on other acts to which it responds. To understand actual performances as a connected series of events is to see these acts as composing a historical narrative in which individual occurrences acquire significance as the contingent outcome of their antecedents. The explanation provided by a history of contingently connected events is one in which the identified antecedents of a performance do not simply account for its occurrence but illuminate its meaning. Positivist theories of historical explanation assume that historical inquiry aims to account for the occurrence of events whose character is already known. But this, Oakeshott insists, is precisely what the historian cannot assume. Historical inquiry is not a matter of explaining already known events — events whose character is simply given. It requires historians to infer the character of an event by relating it, on the basis of what the canons of historical scholarship define as evidence, to its antecedents so that its character is illuminated by the relationship the historian has identified.

This analysis implies a view of history as a mode of explanation distinct from 'scientific explanation'. But it also implies a general philosophy of the social sciences, one that recognizes the importance of meaning in these sciences but distinguishes between treating human practices as systems of meaning and explaining individual performances. Historical understanding, then, is one way of understanding human conduct. How is it related to other ways of understanding conduct?

History and the Human Sciences

For Oakeshott, historical inquiry is not coextensive with the social sciences; it is one idiom among others concerned with human conduct. But the social sciences, when they seek to explain individual performances, are parasitic on historical inquiry. The explanations of human conduct offered by scholars in the social sciences are in effect partial or truncated historical explanations. They fall short as explanations because even though they provide interpretations of conduct, they cannot account for why someone responded in a particular way on a particular occasion, or, in general, why individual actions or individual practices are what they are. Insofar as anthropology, sociology, and other social sciences are concerned with particular practices and with actions made intelligible in terms of such practices, they are 'respectable and somewhat attenuated engagements in historical understanding' (*VLL*, 36).

The failure of the social sciences to provide genuine explanations of individual human actions can be seen most clearly in those disciplines that remain committed to a science of human behavior on the model of the natural sciences, and that rest on the claim that this science can yield generalizations about intelligent action that explain the occurrence of particular acts. In *On Human Conduct*, Oakeshott considers two versions of this claim: the argument that actions can be explained as expressions of human nature — either in general or in the nature of certain categories of human beings (women, for example) — and the argument that they can be explained by an agent's social circumstances.

For Oakeshott, whether we rely on the idea of human nature or on what we believe to be the traits of certain categories of human beings, conceiving an agent as possessing characteristic dispositions has only limited utility in explaining particular acts (*OHC*, 95). The proposition that politicians are characteristically disloyal and dishonest, even if true, tells us little about why Alcibiades or Richard Nixon broke a promise or told a lie. The idea of 'human nature' or ideas concerning the dispositional qualities of a particular class can be used to frame generalizations, but if we want to explain individual performances, these generalizations cannot take us very far. The same point can be said of the efforts of political scientists, market researchers, and others to explain particular acts in relation to an agent's 'social circumstances' — that he or she is college-educated or an immigrant, for example. Such explanations invoke causal relationships between not-intelligent identities — income levels, suicide rates, and other variables that are abstracted from conduct (Durkheim's 'social facts') — not the intelligent choices of agents performing actions. Even when successful, this enterprise has nothing to do with understanding the thoughts and choices of individual persons on specific occasions. Contra Davidson, a person's reason for acting is not its 'cause' in this (scientific) sense of the word.[12] Davidson assumes that in explaining intelligent action we employ the same idea of causation as that used in explaining not-intelligent events. For Oakeshott, in contrast, the presuppositions of causal explanation vary from one mode to another. Historical and scientific causation involve categorially distinct kinds of explanation — explanations that cannot, without incoherence, be brought under a single, equivocal, label.

Implicit in these strategies for salvaging the idea of a natural science of human conduct that can explain individual performances is the unwarranted assumption that an explanation that draws upon statistical generalizations is a scientific explanation. But generalizations about how people in general, people with certain character traits, or people in certain social circumstances customarily behave are not scientific generalizations about a truly time-independent class of phenomena; they are more or less well-disguised descriptions of customs specific to a particular historical situation. To explain an event in terms of the customs it is said to exemplify is to invoke not scientific laws but descriptive generalizations regarding a particular time and place. The same can be said of efforts to predict particular events, like the outcome of an election, where such efforts rely on statistical models that extrapolate data patterns of limited generality. Nor, to extend Oakeshott's point, is statistical social science the only enterprise that seeks to represent intelligent conduct as the unintended outcome of dispositions or social circumstances, for this is also the program of structuralism and poststructuralism in the

[12] See Donald Davidson, 'Actions, Reasons and Causes,' in *Readings in the Philosophy of Social Science*, ed. Michael Martin and Lee C. McIntyre (Cambridge: MIT Press, 1994).

hands of Lévi-Strauss, Foucault, Derrida, and others whose arguments, though diverse and often incompatible, explain human actions in terms of the systems ('structures', 'discourses') that produce them.

When the pretense of scientific generalization is dropped, we are left with historically specific generalizations and with a way of speaking about conduct that is concerned not with actions but with historical situations or practices. Historians, for example, often rely on what Oakeshott calls a 'situational identity' (*OHC*, 57). Situational identities are broad interpretive concepts like 'the civilization of Renaissance Italy' or 'Atlantic republicanism', each of which is a pattern of related occurrences identified by a historian in an effort to answer a historical question. But reconstructing a historical situation is only part of what is involved in framing a historical explanation, for the identified situation gives us a static, unchanging historical past. To explain past events we need an inquiry that goes beyond reconstructing a past situation. It must explain any occurrence, whether a simple performance or a complex situation, as itself a historical event or sequence of events. Because its antecedents are other events, to explain an event historically is not to reveal its place in an unchanging situation but to illuminate its character as the outcome of these events. Like a generalization concerning human nature or social circumstances, then, a situational identity is an interpretive tool that falls short of explaining particular, contingent happenings. The same may be said of efforts to account for human actions as expressions of unchanging structures or discourses.

Many ways of explaining conduct interpret individual performances as expressions of (or reactions to) particular literary genres, architectural styles, moral ideals, etc. Much of what goes on in anthropology, law, cultural studies, and other humanities fields is concerned with actions as subscribing or not subscribing to such practices, understood as patterns ('languages' or 'idioms') of human performance. The human sciences are concerned, each in its own way, with theorizing human conduct in relation to practices. A practice provides what Oakeshott calls a 'map' on which to locate individual acts. But the understanding provided by identifying actions in relation to practices is not a complete understanding: it reveals only their character as performances of a certain kind. In other words, to interpret an action as reflecting a given practice is to reveal its character 'in terms of its "conventionality"' (*OHC*, 99-100). Such an approach is obviously important in the social sciences. But the understanding of human conduct it provides is limited.

The explanation of actions as expressions of practices remains, then, an exercise in open-ended interpretation. It is incomplete and indeterminate for several reasons. First, every action expresses an indefinite number of practices and can be described in an indefinite number of ways. This is one reason arguments in the humanities so often strike both outsiders and insiders as undisciplined and futile. What is the point of a game in which all moves are legal? Coherence in these fields emerges only when the rules of the game are both clear and genuinely restrictive. The challenge in the humanities is to tame the use of metaphor so that something definite can be said. Second, because (as previously intimated) practices are themselves historical occurrences, their meaning is also contextual. That is, although a practice provides a context for understanding individual actions, it is itself a contingent outcome of events. What is said about explaining performances therefore applies, by extension, to practices (*OHC*, 92 n.1, 100 n.1). Third, practices are not independent of the individual actions they are used to interpret, for a practice is itself created and continually modified by its performances. Practices are displayed only in performances: a practice is the continuously generated by-product of its performances. Practices are not 'stable compositions of easily recognized characteristics.' They are 'footprints left behind by agents responding to their emergent situations, footprints which are only somewhat less evanescent than the transactions in which they emerged' (*OHC*, 100). Like other historical identities, the practices that are used to illuminate performances are not immutable; they are themselves more or less slowly changing identities in terms of which to understand change. And, finally, because the conventionality of a performance is only one aspect of its character, no performance can be explained solely in terms of its having or not having a conventional character, and the more original the performance the less mileage we get in attempting to explain it in conventional terms. What works for Agatha Christie may fail for Shakespeare. For all these reasons, there are no conclusive interpretations.

Interpretive theorizing in the social sciences is typically 'an engagement of historical understanding of a certain limited sort' (*OHC*, 24), because it is typically the interpretation of individual human practices and performances. But such interpretation is not historical in a narrower sense of the term — it is not history 'properly so-called' — because it cannot explain why one performance occurred rather than another, or why a given practice came into being, changed, or disappeared. To interpret an action in relation to a practice cannot explain why an agent has chosen to view a situation or to respond to it in a particular way. Practices can provide a context for interpreting a performance, but they are only one aspect of a larger context. They cannot provide more than a very partial and tentative understanding of the character of an action because performances are related not only to practices but also to other performances. What is needed to fill in the free space of interpretation that remains after an action's conventionality (or lack thereof) has been explored is an account of its relationship to other actions, that is, an account that places it in a narrative of contingently related events: a historical explanation proper.

12

Leslie Marsh

Constructivism and Relativism in Oakeshott

What is at Stake?

This paper highlights a troubling tension within the philosophy of Michael Oakeshott.[1] The relativistic stance that informs his radical constructivism gives license to socio-political conclusions we know Oakeshott could not possibly accept.

Politically, Oakeshott cannot accept constructionist social ontologies that are forged in the clamor for rights, an abstract and axiomatic foundationalist conception of rights, which demands a corresponding morality not deduced from morally relevant considerations.

Educationally, Oakeshott laments that the notion of disinterested liberal learning is rendered redundant given the incessant impulse for RELEVANCE, now guaranteed with sociology as its master.

Scientifically, Oakeshott plays both sides and this is most problematic. On the one hand he commends science for its achievement *against* the sociology of knowledge view that science is at best an ideology, at worst, a tool of oppression. On the other hand, the constructivist/relativist Oakeshott berates science for being devoid of any truth-value. Taken thus, bereft of any veritistic notions, Oakeshott is in no position to distinguish good science from pseudo-science. Oakeshott therefore plays into the hands of the scientism that has been the hallmark of his Rationalist and contravenes his own primary philosophical dictum — the error of irrelevance.

For Oakeshott these three dimensions have conspired to create a distinctly *il*liberal intellectual climate, a regime of 'ready-made' or

[1]   This paper has benefited from comments made by Corey Abel, Robert Grant, Anthony Quinton, and Geoffrey Thomas.

approved ideas, 'oppressive uniformities of thought or attitude or conduct.'[2] Behind the ostensibly liberal metaphysic of social constructionism is a reformist program that is not at all benign. Furthermore, behind the familiar appeal to notions of 'social' justice, 'social' conscience, 'social' science and all manner of RELEVANCE, there lies a self-serving *il*liberal divisiveness functional to a realignment of power relations. In a word, 'socialization' is the order of the day — a gross example of an *ignoratio elenchi*.

The question then is, why does Oakeshott's constructivism and relativism not tally with his socio-political conclusions? *Oakeshott accepts all of the philosophical pre-conditions of constructivism yet he cannot accept its natural conclusion.* If Rorty's co-option of Oakeshott's metaphor of 'conversation' in the service of his own radically relativist epistemology has any plausibility, this creates serious problems for Oakeshott: it throws up some surprising socio-political anomalies for those of us attracted to Oakeshott's philosophical politics.

The Sources of Constructivism

Constructivism and relativism tend to be two sides of the same coin but I will try, insofar as it is feasible, to separate out the issues as we go along. In what follows is a quick and highly selective history of constructivism: I do not make any reference to constructivist theories that have currency in developmental psychology (e.g., Piaget) and socio-cultural theory (e.g., Vygotsky).

On some interpretations the constructivism debate is as old as philosophy itself. Its precursors can be found in Protagoras' dictum 'Man is the measure of all things, of the existence of the things that are and the non-existence of the things that are not'; this was ascribed and attacked by Plato as relativistic. Modern constructivist theories take as their starting point Kant's transcendental idealism. We then have the Romantics' rejection of the notions of progress and rationality embodied in the universalizing tendencies of the Scientific Revolution and the Enlightenment. The seeds of social constructivism, implicit in the sociology-of-knowledge tradition, are to be found in Marx, Manheim and Durkheim: all emphasized the causal role of social factors in shaping belief. At the turn of the twentieth century and between Wars with the rise of postmodern-

---

[2] Oakeshott, *The Voice of Liberal Learning: Michael Oakeshott on Education*, ed. Timothy Fuller (Indianapolis: Liberty Press, 2001), 20, 31, 85, 93, 96. Hereafter: *VLL*.

ism, the leitmotif was again the rejection of objective truth and scientific rationality. Mid-century saw 'the silly doctrine' (*VLL*, 22) of the Two Cultures debate.[3] The distant heirs of the first wave of sociology of knowledge theorists have included the later Wittgenstein, Kuhn, Foucault and Rorty — the latter finding in Oakeshott's metaphor of 'conversation' support for his radical relativism. TRUTH for Rorty, scientific truth included, is merely a matter of agreement or 'solidarity,' downgraded from any privileged position. This debate culminated in the Sokal[4] hoax igniting the most disputatious and bitter of debates within and beyond philosophy.[5]

Alvin Goldman identifies six lines of argument that typically feed the contemporary constructivist (and relativist) rejection of truth-based epistemology[6] — to use Goldman's term, their 'veriphobia.'[7] These six criticisms are as follows:

(i) *The argument from social construction*: What we call true is a product of social construction, negotiation, with no consideration to the 'external' features of reality.

(ii) *Language and world making*:[8] Knowledge, reality and truth are the products of language. There is no language-independent reality that can make our thoughts true or false.

(iii) *The unknowability criticism*: If there were any transcendent or objective truths, they would be inaccessible and hence can play no role in practical epistemic evaluation.

(iv) *The denial of epistemic privilege*: There are no privileged or foundational epistemic positions. The arbiter of all claims is convention, tradition and practice.

[3]   C.P. Snow, *The Two Cultures and the Scientific Revolution* (Cambridge: Cambridge Univ. Press, 1959). An equally famous response comes from F. R. Leavis and Michael Yudkin, *Two Cultures? The Significance of C. P. Snow* (London: Chatto and Windus, 1962).

[4]   Alan Sokal and Jean Bricmont, *Intellectual Impostures* (1998; reprinted with a new preface, London: Profile Books, 2003). This generated a voluminous literature — a good starting point is www.physics.nyu.edu/faculty/sokal (accessed 4 April 2004).

[5]   For an overview of the so-called 'science wars' see James Robert Brown, *Who Rules in Science: An Opinionated Guide to the Wars* (Cambridge: Harvard Univ. Press, 2001).

[6]   Alvin Goldman, *Knowledge in a Social World* (Oxford: Oxford Univ. Press, 1999), 9-40.

[7]   Goldman, *Knowledge*, 7.

[8]   See also Michael Devitt, *Realism and Truth* (Princeton: Princeton Univ. Press, 1997), 235-58.

(v)   *The argument from domination*: Appeals to truth are merely instruments of domination, which should be remedied by installing progressive social value.

(vi)   *The argument from bias*: Truth cannot be obtained because all ostensibly truth-orientated practices are tainted and biased by political, economic or other self-serving interests.

Both (i) and (ii) have anti-essentialism at their heart: spatio-temporal boundaries should not be conceived as necessities. Arguments (i) to (iii) are *prima facie* Kantian:[9]

Premise 1: We can know things only as they are related to us,

Premise 2: under our forms of perception and understanding insofar as they fall under our conceptual schemes.

Conclusion: We cannot know things as they are in themselves.

This form of this argument is lampooned by David Stove as the 'Worst Argument in the World,'[10] which he does not expressly pin on Kant.[11] It runs like this:

We can eat oysters only insofar as they are brought under the physiological and chemical conditions that are the presuppositions of the possibility of being eaten.

Therefore: We cannot eat oysters as they are in themselves.[12]

Arguments (v) and (vi) are forms of what Susan Haack calls the 'Passes-for Fallacy.'[13]

Premise 1: Relativists claim that what passes for X (truth, fact, knowledge, evidence, etc.) is often a fiction.

Premise 2: It is those in positions of power that have managed to get people to accept as X.

Conclusion: 'The concept of X is ideological humbug.'

---

[9]   Devitt calls this style of argument 'fig-leaf' realism.

[10]   David Stove, 'Judge's report on the competition to find the worst argument in the world,' in *Cricket Versus Republicanism* (Sydney: Quakers Hill Press, 1995), 66-7. I am indebted to Peter Coleman for bringing Stove's work to my attention.

[11]   James Franklin, 'Stove's Discovery of the Worst Argument in the World,' *Philosophy* 77 (2002): 615-24.

[12]   David Stove, *The Plato Cult and Other Philosophical Follies* (Oxford: Blackwell, 1991), 151, 161.

[13]   Susan Haack, 'Fallibilism, Objectivity, and the New Cynicism,' *EPISTEME* 1, no.1 (June 2004): 36, 40.

The argument is invalid for if, as the conclusion says, 'the concepts of truth, evidence, honest inquiry, etc., are ideological humbug, then the premise couldn't be really-and-truly true, nor could we have objectively good evidence, obtained by honest inquiry, that it is so.'[14]

Goldman and some other leading epistemologists[15] do now acknowledge that there has been a lacuna in epistemology in the Cartesian tradition of individual knowers. They are not denying that there is a social dimension to knowledge. But to dispense with the notion of TRUTH is to submit to an untenable relativism

Oakeshott's Constructivism

Oakeshott commentators have highlighted the continuities between Oakeshott and the arguments that comprise items (i) though (iv) above. Items (v) and (vi), Marxist in inspiration, would have no appeal for Oakeshott.

Consider the following examples from Hacking and Oakeshott. Hacking offers numerous items that have had constructivist claims made on their behalf and includes gender, illness, women, refugees, quarks, Zulu nationalism, Japan, the past, emotions, reality, the child viewer of television, the Landsat satellite system, dolomite, and the self.[16] Oakeshott's examples are:

> A rock-formation, a boy on a bicycle, a waterfall, Westminster Abbey, the circulation of money in an economy, a man going upstairs to bed or posting a letter, or a volume of Racine's plays standing on a bookshelf... [17]

> Stories, poems, works of art, musical compositions, landscapes, human actions, utterances and gestures, religious beliefs, inquiries, sciences, procedures, practices and other artifacts of all sorts... (*VLL*, 9)[18]

Hacking's and Oakeshott's lists are indistinguishable in the sense that people, inanimate objects, states, conditions, events, practices, actions, experiences, relations, substances and concepts are all candidates for constructivist claims.

If the dependence of facts upon human activity means no more than that the facts would not be what they are if people did not do

---

[14] Haack, 'Fallibilism,' 36, 40.

[15] Hilary Kornblith, *Knowledge and its Place in Nature* (Oxford: Oxford Univ. Press, 2002).

[16] Ian Hacking, *The Social Construction of What?* (Cambridge: Harvard Univ. Press, 1999), 6.

[17] Oakeshott, *On Human Conduct* (Oxford: Clarendon Press, 1975), 18. Hereafter: *OHC*.

[18] Cf. *VLL*, 37, 65, 66.

certain things, then it has to be admitted that all facts are constructed. This weak constructivism is mind-numbingly banal. This is not what is being contested. André Kukla distinguishes between *causal* constructivism and *constitutive* constructivism.[19] The former is the view that human activity causes and sustains the facts about the world (including scientific facts); the latter is the view that what we call 'facts about the world' are really just facts about human activity. A more interesting form of dependence is *strong* constructivism, one that insists that *all* facts (artifactual or natural) would cease to exist without the continued presence (and appropriate behavior) of human agents. In other words, there is no independent reality. This is clearly consonant with Oakeshott's idealism.

That Oakeshott subscribes to a strong form of constructivism should not be in any doubt:

> The 'natural world' of the scientist is an artefact no less than the world of practical activity; but it is an artefact constructed on a different principle and in response to a different impulse.[20]

And again:

> Fact is what has been made or achieved; it is the product of judgment ... Fact... is not what is given, it what is achieved ... Facts are never merely observed, remembered or combined; they are always made. We cannot 'take' facts, because there are none to take until we have constructed them.[21]

Indeed, for Oakeshott *everything* is a construction: 'The starry heavens above us and the moral law within are alike human achievements' (*VLL*, 38).[22] To my knowledge only two commentators well-disposed to Oakeshott have expressed discomfort with Oakeshott's constructivism: one is Anthony Quinton, the other, the

---

[19] André Kukla, *Social Constructivism and the Philosophy of Science* (London: Routledge, 2000), 21. Kukla also suggests that there may be an intermediate position whereby the physical *supervenes* on the social.

[20] Oakeshott, *Rationalism in Politics and other essays, new and expanded edition*, ed. Timothy Fuller (Indianapolis: Liberty Fund, 1991), 506. Hereafter: *RIP*.

[21] Oakeshott, *Experience and its Modes* (Cambridge: Cambridge Univ. Press, 1933), 42. Hereafter: *EM*.

[22] Robert Orr points out the allusion to Kant 'who confessed himself to be fascinated equally by the starry heavens above and the moral world within, and admitted his inability to make the twain meet.' Robert Orr, 'A Double Agent in the Dream of Michael Oakeshott' *Political Science Reviewer* 21 (1992): 44-62. Oakeshott uses a similar phrase in 'The Character of a University Education,' in *What is History and other essays*, ed. Luke O'Sullivan (Exeter: Imprint Academic, 2004), 375. Hereafter: *WH*.

late Robert Orr.[23] The Kantian inspired constructivism of *On Human Conduct* is taken to task by Orr: 'This phase three self is the one that invents rather than discovers properties in the natural world.'[24]

Oakeshott argues at length in *Experience and its Modes* for rejecting the realist myth of the self-differentiating object (*EM*, 10-14, 18-19, 23). Oakeshott argues that experience involves both perception and thought. In this sense it is hypothesized. This is a broadly Kantian (and Bradleian) position, and is common coin in most modern attempts to explain the nature of experience.[25] We have learned to reject what Wilfrid Sellars called 'the Myth of the Given.' Experience requires, not just the capacity for sensory awareness stressed by Locke and Hume, but also the capacity to make judgments about what one is aware of. At a minimum this last condition means that, in the current *argot*, observation is theory-laden.

Such a truism would not be worth stating were it not that philosophy in its attempt to articulate reality has been divided by the realist 'myth of the self-differentiating object' and, as I term it, the 'constructivist myth.' The latter is of the view that the inquiring mind does not merely construe reality; it *constructs* it. We all accept Oakeshott's case against the realist myth, but in his fully subscribing to the constructivist myth, Oakeshott poses a false dichotomy and this creates problems for him.

The reason is this: writers in the social constructivist tradition by their own admission tend to be political or reformist; they have a socio-political agenda.[26] This impulse would qualify as Rationalistic on Oakeshott's terms.

Consider the general form of the constructivist position:[27]

(i) X, or X as it is at present, is not determined by the nature of things; it is not inevitable. Furthermore, the natural X and the artifactual X would cease to exist *without* the continued presence and appropriate behavior of human agents.

---

[23] See Anthony Farr's obituary: www.michael-oakeshott-association.org.

[24] Orr, 'Dream', 57.

[25] See *EM*, 54: 'The doctrine, then, that the real is what is independent of experience should be distinguished from the doctrine that the weakness and imperfection of our human faculties place a permanent barrier between knowledge and reality; but it is difficult to say which is the more ridiculous.'

[26] Hacking, *Social Construction*, 6.

[27] Hacking, *Social Construction*, 6, 12; Kukla *Social Constructivism*; and David Wiggins *Sameness and Substance* (Oxford: Oxford Univ. Press, 1980), 147-8.

(ii)   It is conceivable that reality (social or otherwise) might have been articulated and individuated with very different principles; thus, spatio-temporal boundaries should not be conceived as necessities.

(iii)   We would be better off if X were transformed or even abolished.

Now what is odd about Oakeshott's position is this. He subscribes to (i) and (ii), but his anti-rationalism precludes him from accepting (iii). Oakeshott once denied that he had 'an extravagant distaste for normative reflection.'[28] Yet (iii) is the easiest of derivations to make once (i) is accepted.

The anti-essentialism of (i) and (ii) is clear. Take an explicit example of Oakeshott's anti-essentialism. He writes:

> For example, the word 'water' stands for a practical image; but a scientist does not first perceive 'water' and then resolve it into H_2O: *scientia* begins only when 'water' has been left behind. To speak of H_2O as 'the chemical formula for water' is to speak in a confused manner: H_2O is a symbol the rules of whose behaviour are wholly different from those which govern the symbol 'water'. (*RIP*, 514)

Whether or not Oakeshott was familiar with the Kripke-Putnam doctrine of natural kinds I do not know.[29] Their thought experiment goes roughly like this. Imagine a 'twin earth' wherein there is a liquid qualitatively very similar to water, but whose inner constitution is XYZ rather than H_2O and is used for exactly the same purposes. We would not say that this stuff was water. What we mean by 'water' is partly determined by our causal interaction with the relevant kind. The surface phenomena comprise a 'stereotype', or 'reference-fixing device', so that I pick out 'this stuff'. We partly defer to science, so that the meaning of 'water' is not determined solely by the individual thinker but also the 'experts.' Of course, before it was known that water is H_2O people had beliefs about it and referred to it. The essentialist statement that water must be H_2O is a *de re* proposition and an *a posteriori* truth. For Oakeshott, '[S]cientific knowledge...has no contribution to make to our knowledge of reality' (*EM*, 217).

If water is a social construction then it becomes relative to an epistemic community — an interest, a group, a society, a culture. Jus-

---

[28]   Oakeshott, 'Rationalism in Politics: A Reply to Professor Raphael,' *Political Studies* 13 (1965), 89.

[29]   Saul Kripke, *Naming and Necessity* (Oxford: Blackwell, 1980); Hilary Putnam, *Philosophical Papers*, vol. 2: *Mind, Language and Reality* (Cambridge: Cambridge Univ. Press, 1975).

tification is nothing more than a social practice, a convention, conversational, explicitly spurning the question of whether beliefs are veridical or justified. In Oakeshott's discussion of identity, he asserts that 'It is impossible to say . . . where the environment ends and the thing begins' (*EM*, 63). So identities end up being defined not just in terms of the mode to which they belong, but according to a community of inquirers or practitioners: every 'identity' is thus susceptible to revision. This question is, of course, a perennial topic within the identity literature but it should be noted that if Oakeshott abandons the Leibnizian conception of identity and the canonical notions of *identical*, *continuant*, and *individuate*, there arise overwhelming difficulties.

So for Oakeshott the knowledge we have is no more than knowledge in the weakest of senses:

(1)　Knowledge = belief, or

(2)　Knowledge = institutionalized belief

The former variant can be true or false, rational or irrational, agreed to or not agreed to by other members of the believer's community. In the latter, individual believers belong to a community that has a way of bringing order to cognitive affairs. The irony is that (1) and (2) are typically the positions of the sociology-of-knowledge movement, which Oakeshott feels has had a corrosive effect in the areas under discussion.

Compare these formulations to the stronger and orthodox notion of what we mean by knowledge:

(3)　Knowledge = justified true belief (plus)

Mere belief or opinion is not sufficient for knowledge: knowledge also requires truth. Moreover, true belief does not qualify as knowledge unless it is justified, warranted, or acquired in some suitable fashion. (Edmund Gettier showed that knowledge requires even more than justified true belief.[30]) What is crucially missing from Oakeshott (and Rorty's) account of knowledge is the notion of TRUTH in the last sense. And this is perfectly consistent with the view that *truths are fallible and revisable*. At this point it is appropriate to discuss Oakeshott's coherentist theory of truth and attendant relativism.

---

[30]　Edmund Gettier, 'Is Justified True Belief Knowledge?' *Analysis* 23 (1963): 121-3.

Oakeshott's Relativism

Attributions of relativism to Oakeshott are twofold: The first, and the more common attribution, is from the general perspective of viewing Oakeshott as a postmodern relativist. The second, more technical aspect and less familiar attribution, involves the assumption that Oakeshott was a coherentist.

I examine the second view first. On this assumption it is standard to present Oakeshott with the following problem. It is empirically and conceptually possible that there are any number of ethical, political, and social beliefs and activities that form equally coherent systems, with *ex hypothesi* no decidability on grounds of coherence between them. And this is relativism (or one recognizable form of it).

Coherentism can inform both a theory of what we are justified in *believing* and a theory of *truth*. Indeed the two can be, and usually are, linked. We are justified in believing that X is the case if and only if:

(a) The belief that X is the case is consistent with all other beliefs in our system of beliefs; moreover and more strongly;

(b) those beliefs are mutually entailing; and

(c) the system of beliefs exhibits overall simplicity and is relevantly comprehensive.

The real work is done by condition (b), since (b) subsumes (a); and (c) is common to virtually all theories of justification. Then we can go from justification to truth by holding that truth just is the property of belonging to such a system of beliefs or worldview.

A standard problem with coherence as *justification* is that there seems no reason to accept that there is a single fully coherent and comprehensive system of beliefs or worldview from the perspective of a given subject — individual mind or a collectivity of minds — at a given time. A problem about *truth* and coherence is that it fails to do justice to an intuition most of us have about truth — namely that conditions (a), (b), and (c) might all be met, and our belief that X is the case *still* be false.

There are a number of discriminations to be made. Oakeshott might be expected to reject the idea of a single fully coherent and comprehensive system of beliefs or worldview from the perspective of a given subject — individual mind or collectivity of minds — at a given time. This might appear to follow from the possibility, indeed the fact, of different modes of experience — or, later, conversational 'voices' — that are incommensurable. Coherence is to be indexed to a particular mode or voice. Since, for example, science and history are answering modally distinct sorts of questions, there need be no mutual entailment between our answers to scientific questions and our answers to historical questions.

Still the problems about coherence, either for justification or truth, are simply replicated at the modal level. Take science: there seems no reason to accept that there is a single fully coherent and comprehensive system of scientific beliefs or worldview from the perspective of a given subject — individual mind or collectivity of minds — at a given time.

So it matters whether Oakeshott was a coherentist, because (even when we have made these discriminations) he cannot avoid the problems of coherentism concerning justification or truth. He cannot charge us with his favorite criticism: *ignoratio elenchi*.

Two points are relevant to the issue of Oakeshott's coherentism. The first is Terry Nardin's perfectly fair point that Oakeshott's account of the nature of coherence is so indeterminate that 'the idea of coherence necessarily functions as a metaphor, not a technical concept.'[31] This is not quite decisive, however. Oakeshott might be an inadequate explicit theorist of coherence but still, implicitly, employ a specific notion of it.

This leads to the second point. If we consider how Oakeshott conceives, in his famous phrase, 'the activity of being an historian,' we see a non-coherentist account of justification and truth at work. To avoid the problems of coherentism, let's try a different interpretation albeit a somewhat controversial one: the anticipated objections will be considered later. C. Behan McCullagh[32] outlines what he terms the 'correlation' theory of justification and truth. In it I find nothing with which Oakeshott would disagree. Now here is the controversial aspect: I take it to be a form of *inference to the best explanation* (IBE).

IBE holds that we have sufficient reason (i.e., justification) for accepting that hypothesis which, if true, would best explain X, where 'X' is some available evidence that presents a problem of intelligibility. Its logical form is:

X (evidence to be explained)

[31] Terry Nardin, *The Philosophy of Michael Oakeshott* (University Park, PA: Pennsylvania State Univ. Press, 2001), 22; *WH*, 88.

[32] C. Behan McCullagh, *The Truth of History* (London and New York: Routledge, 1998), 46.

Y (hypothesis which, if true, would best explain X)

Therefore Y

Note that IBE is a form of *non*-deductive inference; the premises *probabilify* and do not necessitate the conclusion. We accept Y because it is the best explanation of X available to us; it may still be false.

Now, of course, a whole set of questions immediately presents itself as to what constitutes the 'best explanation'. The matter cannot be fully discussed here; elucidation can be found in Peter Lipton's standard text.[33]

We infer to the best explanation regularly in science, history, and practice. It is formally elusive, indeterminate in its technical expression, but easily recognizable in specific examples. Jack has never liked Jill but suddenly becomes affable towards her. Jill starts to receive invitations to Jack's parties; Jack also sends Jill the occasional solicitous email; Jack asks Jill her opinion on a range of matters and listens carefully to her views. How best to explain this turn of events? We discover that Jack is standing for election to a committee that is likely to be divided on his candidature and on which Jill is likely to have a casting vote. So we infer that Jack has become affable towards Jill in order to secure her vote. From our knowledge of all concerned, this is the best explanation. It may be wrong; perhaps Jack has undergone a moral conversion. But we have no evidence, outside this episode, of any such conversion. If further evidence becomes available, the best explanation may change.

So far as I can make out, this is very much Oakeshott's approach to the nature of both historical and scientific explanation. It is hard to see how else, in science, he could explain why:

> The image of a stationary earth is replaced by that of a stationary sun, iron dissolves into an arrangement of electrons and protons, water is revealed to be a combination of gases and the concept of undulations in the air of various dimensions takes the place of the images of sounds. (*RIP*, 504-5)

These images changed because they provided or supported, according to the evidence available, the best explanation of a range of problems. And the image of the dry wall, invoked in his later

---

[33] Peter Lipton, *Inference to the Best Explanation* (London and New York: Routledge, 1991).

accounts of historical explanation,[34] is exactly apt for IBE. We infer the hypothesis that would, if true, provide the best explanation of the available evidence. *We build the wall (infer the historical hypothesis) that best fits the stones together (explains the available evidence).* (Oakeshott's 'dry-wall' analogy has some resonance with Haack's crossword analogy of scientific justification — her so-called Foundherentism,[35] which allows the relevance of experience to empirical justification *without* postulating any privileged class of basic beliefs or requiring that relations of support be essentially one directional.)

Two objections may be expected to this account of Oakeshott. The first is that it commits the fallacy of supposing that, because IBE fits well with (much of) what Oakeshott says, that therefore he accepts the model of IBE. The reply to this is that we know that Oakeshott cannot be a correspondence theorist about justification, at least with respect to historical explanation, because our historical explanations *cannot* correspond to an inexistent past. If Oakeshott does not subscribe to IBE, then it would be interesting to know what presents itself as a probable alternative, if correspondence is certainly out of the question and coherence were not in play.

Even if Oakeshott were an IBE theorist, relativism returns to haunt him. This is because such inference is indexed to a given subject — an individual mind or a collectivity of minds — at a given time. A dilemma arises for IBE. If it allows for ethical, political, and social justification, then:

(a) it must affirm the empirical and conceptual possibility that different minds or collectivities of minds — or let us say 'different persons', which is a more natural phrase here — may justifiably accept ethical, political, and social beliefs and activities which, when universalized, are inconsistent. That is the logic of the IBE model. Or,

(b) it must exclude the idea of ethical, political, and social justification. This would certainly avoid relativism in these areas.

On a clarificatory point: in the cases of IBE justification considered above, we focused on justification in believing *that* X (believing that something is the case), which may yield knowledge *that* X. It is clear

[34] Oakeshott, *On History and Other Essays* (Oxford: Blackwell, 1983). Hereafter: *OH*.

[35] Susan Haack, *Evidence and Inquiry: Towards Reconstruction in Epistemology* (Oxford: Blackwell, 1993).

that, on Oakeshott's account, justification will operate differently in ethical, political, and social action as involving justification in decision-making or practical reasoning, in deciding how to act, as well as justification in what to believe. This is why the dilemma refers to 'beliefs and activities'. In the background is Ryle's epistemological distinction by which it is widely agreed that Oakeshott was influenced.[36] But the question of justifying practical reasoning still applies. Our dilemma loses none of its force.

Now to the first view: Oakeshott as postmodern relativist. The most famous identification of Oakeshott with relativism came from Rorty in his co-option of Oakeshott's metaphor of 'conversation' in the service of his radical relativism:[37]

> If we see knowing not as having an essence, to be described by scientists or philosophers, but rather as a right, by current standards, to believe, then we are well on the way to seeing conversation as the ultimate context within which knowledge is to be understood. Our focus shifts from the relation between human beings and the objects of their inquiry to the relation between alternative standards of justification. . . . [38]

Rorty's target was twofold: a correspondence theory of truth and foundationalist justification. Yet this was no longer part of the philosophical landscape. Ramsey had long since proposed a reliabilist theory of knowledge.[39] Quine had already challenged analycity,[40] Sellars 'the Myth of the Given;'[41] and Goldman had presented a sec-

---

[36] Gilbert Ryle, *The Concept of Mind* (London: Hutchinson, 1949; reprint, Harmondsworth, England: Penguin Books, 1990), esp. chap. 2: 'Knowing How and Knowing That'; Oakeshott, Review of Ryle, *Concept of Mind*, *Spectator* 184 (1950): 20, 22; J.D. Mabbott, Review of *Rationalism in Politics*, *Mind* 72 (1963): 609. In a cognitive science context this ability distinction has been used in discussion of Frank Jackson's 'knowledge argument;' in 'Epiphenomenal *Qualia*' *Philosophical Quarterly* 32 (1982): 127-36.

[37] Richard Rorty, *Philosophy and the Mirror of Nature* (Princeton: Princeton Univ. Press, 1979; reprint, Oxford: Blackwell, 1994), 264, 318, 389; and *Objectivity, Relativism and Truth* (Cambridge: Cambridge Univ. Press, 1997), 197.

[38] Rorty, *Mirror*, 389.

[39] F. P. Ramsey, 'Knowledge' (1929). Reprinted in *Philosophical Papers*, ed. D. H. Mellor (Cambridge: Cambridge Univ. Press, 1990).

[40] W. V. O. Quine, 'Two Dogmas of Empiricism,' in *From a Logical Point of View* (Cambridge: Harvard Univ. Press, 1953), 37.

[41] Wilfred Sellars, 'The Myth of the Given: Three Lectures on Empiricism and the Philosophy of Mind' (1956). Reprinted in *Empiricism and the Philosophy of Mind* (Cambridge: Harvard Univ. Press, 1997).

ond generation formulation of reliabilism,[42] followed by David Armstrong's version,[43] culminating in Nozick's reliabilism,[44] which was very definitely in the air in the late seventies.[45]

Two recent attempts to rescue Oakeshott from the appellation of postmodern come from Kenneth McIntyre and Efraim Podoksik. McIntyre rejects the contention that there *is* a postmodern Oakeshott. Agreed, Oakeshott does not share the postmodernist predilection for programmatic politics — a point I have been making all along.[46] McIntyre is of the view that those who would claim Oakeshott as a postmodern typically (and mistakenly) seize upon Oakeshott's anti-foundationalism and his conversational metaphor. But Oakeshott is convicted of postmodern tendencies *not* on the grounds of his anti-foundationalism, *nor* on the ostensibly relativistic conversational metaphor (though that may be sufficient), but on the grounds of the relativism generated by his *austere* modality, his coherence theory, *and* his radical constructivism.

Efraim Podoksik[47] has made a compelling case for the view of Oakeshott as a defender of modernity: he seeks to shift our perspective on the familiar views of Oakeshott as conservative anti-modernist or as proto-postmodernist. Podoksik does not claim that these views are simply false, but that they are misleading unless we appreciate the inherent fluidity of these interpretive categories.

For Oakeshott the mark of the modern consciousness is the emergence of a plurality of distinct spheres of knowledge — poetry, science and history (*inter alia*). This plurality, insists Podoksik, should not lead us to derive postmodern relativistic conclusions — each of these domains are constitutive of their own criteria of objectivity and standards appropriate to their own subject matter. But any way you slice it this still sounds pretty much like a relativistic position — the precise contrast with postmodernism is not as clear as Podoksik's

[42] Alvin Goldman, 'A Causal Theory of Knowing,' *Journal of Philosophy* 64 (1967).

[43] David Armstrong, *Belief, Truth, and Knowledge* (Cambridge: Cambridge Univ. Press, 1973), 162-75.

[44] Robert Nozick, *Philosophical Explanations* (Cambridge: Harvard Univ. Press, 1981).

[45] For a survey see Anthony Quinton 'The Rise, Fall and Rise of Epistemology', in *Philosophy at the New Millennium*, ed. Anthony O'Hear (Cambridge: Cambridge Univ. Press, 2001).

[46] Kenneth B. McIntyre, *The Limits of Political Theory* (Exeter: Imprint Academic, 2004), 156.

[47] Efraim Podoksik, *In Defence of Modernity: Vision and Philosophy in Michael Oakeshott* (Exeter: Imprint Academic, 2003).

modernity thesis requires.[48] A marked feature of Podoksik's discussion is the substantial amount of time he devotes to the place of science in Oakeshott's thought. Typically, commentators talk up Oakeshott's anti-naturalist credentials almost as a matter of professional pride. Podoksik rightly views this emphasis as one-dimensional: Oakeshott's animadversions against scientism should be counterbalanced by his intention to maintain the integrity of science, rescuing science from misplaced skepticism and the relativism that is corrosive of one of modernity's great achievements. But as I have already indicated, if this is Oakeshott's view he does not hold it consistently: we will pick up on this in the next section.

Politics, Education and Science Revisited

Discussion of politics, education and science are for the sociologist of knowledge inextricably linked. To this list, one might add history.[49] This unholy mix is for Oakeshott the grossest *ignoratio elenchi*.

Forty years ago, Snow approvingly associated science with the Left and disapprovingly the anti-science literati with the Right. Twenty-five years on the situation was reversed. Gross and Levitt[50] associated much of the left-wing critics (Haack's 'New Cynics') of science with an 'uncritical criticism,'[51] an academic left wing that Roger Kimball termed the 'tenured radical',[52] or in Oakeshott's words 'servants of social purpose' (*WH*, 389). For Kimball these academics, ostensibly concerned with notions of social justice, are no more than a self-serving industry of intellectual obscurity — this obscurity serves as 'badges of intellectual sophistication and moral rectitude.'[53]

---

[48] For a classification of the many forms of relativism, see Susan Haack, 'Reflections on Relativism: From Momentous Tautology to Seductive Contradiction,' in *Manifesto of a Passionate Moderate* (Chicago: Univ. of Chicago Press, 1998), 149-66.

[49] Keith Windschuttle, *The Killing of History: How Literary Critics and Social Theorists Are Murdering Our Past* (San Francisco: Encounter Books, 2000).

[50] Paul Gross and Norman Levitt, *The Higher Superstition: The Academic Left and Its Quarrels with Science* (Baltimore: Johns Hopkins Univ. Press, 1994). See also, Tammy Bruce, *The Death of Right and Wrong: Exposing the Left's Assault on Our Culture and Values* (New York: Three Rivers Press: 2004).

[51] Haack, *Manifesto*, and 'Fallibilism.'

[52] Roger Kimball, *Tenured Radicals: How Politics Has Corrupted Our Higher Education* (Chicago: Ivan Dee, Inc., 1990).

[53] Haack, 'Fallibilism,' 35.

This anti-science Left versus pro-science Right seemed to be a neat dichotomy.[54] But this was never the case — the Right (at least stateside) is inclined towards anti-Darwinism. With Sokal, an eminent physicist with a Leftwing sensibility, the waters were further muddied. Sokal lampooned the worst excesses of Left-wing critics of science, which he felt was undermining serious issues:

> My essay, aside from being . . . 'a hilarious compilation of pomo gibberish,' is also an annotated bibliography of charlatanism and nonsense by dozens of prominent French and American intellectuals. This goes well beyond the narrow category of 'postmodernism,' and includes some of the most fashionable thinkers in 'science studies,' literary criticism, and cultural studies.
>
> In short, there is a lot of sloppy thinking going around about 'social construction,' often abetted by a vocabulary that intentionally elides the distinction between facts and our knowledge of them. . . . My goal isn't to defend science from the barbarian hordes of lit crit . . . but to defend the Left from a trendy segment of itself. . . . We're worried above all for the social sciences and the humanities, not the natural sciences. . . . They conflate science as an intellectual system with the social and economic role of science and technology. They conflate epistemic and ethical issues.
>
> There are hundreds of important political and economic issues surrounding science and technology. Sociology of science, at its best, has done much to clarify these issues. But sloppy sociology, like sloppy science, is useless or even counterproductive.[55]

Sokal, Brown[56] and Oakeshott (*VLL*, 116) are all well aware that patronage has its pitfalls and that the impulse for relevance is equally applicable and corrosive to other domains. For Oakeshott these other domains include state interference and free-marketeers — 'a *danse macabre* of wants and satisfactions', the vulgar consumerism which he characterizes as the relentless pursuit of 'barbaric affluence' (*VLL*, 104, 99).[57] Much ink has been spilled and bile generated by the Sokal affair — I only mention it to highlight that there is much common ground concerning the worst excesses of the sociology-of-knowledge movement between ideologically diverse writers, an example being Sokal and Oakeshott — the former uses the term 'conflation', the latter *ignoratio elenchi*.

---

[54]   Brown, *Who Rules in Science*, 23, 26.
[55]   http://www.physics.nyu.edu/faculty/sokal/reply.html.
[56]   James Robert Brown, 'Money, Method and Medical Research,' *EPISTEME* 1, no. 1 (June 2004): 49-59.
[57]   Cf. 'The Character of a University Education' (*WH*, 390), and 'On Arriving at a University' (*WH*, 334).

Politics

The politics of identity and the attendant political 'correctness' are thoroughly constructionist and run on an abstract appeal to rights. Social ontologies are constantly being fabricated from any number of permutations of collecting features (often essentialist in flavor) in order to secure some new *axiomatic* rights. This manifests itself in *non*-liberal remedies, euphemistically referred to as 'positive discrimination' or 'affirmative action.' Other variants include, the 'epistemic privilege of the disadvantaged'[58] (or the culture of victim-hood), and the ideologies of multiculturalism and feminism (several feminists and queer theorists *do* reject the relativistic aspects of their ideologies). These ideologies are all generated in the name of 'relevance' (VLL, 19), but in fact they are appealing to irrelevant collecting features. Susan Haack:

> Perhaps the bizarre idea that the New Cynicism represents the interests of the oppressed and marginalized owes its influence in part to the fact that, as universities have tried to welcome 'women and minorities,' we have allowed ourselves to be distracted from the entirely admirable goal of making a person's sex or race matter less to our judgment of the quality of her or her mind, and begun looking for ways in which sex or race might themselves be qualifications for intellectual work.[59]

And this so-called 'relevance' is euphemistically called 'political correctness' (PC). PC is in fact an oxymoron: it posits a metric, the implication being that there is an objective standard being referred to which of course is being rejected in the first instance by their inherent relativism. And there is the corresponding appeal to rights — recall Bentham's famous characterization of rights talk as 'nonsense on stilts'? It is not difficult to see that these abstract constructionist tendencies and inadvertent essentialist talk (race, gender, nationality, class, and so on) are anathematic to Oakeshott.

Education

Oakeshott is at his most scathing of the sociology-of-knowledge movement in his essays on education. The targets are their implicit constructionism and attendant relativism. Oakeshott's essays anticipated a whole raft of literature that shares his concerns,[60] often from unlikely quarters (feminists, lesbians and even socialists). The

[58] Haack, *Manifesto*, 116, 126.
[59] Haack, 'Fallibilism,' 45.
[60] Alan Bloom, *The Closing of the American Mind: How Higher Education Has Failed Democracy and Impoverished the Souls of Today's Students* (NY: Simon

notions of 'conversational encounter' and disinterested research, the *sine qua non* of liberal education[61] so dear to Oakeshott, have been compromised by the universities: '"Academic freedom" has become a cant phrase in the mouths of well meaning but muddled advocates' (*WH*, 390). Indeed, the most worthless of all conditions is for universities to be a forum for the discussion of ideologies (*VLL*, 141). Strong words indeed. Clearly, Oakeshott is well aware that if science (and the humanities) are to answer to social imperatives, conversation will be subverted, stymied and muted. The integrative liberal notion of *citizen* is displaced by an anti-liberal divisiveness, a consequence of the teacher *inventing* alternatives that seem more desirable (*VLL*, 83, 42). A clearer statement of Oakeshott's discomfort with the consequences of the constructivist position cannot be found.

Oakeshott's diagnosis for a plethora of 'pseudo-theorizing' is that it coincides with the rise of the professional academic, answering the relentless demand for industriousness in society at large, and often manifest in 'the pursuit of learning for the power it may bring [that] has its roots in a covetous egoism which is not less egoistic or less covetous when it appears as a so-called social purpose. . . .' (*VLL* 113, cf. 152). Academia heaving under the strain of its output 'has led to a proliferation of what may be called semisciences: sociology, anthropology, psychology, economics, politics' (*VLL*, 22-3). Invoking these disciplines, I think Oakeshott is being too flippant here, though it has to be admitted that there are some very dubious academic programs. Susan Haack echoes this sentiment, which she colorfully terms 'preposterism':

> As preposterism has become the way of academic life, conceptions of 'productivity' and 'efficiency' more appropriate to a manufacturing plant than to the pursuit of knowledge have become firmly entrenched. The effect, not surprisingly, has been a gradual erosion of intellectual integrity. We are over-

and Schuster, 1987); Anthony Quinton, 'A Cultural Crisis: The Devaluation of Values', and Anthony O'Hear, 'Education, Value and the Sense of Awe ,' in J. Haldane ed. *Values, Education and the Human World*, St. Andrews Studies in Philosophy and Public Affairs (Exeter: Imprint Academic, 2004); Kimball, *Tenured Radicals*, and *Experiments Against Reality: The Fate of Culture in the Postmodern Age* (Chicago: Ivan Dee Inc., 2000); Haack, *Manifesto*, and 'Fallibilism;' Charles Kors and Harvey Silverglate, *The Shadow University: The Betrayal Of Liberty On America's Campuses* (NY: Perennial, 1999); Tammy Bruce, *The New Thought Police: Inside the Left's Assault on Free Speech and Free Minds* (Roseville, CA: Prima Publishing, 2001).

[61] *VLL*, 15, 16, 28, 30-31, 34, 68, 70-72, 76, 80, 82-83, 94-95, 99, 101, 126: '"liberal" because it is liberated from the distracting business of satisfying contingent wants.'

whelmed by a bombardment of books and journals and a clamor of conferences and meetings in which it is close to impossible, except by sheer luck, to find the good stuff. No wonder that many take the easy way out, conforming to whatever party line will best advance their career, or that many lose their grip on the demands of real inquiry, forgetting that you may work for years on what turns out to be a dead end, and that it is part of the meaning of the word 'research' that you don't know how things will turn out.[62]

This last phrase is a classic mark of Oakeshott's Rationalist. Furthermore, the honorific title 'science' accorded much research beyond the natural sciences, has had a damaging effect 'because, in putting on the mask of "science"' (*VLL*, 26), their recognition is functional to some technological enterprise. Herein lies a tension. On the one hand these theorists berate science for not having any truth-value, yet on the other hand they are impressed with the prestige accorded to science. Oakeshott continues,

> if every department of liberal learning is not itself to be turned into sociology (philosophy into the sociology of knowledge, jurisprudence into the sociology of law and so forth), then, at least, none is as it should be unless sociology were added to it. (*VLL*, 27)

These sociologists of knowledge

> represent themselves as persons who have perceived a 'truth' which prejudice has concealed from others; namely, that everything has a 'social function,' that everything is what its 'social function' *declares it to be*, and that, consequently, there never were and never could be educational as distinct from 'social' considerations. . . . (*VLL*, 102, italics added).

False consciousness indeed! Again, '[E]ducation is not learning how to perform a social function' (*WH*, 390). Furthermore, '[T]he destruction of an educational engagement proceeds behind a veil of conceptual nonsense and historical rubbish . . . designed to persuade us that what is being destroyed never existed' (*VLL*, 103).

These strong words might just as well apply to the anti-essentialist position (to which Oakeshott subscribes): constructivists accept a range of basic sortals[63] and then 'adduce as a reason to depreciate the suggestion that any of these things "had" to be a horse, or a tree or a man, the anthropocentricity of the viewpoint that underlies and conditions the attributes.'[64]

Bona fide liberal education is described by Oakeshott:

---

[62] Haack, 'Fallibilism," 44.
[63] A term introduced by Locke in the *Essay*. A sortal provides a principle for individuating and counting examples of things of a type, e.g., 'tree', 'dog,' 'man'. Adjectives such as 'brown' and 'wooden' are not sortals.
[64] David Wiggins, *Sameness*, 136.

The business of the teacher (indeed, this may be said to be his peculiar quality as an agent of civilization) is to release his pupils from servitude to the current dominant feelings, emotions, images, ideas, beliefs and even skills, not by inventing alternatives to them which seem to him more desirable, but by making available to him something which approximates more closely to the whole of his inheritance . . . to see oneself reflected in the mirror of the present modish world is to see a sadly distorted image of a human being; for there is nothing to encourage us to believe that what has captured current fancy is the most valuable part of our inheritance. (*VLL*, 42)

Science

Oakeshott's position on science is schizophrenic. We are all familiar with Oakeshott's long running critique of scientism. But there are moments when Oakeshott resorts to language that could easily be espoused by his sociology-of-knowledge enemies. For example: '[S]cientific understanding [is] in any case not notable for its integrity and all too eager to be seduced' (*OHC*, 97). Again, '[T]he entire history of science may be seen as a pathetic attempt to find, in the face of incredible difficulties, a world of definite and demonstrable experience. . . .' (*EM*, 169).

One could let these comments slide but it should be recalled from section 3 that Oakeshott fully subscribes to a radical constructivist premises — of this there is no doubt. There is a revisionist/ ameliorant and consequently a relativist critique that is at the very heart of the constructivist. If science is merely a human construction, it should be no surprise that it is amenable or functional to extraneous purpose or caprice, typically political and economic power relations. Science is no longer secure in its modal autonomy, no longer immune from the sham reasoning of Oakeshott's Rationalist. Even if Oakeshott the constructivist does not contravene his own central philosophical admonition of invoking extrinsic or irrelevant considerations, by stripping science of any distinctive epistemological TRUTH-value, Oakeshott is in no position to distinguish good science from pseudo-science.

And yet, there is the other Oakeshott, the protector and admirer of scientific achievement, Podoksik's Oakeshott. For example: '[S]cience cannot be dismissed as having no truth. . . .' (*EM*, 213). In this vein consider science education: '[Science] education has had to resist the seductive advances of enemies dressed up as friends' (*VLL*, 19). Of course, these comments are modally indexed. And despite Podoksik's admirable attempt to rescue Oakeshott from the relativists, the charges of relativism (section 4) still stick. Still, let's allow Oakeshott the point. He admits in *Rationalism in Politics*:

> Nor, finally, do I think that we owe our predicament to the place which the natural sciences and the manner of thinking connected with them has come to take in our civilization. This simple diagnosis of the situation has been much put about, but I think it is mistaken. That the influence of the genuine natural scientist is not necessarily on the side of Rationalism follows from the view I have taken of the character of any kind of concrete knowledge. No doubt there are scientists deeply involved in the rationalist attitude, but they are mistaken when they think that the rationalist and the scientific points of view necessarily coincide. (*RIP*, 34-5)

So whatever the comments of the 'sociology-of-knowledge' Oakeshott, he is not impugning the genuine achievements of science. Very early on Oakeshott writes that 'the development of biology . . . has been hindered by a moral interest' (*EM*, 178). We accept Oakeshott's concerns about the ubiquitous honorific usage of the suffix 'science' attached to all manner of inquiry, but this is a completely separate issue from the fact that some scientists are corrupt, arrogant or incompetent; these are moral failings that have nothing to do with scientific inquiry.

There is nothing that Oakeshott could possibly object to in Haack's suggestion that science should be viewed not

> as privileged, but distinguished epistemically; as deserving, if you will, respect rather than deference. Science is neither sacred nor a confidence trick . ... (Nor, of course, is science the only source of knowledge).[65]

Taken in modal terms, of course science has truth-value for Oakeshott. Oakeshott emphasises the modal differences — i.e., one cannot do science (with its generalizing function and search for universal laws) in the same way one does history.

Where to From Here?

By way of summary, three inextricable points conspire to create difficulties for Oakeshott.

(1) Oakeshott's irreducible plurality of modal worlds forbids any commonalities — the use of relevant evidence, the use of logical inference, etc. Oakeshott seems to rule out the notion that there are *general* virtues of evidence and inquiry that we appeal to regardless of the domain of inquiry (a non-relativistic position) and which does *not* entail scientism or partake in the error of irrelevance. Of course

---

[65]   Haack, *Manifesto*, and *Defending Science*.

the standards of accuracy and relevance will vary between subject matters — e.g., we do not expect probability from a geometer or demonstration from a man of action. This said, a complication arises in Oakeshott's later addition of poetry as a mode — it is just a mode of sensibility devoid of evidence or inquiry.

(2) Given this irreducible plurality Oakeshott relies upon some notion of coherentism. Coherentism in epistemology and metaphysics — i.e., justification and truth — inherits several well-known difficulties. It invites transference to ethics, politics, and society — else we are *in*coherent in having coherentism in one sphere and something different in the other. Coherentism about ethics, politics, and society leads directly to relativism since it is empirically and conceptually possible for there to be any number of sets of ethical, political, and social beliefs and activities which form equally coherent systems, with *ex hypothesi* no decidability on grounds of coherence between them.

(3) Oakeshott's radical constructivism belies a revisionist/ ameliorant and consequently a relativist critique that is at the very heart of the constructivist:

> [A]t the heart of the New Cynicism lies a profound intolerance of uncertainty and a deep unwillingness to accept that the less than perfect is a lot better than nothing at all.[66]

This *is* Oakeshott's Rationalist! The point needs to be re-emphasized: *If science is merely a human construction, it should be no surprise that it is amenable or functional to extraneous purpose or caprice, typically political and economic power relations.*

What is curious is that Oakeshott was well aware of relativism's self-defeating tendency. Writing in 1961, Oakeshott criticizes Carr for over emphasizing a relativistic sociology-of-knowledge approach to historical theorizing: 'the sociology of knowledge cannot swallow up every other attitude towards knowledge without swallowing itself also, and nothing remains' (*WH*, 332). Years later, widening the target, he reiterated:

> [T]he history of thought is not the same thing as what is called the 'sociology of knowledge'. Indeed, the 'sociology of knowledge' is an unredeemed relic (inherently self-destructive) of the intellectual legend of the *Enlightenment* in which all thinking appeared as a 'reflex' determined by so-called 'social' circumstance. (*WH*, 371)

---

[66]   Haack, 'Fallibilism,' 36.

Had Oakeshott adopted a more conciliatory position between the 'myth of realism' and what I term the 'myth of constructionism' he would not find himself subject to criticisms I have outlined here. This conciliation could be along the lines of David Wiggins' 'conceptual realism' already hinted at above — the notion that there 'must still be something we can discover *in spite* of ourselves':[67] 'the mind "conceptualises" objects, yet objects "impinge" upon the mind.'[68] After all, Oakeshott does say, 'reality is what we are obliged to think' (*EM*, 58-9). Only then can one take existence, identity and truth statements seriously. There needs to be a reciprocal relation between our conceptual creativity and nature, allowing nature to intimate, regulate and inform the concepts. The sortal concepts that are brought to bear upon experience determine what we can find there — just as the size and mesh of a net determine 'not what fish are in the sea, but which ones we shall catch.'[69] This is not a species of anti-constructivism that John Dupré characterizes:

> Those most strongly opposed to constructivism are those who believe that interactions with nature completely determine scientific belief and, in connection with proper scientific methodology, determine true beliefs about the world.[70]

Concepts under which experience is articulated and things singled out determine the persistence conditions 'only because such concepts determine "what" is singled out.'[71] This expunges any vestige of idealism, which *ties the persistence condition to the creative act of mind*, and which severely weakens Oakeshott's thought. Wiggins' concern is not merely to act as guardian of objectivity in human thought, but 'to preserve its prospects of passing beyond the most narrowly anthropocentric.'[72] Our concepts are open to being regulated by reality and as a consequence our understanding approaches a realm not sensitive to the practical. This is surely consonant with Oakeshott's modal forewarning of the error of irrelevance.

---

[67] Wiggins, *Sameness*, 67, italics added. Wiggins rejects Geach's relativity thesis by offering his thesis of Sortal Dependency of Identity, a highly elaborate and technical argument with extended preliminaries, qualifications, and amendments.
[68] Wiggins, *Sameness*, 101.
[69] Wiggins, *Sameness*, 141
[70] John Dupré, 'What's the Fuss about Social Constructivism?' *EPISTEME* 1, no.1 (June 2004): 74.
[71] Wiggins, *Sameness*, 141.
[72] Wiggins, *Sameness*, 141.

* * *

Text and interpretation are one, Oakeshott observes in 'The Concept of a Philosophical Jurisprudence,' and of no texts is this truer than Oakeshott's own.[73] Commentators can no longer absolve themselves of critically engaging with Oakeshott on the grounds that because Oakeshott's thought lies within the hermeneutic tradition, some special interpretive approach should be accorded him. Few of us working within the so-called analytic tradition accept the 'the 'continental (hermeneutic) /analytical' divide.[74] To insist otherwise is rather like 'conceiving America as being divided into Business and Kansas.'[75] Of course, one has to enter into sympathy with a target thinker — any thinker. However, Oakeshott's thought can be recast and does offer value to an issue-led style of philosophizing. Commentators' haughty complicity with Oakeshott's well-known lack of engagement with the philosophical establishment does Oakeshott no favors. Furthermore, the suggestive richness of Oakeshott is now beginning to be recognized in areas Oakeshott himself could not have anticipated — whether or not he would approve is neither here nor there.

To read Oakeshott is to sense a distinctive intelligence, to discern a particular attitude. Here, if anywhere, is Pascal's *'esprit de finesse'*. Yet the attitude is often hard to make out in specifics. We readily get a broad sense of what is being rejected, but seldom a precise and unencumbered sense of what is being held. The preceding discussion acknowledges all this and is offered as a reading of a brilliant, profound, but elusive mind. Whatever the criticisms leveled at Oakeshott I am not clear how far any of this would have embarrassed him. He might just as well re-invoke the Latin dictum: *Spartam nactus est, hanc exorna* — 'Sparta is what you have been allotted; do what is best with it' (*RIP*, 60).

---

[73] 'The Concept of a Philosophical Jurisprudence,' *Politica* 3 (1938): 203-22, 345-60.
[74] http://www.philosophicalgourmet.com/analytic.htm (accessed 22 June 2004).
[75] Attributed to John Searle, cited in Barry Smith, 'A Theory of Divides' http://ontology.buffalo.edu/smith/articles/israel.PDF (accessed 11 June 2004).

13

Keith Sutherland

Rationalism in Politics and Cognitive Science

The madman is not the man who has lost his reason. The madman is the man who has lost everything except his reason.

G.K. Chesterton

Introduction

Michael Oakeshott would not have approved of this essay.[1] Given his disdain for the notion of 'political science,'[2] I imagine he would have had little sympathy with the notion of 'cognitive science' and would be actively hostile to a discussion of his best-known essay in terms of such an alien discipline. To Oakeshott, political 'texts' were best studied through the languages of history and philosophy (*RIP*, 212). Given that the main problem with political discourse is the confusion of modalities — practical, scientific, historical and philosophical — why then add further to the existing confusion? Cognitive science itself is the result of a Faustian pact between artificial intelligence (an engineering discipline) and psychology (at roots a philosophical discipline), so what is the point of using one confusion to illuminate another? However, Oakeshott himself sometimes blurred the boundaries between the different modes of discourse. As Timothy Fuller put it, Oakeshott may have remained faithful to *Experience and its Modes* in spirit, but not always in the detail.

[1]   My thanks to Anthony Freeman, Maurice Goldsmith, Leslie Marsh, James Newman, James Rutherford and Ben Wempe for comments on an earlier draft.
[2]   Oakeshott, 'The Study of "Politics" in a University,' in *Rationalism in Politics and other essays, new and expanded edition*, ed. Timothy Fuller (Indianapolis: Liberty Press, 1991). Hereafter: *RIP*.

Although Fuller, Greenleaf[3] and Franco[4] argue that Oakeshott preserved a broadly consistent approach throughout his life, other authors have taken issue with this viewpoint. According to Steven Gerencser, Oakeshott may have started his philosophical career as a modal purist, but by the time he wrote his essay on poetry,[5] the modes had softened into the metaphor of 'voices in conversation', in which philosophy was just one voice amongst many.[6] This led Richard Rorty to applaud Oakeshott's latter-day renunciation of the foundational claims of philosophy.[7] Whereas in *Experience and Its Modes*, cross-modal leakage was just responsible for confusion or irrelevance, by the time he wrote 'The Voice of Poetry,' the danger was *superbia* (pride), whereby each voice (including philosophy) tries to laud it over all the others. Tariq Modood agrees that in 'The Voice of Poetry' Oakeshott temporarily 'abandons the idea of a monistic system of absolute coherence,' but returns to it in *On Human Conduct*, albeit in a less dogmatic form.[8]

Most of these authors,[9] however, would agree with Franco over 'the distinctively Oakeshottian gulf between theory and practice.'[10] When asked by Robert McKenzie whether he favored British entry into the European Community, Oakeshott responded, 'I do not find it necessary to hold opinions on such matters.'[11] I'm sure that Oakeshott the man would have been prepared to enter into conversation with a London cabbie or his barber or bartender on all of the perennial favorites. But such was his concern that philosophy should not be corrupted by practical or political considerations that he refused to discuss such topics when he was wearing his philoso-

---

[3]   W. H. Greenleaf, *Oakeshott's Philosophical Politics* (NY: Barnes and Noble, 1966).

[4]   Paul Franco, *The Political Philosophy of Michael Oakeshott* (New Haven: Yale University Press, 1990).

[5]   Oakeshott, 'The Voice of Poetry in the Conversation of Mankind,' in *RIP*.

[6]   Steven A. Gerencser, *The Skeptic's Oakeshott* (London: Palgrave Macmillan, 2000), 38.

[7]   Richard Rorty, *Philosophy and the Mirror of Nature* (Oxford: Blackwell, 1980), 389.

[8]   Tariq Modood, 'Oakeshott's Conceptions of Philosophy,' *History of Political Thought* 1 (1980), 318. See also Jeremy Rayner, 'The Legend of Oakeshott's Conservatism: Sceptical Philosophy and Limited Politics,' *Canadian Journal of Political Science* 18 (1985): 313-338.

[9]   See also: Neal Wood, 'A Guide to the Classics: The Scepticism of Professor Oakeshott,' *Journal of Politics* 21 (1959); Tariq Modood and Dale Hall, 'Oakeshott and the Impossibility of Philosophical Politics,' *Political Studies* 30 (1982): 162.

[10] Franco, *The Political Philosophy of Michael Oakeshott*, 161.

[11] Cited in Joanna Mack, 'The LSE: A Monument to Fabian Socialism?' *New Society* (15 June 1978): 590.

pher's hat. However it would strike most people as plausible that Oakeshott's Hobbesian meditations on the acknowledgement and recognition of authority[12] would have practical implications for, say, the 'peace process' in Northern Ireland. Similarly, his observations on the dangers inherent in supernatural religions have undeniable policy implications in the light of the attack on the World Trade Center by Islamic fundamentalists. If history and philosophy enable us to understand the 'texts' of political discourse then surely we can profit from such understanding in the pursuit of practical politics, even if the understanding has an entirely skeptical outcome. Oakeshott acknowledges during his ironical discussion of Plato's allegory of the cave that when the theorist returns from the Olympian heights 'he is clearly recognizable [to the cave dwellers] as a clever fellow from whom there is much to be learned' (*OHC*, 30). This doesn't mean that the cave dwellers cannot learn from the theorist (or vice versa), but that 'neither party has authority in the conversational meeting-place that they share.'[13] The alternative to this compromise is to agree with Bernard Crick that Oakeshott's skepticism is in fact nihilism in disguise.[14]

To Oakeshott, 'modern rationalism' was a disease and the purpose of his polemic on the topic was both preventative and disinfective. The basic approach of immunology and antibiotics is to combat infection by introducing another virus and leaving it to do battle with the immune system. I would like to attempt a similar cure in this essay and introduce some insights from the strange, Faustian, cross-modal hydra which we call 'cognitive science' to cast some (artificial) light on some of the problems that Oakeshott identified in the field of political philosophy. If this risks offending modal purists, then that is a risk I will have to take.[15]

---

[12] Oakeshott, 'The Authority of the State,' in *Religion, Politics and the Moral Life*, ed. Timothy Fuller (London: Yale Univ. Press, 1993); 'The Rule of Law,' in *On History and Other Essays* (Oxford: Basil Blackwell, 1983). Hereafter: *OH*. 'Introduction to Leviathan,' in *Hobbes on Civil Association* (Berkeley: Univ. of California Press, 1975). Hereafter: *HCiv*. *On Human Conduct* (Oxford: Clarendon Press, 1975). Hereafter: *OHC*.

[13] Gerencser, *The Skeptic's Oakeshott*, 50.

[14] Bernard Crick, 'The World of Michael Oakeshott, or The Lonely Nihilist,' *Encounter* 20 (June 1963): 74.

[15] I also take encouragement from Jon Elster's recent study of rationality and emotion, in which he laments the fact that scientific psychologists and Aristotle scholars ignore each other and that neither discipline ever refers to Jane Austen or

Following the so-called 'cognitive revolution' of the 1950s, psychology returned to its rationalist roots, with a view of cognition that was fundamentally disembodied and ahistorical. Human cognition could, in principle, be expressed by symbolic logic and implemented in any (computational) medium. Although few scientists would acknowledge themselves as dualists, this view of cognition was drawn straight from the seventeenth century. Cognition was viewed as an abstract, disembodied process that bears the same relationship to the brain as does a computer program to its underlying hardware.

This view, known as computational functionalism, drew support from Hubel and Wiesel's discovery that certain cells in the primary visual cortex were only responsive to very specific visual stimuli. Moreover the 'all-or-nothing' firing pattern of the cells seemed to be the perfect example of a digital logic gate. If, then, the brain's hardware was so like a computer, then the mind — the spooky stuff — could best be explained as the software. This theory has been taken to its (risible) limits in the writings of Frank Tipler,[16] who has painted a science-fiction scenario of human beings gaining immortality through downloading their 'neural code' to silicon.

Only comparatively recently — as the result of the 'scandalous' failure of classical artificial intelligence[17] and the phenomenological agenda of the new discipline of consciousness studies — has the cognitivist/rationalist paradigm come under concerted attack. Early indications are that the abstract rationalism of cognitive science may need to be drastically modified by the new emphasis on embodiment, evolution and emotion, and in this paper I would like to explore some of the parallels between this and Oakeshott's attack on 'rationalism' in politics.

Rationalism in Politics

In his essay 'Rationalism in Politics' Oakeshott argues that western political thought since the seventeenth century has been infected by a disease called 'modern rationalism' and that the epidemiology of the modern strand is qualitatively different from both its classical and scholastic forms.

George Eliot. See Jon Elster, *Alchemies of the Mind: Rationality and the Emotions* (Cambridge: Cambridge Univ. Press, 1999).

[16] F.J. Tipler, *The Physics of Immortality* (NY: Anchor Books, 1995).

[17] Jerry Fodor, *The Mind Doesn't Work that Way: The Scope and Limits of Computational Psychology* (Cambridge, MA: Bradford Books, 2000), 37.

Oakeshott traces the origins of 'modern rationalism' back to the dawn of the scientific era. Early in the seventeenth century Francis Bacon observed that the fundamental obstacle to the development of knowledge was the lack of a *technical procedure* to attain 'certain and demonstrable knowledge....Such knowledge is not possible for "natural reason", which is capable of only "petty and probable conjectures"' (*RIP*, 19).[18] This was primarily based on his observations on the corrupting power of *language* — Bacon believed 'that words had insinuated themselves into our understanding and perverted our judgment,'[19] and the task was how to overcome the 'cheat of words.' Some scholars advocated the recovery of linguistic purity through the 'cabalistic' study of Adam's original and magical language, while others proposed the construction of a new artificial language. Bacon's chosen solution, however, was to formulate a *technique of research*, the rules of which could be applied in a purely mechanical way and are universal, as they are independent of the linguistic subjectivity of the enquirer. Just as the technique of the syllogism can be applied to ascertain the truth of arguments, the same procedure applied to science will ascertain the truth of 'things'. 'The business of interpreting nature was "to be done as if by machinery"' (*RIP*, 20).[20] What differentiated scientific rationalism from the rationalism of Plato or Aquinas was that the method for the first time attempted to break free of the constraints of language, culture and history.

Oakeshott notes that the seventeenth century introduced a new connotation to the word 'reason'. Bacon was interested in the development of instrumental rationality — 'a faculty of calculation by which men conclude one thing from another and discover means of attaining given ends not themselves subject to the criticism of reason, a faculty by which a world believed to be a machine could be disclosed' (*RIP*, 22-3 n. 24). This conception of rationality had little in common with 'the Reason of Hooker' (*RIP*, 22), or with 'the divine

---

[18] Oakeshott here cites Bacon, *Novum Organum*, 184. Oakeshott mentions Fowler, probably the edition published by Oxford: Clarendon Press, 1878. Citations here follow Oakeshott's. The late sixteenth century was characterized by a widespread skepticism, which found its expression in the rejection of Aristotelian science and medieval scholasticism over the possibility of ever gaining valid knowledge (of either the natural world or moral principles).

[19] P. Moloney, 'Leaving the Garden of Eden: Linguistic and Political Authority in Thomas Hobbes,' *History of Political Thought* 18 (1997): 255.

[20] Oakeshott cites Bacon, *Novum Organum*, 168.

illumination of the mind that united man with God,' which still
belonged to 'the great Platonic-Christian tradition' (*RIP*, 245). Oakeshott claimed that much of the plausibility of *modern* rationalism (the
'oracle whose magic word is truth,' [*RIP*, 105]) resulted from the
'tacit attribution to the new "reason" of the qualities that belong properly to the Reason of the older intellectual tradition' (*RIP*, 22-3 n. 24).

Oakeshott would have agreed that as philosophy was a rational
undertaking, he was therefore a rationalist himself in his role as philosopher. But this depended on a limited, Hobbesian view of rationality, which drew on the skeptical nominalism of the late scholastic
tradition. Reasoning (to Hobbes) was 'nothing but the addition and
subtraction of names' (*RIP*, 242).[21] Language is the giving of names
to thoughts or images in the mind, not things in the world, and language is what makes conscious thought itself possible. Philosophy is
the manipulation of a system of tokens, which may or may not have
any external correspondence: 'Words are wise men's counters, they
do but reckon by them: but they are the money of fooles.'[22] Thus, for
Hobbes (and the same is probably true for Oakeshott, despite nods
in another direction), 'philosophical knowledge . . . is conditional,
not absolute' (*RIP*, 244).

Jon Elster draws the distinction between rationality ('the instrumentally efficient pursuit of given ends') and reason ('any kind of
impartial motivation or concern for the common good.')[23] La
Bruyère, Montaigne, La Rochefoucauld and the other French moral-
ists on the whole respected this distinction, but Oakeshott's critique
of 'modern rationalism' tends to use both terms interchangeably
because, in practice, the limited concept of efficient rationality is still
(mis)associated with the oracular qualities of Reason.

However, the most important thing for Francis Bacon was to set
aside received opinion and to 'begin anew from the very foundations.'[24] Descartes was equally concerned with providing a similar
foundation of certainty for knowledge. Although his *cogito* is usually
discussed as the source of the dualism that has plagued the philosophy of mind ever since, Descartes was more concerned with the sort
of intellectual enema that Bacon was advocating. The *cogito* is the
starting certainty upon which to build a methodical approach to the

---

[21] Oakeshott, 'Introduction to *Leviathan*,' in *RIP*.
[22] Thomas Hobbes, *Leviathan*, ed. C.B. Macpherson (London: Penguin Books, 1968),
      106.
[23] Elster, *Alchemies of the Mind*, 102.
[24] Bacon, *Novum Organum* I, Aphorism XXXI.

acquisition of knowledge. The technique of enquiry is to be followed in a similar blind, mechanical way to the one that Bacon proposed.

If Bacon and Descartes were concerned with rationalism in the field of scientific enquiry, it was Kant who went on to develop the idea as the foundation of the modern discourse of moral and political philosophy: 'Kantian moral theory emphasizes the primacy of the rational self. . . . The moral agent, for Kant, is first and foremost a rational agent; an agent who purportedly has a certain level of self-knowledge and a capacity to derive the moral law for itself.'[25]

Although the Enlightenment was predominately rationalist and optimistic, it was also characterized by a skeptical empiricism. Indeed the advocates of the new empirical approach to science sought to distance themselves from the rationalisms of scholasticism and classical Greece. But Oakeshott argues that 'modern rationalism' and empiricism are two sides of the same coin, as the goal is to reduce the 'tangle and variety of experience' to a set of principles: 'Like Midas, the Rationalist is always in the unfortunate position of not being able to touch anything, without transforming it into an abstraction; he can never get a square meal of experience' (*RIP*, 31 n. 30).

The true contrast, derived from Thucydides, is between the rational-empirical approach of 'technical knowledge' and the practical approach of 'traditional knowledge'. Technical knowledge is rule-based and procedural, whereas traditional knowledge can only be passed on empathically from master to student, or else acquired the hard way — through the university of life. A great chef can write any number of cookery books, but there is no substitute for hands-on experience.[26]

As the distinction between technical and practical knowledge is an important one for Oakeshott, it will be helpful at this stage to describe it in some detail:

> Every science, every art, every practical activity requiring skill of any sort, indeed every human activity whatsoever, involves knowledge. And, universally, this knowledge is of two sorts, both of which are always involved in any actual activity. It is not, I think, making too much of it to call them two sorts of

---

[25] Christine James, 'Irrationality in Philosophy and Psychology: The Moral Implications of Self-defeating Behaviour', *Journal of Consciousness Studies*, 5, no.2 (1998): 224-34.
[26] Gilbert Ryle expressed this as the difference between 'knowing that' and 'knowing how' in *The Concept of Mind* (New York: Barnes and Noble, 1949). Cf. the distinction between declarative and procedural memory, usually associated with Larry Squire, e.g. *Memory and Brain* (Oxford: Oxford Univ. Press, 1987), chap 12.

knowledge, because (though in fact they do not exist separately) there are certain important differences between them. The first sort of knowledge I will call technical knowledge or knowledge of technique. In every art and science, and in every practical activity, a technique is involved. In many activities this technical knowledge is formulated into rules which are, or may be, deliberately learned, remembered, and, as we say, put into practice; but whether or not it is, or has been, precisely formulated, its chief characteristic is that it is susceptible of precise formulation, although special skill and insight may be required to give it that formulation. The technique (or part of it) of driving a motorcar on English roads is to be found in the Highway Code, the technique of cookery is contained in the cookery book, and the technique of discovery in natural science or in history is in their rules of research, of observation and verification. The second sort of knowledge I will call practical, because it exists only in use, is not reflective and (unlike technique) cannot be formulated in rules. This does not mean, however, that it is an esoteric sort of knowledge. It means only that the method by which it may be shared and becomes common knowledge is not the method of formulated doctrine. And if we consider it from this point of view, it would not, I think, be misleading to speak of it as traditional knowledge. In every activity this sort of knowledge is also involved; the mastery of any skill, the pursuit of any concrete activity is impossible without it. (*RIP*, 12)

However, 'Rationalism is the assertion that what I have called practical knowledge is not knowledge at all, the assertion that, properly speaking, there is no knowledge which is not technical knowledge' (*RIP*, 15).

Rationalism in Cognitive Science

The research agenda of classical artificial intelligence (AI), which had a dominant impact on cognitive psychology during the second half of the twentieth century, was based on the same (rationalist) assumptions. According to this (now discredited) viewpoint,[27] explicit, conscious processes — in particular those specialized processes connected with verbal report — are 'the central arena for the mental solution of problems.'[28]

The classical AI program had some modest success in the design of scholarly and scientific expert systems — particularly in the field of medical diagnostics. But researchers in the field had broader ambitions — an early attempt to develop an expert system for

---

[27] Cf. Hubert Dreyfus, *What Computers Can't Do: The Limits of Artificial Intelligence* (NY: Harper and Row, 1979); T. Winograd and F. Flores, *Understanding Computers and Cognition: A New Foundation for Design* (Norwood, NJ: Ablex Pub. Corp., 1986).

[28] Donald Michie, 'Consciousness as an Engineering Issue, part 1', *Journal of Consciousness Studies* 1, no.2 (1994): 182.

commonsense reasoning being John McCarthy's 'Advice Taker'.[29] Broadly speaking, McCarthy felt that the development of expressive formal languages and high-speed electronic computing would enable AI to go further than Leibniz's Enlightenment project for the codification of declarative knowledge. In Oakeshottian terms, this would involve the codification of practical knowledge as well as technical knowledge.

Unfortunately it remains the case that most human 'commonsense' activity is not amenable to symbolic reasoning, partly on account of the fact that most mental representation is non-linguistic, and most knowledge is tacit and procedural ('practical' knowledge, in Oakeshottian terminology). There was also the problem of 'scaling up' symbolic approaches to open-ended knowledge domains. As a consequence, attempts to implement commonsense reasoning using symbolic artificial intelligence have largely been abandoned.[30]

One of the most strident critics of the limitations of AI has been Jerry Fodor, himself one of the key advocates of (symbolic) computationalism as 'the only show in town.' Although Fodor is a committed rationalist (he is even more rude about connectionism,[31] the new kid on the block from the associationist camp) he has always acknowledged the inability of AI to model holistic mental properties ('abduction' to the cognoscenti, 'commonsense' or 'flexibility' to the rest of us). To Fodor, cognition cannot be just a mechanical syntactic operation on a local database, as how then do we account for the properties of a thought 'that are sensitive to *which belief systems* it's embedded in?'[32]

The failure of classical AI is partly the cause and partly the consequence of a reevaluation of the role of explicit conscious processes in human cognition. The Enlightenment model of human psychology, in which the 'main engines of knowledge acquisition and problem solving are just the verbally articulate processes described as con-

---

[29] John McCarthy, 'Programs With Common Sense,' reprinted in M. Minsky (ed.), *Semantic Information Processing* (Cambridge: MIT Press, 1968).

[30] Other examples include Japan's Fifth Generation project and the MCC CYC project in Austin, Texas.

[31] See Fodor, *The Mind Doesn't Work That Way*: 'It must be the sheer magnitude of their incompetence that makes them so popular' (47), and 'If you want to understand even less about the cognitive mind than Connectionism does, I suppose you will have to become a behaviorist' (52). Fodor's polemical and journalistic style makes this essay a useful foil for Oakeshott's equally polemical assault on modern rationalism.

[32] Fodor, *The Mind Doesn't Work That Way*, 28.

scious thought,'[33] has largely been displaced by a tacit learning model, best expressed by Francis Galton's observation that 'the position of consciousness appears to be that of a helpless spectator of but a minute fraction of automatic brainwork.'[34] Galton's observation has since been confirmed by a large volume of work in experimental psychology, starting with Nisbett and Wilson's findings that most human skills are largely procedural and tacit, leaving consciousness little more than the role of confabulating *ex post facto* narratives for cognitive events which were taking place below the threshold of consciousness and rationality.[35]

The failure of classical artificial intelligence and the success of the psychological research program in tacit learning has led modelers in cognitive science to develop new models which are more biologically accurate than the tradition of disembodied, abstract cognition inherited from Enlightenment rationalism. Psychologists have always borrowed their models from their colleagues in the hard sciences, and it would appear that most of the inspiration is now coming from biological science and evolutionary theory.

The new buzzwords in AI and robotics are thus terms like 'connectionist', 'situated', 'behavior-based', and 'animat'. They tend to be data-driven and reactive, as opposed to model-driven, and 'limit themselves to the automatic solution of problems by structured repertoires of reflex-like responses' which then 'evolve' along Darwinian lines.[36] As this work is in its infancy, of necessity it is addressing simple behavioral repertoires, but scientists are confi-

---

[33] Michie, 'Consciousness as an Engineering Issue, pt. 1' 191.

[34] Francis Galton, *Inquiries into Human Faculty and its Development* (London: Macmillan, 1883).

[35] R.E. Nisbett and T.D. Wilson, 'Telling More Than We Can Know: Verbal Reports on Mental Processes,' *Psychological Review* 84, no.3 (1977), 231-59. This idea — at least in a societal context — has its origins in the thinkers of the Scottish Enlightenment, in particular Adam Smith and Adam Ferguson. Ferguson conceived of people working subrationally to secure order, and regarded the idea of 'the Great Legislator' as a rationalist historical fiction. See Lisa Hill, 'Adam Ferguson and the Paradox of Progress and Decline,' *History of Political Thought* 18 (1997), 677-706. The psychological notion of *ex post facto* confabulation (Michael Gazzaniga's left-hemisphere 'narrative interpreter') was anticipated by Pascal's close friend Jean Domat: 'We do not act by reason, but by love, because it is not the mind that acts, but the heart that governs, and the deference of the heart towards the mind is such that even if it does not act by reason it must at least believe that it acts by reason.' (J. Lafond, ed., *Moralistes du XVIIe Siècle* (Paris: Robert Laffont, 1992), 611.

[36] Donald Michie, 'Consciousness as an Engineering Issue, part 2', *Journal of Consciousness Studies* 2, no.1 (1995), 55.

dent that the models can be developed to include sophisticated cognitive processes. One of the most promising conceptual tools is that of 'structured induction', whereby theory is derived from intuition (rather than logical deduction from first principles). Researchers like Alen Shapiro claim that this is the best tool for modeling how chess masters function — it is far easier to reliably predict the outcome of a move than it is to describe in detail how it is done.[37]

The other main trend in artificial intelligence is the rapid development of neural network and connectionist modeling. These approaches eschew rule-based symbolic programming in favor of an inductive approach. The connectionist machine 'learns' from a series of actual cases, in a similar way to human agents. Stephen Turner eloquently describes the confluences between connectionism and Oakeshott's view of human practitioners and of tradition as an evolving process:

> Change is continuous because learning is continuous, and the history of experience — its 'authority', so to speak, is built into the weightings that are produced and thus into what is learned: the past is thus always in a sense present, but as a consequence of the modifications it has produced that are retained in the weightings of the connections.[38]

As cognitive science is a hybrid discipline (at my *alma mater* philosophy is now taught in the computer science department), a number of writers have started to explore the philosophical implications of the move towards a 'situated' and 'embodied' robotics and cognitive science.[39] The first biologically inspired robot, embodying cybernetic control principles like learning, homeostasis and goal-seeking behavior, was developed by Grey Walter in the 1950's. However, due to the domination of symbolic AI, such approaches were largely ignored until revived by Rodney Brooks at MIT during the late 1980s. It remains to be seen whether connectionism and/or the new wave of situated, embodied and evolutionary robotics will return to

---

[37] Alen Shapiro, *Structured Induction in Expert Systems* (Boston: Addison-Wesley Longman, 1987).

[38] Stephen Turner, 'Tradition and Cognitive Science: Oakeshott's Undoing of the Kantian Mind,' *Philosophy of the Social Sciences* 33, no. 1 (2003): 53-76.

[39] Andy Clark, *Being There: Putting Brain, Body and World Together Again* (Cambridge: MIT Press, 1997); Rafael Nuñez and Walter J. Freeman, ed., *Reclaiming Cognition: The Primacy of Action, Intention and Emotion* (Exeter: Imprint Academic, 1999), Francisco J. Varela, Evan Thompson and Eleanor Rosch, *The Embodied Mind: Cognitive Science and Human Experience* (Cambridge: MIT Press, 1991).

artificial intelligence some of the status it has lost since the disap-
pointments of the classical period of the discipline.

Rationalism in Neuroscience

Oakeshott's primary target running through his several essays on
rationalism is the following notion:

> It has been supposed that the human mind must contain in its composition a
> native faculty of 'Reason', a light whose brightness is dimmed only by educa-
> tion, a piece of mistake-proof apparatus, an oracle whose magic word is truth.
> (*RIP*, 105)

Oakeshott argues that this is a relic of a belief in magic (*RIP*, 113).
However, Anthony O'Hear claims that it is, in fact, a distortion of
Greek and Hebrew religious intuitions.[40] Plato and Aristotle agreed
that the supreme form of human life was the exercise of rationality in
the contemplation of divine, eternal truths. The Greeks, however,
had no notion of linear progress, and were more inclined to look
back to a golden age or adopt a cyclical model. The Western notion of
linear progress (which led directly to the Enlightenment view of
rationalism) has its origins in Hebrew messianism. Since leaving
Egypt, the Israelites focused on the notion of the Promised Land, but
could never quite make up their minds whether the New Jerusalem
was for this world or the next.

The merging of Greek rationalism with the Hebrew notion of mes-
sianic progress is the product of our Christian heritage.[41] For many
centuries constrained by the authority of the Catholic Church, it took
the Reformation and Enlightenment to liberate the notion of messi-
anic progress from the restraints of tradition. Thus, rather than having its origins in a belief in magic, the Enlightenment concept of
rationality was a direct consequence of the development of Christian
doctrine. Given its providentialist origins, the faith in rationalism
did not long survive the loss in religious faith, from which it derived
its moral force. The decline of Enlightenment optimism and rational-

---

[40] Anthony O'Hear, *Beyond Progress: Finding the Old Way Forward* (London:
Bloomsbury, 1999).
[41] Although Oakeshott usually prefers the more rhetorical claim that faith in
rationalism is a relic of a belief in magic, on at least one occasion he conceded that
it is 'closely allied with a decline in the belief in Providence: a beneficient and
infallible technique replaced a beneficient and infallible God' (*RIP*, 23).

ism and the growth of the 'hermeneutics of suspicion'[42] with its increased attention to irrationality have their origins in the writings of Marx, Nietzsche and Freud:

> Freud overturned a view of reason, common since antiquity, according to which it is a completely independent force. Evidently, it is a force that is stronger in some people than in others, and, when it comes to action, it is less often frustrated in some agents than in others. But the old idea was that there is no interfering with its inner working.[43]

Although the Freudian view of irrationality, with its positing of the dynamic unconscious and other such sub-agents, is now dismissed by psychologists, nevertheless after Freud there was no escaping the fact that reason had descended from the Platonic realms and was now incarnate, though there is ongoing debate as to whether this is a matter for neurology or sociology. One of the most widely discussed books on the topic is Antonio Damasio's *Descartes' Error*.[44] Damasio examined the clinical records of the unfortunate Phineas Gage, who suffered a massive injury to the ventromedial pre-frontal area of his brain and consequently developed serious personality disorders (although his basic cognitive faculties were largely unchanged). Although the damage was in an area that is normally associated with emotion, Damasio discovered that, in contemporary patients with similar lesions, the ability to take rational decisions was severely impaired by the damage to the social-emotional regions of their brains. 'Descartes' error,' according to Damasio, was to separate our rational souls from their physical and social context. Modern neurology tells us that reason is embodied and cannot be separated from social and affective processes.

Damasio proposed a 'somatic marker' (gut reaction) hypothesis to account for the claimed causal connection between the emotional flatness of some brain-damaged patients and impaired social rationality. According to this theory, such patients are unable to be motivated by mental representations of future states, as the normal physiological process whereby a bad outcome is connected with (say) an unpleasant gut feeling fails to operate.[45] In the case of the well-known gambling experiment, where brain-damaged patients

---

[42] Paul Ricoeur, *Freud and Philosophy: An Essay on Interpretation* (New Haven: Yale Univ. Press, 1970).
[43] David Pears, *Motivated Irrationality* (Oxford: Clarendon Press, 1984).
[44] Antonio Damasio, *Descartes' Error: Emotion Reason and the Human Brain* (NY: Grosset/Putnam, 1994).
[45] A derivation of the James-Lange theory of emotionality.

ignored the inevitable bankruptcy that resulted from selecting cards from the 'high risk' decks, patients lacked the ability to represent future states. Although such patients demonstrated normal skin conductance reactions to actual monetary loss, they differed from normal subjects in having *'no anticipatory responses whatever'* in the period immediately preceding their selection of a card from a bad deck.[46]

Such cortically damaged patients tend to act recklessly or, on the other hand, to be unable to make even trivial decisions, such as the scheduling of the next appointment with their neurologist. A similar model by Ronald de Sousa argues that 'emotion limits the range of information that the organism will take into account, the inferences actually drawn from a potential infinity.'[47] Without emotion, according to Damasio and de Sousa, there would be no soluble problems for human agents, as emotion acts as a tiebreaker in cases of indifference, incommensurability or other forms of indeterminacy. On the basis of the clinical evidence, Damasio and de Sousa claim that the traditional opposition between emotion and reason is a false dichotomy and that the fictitious Mr. Spock — the ultimate 'cool head' — would be incapable of practical reasoning. The traditional view — that emotion interferes with rational choice — is now more difficult to support. Rather than emotions being the 'sand in the machine'[48] it looks more like a case of the grit in the oyster. 'The cool strategy advocated by Kant, among others, has far more to do with the way patients with prefrontal damage go about deciding than with how normal humans operate.'[49]

Damasio's 'somatic marker' hypothesis is not without its critics. Jon Elster claims that he is making the old error in social science explanation of mistaking correlation for causation.[50] It is perfectly possible, Elster claims, that the same brain damage that is the cause of emotional flatness could also (independently) cause the lack of ability to be motivated by the representation of absent events that leads to defective decision making. According to Elster, Damasio has no evidence to support his stronger *causal* claim, and the psychological mechanism of reinforcement — which Damasio claims links

---

[46] Damasio, *Descartes' Error*, 221 (his italics).
[47] Ronald de Sousa, *The Rationality of Emotion* (Cambridge: MIT Press, 1987), 195.
[48] Elster, *Alchemies of the Mind*, 284.
[49] Damasio, *Descartes' Error*, 172.
[50] Elster, *Alchemies of the Mind*, 297.

emotions and decisions — 'seems too coarse for the range of cases it is supposed to explain.'[51]

Of course Elster is right — Damasio has no direct evidence to support his causal claim. However if this is the case, then the emotions involved must surely be epiphenomenal 'spandrels' — if the 'gut feeling' does not help in the decision-making process, then why has this (or any other) emotion been selected for? As natural selection only operates on functional properties are we to see emotion research end up in the same epiphenomenal blind alley as consciousness studies? In the latter field no one has yet managed to exorcise Huxley's ghost, and consciousness still seems to be like the 'steam whistle, which accompanies the work of a locomotive [but] without influence upon its machinery.'[52]

Elster also claims that Damasio (and several other emotion researchers)[53] are setting up a 'straw man' by opposing gut feeling to 'hyperrational cost-benefit calculation.'[54] After all there are plenty of rules of thumb and other heuristic devices that can be employed in the decision-making process, without recourse to ideal types like 'impeccable rationality' or an 'addiction to reason' (of itself irrational). 'What we may observe here, however, is not emotion doing what reason cannot do, but rather emotion doing what reason could also do, only differently.'[55] But this is perhaps to misrepresent Damasio's primary intention — as a neurologist his task is to identify mechanisms that human agents actually use (and to speculate on their evolutionary origins). The question of whether such biological markers are 'optimal' and whether reason *could* do what emotion appears to be doing is a topic for engineering disciplines, rather than biological science. Damasio chooses the dilemma of the businessman who is 'faced with the prospect of meeting or not with a possible client who can bring valuable business but also happens to be the arch-enemy of your best friend,' to illustrate his 'somatic marker' hypothesis.[56] The gut reaction may well predispose the businessman

---

[51] *Ibid.*
[52] T. H. Huxley, 'On The Hypothesis that Animals Are Automata, and its History,' *Collected Essays*, vol. 1 (London: Macmillan, 1893).
[53] De Sousa, *The Rationality of Emotion*; Joseph LeDoux, *The Emotional Brain* (NY: Simon and Schuster, 1996); Philip Johnson-Laird and Keith Otley, 'Basic Emotions, Rationality, and Folk Theory,' *Cognition and Emotion* 6 (1992): 201-23.
[54] Elster, *Alchemies of the Mind*, 295.
[55] Elster, *Alchemies of the Mind*, 290.
[56] Damasio, *Descartes' Error*, 170.

to decide against the meeting, and this may well be a non-rational decision from the perspective of cost/benefit analysis. Nevertheless if this is how actual living human agents take decisions then Damasio is right to focus on this mechanism.

Elster offers another objection to the somatic marker hypothesis in his discussion of developmental sociopathy, where he prefers Robert Frank's explanation, whereby sociopaths emphasize rewards in the present moment, in preference to future payoffs.[57] The British neuropsychologist James Blair has also cast doubt on the somatic marker hypothesis.[58] He also questions Damasio's claim that similar mechanisms underlie both psychopathy and those, like Phineas Gage, who acquire similar symptoms as a result of cortical damage (acquired sociopathy). While both cases are associated with emotional impairment, the impairments are different.

But, notwithstanding the above caveats regarding the specific mechanisms interfacing reason, emotion and the body, most researchers in cognitive science would agree that reason is an embodied state, by contrast to Oakeshott's portrayal of the rationalist: 'His mind has no atmosphere, no changes of season and temperature; his intellectual processes, so far as possible, are insulated from all external influence and go on in the void' (*RIP*, 7). To Oakeshott, it is impossible to separate out the mind from its contents and context, both in terms of human biology and culture. And there is increasing evidence to support this view.

Modularity of the Mind

According to Oakeshott the prevailing view of the mind as an 'apparatus for thinking,' a (computationally-derived) general intelligence, was 'a fiction; . . . a hypostatized activity.' As he says, 'The notion is: that first there is something called "the mind", that this mind acquires beliefs, knowledge, prejudices — in short, a filling — which remain nevertheless a mere appendage to it, that it causes bodily activities, and that it works best when it is unencumbered by an acquired disposition of any sort' (*RIP*, 109).[59]

---

[57] Robert Frank, *Passion Within Reason* (NY: W. W. Norton and Co., 1988).

[58] R.J.R. Blair and L. Cipolotti, 'Impaired Social Response Reversal: A Case of "Acquired Sociopathy",' *Brain* 123 (2000): 1122-41.

[59] Oakeshott would have agreed with Gilbert Ryle's argument that this is the same sort of category error as the continuing search for 'Oxford University' even after

In ridiculing this view, Oakeshott was remarkably prescient of the view of cognition that came into prominence some fifty years later. Cognitive theorists, for the most part, would accept Oakeshott's view that the mind is not in fact some sort of general-purpose information-processing device.[60] Rather than using the analogy of the digital computer, theorists now tend to regard 'the mind' as more like a Swiss army knife — a collection of domain-specific modules, which developed along Darwinian lines.[61] As there appear to be modules for concrete and highly specific functions such as face recognition and 'cheater detection', evolutionary psychologists would agree with Oakeshott's view that it is a piece of nonsense to try and draw a separation between 'the mind' and its 'contents'. Although some choose to criticize the new discipline of 'evolutionary psychology' as little more than Kiplingesque 'Just So' stories,[62] nevertheless there is much evidence from clinical lesion studies to underpin the claim that mental processes are modular from the point of view of brain structure and function, even though we may only speculate as to the provenance of our cognitive abilities.

Neuropsychology

Some scientists have claimed that rationality is just another cognitive state that can be accurately placed on a biological continuum not a long way removed from autism. For example, Simon Baron-Cohen and his team at Cambridge have attempted to highlight the neurological basis of autism, which often manifests as compulsive rational-analytic behavior.[63] Baron-Cohen concludes that the evidence suggests that autism involves a breakdown in a loop involving the orbito-frontal cortex, the superior temporal sulcus and the amygdala (areas which were also implicated in Damasio's work on emotion and social judgment). According to Baron-Cohen, there is a psychological continuum with the traditional 'female' characteris-

one has visited all the colleges. The Rylian view of the mind, as popularized by his student Daniel Dennett, is now widely accepted by philosophers of mind.

[60] Daniel Dennett prefers to view the mind as an 'army of idiots,' rather than a single intelligent homunculus. See his *Consciousness Explained* (Harmondsworth: Penguin Books, 1993).

[61] Jerome H. Barkow, Leda Cosmides and John Tooby, ed., *The Adapted Mind: Evolutionary Psychology and the Generation of Culture* (Oxford: Oxford Univ. Press, 1992).

[62] Hilary and Steven Rose, *Alas Poor Darwin* (London: Vintage Books, 2001).

[63] Simon Baron-Cohen, *Mindblindness*, (Cambridge: MIT Press, 1995).

tics of intuition and empathy at one end and the socially isolated state of the autistic at the other, with normal males somewhere in the middle (the stereotype 'computer nerd' would be positioned half-way between the normal male and the autistic).[64]

Conclusion

At the heart of 'modern Rationalism' is the preoccupation with the quest for *certainty* — and this can be traced back to the work of Bacon and Descartes. However, contemporary science has thrown in the towel on this quixotic project — Descartes' first critic, Pascal, was right all along.[65] Our best understanding of the physical world, quantum theory, has probability at its very core, the firing of a nerve cell is equally probabilistic and the rapid development of nonlinear dynamics has made even the calculation of probabilities fraught with problems. In the light of all this, a philosophical system with 'certainty' as its starting point and its goal is beginning to look like a quaint anachronism.

When Oakeshott wrote his famous essay, he was out of line with the emerging paradigm of cognitive science, not to mention the general 'progressive' *zeitgeist* of the post-war corporatist-collectivist consensus. However, rather than being a relic of an age of fusty idealist philosophy, Oakeshott was a prophet before his time. Students from a wide variety of disciplines who first turn to his work at the start of the twenty-first century are likely to be surprised by its freshness and relevance.

---

[64] Notwithstanding the use of scare quotes, autism is far more prevalent among males, although there are some well-known female cases, including Temple Grandin, who describes how she tries to overcome her lack of natural social empathy by trying to 'compute' others' intentions and states of mind. By contrast, she feels quite at home in a 'male' scientific-rational or technological context (she is a designer of cattle-handling equipment). Reported in Oliver Sacks, *An Anthropologist on Mars* (London: Picador, 1995), 258. Baron-Cohen's work also suggests there may be considerable undiagnosed mild autism in the community. Although this is no more than speculation, the point I wish to make here is that qualities we normally call 'rational' are biologically-based rather than transcendental and can be accurately positioned on a continuum that includes a gender and developmental component.

[65] Blaise Pascal, *Pensées* (Braunschweig: G. Westermann, 1873), 1.76.

14

Martyn P. Thompson

Intimations of Poetry in Practical Life

Oakeshott's discussion of *The Voice of Poetry in the Conversation of Mankind* (1959)[1] has been frequently misunderstood. Those, like Valerie Minogue, who read it as a comprehensive account of Oakeshott's philosophy of art are bound to come away disappointed. So much is missing; so much is left unexamined.[2] Others, like Steven Gerencser, who read it as Oakeshott's attempt to refashion his conception of philosophy, a conception that was supposedly too rigid and too Idealist in *Experience and Its Modes*, mistake the main purpose of *The Voice of Poetry*.[3] To be sure, when Oakeshott included 'The Voice of Poetry' in the first edition of *Rationalism in Politics* (1962), he noted that the 'essay on poetry is a belated retraction of a foolish sentence in *Experience and Its Modes*' (*RIP*, xi).[4] But that retraction required neither a comprehensive elaboration of a philosophy of art nor any major overhaul of the philosophical argument in which the sentence had occurred. The foolish sentence Oakeshott retracted was that in 'art, music and poetry...we are

---

[1] Oakeshott, *Rationalism in Politics and other essays, new and expanded edition*, ed. Timothy Fuller (Indianapolis: Liberty Press, 1991), 488-541. Hereafter: *RIP*. The essay was originally published as *The Voice of Poetry in the Conversation of Mankind* (London: Bowles and Bowles, 1959).

[2] Valerie Minogue, 'Philosopher Go Home!' *The Twentieth Century* 167 (March 1960): 226-34. Minogue finds Oakeshott's greatest omission to be any discussion of the 'process' of artistic creation or production. She is quite right. But to expect any such discussion in the essay is to miss its point.

[3] Steven A. Gerencser, *The Skeptic's Oakeshott* (NY: St. Martin's Press, 2000), esp. 2-3, 38-42.

[4] 'Preface to the first edition.'

wholly taken up with practical life.'[5] So the main point of 'The Voice of Poetry,' it would seem, is to offer a philosophically better or more appropriate account of the relationship between poetry and practical life than that given, as little more than an aside, in *Experience and Its Modes*.

I shall argue that this, indeed, is the main point of the essay. But in sketching what I take to be a more appropriate reading of the complex arguments of 'The Voice of Poetry,' I shall emphasize two further points. First, the essay is more concerned to refine our understanding of the character of practical life than to develop anything approaching a comprehensive philosophy of art. Second, despite Oakeshott's repeated insistence that philosophy has no direct practical impact, 'The Voice of Poetry' is explicitly concerned to show that it may have a significant indirect impact on human conduct.

This second point is bound to be controversial. But I am not alone in advancing it. Several years ago, Timothy Fuller made a similar point with respect to Oakeshott's philosophical account of history as a mode of thought. While not disagreeing with Oakeshott's contention that an historian's concern with an historical past meant that history had no lessons for the practical present, Fuller went on to suggest that this did not mean that a philosophical account of history had no indirect practical significance. I shall repeat Fuller's two main points since I shall draw upon them at the end of this essay.

Fuller identifies two different sets of practical impacts on two different kinds of practice that might be said to result from Oakeshott's thinking about history and philosophy. The first kind of practice is that of historians themselves. Fuller quotes an unpublished paper by Oakeshott in which he refers to the 'reciprocal' relationship between the philosopher and the historian. Here Oakeshott acknowledges that 'the historian, in his own enquiry, may, perhaps, benefit from the philosophical criticism of some of his more general ideas — ideas such as cause and effect, growth and decay, development, change, progress, success and failure.'[6] The second kind of practice is that of political activity and here Fuller points to a more indirect impact of

---

[5]   Oakeshott, *Experience and Its Modes* (Cambridge: Cambridge Univ. Press, 1933), 297. Hereafter: *EM*.

[6]   Quoted in Timothy Fuller, 'The Practical Impact of Oakeshott's Thought on History and Philosophy (Despite His Intent?),' delivered at the CSPT conference on 'The Politics of History', Tulane University, New Orleans, 22–4 March 1996 (typescript, 4).

Oakeshott's 'philosophical skepticism.' This philosophical skepticism, Fuller argues, might well lead readers to foster tolerance, to exercise self-constraint in public and private affairs and, in general, contribute to the revival of 'the politics of skepticism against the currently dominant politics of faith.'[7] This all seems persuasive to me and, in considering 'The Voice of Poetry,' I shall suggest that here too we encounter the recognition of similar kinds of indirect impact of philosophical thought on practical activity. But there is, I believe, a still more general point to be made about the relationships between philosophy and practical activity in Oakeshott's thinking. This general point, I shall suggest, revolves around the characteristic activities, attitudes and manners of the ideal of an educated person that Oakeshott envisages. For this ideal is explicit in some and implicit in all of Oakeshott's writings. The speaker, that is to say, is always this person but so, too, is the implied reader who is addressed in all of Oakeshott's published works.

So I propose to look again at 'The Voice of Poetry.' My ultimate concern will be to explore a little further the grounds for believing that Oakeshott's philosophical thinking does have some practical impact, of some sort or another. 'The Voice of Poetry' is particularly appropriate for reflections of this kind because it raises and, I think, answers exactly this question. It begins with an image of civilization under attack from the forces of barbarism. And it offers as a defense of civilization something rather unpromising. It offers a philosophical enquiry into the 'voice' of poetry or art. The forces of barbarism are identified as science and practical activity. But if, as Oakeshott often says, philosophy itself has no practical impact whatsoever, how can a philosophy of poetry even begin to engage these barbaric forces? The short answer is indirectly. The engagement with these forces occurs in the activities that may, but need not, flow from an educated understanding of the world. But what this means, why a philosophy of poetry should be the chosen vehicle to do the trick, and how it all might work are best examined in terms of the interplay between the various themes of 'The Voice of Poetry.' There are good reasons why Oakeshott looks at poetry in this essay; reasons that have very little to do with his desire to correct the judgment in *Experience and Its Modes* that poetry is a kind of practical activity.

'The Voice of Poetry' has at least four interrelated themes. Two are obvious; two perhaps less so. The first theme, which frames the

---

[7]   Fuller, 'The Practical Impact,' 16.

essay, is a theme of cultural decline and the suggestion for an appropriate response. The second theme is the philosophical elucidation of the 'voice' and distinctive idiom of poetry or art in the 'conversation of mankind.' Philosophical elucidation involves identifying the 'quality' of the voice of poetry and its relationship to the other voices, mainly practice and science. The third theme identifies similarities between the voices of poetry, philosophy, history and science and it explores their differences from the voices of practical activity and science corrupted by practical concerns. In noticing this theme, I shall draw on Oakeshott's recently published essay 'Work and Play.' The fourth theme is educational. It is here, in the activities and characteristic attitudes of the educated person, that Oakeshott's ideas offer a model for civilized human conduct in practical as well as intellectual pursuits. Let me turn to the first theme.

The Theme of Cultural Decline

The essay starts with a theme of cultural criticism. Over the past few centuries, we are told, intellectual life in both public and private has become increasingly 'boring.' The greatest of intellectual achievements which was once a more or less flourishing conversation between the distinct, different, but equal voices of practice, science, philosophy, art and so on, has degenerated into an argument or dispute monopolized by just the voices of practice and science. Everything in human affairs has been impoverished as a result, even the worlds of science and practice. The world of politics, for example, from being understood once (in ancient Greece) as a poetic activity and later (in Machiavelli, for example) as an heroic activity, has now been almost completely assimilated to a dull kind of practical activity (*RIP*, 493-4 n. 1). This particular theme is very familiar to readers of 'Rationalism in Politics.' But Oakeshott's point in 'The Voice of Poetry' is to draw attention to a much more widespread cultural decline. The conversation that is the height of human achievement has fallen into a 'bog,' he says. There is no obvious way out. Any rescue, he notes, 'would require a philosophy more profound than anything I have to offer.' And given the absence of such a profound philosophy, he decides to pursue a much more 'modest' proposal for assistance. He will reconsider philosophically, he says, 'the voice of poetry…as it speaks in the conversation' (*RIP*, 494).

Now, there is something odd in this suggestion. Oakeshott, like Hegel, always insisted that philosophy makes nothing happen. So if the shape of our intellectual life has grown old and has become bogged down by boring distractions, no philosophy, no matter how profound, could possibly rejuvenate it. How, then, might his more modest philosophical undertaking even begin to contribute to some partial rescue of human intellectual achievement from the bog into which it has fallen? He is clearly claiming that it will help in some way or another. The problem is compounded by the time we reach the end of the essay. For by then we have learned that poetry is 'a sort of truancy, a dream within the dream of life, a wild flower planted among our wheat' (*RIP*, 541). It is an activity of contemplation, of delight. It is not a source of pleasure, such as the practical world offers. Nor is it a source of knowledge, such as science offers. It has apparently no practical import whatsoever. So poetry, for Oakeshott as for the chastened Auden in the late 1930s, 'makes nothing happen: it survives / In the valley of its making where executives / Would never want to tamper.'[8] And it is perhaps worth noting here that had Oakeshott chosen to advance his philosophy of history against the forces of barbarism, the same problem would have arisen. So, too, with his philosophy of science. For in the accounts in both *Experience and Its Modes* and in *Rationalism in Politics*, neither history nor science ('pure science,' we might want to say) make anything happen. So how, once again, can a philosophy of art help lift us out of the bog?

Let me reject one possible answer. One might be tempted to link this first theme with T.S. Eliot. One might, that is, search Oakeshott's writings for several 'fragments' which he had rescued from the encroaching decay. Amongst them might be the voice of poetry, the voice of history, and so on. And we might imagine Oakeshott to have been saying not quite Eliot's 'These fragments I have shored against my ruins', but something like 'These fragments may shield us from the bores.' But it would be a mistake to do this. Modernity, for Oakeshott, is not a 'Waste Land.' The springs of culture have not dried up. There is no resignation, anger or despair in Oakeshott's voice. Quite the contrary. As 'On Being Conservative' makes clear, there was just as much joy, adventure and fulfillment to be had in the modern world as in any other. You just needed to know where and how to look for them. Youth sends you one way, old age another. Politics, increasingly dominated by modern rationalists and increasingly conducted in an ideological style, was an unpromising place to try to find them. So, too, was the world of practical activity in gen-

[8]   'In Memory of W.B. Yeats,' 1939, lines 36-8.

eral, which Oakeshott often characterized as a continuous cycle of
wants, satisfactions and inevitable frustrations ending only in death.
This is not, of course, to say that fulfillment is never to be found in
political or practical activity. Of course it is, especially if, as
Oakeshott notes, 'we are so inclined and have nothing better to think
about' (*RIP*, 437). It is rather to say, as his argument in 'The Claims of
Politics' suggests, that it is perhaps more readily to be found in some
other activities like those of literature, philosophy and art.[9]

A better way to understand the contribution that a philosophical
enquiry into artistic experience might make to resisting cultural
decay is simply to take it for what it undoubtedly is: a contribution to
the education of both writer and audience. It is still, of course,
unclear how the desired effect is to be achieved. But I must postpone
offering my suggestions until I have looked at the interplay between
the essay's main themes. Let me turn to the second.

The 'Voices' in the Conversation of Mankind

Oakeshott's thought runs something like this. We grow up in a rich,
diverse and bewildering world. But we are never without some
guidance as to how to make sense of it and how to act in it with some
likelihood of success. There are always people who have been here
longer and whose experience can help us first hand. And there were
always people before them who have left records that can serve us as
guides. Over the decades and centuries, these guides to acting in and
understanding the world have established themselves as durable,
often highly institutionalized, practices. They include the modes of
experience examined in *Experience and Its Modes*, the conditional
platforms of understanding that appear in *On Human Conduct*, and
the various conversational 'voices' which appear in 'The Voice of
Poetry.' Their appearance was in no sense accidental although their
fortunes have changed with changing historical circumstances. For
each is intimated in some sense in our everyday experiences. There is
no hierarchy in these modes, platforms or voices. Each has come to
constitute a distinct, different and autonomous world of experience.
And the surest recipe for confusion and frustration in the world is to
mix the modes together. The modes and voices that Oakeshott
explored in most detail were those of practice, science, history and
poetry. Let me glance at each in turn.

[9]   'The Claims of Politics,' in Oakeshott, *Religion, Politics and the Moral Life*, ed.
       Timothy Fuller (New Haven: Yale Univ. Press, 1993), 91-6. Hereafter: *RPML*.

We spend most of our waking lives inhabiting the world of practice: the world of desire and aversion, of approval and disapproval. It is the world in which we must live, if we are to live at all. Indeed, this is the only world in which we could, if we so chose, spend all of our lives. Of course, we have to learn how to live in this world. We have to learn the language of appetite and morality. And we can do this mainly, though not necessarily very efficiently, just by imitating others in the so-called 'school of life.' Of course, our needs have long since become wants. The search for satisfactions and moral evaluations often require considerable sophistication. The practical world is not a simple world. Rather, it is a rich and varied world of satisfactions and frustrations, of never-ending attempts to change 'what is' into what we imagine it 'ought to be.' It is the world considered in its relationship to our wants. But it is not the only world available to us.

The world of science is the world understood in its independence from us. It emerges when the desire to acquire knowledge in order to get what we want gives way to the impulse to explain the world as a rational system of concepts, causally related to one another, exhibiting universal laws of nature. It is a constructed world, a universe of discourse, as all the other worlds are. We have to learn the language of science if we are to spend any time here. That language, that voice, is a particular kind of explanatory language, one that aims at complete communicative precision. It requires the removal of everything personal, esoteric or ambiguous, because it presupposes that what is said in science can best be said in terms of mathematical symbols.

The world of history is also a world understood in its independence from us. But, unlike science, it emerges when the desire to acquire knowledge either to get what we want or to justify what we do gives way to the impulse to explain the past in terms of its pastness. The world of history is comprised of images that have to be constructed. They are images of particular and unrepeatable past occurrences which all the available present-day historical evidence obliges us to believe occurred. History, too, has a language and hence a voice of its own. It is one in which the practical language of desire and aversion, approval and disapproval is irrelevant and in which the scientific language of universal laws of cause and effect can have no place.

The languages of practice, science and history are all symbolic languages of one kind or another. They all presuppose a distinction

between fact/not-fact, fact/fiction, true/false. But truth is different
in each language. Practical truths are not scientific truths, historical
truths are not practical truths, and so on. But all this is absent from
the language of poetry/art. The world of art is the world of contem-
plating or delighting. Everything in this world is fiction. It is a
'dream within a dream.' Works of art do not stand for other things.
They do not represent or express things. They are what they are,
imaginative images to which the appropriate response is delight and
nothing else. So the language of art is not symbolic. For want of a
better term, Oakeshott calls it strictly metaphorical, where words are
fictional images not signs for other images (*RIP*, 527–8). It, too, is a
language that has to be learned. In learning it, as in learning the language of history, philosophy is not entirely irrelevant. The concern
of the literary critic, Oakeshott says, 'is to quicken the hearing we
give to the voice of poetry and to explore the qualities of a poem. In
this it is not a bad thing to be something of a philosopher; philosophic reflection may perhaps hinder the critic from asking irrelevant questions and from thinking and speaking about poems in an
inappropriate manner, and this (though it does not carry us very far)
is something not to be despised' (*RIP*, 495).

But as it turns out, the voice of poetry has been particularly
ill-served by even its most prominent literary-critical apologists. For
some of these have actually assisted the forces of science and practical activity to take over the 'domain of the poetic.' On the one side,
for example, advancing the claims for some superior 'poetic truth'
simply assimilates art to science. On the other side, for example,
insisting that poets are, say, the 'unacknowledged legislators of the
world' simply assimilates art to the world of practical activity (*RIP*,
532-4). So aided by its supposed defenders, the voice of poetry has
proved to be most vulnerable to the encroachments of practice and
science. By abandoning the distinctive voice of poetry, these 'defenders' have made it almost impossible for that voice to be heard
and understood by its conversational partners. They have encouraged asking artistically irrelevant questions about art, questions that
would anyway have been asked by others. And they have encouraged artistically inappropriate talk about art by engaging in it themselves. Hence the urgent need for Oakeshott's modest philosophical
project with respect to poetry, rather than, say, with respect to history. The project might help, in the circumscribed way he suggests,
to aid the most vulnerable of contemporary intellectual voices to

regain a hearing. This, after all, is the voice that has allowed itself to fall deepest into the bog.

Now, one might well say, given the initial responses to 'The Voice of Poetry' and the subsequent developments in English departments, Cultural Studies departments and all the rest, that Oakeshott was singularly unsuccessful in this particular project. But this would be premature. I want to suggest that his modest project in 'The Voice of Poetry' is part of a much larger project, one where success and failure are of a different order. This larger project emerges in the essay's third theme.

Work and Play

The first theme in 'The Voice of Poetry' identified the increasing predominance of practical concerns and scientific ways of thinking as a threat to civilization. The second theme identified the ways in which this dual threat has all but silenced the 'voice' of poetry/art by appropriating its domain. But it has done much more than this as well. It has drawn a significant distinction between the quality of the current voices of practice and science on the one side, and the quality of the current voices of poetry, art, philosophy (and I have added history), on the other.

The worlds of discourse that are under threat are distinct and different worlds but they do share several common characteristics. They are all worlds that have been constructed without concern for the satisfaction of our wants. They are not worlds in which we could spend all of our lives. Like the world of practice, we have to learn the appropriate language to inhabit these other worlds. But in a different way from the language of practice, we must *choose* to learn their languages. Even the world of science shares these few characteristics and it quite understandably occupies an ambiguous position in Oakeshott's battle between civilization and barbarism. Science reduced to, or mistaken for, the servant of practice is really the partner in barbarism, not science properly understood. So all of the voices, save that of practical activity, share the common characteristic that they are each, in their different ways, emancipated from the concerns of practical life. They are play, not work.

What distinguishes 'the civilized man from the barbarian,' Oakeshott tells us, is 'the ability to participate in the conversation' of mankind. He goes on immediately to add that education, 'properly speaking, is an initiation into the skill and partnership of this conversation in which we learn to recognize the voices, to distinguish the proper occasions of utterance, and in which we acquire the intellectual and moral habits appropriate to conversation' (*RIP*, 490-1). The characteristic that Oakeshott constantly underlined as necessary for successful conversation was 'playfulness.' Of all the voices in the conversation, it is the voice of practical activity that has the least playfulness in it, followed closely by the corrupted voice of science: science in the service of relevant or 'useful knowledge.'

The concept of play here is, of course, similar to Huizinga's. Play is the form of culture. Culture, Huizinga writes, 'arises in the form of play...it is played from the very beginning. Even those activities which aim at the immediate satisfaction of vital needs — hunting, for instance — tend, in archaic society, to take on the play-form. . . . It is through this playing that society expresses its interpretation of life and the world.'[10] And so on. So play is a very serious and significant matter. For Huizinga, the enemy of play is the dull seriousness of ordinary life. Like Oakeshott, he sees modern civilization in decline. Modernity reached its playful zenith in the eighteenth century. For Oakeshott, decline set in two centuries earlier as work, not play, came gradually to be regarded as 'the great business and occupation of life.' Work, here, is understood as the 'activity of exploiting the natural resources of the world for the satisfaction of human wants.' Instead of being the partner of *homo ludens*, *homo laborans* became his enemy and eventually his self-appointed master. As a result, the pursuit of the happiness that comes from the satisfaction of human wants has all but eclipsed the pursuit of that other sort of happiness that comes from playfully participating in the great intellectual achievements civilization has to offer. But the happiness derived from work is at best fleeting. It generates its own frustration and anxiety. Only the happiness that comes with play has duration. For play 'offers satisfactions that are not at the same time frustrations.'[11]

For Huizinga, who was writing at a time when European societies seemed to be 'rapidly goose-stepping into helotry,' what remained of the play-element in culture had turned into 'false play,' almost

---

[10] Johan Huizinga, *Homo Ludens: A Study of the Play-Element in Culture* (London: Routledge, 1949), 46.

[11] Oakeshott, 'Work and Play,' at: www.firstthings.com/ftissues/ft9506/ articles/oake.html. Oakeshott is quoting Aristotle. 'Work and Play' has also been published in Luke O'Sullivan, ed., *What is History? and other essays* (Exeter: Imprint Academic, 2004), 303-14. Hereafter: *WH*

'non-play.'[12] Oakeshott was by no means this pessimistic. A defense against barbarity still existed in educational institutions and practices which remained committed to 'liberal studies' or studies liberated from the concerns of practical doing, studies concerned with the activities that belong to 'play'.[13] This ancient educational tradition, 'that has not quite gone out of fashion,' needed to be supported and rejuvenated. Everything that Oakeshott wrote seems designed to serve this purpose. It constitutes the fourth theme, implicit more than explicit, in 'The Voice of Poetry.' Let me turn to examine what I take to be involved here.

Liberal Education and Human Conduct

I have suggested that the modest proposal in 'The Voice of Poetry' to stem the tide of barbarism is a part of this larger project to advance the cause of liberal education. How might the modest proposal work and how is it related to liberal education? As in Fuller's discussion of 'The Practical Impact of Oakeshott's Thought on History and Philosophy,' so here too there are two levels of impact. As I have indicated, Oakeshott believed that his philosophical account of the 'domain' of art could usefully serve the practice of literary criticism by identifying irrelevant questions and 'inappropriate' ways of speaking. But as with the historian, so too with the critic or poet. Oakeshott did not believe that it was their main business, or even an important part of their business, to pay heed to the words of the philosopher, even though they might well benefit from them. In this, they were unlike the philosopher, since a philosophy of art is impossible without attending to the works of artists and critics.

But there is also an impact of a broader kind, paralleling the impact that Fuller suggested might follow from Oakeshott's philosophical skepticism on the conduct of political life. At the end of 'The Voice of Poetry,' Oakeshott points to what I have in mind. Poetic activity, he says, has no part in the 'struggle' which is practical life:

> [I]t has no power to control, to modify, or to terminate it. If it imitates the voice of practice its utterance is counterfeit. To listen to the voice of poetry is to enjoy, not a victory, but a momentary release, a brief enchantment. And perhaps, obliquely, it is to enjoy something more. Having an ear ready for the voice of poetry is to be disposed to choose delight rather than pleasure or vir-

---

[12]   Huizinga, *Homo Ludens*, 206.
[13]   Oakeshott, 'Work and Play,' 8.

tue or knowledge, a disposition which will reflect itself in practical life in an affection for its intimations of poetry. (*RIP*, 540)

This reveals, I believe, how poetry (or, for that matter, any of the other cultured, emancipated, 'playful' voices) might help, albeit obliquely, as Oakeshott says, to find a way out of the 'bog' into which we have fallen. It might do so by restoring to people increasingly engaged in practical life the ability to detect even here its own 'intimations of poetry' and hence its own 'playfulness.' If they can do this, the voice of practice can once more become an equal partner in the conversation of mankind instead of the ill-mannered, domineering bore it currently seems to be.

Now this immensely important disposition to find, to enjoy and to cherish what is playful in the manifold activities of life is, it seems to me, exactly the disposition which characterizes the ideal of a liberally educated person that appears in all that Oakeshott wrote in defense of liberal education.[14] So all of the practical effects that may, but need not, manifest themselves in, say, political conduct — tolerance, self-restraint, civility, a preference for the politics of skepticism, and so on — these might all be understood as something more than just the likely outcomes from accepting 'philosophical skepticism.' They are also the likely outcomes of that reflection in practical life of the disposition to attend to the play-element in culture. The person with this disposition is the liberally educated person. This is the person sufficiently cultured, sufficiently sensitive, and sufficiently self-aware to have 'an ear ready' to hear the voice of poetry in the otherwise repetitive life of satisfactions gained and frustrations encountered that is practical activity. And to the extent that everything Oakeshott wrote was written for the liberally educated person, to that extent at least, his philosophical writings were designed to have this indirect impact on the conduct of practical life.

[14] See Oakeshott, *The Voice of Liberal Learning*, ed. Timothy Fuller (Indianapolis: Liberty Fund, 2001).

15

Robert Grant

Oakeshott on the Nature and Place of Aesthetic Experience

A Critique

Michael Oakeshott was Professor of Political Science at the London School of Economics from 1952 to 1969. He died in 1990, a week after his eighty-ninth birthday, and is now widely recognized as a classic. It is still not generally realized, however, that his politics are only one aspect of the philosophical idealism which pervades all his thought. Still less is it known that, in revising his master-conception, Oakeshott also made an original contribution to aesthetics. That is our present subject, but, since his aesthetics are best understood in relation to his 'core' philosophy, I shall begin with that.[1]

Oakeshott set out his basic world view in *Experience and its Modes*.[2] This precocious work was an attempt, in the manner of Collingwood's *Speculum Mentis*,[3] to map out experience, its scope, contours and local varieties. Experience, for Oakeshott, is epistemologically primitive. As in Hegel, there is nothing outside it, nothing prior to it, nothing transcendental.[4] Even so-called 'immediate' experience

---

[1]   This paper was also delivered at the International Congress of Aesthetics at Kanda University, Tokyo, just before the Burton Gray Memorial Conference at LSE in 2001. The author gratefully acknowledges the British Academy's award of an Overseas Conference Grant for his travel to Japan.

[2]   Oakeshott, *Experience and its Modes* (Cambridge: Cambridge Univ. Press, 1933). Hereafter: *EM*.

[3]   R. G. Collingwood, *Speculum Mentis* (Oxford: Clarendon Press, 1924).

[4]   Or if there is, then it is purely hypothetical and therefore, as Wittgenstein said, of no interest to us. Cf. *Philosophical Investigations*, I, §126.

comes to us in the form of thought or judgment, and never as pure, unqualified 'sensation'. If we then deduce other things from it, those are still part of experience as a whole. And the same is true of your immediate experience, which must naturally differ from mine. Oakeshott, here, is no solipsist or subjectivist, because experience, simply *qua* experience, is prior to both subject and object.[5]

For Oakeshott, human experience is composed of a number of distinct 'modes' or discourses. The main ones are history and science, which are purely theoretical, and practice, which is the value-laden world of everyday life. In Oakeshott's original scheme art belonged, with morality and religion, to practice. But he later assigned art and aesthetic experience to a new mode, Poetry, whose sole end is contemplative 'delight'. Anything, not only art, but also nature, may be viewed 'poetically'.

Experience as a whole, or absolute reality, is accessible only to philosophy. (Strange, then, how few philosophers, if any, seem to have gained access to it.) Otherwise experience comes to us only *via* a multiplicity of differing perspectives, which Oakeshott here calls 'modes', but later calls 'activities', 'practices', 'imaginings', 'idioms', 'universes of discourse', or 'voices'. A mode, says Oakeshott, is a settled 'direction of attention,' a particular way of approaching the world, conceiving it and (what follows) dividing it up.[6]

The modes are potentially infinite in number but, as aforesaid, three predominate. Loosely speaking, science and history are contemplative modes. They focus on the world as it appears independently of human self-interest, that is, as freed from all practical considerations of profit, use, value and present action. In science the world appears to us as 'nature', as quantitatively conceived and governed by general physical laws. In history we deduce a past world from present evidence, events being understood as the outcome of choices made intelligible by contiguous prior events.

---

[5]   As in Hegel and Heidegger, whose joint predecessor Lichtenberg had acutely noted that Descartes' *cogito* begs the question. The foundational intuition is not 'I think', but 'there is a thinking.' The 'I' is derivative.

[6]   Unlike Kant's categories, Oakeshott's 'modes' are not innate, but collective human inventions. They resemble Wittgenstein's 'language-games', except that they may encompass every kind of utterance or performance. The phrase 'direction of attention' comes, not from *EM*, but from 'The Activity of Being An Historian,' in *Rationalism in Politics and other essays* (London: Methuen, 1962), 137, 139. Hereafter: *RP*. Nevertheless, it answers very well to what Oakeshott means by 'mode' in the earlier book.

We exploit nature and distort the past, but in their inmost constitution both are impervious to our will. Although Oakeshott claims that each mode is a limited perspective on the whole of experience, it is hard to see just what he means. Science aspires to view everything in physical terms, but its success, surely, is largely due to its discounting whatever cannot be so viewed. As for history, the future, at least, cannot fall under its scrutiny. The very fact that each mode is an ineluctably partial perspective should invalidate the idea that its object can simultaneously be the totality of experience. Maybe what Oakeshott means is merely that, while we inhabit a particular mode, we *think* of it as all-inclusive, though even this must be doubtful, since, from constantly switching between modes, we know that none can be that.

There is no escape from modal experience, not even for the philosopher. One reason for this lies in practice, the mode that we inhabit most of the time. Since its chief function is to ensure our survival, we cannot permanently ignore or opt out of it. Practice is precisely that immediate world of profit, use, value, action, self-interest, good and bad, pleasure and pain, which history and science exclude.[7]

Each mode, says Oakeshott, has its own presuppositions and procedures. These are uniquely appropriate to, and valid for, whatever falls within the given mode's legitimate competence. Perhaps surprisingly, nothing can belong to more than one mode. The scientist's 'H_2O' and the practical man's 'water' are two entirely different concepts or 'things', inhabiting totally different universes and behaving according to totally different rules. But (says Oakeshott) every mode, being an attempt to comprehend the whole of experience under its own perspective, has a tendency, not merely to exclude other modes, but actually to invade their territory. (If you scent a political analogy here, you are right.)[8]

This modal imperialism is a perennial source of error and confusion, and leads to the gravest of all sins in the Oakeshottian canon, namely irrelevance, or a failure to observe the limits of one's present

---

[7]   As in Hobbes, a major influence on Oakeshott, the worst that can happen to us in the practical world is death. But this is true of any mode, since death is the end of all experience.

[8]   It is actually more than an analogy, because this tendency can have real political consequences. It leads, first, to collectivism, 'the mobilization of a society for unitary action' (the said society being conceived as existing in a single mode), and thence to 'the condition of things in which it is appropriate,' i.e., war. See 'The Political Economy of Freedom' (*RP*, 53-4).

discourse. For example, morality, religion, politics and commerce all belong to practice. Nevertheless, enthusiasts for each will read science, history and everything else in the light of their particular preoccupation. Again, people impressed by the success of science in its own sphere will offer us 'scientific morals' (usually some version of utilitarianism) or 'scientific history' (that is, historical positivism, under which events supposedly conform to comprehensive, quasi-scientific 'laws'). And so on.

In all this, although the philosopher's ultimate task is to remove our modal blinkers, his day-to-day job is to point out irrelevancies and to pull us up short when we commit them. Though every kind of modal thinking naturally pushes beyond its limits, and defective though it is in the philosophical overview, within those limits its competence is real.

Such is the burden of *Experience and its Modes*. Oakeshott never returned to a full-scale, systematic treatment of modality. He did, however, continue to tinker with the details, notably in two essays from the 1950s: one, 'The Activity of Being an Historian,' on historiography; and the other, 'The Voice of Poetry in the Conversation of Mankind,' on the place of the aesthetic in experience.[9] In 'The Voice of Poetry' Oakeshott's focus shifts, radically if unobtrusively, from the idealist Absolute — that is, from experience considered as a single, integral whole — to something much more dynamic, fluid and (consequently) elusive, which he calls 'conversation'. This latter idea, along with allegedly similar notions in Heidegger and Wittgenstein, has been picked up by the American pragmatist and self-confessed post-modernist Richard Rorty, and promoted by him as a suitable philosophy, or anti-philosophy, for our times.[10]

Oakeshott's aesthetics accompany, and illustrate, the conversational paradigm elaborated in 'The Voice of Poetry.' As far as I know I am the only person who has written about them at any length.[11] One reason for their neglect may be that, by Oakeshott's normal standards, they are both incoherent and implausible. But, as

---

[9]   Both are in *RP*.

[10] Richard Rorty, *Philosophy and the Mirror of Nature* (Oxford: Basil Blackwell, 1980).

[11] This was true at the time of writing (2001), the reference being Grant, *Thinkers of Our Time: Oakeshott* (London: Claridge Press, 1990), chap. 7. Since then there have been Glenn Worthington, 'The Voice of Poetry in Oakeshott's Moral Philosophy,' *Review of Politics* 64 (2002), and several conference papers by various hands.

Oakeshott has said elsewhere, echoing Cervantes, it is better to travel than to arrive. There is much of interest in 'The Voice of Poetry,' and, as with Rousseau's *The Social Contract*, Oakeshott's twists and turns may be due more to his correcting himself as he goes along — that is, to his intellectual honesty — than to any radical failure of understanding. In fact, he *does* arrive at a plausible conclusion, which I shall articulate in due course. My only complaint is that it does not follow from his premises, though Oakeshott virtually admits as much, as we shall see.

There are difficulties in Oakeshott's conversation paradigm,[12] but only one concerns us here. Originally, the modes were radically immiscible, in keeping with the all-important notion of relevance. But in Oakeshott's revised view they become 'voices' in a 'conversation'. Logically considered this should be no more than some kind of mutual recognition, since if there were any substantive dialogue they would no longer be modally distinct.

However, some things make the conversation metaphor plausible. One is, that since each person knowingly switches between modes without losing his identity, those modes must somehow be related, if only through him. Secondly, Oakeshott's educational model, in his writings on the universities, is conversational. Even today it still answers to a recognizable reality. Each separate discipline or subject group constitutes something like a mode. So why gather them together in one place unless they have, if not some common substance, at least a common spirit?

Thirdly, Oakeshott's ethics and politics are conversational. Like Oakeshott's preferred model of society, a conversation has rules of a sort, but no goal except participation. It may take any turn without irrelevance; indeed, in the conversation as a whole (as opposed, say, to a local passage of argument) nothing can be irrelevant, just because the conversation, like its predecessor the Absolute, embraces everything. And one may withdraw from it indefinitely, so long as, on re-entry, one once more observes its conventions.

Finally, science and history are *not* conversational, at least not internally. This is because they are *enterprises*. Their domestic business is not conversation, but inquiry and argument, which press forward endlessly to conclusions (albeit temporary ones). For this reason science and history are not fully 'contemplative'. They may seem so in comparison with practice, but, like practice, they are still

---

[12]   I have attempted to resolve them in Grant, *Oakeshott*, chap. 5.

dynamic, still 'going somewhere'. They are not content simply to rest in the present moment, unlike Oakeshott's new mode, poetry. This Oakeshott now identifies as pre-eminently conversational and exclusively 'contemplative'. Poetry, in fact, is simply aesthetic experience generally, and therefore is not limited to artifacts. It seems that anything may be viewed aesthetically by one so minded. This puts the spectator, rather than the author or the object, in the driving seat, so that Oakeshott's idealism here takes an unwontedly subjectivist or postmodernist turn.

In *Experience and its Modes* art, like religion and morality, belonged firmly to practice. Having returned to the topic twenty-six years later, Oakeshott now describes 'The Voice of Poetry' as a belated retraction of his earlier view, which he calls 'foolish.'

Actually, his earlier view does not seem all that foolish, for many other intelligent people have thought that art and life (that is, practice) were connected. On the other hand, Oakeshott might reply, what is the commonplace distinction between 'fiction' and 'reality' but a statement to the effect that art has nothing to do with so-called 'real life'? If art truly belonged to practice, he now says, it would make sense to ask what Hamlet's bedtime was, or to approve or disapprove of Anna Karenina's behavior. However, these are not at all the same kind of question, and in combination appear somewhat disingenuous. The first, concerning Hamlet's bedtime, is clearly absurd, not least because, unlike *Macbeth*, the play makes no mention of the hero's sleeping habits. But the second, concerning Anna's behavior, is far from absurd, since Tolstoy has described her thoughts and actions at several hundred pages' length. To have done so is virtually to have invited a moral response, almost as if the events narrated had been 'real'.

Oakeshott accompanies his aesthetic exposition with a detailed — though also, to my mind, ill-thought-out and largely superfluous — idealist phenomenology. The world consists of 'selves' on the one hand and 'images' on the other. (Note, by contrast with *Experience and its Modes*, that selves, or subjects, are now primordial 'givens', rather than abstractions from experience as a whole, and thus derivative.) Selves create images, imagining is an activity, and activity is imagining. (As in Gilbert Ryle,[13] with whom Oakeshott has several

[13] Oakeshott reviewed Ryle's *The Concept of Mind* (London: Hutchinson, 1949) in glowing terms, in the *Spectator* 184 (1950): 20, 22. Ryle, so Oakeshott told me, was one of the few professional philosophers with whom he

affinities, emotions amount merely to 'being active in a certain manner'; and they too, it seems, are 'images'.) All 'images' initially appear as 'not-self'.[14] But some examples of 'not-self' come to be recognized as *other* selves, and this calls (first) prudential and (subsequently) moral considerations into play.

History, science and practice, Oakeshott now says, all distinguish images understood to be 'fact' from others understood to be 'not-fact'. This is plausible, up to a point. For activity in each of these modes is concerned precisely to *establish* something: in practice, whether an action will be safe or profitable; in history, whether something actually happened or was the case; in science, whether an observed occurrence confirms or establishes some general law.

But what exactly does Oakeshott mean by 'fact'? Idealism generally points away from a correspondence theory of truth. Since *everything* is an 'idea' or an 'image', nothing can be tested for its factual status against something which is neither. How can we know which images are 'facts', and why should we continue to refer to those which are as 'images'? Why not reserve the term 'image' for things, such as dreams, hallucinations, depictions, and so on, which are known to be illusory or fictitious? In practical experience, says Oakeshott cursorily, the criterion of 'fact' is pragmatic: 'an image is "fact" if by regarding it as "fact"...the desiring self is preserved for future activity' (*RP*, 207). If that answer satisfies you, then so may pragmatism; but neither will do so if you are a realist, and require something more objective.[15]

Obscure though Oakeshott's fact/not-fact distinction is, it seems to bear on a further one between things and signs. Science, history and practice are symbolic discourses. Each employs a fairly stable, conventional repertoire of images — symbols, words, and gestures respectively — to signify or refer to another set of images, generically distinct, which a realist would simply call 'things'.[16] Poetry, by contrast, recognizes no distinction between 'fact' and 'not-fact'. Its

---

maintained a personal acquaintance. Oakeshott himself never belonged to a philosophy department. His official subject at Cambridge was history, and at LSE politics.

[14] Oakeshott does not say whether the self ever perceives itself as an 'image', in the manner of Kant's 'empirical ego'.

[15] One might add that a belief's survival value is no automatic test of its truth or factual status. Many false beliefs have a high survival value.

[16] A distinction, I have subsequently learnt, once urged against Oakeshott in conversation by the Australian poet and man of letters A.D. Hope (information from Prof. Conal Condren).

words and images, in Oakeshott's view, do not signify or refer to 'things' at all. Further, an object in itself, not signified at all but simply present, can become a poetic 'image'. Poetic images are just that, mere images, to be enjoyed, elaborated and delighted in for their own sake.[17] Therefore, and despite the traditional literary-critical usage, the language of poetry is not truly or literally 'symbolic'.

Some of this seems counter-intuitive. One reason may be that Oakeshott has extended the term poetry to embrace not merely artifacts, that is, fictions, but also natural and found objects, which, when regarded normally, are 'fact'. But, when considered 'poetically', they too become 'fictions', in the sense of being transformed or re-created in the spectator's imagination. And the same is true of artifacts, which regularly lose their historic, intended meanings (which were once, perhaps, religious or practical) and acquire new, purely aesthetic ones. Congo fetishes and Russian icons are obvious examples of this process,[18] but of course it is always and everywhere at work, only less obtrusively.

Oakeshott's 'poetic images', then, are effectively all fictions of the experiencing self, whether or not they also have an author. Nevertheless, he insists repeatedly that they are neither fact nor not-fact, even though the terms 'fiction' and 'not-fact' overlap.[19] Furthermore, the fact/not-fact distinction is crucial to something that Oakeshott wishes absolutely to exclude from poetry, namely make-believe. For make-believe, Oakeshott rightly says, self-consciously treats not-fact as though it were fact. Presumably this is objectionable for the reason that make-believe must thereby verge on practice. And make-believe certainly does provoke emotions of an unmistakably practical nature, such as fear, pity, suspense, approval and disapproval, even though, unlike genuine belief, it refrains from translating them into action, since it knows perfectly well that their objects are not real (i.e., are not 'fact').

-----

[17] If anything could make this claim plausible, it would be the nursery rhyme 'Hey, diddle diddle', which is (a) wholly delightful, and (b) semantically totally opaque.

[18] Other examples might be vintage cars and Oxfam 'retro-chic' clothing (things which in their own time were merely 'cars' and 'clothes'), but of course their 'new' meaning is more than just aesthetic, being primarily a matter of display, and thus 'social.'

[19] The reason, one supposes, is that to classify poetry as 'not-fact' would in effect return it to the domain of practice, where such categories apply.

My own view is that probably none of this much matters, and that, as Kendall Walton has illustrated at length,[20] make-believe is an important component, if not of aesthetic experience *per se*, then at least of very many representational artworks. (It is also valuable in encouraging empathy.) Oakeshott's modal rigorism, which has prompted his search for each mode's *differentia specifica*, that is, for the one indispensable defining feature possessed by everything belonging to it, may have led him astray.

Science and history have something important in common, namely disinterested inquiry, but they are still modally distinct. Suppose that art and nature also are. Both provoke aesthetic emotion, but the one does so deliberately, the other not. How, then, except by a modal distinction based on that between art and nature (or on similar distinctions between art and life, fiction and non-fiction), do we account for the fact, famously remarked by Lessing,[21] that events which would be unambiguously painful in real life may nevertheless afford us a legitimate pleasure when artistically represented? Or that an ugly thing, or scene, or person may seem beautiful even when accurately depicted? And do we not also feel that there are 'real-life' events from which it would simply be depraved to extract aesthetic pleasure, even if one had not contrived them for the purpose, as the Emperor Elagabalus allegedly did, in having randomly selected slaves beheaded on his lawns, because he liked the contrast of red against green? This example also suggests that one mode may after all have the 'right' to interfere in another. In this instance morality, or practice, would trump the aesthetic, or poetry.[22]

It is tempting to regard Oakeshott's revised position as 'aestheticist'.[23] Oakeshott certainly seems to believe, with Kant, that the defining feature of the aesthetic is that it is 'disinterested' in a unique and specific way. Like Roger Fry and Clive Bell, the Bloomsbury aes-

---

[20] Kendall Walton, *Mimesis as Make-Believe: On the Foundations of the Representational Arts* (Cambridge: Harvard Univ. Press, 1990).

[21] G. E. Lessing, *Laocoön* (1766; Baltimore: Johns Hopkins Press, 1984).

[22] In Oakeshott's last full-scale work, *On Human Conduct* (Oxford: Clarendon Press, 1975), all human activity is seen as ultimately subject to ethical constraints.

[23] As a Cambridge undergraduate, Oakeshott chose for his History Tripos Prize the complete works of Walter Pater, the leading advocate of 'art for art's sake' (see esp. Pater, *The Renaissance*, 1873). He particularly admired Pater's novels *Marius the Epicurean* and *Gaston de Latour*, and quotes from them extensively in his notebooks.

thetes and formalists of an earlier generation,[24] Oakeshott repeatedly maintains that ethical considerations belong solely to practice,
and that the whole point, and indeed value, of aesthetic experience,
as also (in their different ways) of science and history, is that it offers
an *escape* from the imperatives of practical existence.

There are obvious problems here. First, value belongs to practice,
yet aesthetic experience, which does not, is said to be valuable. Secondly (a related point), disinterestedness is central to all the
non-practical modes, yet it is also regarded as ethically, which is to
say practically, admirable. Maybe ethics, like disinterestedness,
exists precisely to counter the prevailingly egoistic, survival-orien-
tated ethos of practice. But if so, is ethics then really part of practice?
Yes, says the original theory, otherwise ethics must be ineffectual.
Maybe not, says the revised theory, since modal boundaries now
seem both less fixed and more permeable.

One reason, says Oakeshott, why poetry is the most 'conversable'
of the voices is that so many other valued and desirable things, such
as love, friendship, and moral goodness contain intimations of it.
Moral goodness, like religion in *On Human Conduct* (where it
appears as a vague Romantic piety), is characterized in the very
same words, as being a release from 'the deadliness of doing', in
other words, as yet another escape from practice. If these things are
implicitly 'poetic', then why should our approvals and disapprov-
als, our quasi-ethical responses to fictional representations of them
and their opposites, not equally count as part of the 'poetic' experience?

The reason, I suspect, is that Oakeshott is determined to include
under poetry what is often our wholly abstract, non-ethical appreciation of natural beauty, such as that of a flower, a sea-shell, or something similarly small and unthreatening.[25] And of course abstract or
decorative artifacts, such as a Japanese pot, may elicit a similarly
'pure' response. But why assume that this peculiar, non-moral,
self-sufficient experience is necessarily the 'core' one? Doubtless a
work from which such contemplative 'delight' is totally absent — a
novel by Theodore Dreiser, say — will not be very good or success-

---

[24] Clive Bell, *Art* (London: Chatto and Windus, 1914); Roger Fry, *Vision and
      Design* (London: Chatto and Windus, 1920).
[25] Kant did not exclude from the realm of the aesthetic quasi-moral responses
      to natural phenomena, such as sympathy, terror, and gratitude. But the
      phenomena concerned tended to be on a scale large enough to justify the
      responses (and their fanciful character).

ful, but it will still be art, and not something else. And it might, even if by Dreiser, still contain representations capable, on account of their 'poetic' quality (in Oakeshott's extended, quasi-ethical sense), of engaging our sympathy, approval, and the rest. One is reminded of Nabokov's curious postscript to *Lolita*, in which, having just identified his aim as 'aesthetic bliss', he then goes on to locate its source in some very familiar moral virtues and sentiments, among them kindness and tenderness.

Oakeshott's aesthetics, as a piece of pure theory, are surely unsatisfactory. There are too many loose ends, cul-de-sacs, and contradictions, the most striking being that (unless this is a religious paradox) we cannot have an ethics that shall simultaneously be part of practical experience and deliver us from it, nor a conception of the aesthetic that both excludes and includes the ethical. The effect is of a constant moving of the goalposts.

But the most extraordinary thing is that Oakeshott eventually concedes that the aesthetic, or at least the forms under which we apprehend it, is not to be reduced to a single formula after all. (Perhaps, we might suggest, it is a 'family resemblance' term.) Poetry remains ambiguous, paradoxical, and (like conversation) plural. It is ultimately not divorced from 'real life' and its values — whether or not we identify that with Oakeshott's practice — precisely because, as with conversation and liberal education, its autonomy, its ability to liberate us more completely even than science and history from 'the deadliness of doing', itself constitutes a 'value'. (Like those things, it belongs to Aristotle's *scholē* , or 'leisure', the true, if non-practical purpose of human life, which practice exists to serve.)

Oakeshott admits as much in commending Schiller's views on the 'social value' of art, and his 'thoughts on the usefulness of a "useless" activity' (play). And he abandons all his aestheticism — not to say his entire theory — in observing that Shelley's claim, to the effect that poets are '"the unacknowledged legislators of the world"',' may after all be 'merely a reflection of the manifold character of Apollo' (*RP*, 240 n. 2). A manifold character, at the beginning of Oakeshott's discussion in 'The Voice of Poetry', was just what Apollo was supposed *not* to have.

Several commentators have suggested that there is something postmodernist about Oakeshott, and Rorty's championing him confirms this suspicion. Idealism generally has a subjectivist tendency that is due to the immense constitutive importance it accords to imagination in producing the world as we experience it. For idealism there is no authentically 'external' world to correct our ideas of it, for ideas are all that we have. Of course, that we each have our own, and know that others have different ideas, acts to constrain our fantasy; but in a uniform, coercive, collectivist society such as that of George Orwell's *Nineteen Eighty-Four*, that constraint is lacking, and the most enormous untruths subsist unchecked, simply through fear, peer pressure, mass hysteria, and political will.

Some postmodernists, such as Foucault, apply this diagnosis, not to totalitarian, but to liberal societies. Our freely chosen beliefs reflect no independent reality, but both serve and further conceal the only true reality, viz. the hidden interests diffused through every cell of the social organism and the secret, 'capillary' power by which they are advanced. For Foucault, therefore, as not for Oakeshott, everything is practice (that is, relative to power and will), and disinterestedness is an illusion. Since this must also apply to Foucault himself, he has virtually asked us not to believe him. That being so, it is scarcely worth investigating a possible resemblance between Foucault's *epistemes* and Oakeshott's modes, so I mention it only for whatever little of interest it may contain.

Oakeshott's postmodernist affiliations are mostly to be found in his idealist anti-foundationalism and his aesthetics, or at least in some aspects of them. Subject only to some few genuinely 'external' circumstances, such as our need to survive, the world of experience as a whole, and also particular aesthetic experiences, are very largely what we make them, in the first case as a culture, and in the second, individually. In these areas, as also, incidentally, in his Chicago economics, Oakeshott appears as a liberal advocate of 'consumer sovereignty'.[26]

Relative to the interpretation of works of art, this radically antisemantic position, if taken seriously, amounts virtually to Roland Barthes' celebrated 'death of the author',[27] a theory whose own death is long overdue.[28] It should be remembered, however, that

---

[26] See 'The Political Economy of Freedom' in *RP*.

[27] Oakeshott is not consistent about this. In other essays than 'The Voice of Poetry' he is quite prepared to cite what he evidently sees as the author's meaning in support of some contention of his own. For example, he uses a discussion about agricultural methods in *Anna Karenina* as evidence of the folly of what he calls 'rationalism' (*RP*, 96 n).

[28] See Seán Burke, *The Death and Return of the Author: Criticism and Subjectivity in Barthes, Foucault and Derrida* (Edinburgh: Edinburgh Univ. Press, 1992).

outside fiction and aesthetics, in matters of propositional or declarative discourse such as we find in science, history and practice, Oakeshott is a linguistic realist.[29] Even if 'things' are a special type of 'image', words are still distinct from them and signify (or 'symbolize') them in a reasonably objective, convenient, and predictable manner. There is nothing in Oakeshott resembling, say, Derrida's linguistic Pyrrhonism. The idea that in the ordinary way words, and thus meanings, are intrinsically unstable would have seemed to him literally absurd, a proposition logically incapable of statement. Doubtless he would have accused Derrida of the greatest of intellectual crimes, irrelevance. For what else is it but irrelevance, an inaptitude for distinctions, to treat all language as though it were fictional, as Derrida does? Is that not as crass as its opposite, the Philistine's inability to understand anything except in a literal sense?

---

[29] Even metaphysically he might be regarded as an 'internal realist', a position compatible with at least a modest Kantian idealism.

16

Wendell John Coats, Jr.

Michael Oakeshott and the Poetic Character of Human Activity

In this paper I try to make clear a phrase I have used elsewhere as a summary expression indicating Oakeshott's comprehensive critique of 'Rationalism' in politics and morals.[1] The phrase, 'the poetic character of human activity,' has not been clear to some readers, and is also sometimes mistakenly taken to imply a highly aesthetic view of political and moral life. In what follows, I try to reconstruct Oakeshott's critique of modern Rationalism from the standpoint of his account of the recurring structure of all mediated human experience, including settled patterns of practical activity and skill. I begin by summarizing Oakeshott's critique of the errors of modern Western Rationalism in the political and moral life of especially the past four centuries, and then go on to show how the critique flows from Oakeshott's account of mediated experience generally; in what sense the structure of mediated human experience (including settled skills) is poetic or fluid, rather than prosaic and 'wooden'; and what are some of the implications of this viewpoint for contemporary practical (including political) life. This summary is drawn from the essays of Oakeshott's 1962 book, *Rationalism in Politics and Other*

---

[1]   The latest instance is in the conclusion to Wendell J. Coats, Jr., *Oakeshott and His Contemporaries* (London: Associated Univ. Presses, 2000).

Essays. I have also drawn upon formulations of Oakeshott's critique of Rationalism I have made in previously published writings.[2]

Oakeshott uses the expression 'modern Rationalism' to refer to a post-Renaissance intellectual tradition first clearly discernible in the thought of Bacon and Descartes, and (without their reservations) characterized by the belief in the importance of certain and sovereign techniques of knowledge, capable of being applied by almost anyone to almost any subject matter. Oakeshott distinguishes this rationalism from its ancient and medieval varieties by suggesting that it has combined the worst of the claims for reason of both — broadness of scope, and scholastic rigidity, respectively.

Oakeshott characterizes Rationalism as the belief that all real knowledge is technical knowledge susceptible of formulation in precepts capable of universal application at distinct starting and ending points; and contrasts it with his own view that all concrete knowledge and skill is fluid, and consists of both technical knowledge that *can* be put in precepts and books, and practical knowledge of timing and context that is so general and subtle that it can only be acquired in patient practice and apprenticeship. Oakeshott is careful to distinguish Rationalism from modern science and the modern industrial economy, both of which, insofar as they enable the practice of real skill, also contain elements of both technical and practical knowledge. When their insights are put in books, of course, all that is passed on is the technical part of knowledge.

Oakeshott makes both a philosophic and practical critique of this approach to knowledge. Philosophically, he suggests that Rationalism's claim of certainty and control through distinct beginnings and endings is an illusion, and he cites Pascal's view that in human affairs the probable is more certain than the certain. Oakeshott also suggests that Rationalism has an erroneous view of the human mind in conceiving of a method of reason that can be clearly separated from its historically acquired subject matter. Finally, Oakeshott suggests that Rationalism makes a practical error in thinking that making conduct self-conscious and bringing it before the bar of reason is always desirable — usually self-consciousness about an activity results in the loss of fluid rhythms that are the basis of skillful practical action. Except in crises, when balance is already lost, the proper

---

[2]   Especially 'Michael Oakeshott's Critique of Rationalism in Politics,' in Wendell J. Coats, Jr., *The Activity of Politics and Related Essays* (London and Toronto: Associated Univ. Presses, 1989), 34-41.

place of conscious intellect is as critic, not generator, of practical action, in the lives of both individuals and entire peoples. Oakeshott suggests that Rationalism's invasion of politics, a realm of diplomacy traditionally grounded in the makeshift has come by way of the combination of political inexperience and political opportunity over the past four centuries, and has become the dominant political orientation — not to have a rational plan or doctrine now signifies a lack of seriousness or proper preparation. Oakeshott discusses three well-known European political 'cribs' constructed to deal with the political inexperience of 'the new ruler, of the new ruling class, and of the new political society' — those of Machiavelli, Locke, and Marx and Engels, respectively; he suggests that each successive crib has become more abstract and 'rationalist', naming that of Marx and Engels as 'the most stupendous of our political rationalisms.'[3]

In its political form, Rationalism has become the politics of the 'felt need' interpreted by an ideology, and in its moral form, the self-conscious pursuit and application of ideals and precepts. Oakeshott's critique of these activities follows from his critique of Rationalism in general. Mistaking its origins for 'nature' or 'truth' or 'reason', rather than some historically evolved way of living, Rationalism deceives itself into thinking that it can self-consciously and successfully recreate its own political and moral life from new beginnings. Lacking the insight that unself-conscious traditions are flexible with regard to change, it resolves political life into a succession of crises or problems to be resolved by yet another *tour de force* of 'unaided' reason, with the attendant loss of skill and balance. Additionally, as the traditions of a society over time became Rationalist themselves, the view of life as a series of problems to be solved becomes even more plausible, though still at the expense of genuine skill.

Oakeshott does not seem optimistic about the recovery of political balance for an age in which the Rationalist 'political' vocabulary of war and crisis management retains center stage owing to its own generation of a world situation of almost permanent war and crisis, in the name of 'rational' solutions to further crises. Even where new rulers sense the shortcomings of the 'book' and fall back on their own experience, it is usually experience acquired in a profession other than politics (such as the military, the business corporation, or the pulpit), and hence not appropriate.

---

[3]   Oakeshott, *Rationalism in Politics and Related Essays* (1962; reprinted, London: Methuen and Co., Ltd., 1977), 26. Hereafter: *RP*.

Critique of Platonic Rationalism

Before delving into the account of mediated human experience which supports Oakeshott's critique of Rationalism, it is instructive to look at his critique of Platonic Rationalism for its failure to grasp the creative character of human experience and activity. This critique occurs in his long 1959 essay, 'The Voice of Poetry in the Conversation of Mankind,' and draws upon some of the work of the twentieth century English political philosopher, M.B. Foster, whose characterization and critique of Platonic craft or *technē* (for the same blindness) it will also be illuminating to inspect in this connection.

The moderately skeptical Oakeshott is obviously dubious of any view (such as the Platonic), which would assign preeminence in human life to bald inquiry and the pursuit of 'Truth.' He implies that the satisfaction hoped for in such activity could be better sought in poetic or aesthetic contemplation, and without the attendant dangers of the vulgarized search for 'Truth' in political existence. Yet Oakeshott has an even more specific critique to make of Platonic discussions of the form or *eidos* of a thing. It is Plato's failure to see the creative character of all human experience, and the subsequent attempt to conceive all human activity as craft or *technē*, which copies an already existing archetype.

On Oakeshott's view, the substantive and formal aspects of experience, what is experienced and *how* it is experienced, arise simultaneously or 'poetically' — hence the difficulty of finding distinct beginnings to which to apply a 'rational' method. The method and subject matter of all activity arise in a fluid interaction, driven by the 'desire' of both the method and the matter, the *how* and the *what*, for the unattainable goal of assimilating the other. For Oakeshott, Plato's theoretical articulation of an archetype was in fact a kind of aesthetic contemplation, and Plato mistook the unique character of a poetic or artistic creation, which momentarily unified the *how* and *what* of experience, for a blueprint to be copied, however perfectly or imperfectly. But for Oakeshott, 'there is in fact no way of determining an end for an activity in advance of the activity itself' (*RP*, 91). Hence, in the end, a critique of modern Rationalism requires tracing back its central error in the peculiar blindness of Greek *theoria*, the failure to grasp the poetic character of human experience and activity; or said differently, assigning a priority to *theoria* in areas of human activity for which it is not appropriate. Before saying in more detail what Oakeshott means by this phrase, let us look briefly at the critique of Platonic *technē* in *The Republic* and other dialogues, by M.B. Foster, whose work Oakeshott's cites in his criticism of Plato. Foster arrives at a conception of the creative — and at a critique of Plato's failure to articulate it — in more philosophic and less metaphorical terms than Oakeshott.

The brunt of Foster's critique is to show that in *The Republic* Plato moves within an ontologically dualist pattern for action and production conceived on the model of the Greek idea of craft or *technē* (in spite of some occasional impulses towards the subjective and creative). The assumptions of the outlook are that human making (including ruling) involves the shaping of matter or subject matter into pre-existing forms or patterns, in the fashion, for example, by which a sculptor shapes marble into a human-like form, or a potter shapes clay into a pot. The matter (or citizen subject-matter in ruling) is always accidental or extrinsic to the essence of the object being crafted, and resides in the form, which is grasped in thought, and imitated by the craftsman. Additionally, the matter being crafted requires no knowledge or understanding of the form into which it is being informed. This is obvious when the matter involved is glass or marble, but less so when the 'matter' is human beings in the art of ruling.

Foster distinguishes the Greek conception of *technē*, including its cosmological dimensions in Plato's *Timaeus*, from the Hebraic and later Christian conception of creation, observing that the idea of creating entails the existence of creatures whose particularity is not simply accidental, but a part of their essential being. On this view, then, the existence of an idea or form would add to its perfection (as in Anselm's famous ontological proof for the existence of God). Foster argues that when this cosmological account of creation finally enters the political realm, it generates the modern idea of sovereignty, understood as the ability of a people to 'create themselves,' i.e., give themselves their own political forms or constitutions, rather than passively receive forms by a political craftsman, founder or legislator, as on the *technē* model.[4] Foster spends some time indicating passages in *The Republic* where Socrates moves toward transcending the *technē* model, but, of course, cannot ever explicitly do so. One of Foster's most interesting arguments, in this connection for example, involves Socrates' statement to Glaucon that if the city they are

---

[4]   M. B. Foster, *The Political Philosophies of Plato and Hegel* (Oxford: Oxford Univ. Press, 1935), 188-93.

building in words is ever to come into being and sustain itself, some element of the city must possess the understanding of its form possessed by Socrates and Glaucon (and even they are not creating its form, but only discerning it in nature). Foster observes, however, that if an element of the city were capable of intellectively grasping the pattern into which it was being shaped, at least a portion of the *technē* model would have been transcended in a more 'creative' or 'subjective' direction.[5]

It is not necessary here to pursue Foster's critique further in this regard. The aim has been merely to give enough of it to illuminate Oakeshott's claim that artistic creation is not like the copying of models or archetypes evident in the Platonic account, but involves a single activity (not first grasping the form, then informing the matter) in which the form and content (not matter as on the dualist account) of an activity or idea arise or evolve simultaneously and fluidly, and are of equal or essential importance in what is created, i.e., in the creation.

Oakeshott's Account of Poetic or Artistic Experience

At this point, it is useful to explain more fully Oakeshott's account of poetic experience, in order to show subsequently in what sense for him all mediated human experience has affinities to poetic mediations. In 'The Voice of Poetry in the Conversation of Mankind,' Oakeshott lays out a conception of poetic experience (including poetry, dance, sculpting, painting, and so on) as a particular way of being active which has always been in human experience but only relatively recently been recognized as a distinct activity. On Oakeshott's view, poetic experience is the experience of contemplative imagining, distinguished from image-making in some other mode, such as the practical, religious, scientific, and so on. It is an activity completely released from any sort of practical, moral, emotional, or scientific concerns, regardless of whether the object of contemplative delight was expressly intended as an artistic or poetic creation.

It is characterized by the absence of any pre-meditated design, and by the creation or production of a unique individual object (not a mere concretion of qualities which might be duplicated or substituted for), which induces contemplative delight in the creator and

[5]   Foster, *The Political Philosophies of Plato and Hegel*, 39-71.

beholder. Its creations are not symbolic. In poetry, for example, the word itself is the image, and writing, saying, or reading it is poetic imagining if it creates the experience of contemplative delight for its own sake. On Oakeshott's view, a poet or artist does not first have a feeling or idea and then express it. Rather,

> as I understand it, a poetic utterance (a work of art) is not the 'expression' of an experience, it is the experience *and the only one there is*. A poet does not do *three* things; first experience . . . an emotion, then contemplate it, and finally seek a means of expressing [it]; he does one thing only, he imagines poetically. (*RP*, 232, italics added)

In poetic experience or imagining (always an intermittent or fleeting activity) what the poet is saying and how he is saying it are momentarily unified in images of contemplative delight, devoid of any concern about the truth of assertions, or moral responsibility, or the accuracy of its depictions, and so on. To say this more formally, on Oakeshott's account of poetic experience, the form and content of activity arise simultaneously, are inseparable except in analysis, and are of equal importance in the experience generated.

I want to try to show next that Oakeshott's general account of skillful experience in his early work *Experience and Its Modes* (in which ironically he did not yet see the place of poetry), and in 'The Voice of Poetry' and elsewhere, has affinities to the account of poetic experience in regard to the characteristics just enumerated. Said differently, I think Oakeshott is implying by his phrase 'the poetic character of human conduct' that the structure of all mediated human experience is creative, but that in poetic imagining we can see this experiential structure most clearly. This insight then becomes the basis for Oakeshott's critique of a prosaic Rationalism's disruption of the fluid skill and rhythm of evolved and settled professions and practices.

Oakeshott's Account of the Structure of Experience, and its Relation to his Critique of Rationalism

Oakeshott's account of experience and its modalities appears in his early work, *Experience and Its Modes*, and in the essays of *Rationalism in Politics*, especially 'The Voice of Poetry.' This account falls squarely within the philosophical idealist school of thought, and although in later works Oakeshott changes his emphases, he never retracts this account, nor writes anything that contradicts it.

For Oakeshott, experience is always a present world of ideas constituted in the tension between a self and what it experiences. Apparently qualitative differences in subject matter, or what is experienced, are illusory — what is known is always our experience in whatever modalities or forms of mediation it comes. Even sensation, on this non-dualist idealist account is simply incipient judgment; and action is, carefully speaking, a practical modification of thought.[6]

In spite of urges toward something more unified, experience, except for fleeting poetic moments, comes always in specific mediations or modifications of experience. Some of these modifications or modalities of experience have become settled over time, such as those of history, and science: one, that of practical experience — the world of desire and aversion, good and bad — is unavoidable. Each mediation of experience orders it on some relatively (though partially) coherent and consistent principles, such as quantity, or continuity, or contemplative delight. In spite of the fact, then, that all experience is a single world of ideas, so to speak, in mediation it is divided into a form and content of consciousness and activity. For example, in the modality of scientific experience, a falling apple is studied as an abstraction called 'mass,' created on the scientific principle of 'quantity,' or quantity-like (i.e., up-down, light-heavy, and so on). The point here is that, as in the case of poetic experience summarized above, science, like all settled activities, creates its own subject matter in the way it mediates experience — for there is no common subject matter 'out there'; all experience is had in specific mediations. Additionally, even the *forms* or principles of science (or history) evolve poetically, or creatively, with no pre-meditated end in sight, and often at least differently from what pre-meditated end may have been in some scientific pioneer's mind:

> It is not to be supposed that the self in scientific activity begins with a pre-meditated purpose.... The so-called 'methods' of scientific investigation emerge in the course of the activity... and in advance of scientific thought there are no scientific problems.... All that exists in advance of scientific inquiries is the urge to achieve an intellectually satisfying world of images. (*RP*, 214-15)

Thus, although the form and content of experience in modalities other than poetic or artistic experience are more easily separable in

---

[6]   Oakeshott, *Experience and Its Modes* (Cambridge: Cambridge Univ. Press, 1933), 251.

analysis than in the poetic case, they are ultimately inseparable, since each modality creates its own subject matter by its distinctive method. The form and content of all activity evolve simultaneously and fluidly, unless conscious efforts are made to disrupt this evolution, and even such efforts may over time be unreflectively re-converted into more 'poetic' forms.

It is this account of the poetic structure of all mediated human experience that provides the basis for Oakeshott's critique of Rationalism in political and moral life. The attempt to abstract a moral code or political ideology from an historically evolved, concrete activity and then woodenly use it to initiate and govern that and other activities denies 'the poetic character of human conduct'; denies the poetic structure of all mediated, human experience, which is to say virtually all human experience for Oakeshott, except for unified fleeting poetic moments.[7] This is the reason Rationalism is often unskillful and imbalanced — it overestimates the role of conscious intellect in activity (making it the generator rather than the critic of action); and it ruptures the fluidity of action by mechanically breaking down into discrete, accessible steps what is spontaneously, and for the most part, unreflectively, done by adepts. This is also one of the reasons that in his more expressly political writing Oakeshott evinces a preference for the idea of civil association under general and formal law as a paradigm for the modern state, over the idea of an enterprise association with substantive purposes to accomplish — the latter's Rationalist planning will inevitably be more destructive of evolved, settled skills and practices, and of 'the poetic character of human conduct.'

I have used the expression 'the poetic character of human activity' here and elsewhere as a summary expression for relating and showing the consistency and coherence of many of Oakeshott's themes. This is a good place to rehearse what is entailed in (and compacted in) this expression. A quick way to do so is to reproduce a concluding paragraph from another of my writings on Oakeshott:

> To refer then to the 'poetic character of all human activity' is to refer to a complex of ideas: it is to refer to the historic way in which all settled activity evolves; to insist upon the inseparability of the form and content (in the prin-

---

[7] The activity of genuinely philosophizing, or investigating the postulates of various other activities, can have no direct influence upon practical action for Oakeshott, since the two activities do not share a common subject matter — at most philosophy can tell us what *not* to do in practical life, can tell us when we are being irrelevant.

ciple of experiential mediation) of any settled activity; to insist that there is no goal or end of an activity in advance of the activity (i.e., to reject teleological explanations, natural or supernatural, of human activity); to deny Reason or Theoretical Intellect the capability to intellect the essence of any activity (and separate it from its accidents); to value the unreflective springs of action in any settled activity as a source of skill and good timing; to downplay the role of calculating intellect except as a critic (not originator) of action; and , hence, to value detailed knowledge of historic and professional practices for the indirection and oblique approach they permit their practitioners.[8]

I have been trying to show that Oakeshott's critique of Rationalism in politics and morals is based upon an argument or insight into the fluid and creative character of all human experience and activity, a character which Rationalism is seen to deny in its prosaic and wooden approach to organizing and originating human action, in its denial of the poetic character of human activity and conduct. As we have noted, although this character is most apparent in the poetic or artistic mode of imagining, it is still implied to some degree in all settled forms of human activity, even in moments of practical experience, the form of experience which might seem the least 'poetic'. This is true of all practical craft, but even more so in moments of love and friendship. I will close this essay with some lines of Oakeshott indicating the poetic-like character of human love and friendship, forms of experience concerned with desire and pleasure, and hence still nominally practical for Oakeshott. In loving, the

> object is individual and not concretion of qualities: it was for Adonis that Venus quit heaven. What is communicated and enjoyed is not an array of emotions ... but the uniqueness of a self ... *the image in love and friendship* ... is more than any other engagement in practical imagining 'whatever it turns out to be' ... *these are at least ambiguously practical activities which intimate contemplation and may be said to constitute a connection between voices of poetry and practice.* (RP, 244)

---

[8]   Coats, *Oakeshott and His Contemporaries*, 105.

Index

A

Africa
  colonial influences, 201-2, 204-5, 219
  development imperative, 215-6
  morality of communal ties in, 217-8
  nationalism, 203, 212
  political discourse
    warlike, 214-5
    rationalism in, 210 n. 18
  political traditions, 203, 205-6
  pre-colonial, 204
  states as enterprise associations,
    209-16, 219
Aristotle
  and civil association, 56-7, 60,
  conduct and character, 42-3, 46, 48
    n. 23, 49, 52, 55, 58
  and critique of rationalism, 43, 46
  on *polis*, 31, 47, 48 n. 24, 55
    and Greek ethical life, 51, 53
  and enterprise association, 57-8
  eudaimonia, 42, 46, 58-9
  freedom in, 44 n. 15, 52-4
  friendship, 59, 60, 111, 147
  and idealism, 53-4, 55
  nature and convention, 30, 51-2
  philosophy and religion, 59, 60 n.
    46, 274
  play, 49, 289-91
  political discourse, 40-1, 78, 88, 146,
  and politics of faith and skepticism,
    43 n. 14
  phronesis, 43, 109
  in relation to Hobbes, 49, 51
  skepticism of, 59
Arnold, Matthew, 133, 136, 189
art. *See* poetry
artificial intelligence, 267-72
Athens, 29-30, 40-1, 57
Augustine, Saint, vii, 3, 38, 163
authority
  of law
    to promulgate, enact, 165

recognition of, viii, 23, 58, 60, 128,
  156, 167, 169, 174 n. 11, 180,
  208, 265
distinct from desirability127, 129,
  165, 168, 208
divine, 166
and liberty, 50, 73, 122, 127-8, 158
as mode of relationship, vii
of state (as social whole), 149
in tradition, 150, 199, 273
and power, 141-3, 152, 157, 209-10,
  219
in religious and other institutions,
  185-7
and wisdom, 127-8, 166

B

Babel, Tower of, viii, 159
Bacon, Francis, vii, 144, 267-9, 280, 307
Bentham, vii, 124, 133, 143, 255
Berkeley, George, 24, 139
Bosanquet, Bernard, 24-8, 30, 32, 35,
  53, 119, 120-22, 127, 128
Boucher, David, 26
Bradley, F. H., 3, 26, 32, 44, 89, 94-5,
  114, 117, 244
Brentano, Franz, 225 n. 6
Browning, Robert, "Easter Day," 66
Burke, Edmund, 3, 124, 143
Butler Act of 1944, 184

C

Catholicism, 134, 136
cause (-ality)
  Spinoza's God, 92-4
  in historical and scientific
    explanation, 234, 282, 287
  and perception, 66 n. 10
  and reasons for acting, 234
Cervantes, Miguel, 3, 297
character

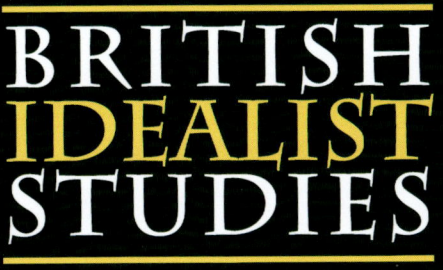

uke O'Sullivan: Oakeshott on History

his book challenges the common view that Michael Oakeshott was mainly of importance as political philosopher by offering the first comprehensive study of his ideas on history. It rgues that Oakeshott's writings on the philosophy of history mark him out as the most uccessful of the philosophers who attempted to establish historical study as an autonomous rm of thought during the twentieth century. For the first time, extensive use has been made unpublished material in the collection of Oakeshott's papers at the LSE.

'Oakeshott's later philosophy is immensely dense and intricate, and is already provoking a notable literature of interpretation. O'Sullivan's *Oakeshott on History* is a most impressive contribution to it.' Kenneth Minogue, *TLS*
'This scholarly and carefully written book provides a more sustained and comprehensive treatment of Oakeshott's views on history than any so far attempted.' *Hist. Pol. Thought*
'A very helpful and welcome volume.' Michael Bentley, *English Historical Review*

308 pages £25/$49.90 0-907845-290

oy Tseng: The Sceptical Idealist

his is the first book-length study to provide a structured interpretation of akeshott's critique of the Enlightenment. The author argues that Oakeshott's famous ritique of *philosophisme* and Rationalism in fact expresses a sense of the crisis of hilosophical modernity. Oakeshott has never altered his analysis of two key themes: hilosophy as the persistent re-establishment of completeness by transcending bstractness, and the modes of experience as self-consistent worlds of discourse.

'Meticulously reconstructs Oakeshott's views across their full range and adeptly weaves the disparate strands together into a coherent and plausible whole.' *Political Studies Review*

320 pages £25/$49.90 0-907845-223

an Tregenza: Michael Oakeshott on Hobbes

his book offers an account of Oakeshott's political theory and examines the way in which it hanges and develops—from a broadly Hegelian to a Hobbesian character. Oakeshott's own heory is shown to mirror changes in his reading of Hobbes and many of the distinctive eatures of Oakeshott's thought—including the modal and sceptical conception of human nowledge, the concern with moral individuality, the rule-based account of modern authority, nd the critique of rationalism—all find a fascinating focal point in his writings on Hobbes.

'This is a skillfully posed and smartly analysed work that offers a definitive analysis of neither Oakeshott nor Hobbes but confronts the reader with an intriguing view of a philosophical relationship.' Steven Gerencser, *History of Political Thought*
'A history of ideas that ranges with formidable learning.' Peter Coleman, *Quadrant*
'This meticulous study shows how Oakeshott deployed selective readings of Hobbes to support his own developing ideas.' Mark Garnett, *Conservative History Journal*

250 pages £25/$49.90 0-907845-592

Efraim Podoksik: In Defence of Modernity: Vision and Philosophy in Michael Oakeshott

Although Oakeshott's philosophy has received considerable attention, the vision underlying has been almost completely ignored. This vision cements his ideas into a coherent whole and provides a compelling defence of modernity. The main feature of Oakeshott's vision of modernity is seen here as radical plurality resulting from 'fragmentation' of experience and society. For Oakeshott, this radical plurality should be recognised and enjoyed.

- 'This is an excellent and illuminating book.' John Charvet, *History of Political Thought*
- 'The book as a whole is a major contribution to the scholarly literature on Oakeshott' *Society*

260 pages £25/$49.90 0-907845-66

Kenneth B. McIntyre: The Limits of Political Theory: Oakeshott's Philosophy of Civil Association

This book examines Oakeshott's political philosophy within the context of his more general conception of philosophical understanding. It suggests that Oakeshott's philosophy of political activity cannot be reduced to conservatism, liberalism, or postmodernism or a theor which fits neatly into any conventional school, like that of Idealism or Skepticism. Oakeshott's philosophy of political activity is a provocation to all of the currently dominant schools of political theory and political practice. It questions their presuppositions and exposes as ambiguous, arbitrary, or confused all of the supposed certainties which they take for granted

210 pages £25/$49.90 1-84540-010-

Suvi Soininen: From a 'Necessary Evil' to an Art of Contingency: Michael Oakeshott's Conception of Political Activity

This book presents a comprehensive study of Oakeshott's conception of political activity. The author first examines Oakeshott in the contexts of liberal, conservative and Idealist thought, and then presents a detailed interpretation of the change in his conception of politics in the context of British postwar political thought. It is argued that Oakeshott's conception of political activity shifted from a near contempt of politics towards the applaudin of politics as a deliberative and reflective activity — his later work presents an important and original view of politics as an art of contingency.

300 pages £25/$49.90 1-84540-006-2 July 200

Glenn Worthington: Religious and Poetic Experience in the Thought of Michael Oakeshott

Much of the scholarly attention attracted by Michael Oakeshott's writings has focused upon his philosophical characterisation of the relations that constitute moral association in the modern world. A less noticed aspect of Oakeshott's moral philosophy is his account of the persona required to enter into and enjoy moral association. The book argues that Oakeshott's characterisations of religious and poetic experience provide a more detailed account of the type of persona that emerged in response to what it perceived as an invitation to participate in moral association in the modern world.

300 pages £25/$49.90 0-907845-622 November 200

Andrew Sullivan: Intimations Pursued: The Voice of Practice in the Conversation of Michael Oakeshott

In this book Andrew Sullivan examines Oakeshott's transition from his original emphasis on philosophy as providing what was ultimately satisfactory in experience to his later emphasis on practical life. This satisfaction is best achieved by a fusion of the modes of poetry and practice, leading the author to examine Oakeshott's view of religious life as the consummation of practice in its most poetic incarnation. Andrew Sullivan writes regularly for the *New York Times* and the *Sunday Times*. He was previously editor of *The New Republic*.

300 pages 0-907845-282 t.b.a